Predictive Cooperative Control for High-Order Fully Actuated Multiagent Systems

Da-Wei Zhang • Guo-Ping Liu

Predictive Cooperative Control for High-Order Fully Actuated Multiagent Systems

Springer

Da-Wei Zhang
Southern University of Science and Technology
Shenzhen, China

Guo-Ping Liu
Southern University of Science and Technology
Shenzhen, China

ISBN 978-981-95-1694-0 ISBN 978-981-95-1695-7 (eBook)
https://doi.org/10.1007/978-981-95-1695-7

This work was supported in part by the National Natural Science Foundation of China under Grant 62188101, Grant 62173255, and Grant 62503215; in part by the Shenzhen Key Laboratory of Control Theory and Intelligent Systems under Grant ZDSYS20220330161800001; in part by the China Postdoctoral Science Foundation under Grant 2025M771730 and Grant GZB20250437; in part by the Shenzhen Science and Technology Program under Grant JCYJ20241202125309014 and Grant KQTD20221101093557010; and in part by the Guangdong Provincial Key Laboratory of Fully Actuated System Control Theory and Technology under Grant 2024B1212010002.

This Springer imprint is published by the registered company Springer Nature Singapore Pte Ltd.
The registered company address is: 152 Beach Road, #21-01/04 Gateway East, Singapore 189721, Singapore

Preface

With the further integration and flourishing development of automatic control technology, the Internet of Things technology, and the communication technology, the cooperative control for multiagent systems (MASs) has been one of the most popular research hotspots. It has been widely applied to numerous fields in relation to the national economy and people's livelihood, such as logistics and supply-chain management, smart grid, intelligent transportation and aerospace, etc. It means that it is with importantly theoretical significance and great engineering value to advance the study on cooperative control for MASs in depth. However, considering the increasing complexity of application scenarios of cooperative control for MASs, the agent structure, cooperative control tasks, working conditions, and other factors have become more and more complex, such that the dynamic model of MASs is with strong and coupled nonlinearities. Significantly, it is noted that the design of cooperative control protocol has become more and more difficult. What is more, the satisfactory cooperative control performance cannot be usually achieved.

Aiming at this dilemma, the high-order fully actuated system (HOFAS) theory is creatively proposed by Prof. Guang-Ren Duan as a novel framework for the control theory. It is concerned with the combination of the modeling, analysis, design, and applications of control systems. Based on the HOFAS theory, the originally open-loop nonlinearities can be directly eliminated to obtain a linear constant system with the desired closed-loop performances. Especially, the HOFAS predictive control is a class of predictive control algorithms developed by the HOFAS theory. It is of the advantages of both HOFAS theory in handling the complex nonlinearities and predictive control in addressing the constraints. By introducing the HOFAS predictive control into the cooperative control for MASs, the cooperative control design can be effectively simplified and the cooperative control performance can be obviously improved by using the rolling optimization principle.

This book is devoted to the cooperative control problems of MASs with multiple constraints by means of a HOFAS predictive control approach. First of all, a HOFAS model of MASs, called the high-order fully actuated MASs (HOFAMASs), is constructed to provide a model foundation for the HOFAS theory-based cooperative control design. Then, the corresponding HOFAS predictive control protocols can be developed to achieve the cooperative control under different cases, containing the communication constraints, cyberattacks, and uncertainties. Further, the sufficient conditions can be derived to analyze the simultaneous consensus and stability of the closed-loop HOFAMASs for different cases. Finally, the feasibility and practicability of the proposed HOFAS predictive control can be demonstrated through the formation control experiments of three air-bearing spacecraft simulators. Based on the above studies, the theoretical results and experimental verification can be provided as the support for the large-scale applications of practical spacecraft control.

This book is divided into three parts with eight chapters; a brief is provided as follows.

- Chapter 1 summarizes the research status and developments of the HOFAS theory and the cooperative control for MASs.
- Part I is composed of Chaps. 2 and 3 and is considered as the basic methodology. Chapter 2 proposes the basic framework of HOFAS predictive control for nonlinear and linear HOFASs. Chapter 3 addresses the fundamental problem of predictive cooperative control for HOFAMASs.
- Part II, including the Chaps. 4 and 5, aims to deal with the predictive cooperative control for HOFAMASs with communication constraints. Chapter 4 designs a proportional-integral predictive control to ensure the cooperative control performance under fixed communication delays, and Chap. 5 further provides an observer-based predictive control to achieve the cooperative control with time-varying communication constraints and immeasurable states.
- Part III consists of Chaps. 6–8 to address the cooperative control of HOFAMASs under cyberattacks and uncertainties. Chapter 6 presents a packet-based HOFAS predictive control to achieve the secure cooperative control against random DoS attacks, Chap. 7 constructs a HOFAS sliding-mode predictive control to cope with random deception attacks, and Chap. 8 develops a HOFAS terminal sliding-mode predictive control for robust cooperative control of HOFAMASs under uncertainties.

The FAS Approach Book Series

This book is one of the following FAS Approach Book Series:

Fully Actuated System Approach for Control and AI

which is to be published with Springer. As planned, each year within the executing period there will be four to six books on this topic published. The following titles are planned to appear in 2026:

1. *Fully Actuated System Approach*—A New Framework for Control,
    - Volume I. Global Fully Actuated Systems

- Volume II. Sub-Fully Actuated Systems
- Volume III. Unidirectionally Connected FASs

by Guang-Ren Duan, Harbin Institute of Technology

2. *Predictive Cooperative Control for High-Order Fully Actuated Multiagent Systems*,
by Da-Wei Zhang and Guo-Ping Liu, Southern University of Science and Technology
3. *Fault-Tolerant Control for Fully Actuated Systems*,
by Dong-Hua Zhou and Miao Cai, Tsinghua University
4. *Adaptive Constrained Control for High-Order Fully Actuated Nonlinear Systems*,
by Chang-Chun Hua, Liu-Liu Zhang, and Peng-Ju Ning, Yanshan University
5. *Cooperative Safety Control for Muliagent Systems*—A Fully Actuated System Approach,
by Ke Zhang, Bin Jiang, Yong-Hao Ma, Yu-Hang Xu, and Yuan Lu, Nanjing University of Aeronautics and Astronautics
6. *Control of Renewable Power Systems*—A Fully Actuated System Approach,
by Yi Yu, The Hong Kong Polytechnic University,
Guo-Ping Liu, Southern University of Science and Technology,
Josep M. Guerrero, Zhejiang University

Acknowledgments The authors would like to gratefully acknowledge the generous financial support provided by the National Natural Science Foundation of China under Grant 62188101, Grant 62173255, and Grant 62503215, the Shenzhen Key Laboratory of Control Theory and Intelligent Systems under Grant ZDSYS20220330161800001, the China Postdoctoral Science Foundation under Grant 2025M771730 and Grant GZB20250437, the Shenzhen Science and Technology Program under Grant JCYJ20241202125309014 and Grant KQTD20221101093557010, and the Guangdong Provincial Key Laboratory of Fully Actuated System Control Theory and Technology under Grant 2024B1212010002.

Meanwhile, the authors' thanks would go to Dr. Lei Cao for his contributions to the design and verification of formation control experiments. Finally, the authors would also express the great gratitude to all readers. The authors would be indeed very grateful if the readers could possibly provide the feedback about any problems, comments, suggestions, or bugs via the email *zhangdw@sustech.edu.cn*. Your help will certainly make any future editions of the book much better.

Competing Interests The authors have no competing interests to declare that are relevant to the content of this manuscript.

Shenzhen, China

Da-Wei Zhang
Guo-Ping Liu

Contents

List of Main Symbols and Abbreviations

List of Main Symbols

$\mathbb{R}$	A set of all real numbers
$\mathbb{Z}$	A set of all integral numbers
$\mathbb{R}^n$	A set of all real vectors with dimension n
$\mathbb{R}^{n\times m}$	A set of all real matrices of dimension $n \times m$
$\in$	Belong to
$\exists$	Exist
$\forall$	Arbitrary chosen
$\succ$	Positively definite
$\Longleftrightarrow$	If and only if
M^{-1}	The inverse of matrix M
M^{T}	The transpose of matrix M
$\det(M)$	The determinant of matrix M
$\mathrm{Blockdiag}\{M_1, M_2, \cdots, M_n\}$	A block diagonal matrix with diagonal elements $M_i, i = 1, 2, \ldots, n$
$\|\cdot\|$	The Euclidean norm
0	A zero matrix with appropriate dimensions
I	An identity matrix with appropriate dimensions
$\aleph_y$	A prediction horizon of the output
$\aleph_u$	A prediction horizon of the input
q	A time operator, i.e., $q^{\eta}\varpi(t) = \varpi(t+\eta)$, $\eta \in \mathbb{Z}$, where $\varpi(t)$ is an arbitrary signal
$\Delta = 1 - q^{-1}$	A difference operator, such that $\Delta\varpi(t+1) = \varpi(t+1) - \varpi(t)$ is an increment of $\varpi(t)$
$\hat{\varpi}(t+\eta_1\|t-\eta_2)$	The η_1-th ahead prediction of $\varpi(t)$ based on $t-\eta_2$ time, $\eta_1, \eta_2 \in \mathbb{Z}$

$\varpi^{\lfloor \eta_1, \eta_2 \rfloor}(t)$	$\{\varpi(t+\eta_1), \varpi(t+\eta_1+1), \ldots, \varpi(t+\eta_2)\}, \eta_2 > \eta_1, \eta_1, \eta_2 \in \mathbb{Z}$
$\varpi^{\lceil \eta_2, \eta_1 \rceil}(t)$	$\{\varpi(t-\eta_2), \varpi(t-\eta_2+1), \ldots, \varpi(t-\eta_1)\}, \eta_2 > \eta_1, \eta_1, \eta_2 \in \mathbb{Z}$

List of Main Abbreviations

DoS	Denial-of-Service
MAS	Multiagent System
ABSS	Air-Bearing Spacecraft Simulator
HOFAS	High-Order Fully Actuated System
IHOFAS	Incremental High-Order Fully Actuated System
HUN-MAS	Heterogeneous Uncertain Nonlinear Multiagent System
HOFAMAS	High-Order Fully Actuated Multiagent System
HUN-HOFASMAS	Heterogeneous Uncertain Nonlinear High-Order Fully Actuated Multiagent System

Chapter 1
Overview

1.1 Introduction

The multiagent system (MAS) refers to a system that is composed of multiple agents with autonomous decision-making ability and information sharing using communication network; its general structure is shown in Fig. 1.1. Compared to the traditional control systems, the MAS has a range of advantages, such as parallelizability, high efficiency, high fault tolerance, etc., and can achieve the seamless combination between cyberspace and physical devices to reduce the complexity and the constraints of space and cost on designing and establishing the control systems. Meanwhile, the controllers can realize the information interaction and data sharing by means of the communication network, which has contributions to the top-level scheduling and decision-making.

With the rapid development of many emerging techniques, such as digital-twin (Lei et al. 2024), ChatGPT (Wang et al. 2023b), and blockchain (Yu et al. 2024), the interaction and coupling between cyberspace and physical world have become more and more close. It causes that the study on the MASs has been one of the most popular fields and has widely used in various areas during the production and practice, containing formation control of unmanned aerial vehicles (UAVs) (Hwang and Abebe 2022), voltage and power distribution of microgrid (Zhao et al. 2022), robotic control (Ta and Chea 2020), and other applications (Belkacem et al. 2020; Thakoor et al. 2020). Among them, the cooperative control for the MASs is regarded as a longstanding concern, which aims to achieve the individual objective of each agent and the global objective of MASs by designing a consensus control protocol (see Jin et al. 2022a; Lederer et al. 2023, and the references therein). In practical applications, satellite formation (Zhao et al. 2023a), containment control (Zhang et al. 2024), photovoltaic inverter (Mahdavi et al. 2021), and other problems can be analyzed and designed in the view of cooperative control for the MASs. However, a number of network-induced constraints, including communication constraints, packet dropouts and disorders, cyberattacks, data quantification, time-varying trans-

D.-W. Zhang, G.-P. Liu, *Predictive Cooperative Control for High-Order Fully Actuated Multiagent Systems*, https://doi.org/10.1007/978-981-95-1695-7_1

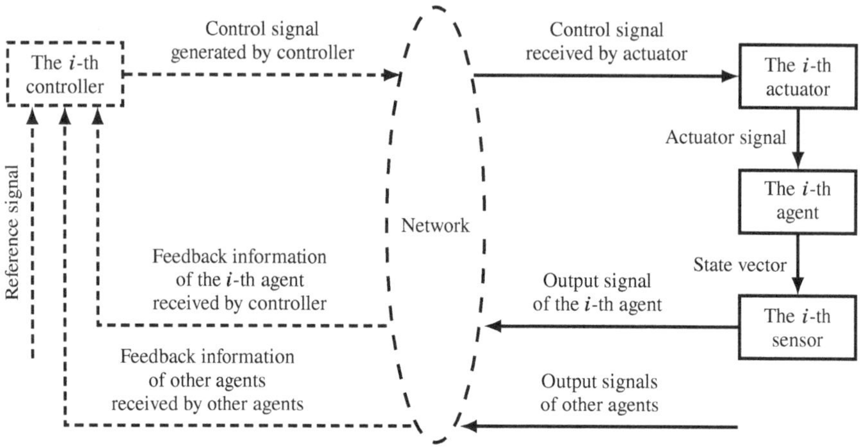

Fig. 1.1 The general structure of the MASs

mission intervals, and competition of multipoint access network, will be caused because of introducing the network into the control systems, which causes that the analysis and design of cooperative control for the MASs become more and more complex. Hence, it has importantly theoretical value and inspiration to construct a cooperative control law in a more simple and general way for overcoming these constraints to develop and perfect the cooperative control for the MASs. Meanwhile, it also has great engineering value to promote the informationization and intelligence enabling transformation of modern industry by combining the cooperative control for the MASs with cloud computing, digital-twin, big data, and other emerging techniques.

The high-order fully actuated system (HOFAS) theory has been creatively proposed by Prof. Guang-Ren Duan (Duan 2021a) as a novel framework for the analysis and design of control systems. Its origins, development, and status are summarized in Duan (2024c) in detail. A critical step of the HOFAS theory is to establish a HOFAS model of the considered systems for guaranteeing the full actuation feature, which can be used to eliminate the originally open-loop nonlinearities for obtaining a linear constant system with the desired closed-loop performances in a simple way. In fact, the full actuation feature is origin from the following aspects:

1. Many physical laws for modeling are in essence second-order fully actuated, such as Newton's Law, Euler-Lagrange Equation, Kirchhoff's Law, Navier-Stokes Equation, etc., and the dynamic models directly modeled or coupled from the above laws are in fact second-order or high-order fully actuated.
2. Through the extension in mathematics, the full actuation feature can also be obtained from some underactuated systems by constructing a diffeomorphism or an elevating-order and eliminating-variable transformation.

Because of its superiority, many scholars pay close attention to the integration and expansion between the HOFAS theory and numerous advanced control approaches and have obtained some newest progress in theoretical studies (Liu et al. 2024c; Zhang and Duan 2024) and practical applications (Cui et al. 2024; Tian et al. 2024). By introducing the HOFAS theory into the cooperative control for the MASs, a new and interesting research hotspot will be opened up, such that a range of popular problems in the relevant fields will be reconstructed and resolved with a satisfactory solution.

Meanwhile, the HOFAS predictive control is a kind of predictive control algorithms developed by the HOFAS theory, which is of the advantages of both the HOFAS theory in handling the complex nonlinearities and predictive control in addressing the constraints. By introducing the HOFAS predictive control into the cooperative control for the MASs, the cooperative control design can be effectively simplified, and the cooperative control performance can be obviously improved by using the rolling optimization principle.

Following the above idea, this book is devoted to the research on predictive cooperative control for the MASs with the help of the HOFAS theory, where a HOFAS model of MASs, called the high-order fully actuated MAS (HOFAMAS), is firstly established to provide a model foundation for the cooperative control design. Then, the corresponding HOFAS predictive control protocols are developed to implement the cooperative control under different situations, containing the communication constraints, cyberattacks, and uncertainties, and the sufficient conditions on the simultaneous consensus and stability for different situations are derived. Finally, the feasibility and practicability of the proposed HOFAS predictive control can be demonstrated via the formation control experiments of air-bearing spacecraft simulators.

By deeply considering the cooperative control for the HOFAMASs, a more general and simple control protocol can be obtained within the framework of the HOFAS theory, which is with great value in promoting and perfecting the theoretical studies and practical applications of cooperative control for the MASs.

1.2 Development of HOFAS Theory

As we all know, control and optimization are regarded as two timeless themes in the system and control theories. However, the implementation of them has been more and more difficult because of strong and coupled nonlinearities in dynamic models. The state-space approach established by R. E. Kalman (Kalman 1959) pays close attention to the solution, response analysis, and the related estimation problems of state vector because it presents a state-space model to describe the dynamics of the considered systems. However, the convenience of solving the control input and its physical realizability are ignored.

Aiming at this dilemma, the HOFAS theory has been proposed as an innovation for the system and control theories, which is concerned with the modeling,

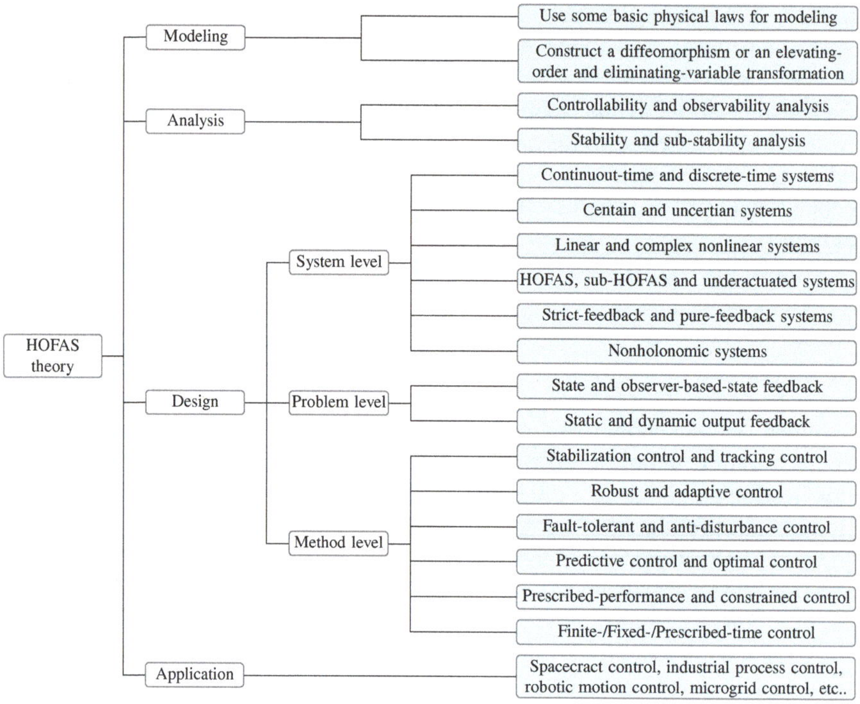

Fig. 1.2 The framework of the HOFAS theory

analysis, design, and application of control systems (see Fig. 1.2). Its physical background, basic foundation, theoretical framework, and application range have been expounded in detail (Duan 2021a, 2024c), and a range of classical problems in control theory, containing the robust control (Duan 2021b,d), adaptive control (Duan 2021c,d), disturbance attenuation and decoupling (Duan 2021e), discrete-time system control (Duan 2022c), etc., have been reexplored and resolved by Prof. Guang-Ren Duan.

To further enrich the HOFAS theory, Prof. Guang-Ren Duan also developed other significant and interesting explorations. Specifically, Duan (2023a,b) provided the single-order and multiple-order HOFAS model of continuous-time time-delay systems and then constructed a global stabilization control with the desired closed-loop performances. Duan (2023c) used the HOFAS theory to consider the robust stabilization of uncertain time-delay systems and realized the uniformly asymptotic input-state stability via a robust state-feedback control. Duan (2023d, 2024d) presented the definitions of sub-HOFAS and its feasible set and singular set, sub-stabilization, and sub-stability and then constructed an exponential attraction domain to ensure that all initial values in this domain can realize the exponential stability by designing a sub-stabilization controller. Duan (2024a,b) proposed a HOFAS theory-based controller to implement the uniformly exponential stability for a type of generalized chained nonholonomic systems. Duan (2022a,b) established a theoretical framework of the HOFAS theory for discrete-time time-delay systems, which included the HOFAS modeling, control design, and stability analysis. Duan (2025a,b,c) continued to consider the problems of the modeling, sub-stabilization control, and practical applications for a kind of constrained unidirectionally connected HOFASs, which further developed the intension and extension of the HOFAS theory.

Inspired by the idea of Duan (2021a), a number of scholars are devoting to the HOFAS theory and its related works and have obtained a string of representative achievements on theoretical study and basic study for applications. The corresponding briefs have been extracted and summarized as follows.

1.2.1 Theoretical Study

Actually, fault-tolerant control is crucial for guaranteeing the safe operation and maintenance of control systems, such that many works focus on the combination between the HOFAS theory and fault-tolerant control strategy. For example, Cai et al. (2023a) established a closed-loop dynamical data model for uncertain HOFAS with nonlinear measurements and faults and then used this model to propose a novel framework of active fault-tolerant control. Aiming at the HOFAS under multiplicative and additive actuator faults, Cai et al. (2023b) realized the fault-tolerant tracking control by designing a differential tracker and an extended state observer. Cai et al. (2023c) presented a nonlinear extended state observer to estimate the actuator faults and disturbances and then constructed a low-power observer-based HOFAS controller to reduce the dependence of model accuracy during the fault-tolerant control. Liu et al. (2022c) designed a middle observer to achieve the estimation of state vector and actuator faults and utilized the perturbation analysis and Lyapunov stability theory to ensure the globally uniformly ultimately bounded stability of closed-loop system for realizing the adaptive fault-tolerant control. For the HOFAS with sensor faults, Cai et al. (2024) proposed a self-healing fault-tolerant control via a redundancy framework to maintain the uniformly ultimately bounded stability of tracking error. Gong et al. (2025) used a HOFAS multicontroller switching fault-tolerant control based on a linear singular set to achieve the stability of the closed-loop systems with additive and multiplicative actuator failures. Liu et al. (2025b) proposed a new adaptive control by means of a generalized martingale method to address a fault-tolerant control problem of nonlinear HOFASs under stochastic fast time-varying actuator failures. Yuan et al. (2024) designed a prescribed-time disturbance observer to achieve the estimation of composite disturbance composed of actuator failures and external disturbances and then established a HOFAS approach-based fault-tolerant control to realize the formation control of 6 degrees of freedom unmanned helicopters.

In practice, the disturbances always exist to affect or even destroy the stability, control accuracy, and other performances, such that it is significant to further investigate the anti-disturbance control methods for enhancing the control performances with high accuracy and high reliability. From Chen et al. (2016), the disturbance compensation method can obtain a less conservatism control performance than that of the disturbance rejection one, where a critical technique is to design a disturbance observer to estimate and compensate for the disturbances. Based on this idea, HOFAS theory also make contributions to the disturbance observer-based anti-disturbance control. For instance, Zhang and Duan (2024) designed a finite-time disturbance observer to achieve the fast estimation and then established a finite-time HOFAS stabilization controller of nonholonomic systems with disturbances. In Jiang et al. (2024b), a joint design way of state and disturbance observers was constructed to obtain the state and disturbance estimations, which were used to design a stabilization controller for nonlinear HOFASs with disturbances. Cui and Duan (2024) gave two disturbance observers for the estimations of input and external disturbances, respectively, and provided a compensation-based HOFAS control for combined spacecraft. Li and Duan (2024) utilized a HOFAS theory-based dynamic compensator and an extended state observer to implement the precision control of servo systems. Jiang et al. (2024a) presented a generalized proportional-integral extended state observer to simultaneously estimate the state and external disturbances and then provided an observer-based HOFAS controller to ensure the uniformly ultimately bounded stability. In Wang et al. (2024b), a disturbance observer was adopted to estimate and compensate for the lumped disturbance and the approximation error of neural network, and a neuroadaptive HOFAS control was established to guarantee the semi-globally uniformly bounded stability. Jiang et al. (2025) constructed a reduced-order unknown input observer with an integral item to address the uncertainties and noises and proposed a HOFAS robust adaptive controller to ensure the uniformly ultimate boundedness of the closed-loop signals.

Among the study on nonlinear systems, the control of strict-feedback systems is one of the most popular concerns, which can be addressed very well by introducing the HOFAS theory. Specifically, Liu et al. (2023b) ensured the uniform ultimate boundedness of closed-loop strict-feedback systems by designing a high-order command filtered backstepping control based on the HOFAS theory, such that the “differential explosion" can be avoided. By using the HOFAS theory, Liu et al. (2022b) proposed a high-order robust command filtered backstepping controller to realize the tracking control of uncertain strict-feedback systems. Further, Zhao et al. (2023b) converted the nonstrict-feedback system with time delay into a strict-feedback one by adopting the neural networks and then designed a HOFAS adaptive neural network controller to guarantee the asymptotic stability based on the Lyapunov-Krasovskki functional. In addition, Liu et al. (2023a) used an adjusting function to construct an adaptive updating law without overparametrization for addressing the parametric uncertainties, such that adaptive control of unknown mixed HOFASs can be achieved. For high-order nonlinear systems with time-varying uncertainties, Hu et al. (2023) proposed a robust adaptive guarantee-cost control to ensure the global boundedness of closed-loop system within a finite time. Zhang et al. (2023b) constructed an adaptive dead-zone inverse to compensate for the dead-zone input and then established a HOFAS controller by applying the Lyapunov-Krasovskii functional.

Moreover, Liu (2022d) adopted a class of discrete-time step-backward HOFAS model to describe the nonlinear cyber-physical systems and then proposed a networked predictive control to actively compensate for time-varying communication constraints for the stabilization control. Wang and Duan (2023) used the HOFAS theory to design a smoothly nonlinear predictive controller with low power, which can be used in the control of underactuated systems. Wang and Duan (2024) constructed an explicit predictive control to realize the optimal control of discrete-time HOFAS with full-state constraints and time-varying delays. Meanwhile, Huang and Sun (2023), Zhou and Duan (2022), Duan and Zhou (2022), Liu et al. (2023c), and their associated studies also made contributions to the progress of theoretical study on the HOFAS theory.

1.2.2 Basic Study for Applications

Based on many physical laws to describe the orbit and attitude dynamics of spacecraft, the dynamical model of spacecraft control is in general fully actuated. Hence, HOFAS theory is naturally applied to the design of spacecraft control, so that the computational complexity and load can be reduced and the degrees of freedom can be fully developed (Zhang and Duan 2023). Among the spacecraft control, the attitude stabilization and maneuvering can be considered as a key guarantee to achieve the attitude adjustment with high precision and high reliability, which has attracted the attention of many scholars. For example, Xiao and Chen (2022) gave a second-order fully actuated system model to describe the attitude dynamics of spherical liquid-filled spacecraft and then designed a HOFAS theory-based controller to realize the attitude stabilization. Zhao and Duan (2022b) implemented the attitude stabilization and maneuvering of flexible spacecraft under time-varying nonlinear inertia be means of the HOFAS theory. Liu et al. (2022a) combined the HOFAS theory with an optimal control method to achieve the attitude tracking of rigid spacecraft subject to actuator saturation. Xiao and Chen (2023) constructed a quaternion model of the attitude dynamics of rigid spacecraft in a fully actuated form and designed a HOFAS controller to ensure the attitude stabilization and tracking and deal with the divergence phenomenon. Liu et al. (2024b) used a fixed-time disturbance observer and a prescribed-performance predictive control to maintain the attitude tracking of second-order fully actuated flexible spacecraft. Liu et al. (2025a) constructed a sliding-mode predictive control to realize the attitude tracking of flexible spacecraft under multiple disturbances.

Further, the attitude joint orbit control of spacecraft is also regarded as an important space task to be investigated. Concretely, Zhao and Duan (2022a) proposed a HOFAS controller combining with an extended state observer to achieve the attitude and position tracking of 6 degrees of freedom spacecraft with unknown disturbances. Wang and Jin (2024) adopted a convex-hull method to deal with the actuator saturation of spacecraft and constructed an extended state observer-based HOFAS controller to guarantee the realization of spacecraft rendezvous. In Xing et al. (2024), an appointed-time controller based on the HOFAS theory was provided to consider the flying-around task of noncooperative target when the external disturbances exist. In addition, the HOFAS theory also had significant impacts in the control of a kind of combined spacecraft. For example, Duan and Liu (2022) designed a HOFAS theory based-optimal control to maintain the attitude and position stabilization of a kind of combined spacecraft. Cui et al. (2024) established an adaptive control by using the HOFAS theory to deal with the stabilization of the combined spacecraft under uncertain parameters. In Cui and Duan (2024), an anti-disturbance control based on the HOFAS theory and disturbance observer was given to realize the attitude and position stabilization of the combined spacecraft with input and external disturbances.

Moreover, the HOFAS theory has been also successfully achieved a string of practical applications in other fields, such as robot manipulators (Tian et al. 2024), servo systems (Li and Duan 2024), quadrotor (Lu et al. 2023a), etc., which provides a solid foundation for basic study for applications and a powerful support for large-scale industrial applications.

1.3 Progress of Cooperative Control for Multiagent Systems

There is no doubt that cooperative control for the MASs is regarded as one of the most important research hotspots because of its significantly theoretical value and widely practical applications. Among so many methods for the design of cooperative control, predictive control is considered as a generally useful one because it simultaneously involves the cooperative control performance in both steady and dynamical processes by using the rolling-horizon optimization, so that a number of scholars pay close attention to the predictive cooperative control for the MASs. Meanwhile, with the rapid development of the HOFAS theory, there are also several previous results that focus on the study of the HOFAS theory-based cooperative control for the MASs. The corresponding briefs have been extracted and summarized as follows.

1.3.1 Predictive Cooperative Control for Multiagent Systems

During the design of cooperative control, predictive control can utilize the historical and current information to construct a multistep ahead predictions on the basis of a prediction model. Then, it adopts the rolling-horizon optimization principle to solve the optimal cooperative control sequence repeatedly in a finite horizon. To prevent the differences of predictions caused by external disturbances and model mismatch, predictive control also provides a feedback correction to update the prediction model

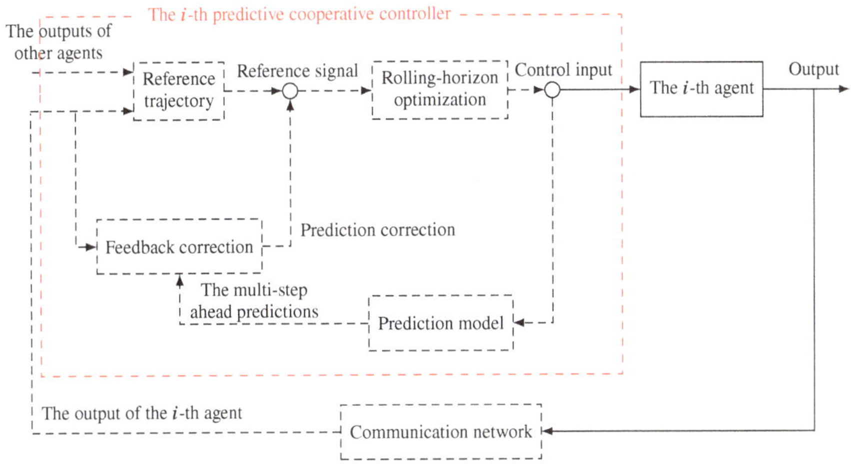

Fig. 1.3 Predictive cooperative control for the MASs

for implementing the rolling-horizon optimization again, such that the optimization of cooperative control performance can be established on an exactly actual model with an accuracy prediction for future information. Summarizing the above implies that predictive control can implement a better cooperative control performance by applying the closed-loop rolling-horizon optimization on the basis of system model and feedback information; the general structure is shown in Fig. 1.3.

Among the associated studies, Prof. Liu firstly proposed a networked predictive control approach to actively compensate for the communication constraints, where broke through the point-to-point single data transmission mode by using the feature that network can transmit the vector data streams (Liu et al. 2006) and also provided the design and implementation procedure for practical applications in Liu et al. (2007), Chai et al. (2008). Further, Liu (2017a) constructed a networked predictive cooperative control scheme for the compensation of communication delays and packet dropouts to realize the output consensus and then presented a sufficient and necessary condition on the simultaneous stability and consensus. Liu (2017b) gave a design method of cloud-based predictive cooperative controller and also derived a sufficient and necessary condition to guarantee the stability and output consensus. Liu (2020a) adopted an observer-based proportional-integral predictive control to realize the cooperative control with the active compensation of communication delays. Liu (2020b) proposed a model-free adaptive predictive control to consider the stability and consensus of nonlinear MASs with communication constraints. Liu (2022a) established a multistep predictors combining with cloud computing to achieve the cooperative control with a low computation load. Liu (2022b) constructed a mist-fog-cloud predictive control based on cloud-edge computing to realize the cooperation for large-scale MASs. Liu (2023) established a proportional-integral-derivative predictive control for the cooperative tracking control of the

MASs. Liu (2022c) used a predictive feedback control based on the HOFAS theory to implement the cooperative control of MASs in a step-backward HOFAS model.

Following the idea of Liu (2017a,b), Pang et al. (2021b) designed an incremental predictive control to deal with random communication delays and data dropouts in the cooperative control. Zhang et al. (2022a) proposed a model-free sliding-mode predictive control to ensure the stability and consensus of time-delay MASs without exact model. Yang et al. (2021a) provided a cloud-based predictive control to handle the denial-of-service (DoS) attacks and quantized signal, so that data losses caused by DoS attacks can be actively compensated to maintain the consensus control of MASs. Furthermore, Zheng et al. (2023) combined time-delay system approach with predictive control to ensure the time-varying formation control under random communication delays and data losses. Pang et al. (2022b) designed a cloud predictive control with input quantization to achieve the time-varying formation control of MASs under random communication constraints and quantized constraints. Aiming at the communication constraints and switching topology, Cao et al. (2023b) gave a proportional-integral predictive control to consider the formation control based on output consensus. Cao et al. (2023c) designed a centralized cloud predictive control to ensure the consensus formation control. Chi et al. (2023) proposed a distributed sliding-mode predictive control to achieve the cooperative formation control. Zhang and Liu (2022) presented an output feedback predictive control to realize the coordination of discrete-time quasi-linear MASs and used a cooperative flying-around task to verify the feasibility.

Additionally, Li et al. (2023a) established an adaptive event-triggering predictive control to realize the consensus in the presence of switched topology, time-varying delays, external disturbances, and input constraints. Li et al. (2023b) provided a tube-based distributed predictive control to maintain the leader-follower full containment control under the leader with a bounded disturbance. Qin et al. (2024) presented an asynchronous event-triggering predictive control to ensure the cooperative control under a parametric synchronization constraint. Wang et al. (2023a) developed a periodic event-triggering predictive control to consider the consensus with bounded disturbances, input, and communication delays. Meanwhile, there are also other literature (Li and Liu 2024; Franzè et al. 2021; Su et al. 2021b) that are intended to the study on predictive cooperative control for the MASs.

1.3.2 HOFAS Theory-Based Cooperative Control for Multiagent Systems

Considering the emergence of the HOFAS theory and its advantages in simplifying the control design and improving the control performance, many scholars are devoting to the cooperative control design based on the HOFAS theory and have obtained many representative previous results. It enriches the theoretical study and basic study for applications of cooperative control for the MASs in depth. During the design process, the first step is to develop the HOFAS model of the MASs, i.e., the HOFAMAS, and the second step is to reconstruct and resolve the cooperative control problems of the HOFAMASs under different cases by adopting various advanced control strategies.

For the cooperative fault-tolerant control against actuator failures, Ma et al. (2023) proposed a hierarchical design scheme to prevent the transmission of failures among all agents and provided a HOFAS adaptive control with a prescribed-time observer. Ma et al. (2024a) provided a HOFAS adaptive control based on a nonlinear approximation using a new neuroadaptive method to consider the leader-follower fault-tolerant cooperative control problem under actuator failure and unmodeled dynamics. In Ma et al. (2024b), a practical prescribed-time control based on the HOFAS theory was further investigated to address the fault-tolerant cooperative control with actuator failure and non-vanishing disturbances. Ma et al. (2025) presented a new prescribed-time control without the estimation of actuator failures to realize the coordination of the HOFAMASs, which allowed for the advance determination of the settling time and the final tracking accuracy as needed. In Liu (2022c), a predictive control strategy using the HOFAS theory was presented to realize the cooperative control with active compensation of communication constraints. Yang et al. (2024) established a controllability condition of the MASs in the finite-time domain by using the HOFAS theory and then designed a cooperative stabilization control protocol. Liu et al. (2024e) implemented the containment control with unknown control directions by applying an adaptive control based on the HOFAS theory, where a neural network method via an RBF function approximates the unknown nonlinear dynamics. Liu et al. (2025c) proposed a prescribed-time containment control with an adaptive prescribed-time observer for the HOFAMASs, which can reduce the computational complexity and can ensure that the followers converge to the convex hull of the leader.

Formation control is considered as one of the most significant directions in basic study for applications of cooperative control, which is applied to various fields, such as smart transportation, intelligent manufacturing, and aerospace. In the formation control of MASs, HOFAS theory has also obtained a lot of important results. Recently, Tan et al. (2025) designed the robust and adaptive control based on HOFAS theory to realize the time-varying group formation control against heterogeneous unknown nonlinearities, respectively. Meng et al. (2025) proposed a distributed observer-based HOFAS fault-tolerant control protocol to implement the formation control of fixed-wing UAVs with actuator failure and communication link failure. In Lu et al. (2024), a prescribed-time disturbance observer was established to estimate the composite disturbances including external disturbance and actuator failure and then provided a fault-tolerant controller based on HOFAS theory to realize the formation control of 6 degrees of freedom helicopters subject to the fixed and switched topology. Liu and Li (2025) constructed an extended state observer to achieve the estimation of actuator failure and environmental disturbances and then designed a compensation-based HOFAS cooperative controller to maintain the robust formation of quadrotor UAVs. Zhang et al. (2025c) firstly transformed the underactuated UAVs into the HOFAS model and then designed a predefined-time bipartite consensus sliding-mode control to realize the formation control of the UAVs. Wang et al. (2025b) provided an adaptive formation control with a distributed observer for the HOFAMASs with unknown dynamics and full-state constraints. Zhang et al. (2025b) constructed a reinforcement learning-based HOFAS optimal control to achieve the formation control of multiple helicopters under actuator failures. Meanwhile, Miao et al. (2024), Li et al. (2024a) and their related results also made contributions to the HOFAS theory-based formation control.

1.4 About This Book

Sections 1.2 and 1.3 have systematically reviewed and summarized the research status and developments of the HOFAS theory, predictive cooperative control, and the HOFAS theory-based cooperative control for the MASs, which implies that the HOFAS theory has great advantages and potential in reducing the complexity of the control design. It can obtain a more complete, simple, and general representation of the control laws, while a precondition and critical step of the HOFAS theory-based control design is to construct a HOFAS model of the considered systems. However, the first-order state-space model is still the most mainstream way to describe the actual dynamics of MASs in the existing studies of cooperative control for the MASs, such that it is difficult to deeply investigate the HOFAS theory-based cooperative control for the MASs.

Meanwhile, predictive control, as one of the most significant approaches for cooperative control of the MASs, can actively compensate for the network-induced communication constraints in the forward and feedback channels to reduce the conservatism and dependence of simultaneous consensus and stability conditions on the communication constraints and can also utilize the rolling optimization principle to improve the cooperative control performance in the dynamic process. But, the existing predictive control methods are hard to directly design a cooperative control protocol for the MASs described by a HOFAS model, because the existing methods are toward a first-order state-space model-based MASs rather than a HOFAS one. When transforming the HOFAS model-based MASs into a first-order state-space one, the computational load and complexity can be increased and some shortcomings, including the ill-conditioned matrices, unstable numerical solutions, and the surge of system dimensions, can be caused, so that it is of great significance to directly propose a predictive cooperative control protocol for the solution to the HOFAS theory-based cooperative control for the MASs.

This book considers the predictive cooperative control for the MASs by means of HOFAS theory, where a HOFAS model of the MASs, called the HOFAMASs, is firstly established to provide a model foundation for the HOFAS theory-based cooperative control design. Then, an IHOFAS prediction model associated with the HOFAMASs can be established by utilizing a type of Diophantine Equation, such that the design and representation of predictive cooperative control protocol can be completed within the framework of the HOFAS theory, named as the HOFAS

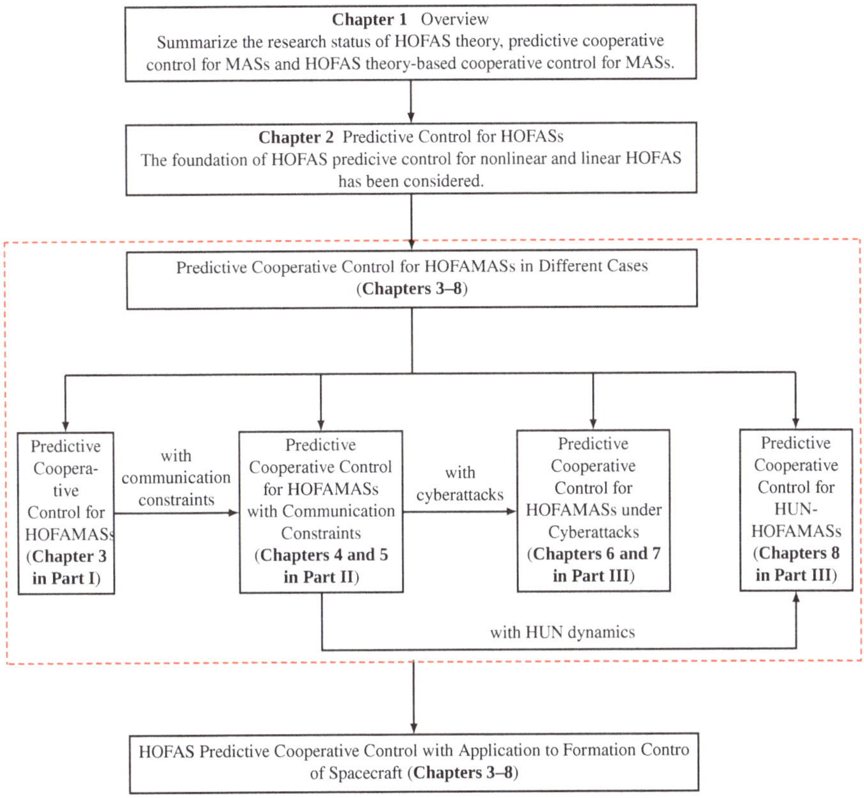

Fig. 1.4 The structure of this book

predictive control. Following the above idea, this book further investigates the predictive cooperative control for HOFAMASs under communication constraints, cyberattacks, and uncertainties and then proposes the correspondingly sufficient conditions to analyze the simultaneous consensus and stability for different cases. Further, the proposed theoretical results are applied to the formation control of air-bearing spacecraft simulators for verifying the effectiveness and practicability. The structure of this book is shown in Fig. 1.4.

The content of this book has been divided into three major parts. In Part I, the basic problem of predictive cooperative control for the HOFAMASs has been investigated. Part II has considered the predictive cooperative control for the HOFAMASs with communication constraints, and Part III has been devoted to the predictive cooperative control for the HOFAMASs under cyberattacks and uncertainties.

This chapter has provided an overview of the HOFAS theory, predictive cooperative control for the MASs, and the HOFAS theory-based cooperative control for the MASs and has summarized the structure and contents of this book.

The foundation of predictive cooperative control for the HOFAMASs has been considered in Part I. Chapter 2 has introduced the basic framework of the HOFAS predictive control for nonlinear and linear HOFASs and then proposed the sufficient condition to analyze the bounded stability and tracking performance. A fundamental problem of predictive cooperative control for the HOFAMASs has been investigated in Chap. 3, where the cooperative control for the HOFAMASs has been achieved by using a HOFAS predictive control and a sufficient condition of the simultaneous consensus and stability has been derived.

Part II has been composed of two chapters, which has been mainly concerned with the predictive cooperative control for the HOFAMASs with communication constraints. In Chap. 4, a HOFAS proportional-integral predictive control has been proposed to achieve the cooperative control for the HOFAMASs with the active compensation of fixed communication delays in the forward and feedback channels, and a sufficient condition on the simultaneous consensus and stability independent of communication delays has been constructed. Chapter 5 has designed a observer-based HOFAS predictive control to address a cooperative control problem of the HOFAMASs with time-varying communication constraints and immeasurable states, where a HOFAS observer has been established by using a time operator-based transformation and a sufficient condition has been derived to analyze the simultaneous consensus and stability.

In Part III, Chap. 6 has developed a packet-based HOFAS predictive control to ensure the secure cooperative control performance of the HOFAMASs under random denial-of-service attacks, such that random data dropouts and disorders caused by random denial-of-service attacks can be actively compensated. Chapter 7 has focused on the secure cooperative control of the HOFAMASs under random deception attacks, where a HOFAS sliding-mode predictive control has been presented and a sufficient condition for the simultaneous consensus and stability has been constructed with the help of the Lyapunov stability theory and a linear matrix inequality method. In Chap. 8, a robust cooperative control problem of heterogeneous uncertain nonlinear HOFAMASs has been addressed via a HOFAS terminal sliding-mode predictive control, which has proposed a sufficient condition of the simultaneous consensus and stability by using the Lyapunov stability theory and a linear matrix inequality method.

Part I
Foundation of Predictive Cooperative Control for High-Order Fully Actuated Multiagent Systems

Chapter 2
Predictive Control for High-Order Fully Actuated Systems

2.1 Introduction

Predictive control, a representative computer optimization control algorithm, plays an important role in the analysis and design of discrete-time control systems with the development of digital and network techniques, which can achieve the optimization of control performances and address some software and hardware constraints. It is also simple for the physical implementation of practical controllers with economy, high efficiency, and other advantages. The general principle of predictive control can be shown in Fig. 2.1, which includes the prediction model, rolling-horizon optimization, and feedback correction.

Because of the advantages of predictive control in theoretical study and industrial applications, numerous scholars focus on this field and have obtained many achievements. Specifically, Zhang et al. (2022b) combined Koopman operator and reinforcement learning to construct a robust predictive control for nonlinear systems with unknown dynamics and state constraints. Zhang et al. (2022c) used a Koopman operator to design a tube-based robust predictive control for addressing the modeling approximation errors and additive disturbances. Wang et al. (2025a) adopted an attention-based deep learning approach to achieve the accuracy modeling based on Koopman operator for unknown nonlinear systems and then proposed a predictive control to optimize the desired control performances. Liu (2024) developed a digital-twin predictive control strategy to implement the tracking control with time delays, unknown dynamics, and communication delays. Zhang and Jia (2025) established a self-healing predictive control on the basis of a control barrier function, so that system can be safety performed under abnormal states and can be asymptotically converged to a predefined safety set. Zhao et al. (2025) presented a robust predictive control to deal with the bounded disturbances and incremental input constraints, which derived an allowable bound of the disturbances and ensured the input-to-state stability. Meanwhile, Thompson et al. (2024), Zheng et al.

D.-W. Zhang, G.-P. Liu, *Predictive Cooperative Control for High-Order Fully Actuated Multiagent Systems*, https://doi.org/10.1007/978-981-95-1695-7_2

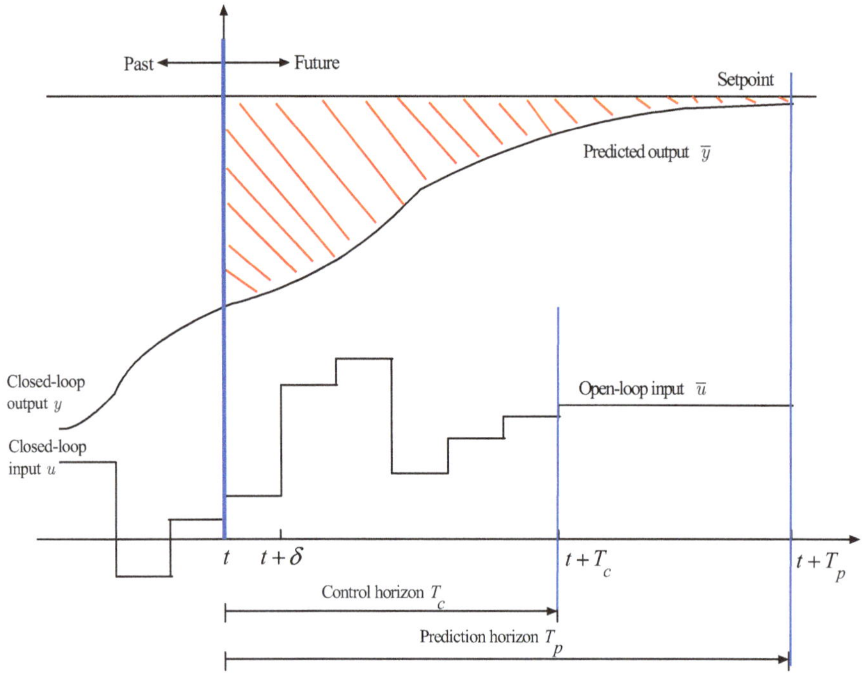

Fig. 2.1 The general principle of predictive control

(2025b), Wang et al. (2024a), and the references therein also make contributions to the theoretical study and basic application study of predictive control.

However, a shortcoming is that the above studies design a predictive control via a state-space model, which means that they must transform the high-order systems into a first-order state-space model and then realize the design of predictive control. Based on Sect. 1.1, the actual dynamic models are almost always high or second order, such that the model reduction can cause the ill-conditioned matrices, unstable numerical solutions, the loss of original physical meanings, the surge of system dimension, and other drawbacks. By introducing the HOFAS theory into the design of predictive control, the drawbacks mentionedabove can be easily addressed, while a key problem is how to represent and design the predictive control law within the framework of the HOFAS theory.

To deal with this problem, this chapter proposes a HOFAS predictive control to achieve the desired tracking control performance, where a highlight is that a type of Diophantine Equation is used to construct an IHOFAS prediction model instead of a first-order one, such that the representation and design of predictive control can be completed in the framework of the HOFAS theory. The main works are drawn as follows. Firstly, a discrete-time HOFAS model is adopted to describe the considered systems, which provides a better model foundation for control design. Based on the HOFAS model, the original dynamics can be eliminated by using the full actuation feature to obtain a linear constant system with the desired closed-loop performances. Then, an IHOFAS prediction model is derived by using a type of Diophantine Equation, such that the multistep ahead predictions are generated to minimize an objective function for generating an optimal tracking controller. Further, a sufficient condition is derived to analyze the bounded stability and tracking performance of the closed-loop HOFAS. Finally, the HOFAS predictive control provides a solution to the tracking control of air-bearing spacecraft simulator (ABSS) for verifying the feasibility and practicality.

2.2 Predictive Control of Nonlinear High-Order Fully Actuated Systems

2.2.1 Problem Statement

Based on Duan (2022c), a type of discrete-time step-forward nonlinear HOFAS is considered as

$$\begin{aligned} y(t+n) =& f\left(y^{\lfloor 0,n-1\rfloor}(t), u^{\lceil p,1\rceil}(t)\right) + g\left(y^{\lfloor 0,n-1\rfloor}(t), u^{\lceil p,1\rceil}(t)\right)u(t), \\ y(t) =& y_0(t),\ u(t) = u_0(t),\ t \le 0, \end{aligned} \tag{2.1}$$

with

$$\begin{aligned} y^{\lfloor 0,n-1\rfloor}(t) &:= \{y(t), y(t+1), \ldots, y(t+n-1)\}, \\ u^{\lceil p,1\rceil}(t) &:= \{u(t-p), u(t-p+1), \ldots, u(t-1)\}, \end{aligned}$$

where $y(t) \in \mathbb{R}^{\tilde{n}}$ and $u(t) \in \mathbb{R}^{\tilde{n}}$ denote the output and input vectors, $y_0(t) \in \mathbb{R}^{\tilde{n}}$ and $u_0(t) \in \mathbb{R}^{\tilde{n}}$ are the relevant initial values of $y(t)$ and $u(t)$, and n and p are two positive integers. $f(\cdot) := f\left(y^{\lfloor 0,n-1\rfloor}(t), u^{\lceil p,1\rceil}(t)\right) \in \mathbb{R}^{\tilde{n}}$ and $g(\cdot) := g\left(y^{\lfloor 0,n-1\rfloor}(t), u^{\lceil p,1\rceil}(t)\right) \in \mathbb{R}^{\tilde{n}\times\tilde{n}}$ are the known nonlinear vector and matrix functions, respectively.

Assumption 2.1 (Duan 2022c) *A1. The output vector of system* (2.1) *is available for the control design. A2.* $\forall t \ge 0$, $\forall y^{\lfloor 0,n-1\rfloor}(t)$, $\forall u^{\lceil p,1\rceil}(t)$, $\det(g(\cdot)) \ne 0$ or ∞.

For system (2.1), a HOFAS predictive control is proposed as

$$u(t) = g^{-1}(\cdot)\left(-f(\cdot) + \Upsilon(A_{0\sim n-1}, y(t)) + v(t)\right), \tag{2.2}$$

where $-f(\cdot)$ is used to eliminate the original nonlinearities, $\Upsilon(A_{0\sim n-1}, y(t)) = \sum_{\eta=0}^{n-1} A_\eta y(t+\eta) \in \mathbb{R}^{\tilde{n}}$ is to adjust the closed-loop performances and $A_\eta \in \mathbb{R}^{\tilde{n}\times\tilde{n}}$ are the adjustment parameters to be determined, and $v(t) \in \mathbb{R}^{\tilde{n}}$ is a tracking control item designed by the proposed HOFAS predictive control. By applying (2.2), the closed-loop HOFAS is achieved as

$$\begin{aligned} y(t+n) =& \Upsilon(A_{0\sim n-1}, y(t)) + v(t) \\ =& \sum_{\eta=0}^{n-1} A_\eta y(t+\eta) + v(t). \end{aligned} \tag{2.3}$$

Then, an objective function $\mathcal{J}(t)$ considering the tracking control performance is designed as

$$\mathcal{J}(t) = \left\| \hat{Y}(t+\aleph_y|t) - R(t+\aleph_y) \right\|_{W_1}^2 + \left\| \Delta\hat{V}(t+\aleph_u|t) \right\|_{W_2}^2, \tag{2.4}$$

with

$$\begin{aligned} \hat{Y}(t+\aleph_y|k) &= \left[\hat{y}^{\mathrm{T}}(t+\aleph_y|t) \cdots \hat{y}^{\mathrm{T}}(t+1|t) \right]^{\mathrm{T}}, \\ \Delta\hat{V}(t+\aleph_u|t) &= \left[\Delta\hat{v}^{\mathrm{T}}(t+\aleph_u|t) \cdots \Delta\hat{v}^{\mathrm{T}}(t|t) \right]^{\mathrm{T}}, \\ R(t+\aleph_y) &= \left[r^{\mathrm{T}}(t+\aleph_y|k) \cdots r^{\mathrm{T}}(t+1) \right]^{\mathrm{T}}, \end{aligned}$$

where $\hat{y}(t+\eta|t)$, $\eta = 1, 2, \ldots, \aleph_y$, and $\Delta\hat{v}(t+\eta|t)$, $\eta = 0, 1, \ldots, \aleph_u$, are the η-th ahead predictions of output $y(t)$ and tracking control increment $\Delta v(t)$ based on t time. $r(t)$ denotes a known reference signal, and $R(t+\aleph_y)$ indicates the related multistep ahead sequence. $W_1 \succ 0$ and $W_2 \succ 0$ are two weighting coefficient matrices. In (2.4), the first item of $\mathcal{J}(t)$ aims to consider the tracking control performance by achieving the approach of $\hat{Y}(t+\aleph_y|t)$ and $R(t+\aleph_y)$, and the second item imposes a constraint on changing the rate and amplitude of $\Delta v(t)$ in the view of algorithm design, which reduces the mechanical losses and ensures the controller's physical feasibility.

Problem 2.1 For nonlinear HOFAS (2.1) with Assumption 2.1, a HOFAS predictive control $u(t, r(t))$ in (2.2) is proposed by minimizing the $\mathcal{J}(t)$ in (2.4) to achieve the bounded stability and tracking performance of the closed-loop HOFAS (2.3), i.e., the following conditions are satisfied:

1. $\forall t \geq 0$, $\|y(t)\| < \infty$ with $\|r(t)\| < \infty$, where $r(t)$ is a known reference signal.
2. $\lim_{t\to\infty} \|y(t) - r(t)\| = 0$.

2.2.2 *Design of HOFAS Predictive Control*

By applying the time operation q, the closed-loop system (2.3) can be equivalently converted into a polynomial one, i.e.,

$$\mathcal{A}\left(q^{-1}\right)y(t)=\mathcal{B}\left(q^{-1}\right)v(t-1), \tag{2.5}$$

where $\mathcal{A}\left(q^{-1}\right)=I-\sum_{\eta=0}^{n-1}A_{\eta}q^{-n+\eta}$ and $\mathcal{B}\left(q^{-1}\right)=q^{-n+\eta}$ are two polynomial matrices in relation to q. Then, a type of Diophantine Equation for system (2.5) is given as

$$\mathcal{E}_{\eta}\left(q^{-1}\right)\mathcal{A}\Delta+q^{-\eta}\mathcal{F}\left(q^{-1}\right)=I, \tag{2.6}$$

where $\mathcal{E}_{\eta}\left(q^{-1}\right) = \sum_{\mu=0}^{\eta-1}e_{\eta,\mu}q^{-\mu}$ and $\mathcal{F}\left(q^{-1}\right) = \sum_{\mu=0}^{n}f_{\eta,\mu}q^{-\mu}$ are two polynomial matrices and also the solutions of Diophantine Equation (2.6) that are generated by the prediction horizon η and the system polynomial matrix $\mathcal{A}\left(q^{-1}\right)$. Multiplying $\mathcal{E}_{\eta}\Delta q^{\eta}$ on both sides of (2.5) yields that

$$\mathcal{E}_{\eta}\mathcal{A}\Delta y(t+\eta)=\mathcal{E}_{\eta}\mathcal{B}\Delta v(t+\eta-1).$$

By taking (2.6) into the above, it is derived that

$$y(t+\eta)=\mathcal{F}_{\eta}y(t)+\mathcal{E}_{\eta}\mathcal{B}\Delta v(t+\eta-1).$$

Let $\mathcal{G}_{\eta}\left(q^{-1}\right)=\mathcal{E}_{\eta}\left(q^{-1}\right)\mathcal{B}\left(q^{-1}\right)=\sum_{\mu=0}^{n+\eta-2}g_{\eta,\mu}q^{-\mu}$, and an IHOFAS prediction model can be established as

$$\hat{y}(t+\eta|t)=\mathcal{F}_{\eta}y(t)+\mathcal{G}_{\eta}\Delta\hat{v}(t+\eta-1|t). \tag{2.7}$$

Based on (2.7), the multistep ahead predictions of $y(t)$ from $t+1$ to $t+\aleph_y$ are obtained as

$$\begin{aligned}\hat{y}(t+1|t)=&\mathcal{F}_{1}y(t)+\mathcal{G}_{1}\Delta\hat{v}(t|t),\\&\vdots\\\hat{y}(t+\aleph_y|t)=&\mathcal{F}_{\aleph_y}y(t)+\mathcal{G}_{\aleph_y}\Delta\hat{v}(t+\aleph_y-1|t),\end{aligned}$$

when $\eta=\aleph_u+1,\aleph_u+2,\ldots,\aleph_y$, $\hat{v}(t+\eta|t)=\hat{v}(t+\aleph_u|t)$ so that $\Delta\hat{v}(t+\eta|t)=0$; thus the above can be compactly summarized as

$$\hat{Y}(t+\aleph_y|t)=P_1y(t)+P_2\Delta\hat{V}(t+\aleph_u|t), \tag{2.8}$$

where

$$P_1 = \begin{bmatrix} \mathcal{F}_{\aleph_y} \\ \vdots \\ \mathcal{F}_{\aleph_u+1} \\ \mathcal{F}_{\aleph_u} \\ \vdots \\ \mathcal{F}_1 \end{bmatrix}, \quad P_2 = \begin{bmatrix} \mathcal{G}_{\aleph_y} & 0 & \cdots & 0 \\ \vdots & \vdots & \cdots & \vdots \\ \mathcal{G}_{\aleph_u+1} & 0 & \cdots & 0 \\ 0 & \mathcal{G}_{\aleph_u} & \ddots & \vdots \\ \vdots & \ddots & \ddots & 0 \\ 0 & \cdots & 0 & \mathcal{G}_1 \end{bmatrix}.$$

Furthermore, an incremental constraint for the tracking control increment $\Delta v(t)$ is defined as

$$\Delta\hat{v}(t+\eta|t) = \gamma_\eta \Delta\hat{v}(t|t), \tag{2.9}$$

where $\gamma_\eta > 0$, $\eta = 1, 2, \ldots, \aleph_u$, denotes a weighting factor, such that P_2 is degenerated as $P_3 = P_2\Gamma$ with $\Gamma = \text{Blockdiag}\{\gamma_{\aleph_u} I, \ldots, \gamma_1 I, I\}$, and $P_2 \Delta\hat{V}(t + \aleph_u|t) = P_3 \Delta\hat{V}(t|t)$ with $\Delta\hat{V}(t|t) = \begin{bmatrix} \Delta\hat{v}^{\mathrm{T}}(t|t) & \cdots & \Delta\hat{v}^{\mathrm{T}}(t|t) \end{bmatrix}^{\mathrm{T}}$. Summarizing the above means that (2.8) can be rewritten as

$$\hat{Y}(t+\aleph_y|t) = P_1 y(t) + P_3 \Delta\hat{V}(t|t). \tag{2.10}$$

Remark 2.1 Actually, the incremental constraint (2.9) provides a proportional hard constraint for the $\Delta\hat{v}(t+\eta|t)$, $\eta = 1, 2, \ldots, \aleph_u$, on the basis of $\Delta v(t)$ to plan the future tracking control increment. The rationality is that only $\Delta v(t)$ is utilized at the current time, and other increments $\Delta\hat{v}(t+\eta)$, $\eta = 1, 2, \ldots, \aleph_u$, are ignored because of the rolling-horizon optimization of predictive control. Meanwhile, the servicing life of mechanical device can also be prolonged because it restricts the change amplitude and frequency of $\Delta v(t)$ via the proportional hard constraint. In the control process, γ_η can be exploited to adjust the control performance of closed-loop system (2.3). In detail, $\gamma_\eta > 1$ can enhance the system robustness because it can inhibit the change of present control by reducing the present control increment $\Delta v(t)$. $\gamma_\eta < 1$ can accelerate the convergence rate of system responses because it can increase the change of present control by raising the present control increment $\Delta v(t)$.

To obtain the optimal tracking control increment $\Delta v(t)$, let

$$\frac{\partial}{\partial \Delta\hat{V}(t|t)} \mathcal{J}(t) = 0.$$

By taking (2.10) into the above, it is yielded that

$$P_3^{\mathrm{T}} W_1 \left(P_1 y(t) + P_3 \Delta\hat{V}(t|t) - R(t+\aleph_y) \right) + \Gamma^{\mathrm{T}} W_2 \Gamma \Delta\hat{V}(t|t) = 0,$$

and then

$$\Delta\hat{V}(t|t) = M_1^{-1}M_2 y(t) + M_1^{-1}M_3 R(t+\aleph_y),$$

where $M_1 = P_3^{\mathrm{T}}W_1P_3 + \Gamma^{\mathrm{T}}W_2\Gamma$, $M_2 = -P_3^{\mathrm{T}}W_1P_1$, $M_3 = P_3^{\mathrm{T}}W_1$. The optimal tracking control increment $\Delta v(t)$ is designed as $\Delta v(t) = \Delta\hat{v}(t|t) = H\Delta\hat{V}(t|t)$, i.e.,

$$\Delta v(t) = HM_1^{-1}M_2 y(t) + HM_1^{-1}M_3 R(t+\aleph_y), \tag{2.11}$$

with $H = \begin{bmatrix} 0 \cdots 0 \; I \end{bmatrix}$.

Remark 2.2 In (2.2), $\Upsilon(A_{0\sim n-1}, y(t))$ is used to adjust the control performance of the closed-loop system (2.3) by stabilizing the system $y(t+n) = \Upsilon(A_{0\sim n-1}, y(t))$. Meanwhile, $\Upsilon(A_{0\sim n-1}, y(t))$ is also utilized to improve the prediction accuracy of IHOFAS prediction model (2.7) by constructing a feedback correction. Summarizing the above means that how to solve the adjustment parameters A_η, $\eta = 1, 2, \ldots n-1$, is also an important problem. A guiding way is to construct a matrix $\Phi(A_{0\sim n-1})$ that is similar to a Schur matrix $\Lambda \in \mathbb{R}^{\tilde{n}n\times\tilde{n}n}$ (Duan 2022c) with

$$\Phi(A_{0\sim n-1}) = \begin{bmatrix} 0 & I & & \\ \vdots & & \ddots & \\ 0 & & & I \\ A_0 & A_1 & \cdots & A_{n-1} \end{bmatrix}, \tag{2.12}$$

and then the adjustment parameters A_η, $\eta = 1, 2, \ldots n-1$, can be solved as

$$\begin{bmatrix} A_0 \; A_1 \; \cdots \; A_{n-1} \end{bmatrix} = \Xi\Lambda^n \begin{bmatrix} \Xi \\ \Xi\Lambda \\ \vdots \\ \Xi\Lambda^{n-1} \end{bmatrix}^{-1}, \tag{2.13}$$

where $\Xi \in \mathbb{R}^{\tilde{n}\times\tilde{n}n}$ is an arbitrary parameter matrix satisfying

$$\det\left(\begin{bmatrix} \Xi \\ \Xi\Lambda \\ \vdots \\ \Xi\Lambda^{n-1} \end{bmatrix}\right) \neq 0.$$

2.2.3 Analysis of Bounded Stability and Tracking Performance

Let $e(t) = y(t) - r(t)$ be the tracking error, such that Conditions 1 and 2 of Problem 2.1 can be equivalent to $\lim_{t\to\infty} \|e(t)\| = 0$. Hence, the bounded stability and tracking performance of the closed-loop HOFAS (2.3) can be transformed into $e(t) \to 0$ with $t \to \infty$. In this view, Theorem 2.1 is proposed to solve this problem.

Theorem 2.1 *The closed-loop HOFAS* (2.3) *can implement the bounded stability and tracking performance if* $\exists W_1 \succ 0$, $\exists W_2 \succ 0$, $\exists \gamma_\eta > 0$, $\eta = 1, 2, \ldots, \aleph_u$, *to guarantee that* $\frac{\partial}{\partial \Delta \hat{V}(t|t)} \mathcal{J}(t) = 0$, *and* $\Phi\left(q^{-1}\right)$ *is a Schur stable polynomial matrix in relation to* q, *where*

$$\Phi\left(q^{-1}\right) = \left(2I + \mathcal{A}_{c,1}\right) - \left(I + \mathcal{A}_{c,1}\right) q^{-1}, \tag{2.14}$$

with $\mathcal{A}_{c,1} = \mathcal{A}_c H M_1^{-1} M_2$ *and* $\mathcal{A}_c = \mathcal{A}^{-1}\mathcal{B}$.

Proof It is generally assumed that $r(\cdot) = r$, such that $\Delta e(t) = \Delta y(t)$, and

$$\begin{aligned} e(t+1) =& y(t+1) - r(t+1) \\ =& e(t) + \Delta y(t+1). \end{aligned} \tag{2.15}$$

Based on (2.5), it is obtained that

$$\Delta y(t+1) = \mathcal{A}_c \Delta v(t),$$

because $\exists W_1 \succ 0$, $\exists W_2 \succ 0$, $\exists \gamma_\eta > 0$, $\eta = 1, 2, \ldots, \aleph_u$, to guarantee that $\frac{\partial}{\partial \Delta \hat{V}(t|t)} \mathcal{J}(t) = 0$, and the optimal tracking control increment $\Delta v(t)$ can be solved in (2.11). By taking (2.11) into the above, it is derived that

$$\begin{aligned} \Delta y(t+1) =& \mathcal{A}_c \Delta v(t) \\ =& \mathcal{A}_c H M_1^{-1} M_2 y(t) + \mathcal{A}_c H M_1^{-1} M_3 R(t + \aleph_y) \\ =& \left(I + \mathcal{A}_{c,1}\right) \Delta y(t) \\ =& \left(I + \mathcal{A}_{c,1}\right) \Delta e(t), \end{aligned}$$

where $\mathcal{A}_{c,1}$ is given below Eq. (2.14). Then, taking the above into (2.15) yields that

$$\begin{aligned} e(t+1) =& e(t) + \Delta y(t+1), \\ =& e(t) + \left(I + \mathcal{A}_{c,1}\right) \Delta e(t) \\ =& \Phi\left(q^{-1}\right) e(t), \end{aligned} \tag{2.16}$$

where $\Phi\left(q^{-1}\right)$ is shown in (2.14).

Because $\exists W_1 \succ 0$, $\exists W_2 \succ 0$, $\exists \gamma_\eta > 0$, $\eta = 1, 2, \ldots, \aleph_u$, to guarantee that $\Phi\left(q^{-1}\right)$ is a Schur stable polynomial matrix, $e(t) \rightarrow 0$ with $t \rightarrow \infty$. Hence, the closed-loop HOFAS (2.3) can achieve the bounded stability and tracking performance.

This completes the proof. □

2.3 Predictive Control for Linear High-Order Fully Actuated Systems

2.3.1 Problem Statement

Based on Duan (2022c) and system (2.1), a type of discrete-time step-forward linear HOFAS is investigated as

$$\begin{aligned} x(t+n) =& - L\left(A_{0\sim n-1}, x(t)\right) + Bu(t), \\ y(t) =& Cx(t), \end{aligned} \tag{2.17}$$

where $L(\cdot) := L\left(A_{0\sim n-1}, x(t)\right) = \sum_{\eta=0}^{n-1} A_\eta x(t+\eta) \in \mathbb{R}^{\tilde{n}}$ is a linear vector function, and $x(t) \in \mathbb{R}^{\tilde{n}}$, $u(t) \in \mathbb{R}^{\tilde{n}}$, $y(t) \in \mathbb{R}^m$ are the state, control, and output vectors, respectively. $A_\eta \in \mathbb{R}^{\tilde{n}\times\tilde{n}}$, $\eta = 0, 1, \ldots, n-1$, $B \in \mathbb{R}^{\tilde{n}\times\tilde{n}}$, $C \in \mathbb{R}^{m\tilde{n}}$ are the known coefficient matrices with the corresponding dimensions.

Assumption 2.2 (Duan 2022c) *A1. The state vector of linear HOFAS* (2.17) *is available for the control design. A2.* $\det(B) \neq 0$.

For system (2.17), a HOFAS predictive control is designed as

$$u(t) = B^{-1}\left(L(\cdot) + \Upsilon\left(K_{0\sim n-1}, x(t)\right) + v(t)\right), \tag{2.18}$$

where $L(\cdot)$ is used to offset the open-loop dynamics, $\Upsilon\left(K_{0\sim n-1}, x(t)\right) = \sum_{\eta=0}^{n-1} K_\eta x(t+\eta) \in \mathbb{R}^{\tilde{n}}$ is to adjust the closed-loop performances and $K_\eta \in \mathbb{R}^{\tilde{n}\times\tilde{n}}$ are the feedback gains to be determined, and $v(t) \in \mathbb{R}^{\tilde{n}}$ is a tracking control item designed by the proposed HOFAS predictive control. By applying (2.18), the closed-loop HOFAS is realized as

$$\begin{aligned} x(t+n) =& \Upsilon\left(K_{0\sim n-1}, x(t)\right) + v(t) \\ =& \sum_{\eta=0}^{n-1} K_\eta x(t+\eta) + v(t). \end{aligned} \tag{2.19}$$

Then, an objective function $\mathcal{J}(t)$ is presented in (2.4) to solve the $v(t)$ for tracking the desired reference signal $r(t)$.

Problem 2.2 For linear HOFAS (2.17) with Assumption 2.2, a HOFAS predictive control $u(t, r(t))$ in (2.18) is designed by minimizing the $\mathcal{J}(t)$ in (2.4), so that the closed-loop HOFAS (2.19) can implement the bounded stability and tracking performance, i.e., the following conditions hold:

1. $\forall t \geq 0$, $\|y(t)\| < \infty$ with $\|r(t)\| < \infty$, where $r(t)$ is a known reference signal.
2. $\lim_{t\to\infty} \|y(t) - r(t)\| = 0$.

2.3.2 *Design of HOFAS Predictive Control*

By applying the time operation q, the closed-loop system (2.19) can be equivalently converted into a polynomial one, i.e.,

$$\mathcal{K}\left(q^{-1}\right)x(t) = \mathcal{B}\left(q^{-1}\right)v(t-1), \tag{2.20}$$

where $\mathcal{K}\left(q^{-1}\right) = I - \sum_{\eta=0}^{n-1} K_\eta q^{-n+\eta}$ and $\mathcal{B}\left(q^{-1}\right) = q^{-n+\eta}$ are two polynomial matrices in relation to q. By applying the Diophantine Equation (2.6) and repeating the process from (2.5) to (2.7), an IHOFAS prediction model can be established as

$$\hat{x}(t+\eta|t) = \mathcal{F}_\eta x(t) + \mathcal{G}_\eta \Delta\hat{v}(t+\eta-1|t). \tag{2.21}$$

Based on (2.21), the multistep state ahead predictions from $t+1$ to $t+\aleph_y$ are obtained as

$$\begin{aligned}
\hat{x}(t+1|t) &= \mathcal{F}_1 x(t) + \mathcal{G}_1 \Delta\hat{v}(t|t), \\
&\vdots \\
\hat{x}(t+\aleph_y|t) &= \mathcal{F}_{\aleph_y} x(t) + \mathcal{G}_{\aleph_y} \Delta\hat{v}(t+\aleph_y-1|t),
\end{aligned}$$

and the corresponding output prediction is yielded as

$$\hat{y}(t+\eta) = C\hat{x}(t+\eta), \quad \eta = 1, 2, \ldots, \aleph_y. \tag{2.22}$$

When $\eta = \aleph_u+1, \aleph_u+2, \ldots, \aleph_y$, $\hat{v}(t+\eta|t) = \hat{v}(t+\aleph_u|t)$ such that $\Delta\hat{v}(t+\eta|t) = 0$, thus the output prediction (2.22) can be compactly written as

$$\hat{Y}(t+\aleph_y|t) = P_1 x(t) + P_2 \Delta\hat{V}(t+\aleph_u|t), \tag{2.23}$$

where

$$P_1 = \begin{bmatrix} C\mathcal{F}_{\aleph_y} \\ \vdots \\ C\mathcal{F}_{\aleph_u+1} \\ C\mathcal{F}_{\aleph_u} \\ \vdots \\ C\mathcal{F}_1 \end{bmatrix}, \quad P_2 = \begin{bmatrix} C\mathcal{G}_{\aleph_y} & 0 & \cdots & 0 \\ \vdots & \vdots & \cdots & \vdots \\ C\mathcal{G}_{\aleph_u+1} & 0 & \cdots & 0 \\ 0 & C\mathcal{G}_{\aleph_u} & \ddots & \vdots \\ \vdots & \ddots & \ddots & 0 \\ 0 & \cdots & 0 & C\mathcal{G}_1 \end{bmatrix}.$$

Similarly, based on (2.9), the output prediction (2.23) can be further rewritten as

$$\hat{Y}(t+\aleph_y|t) = P_1 x(t) + P_3 \Delta \hat{V}(t|t). \tag{2.24}$$

To obtain the optimal tracking control increment $\Delta v(t)$, let

$$\frac{\partial}{\partial \Delta \hat{V}(t|t)} \mathcal{J}(t) = 0.$$

By taking (2.24) into the above, it is yielded that

$$P_3^{\mathrm{T}} W_1 \left(P_1 x(t) + P_3 \Delta \hat{V}(t|t) - R(t+\aleph_y) \right) + \Gamma^{\mathrm{T}} W_2 \Gamma \Delta \hat{V}(t|t) = 0,$$

and then

$$\Delta \hat{V}(t|t) = M_1^{-1} M_2 x(t) + M_1^{-1} M_3 R(t+\aleph_y),$$

where $M_1 = P_3^{\mathrm{T}} W_1 P_3 + \Gamma^{\mathrm{T}} W_2 \Gamma$, $M_2 = -P_3^{\mathrm{T}} W_1 P_1$, $M_3 = P_3^{\mathrm{T}} W_1$. The optimal tracking control increment $\Delta v(t)$ is designed as $\Delta v(t) = \Delta \hat{v}(t|t) = H \Delta \hat{V}(t|t)$, i.e.,

$$\Delta v(t) = H M_1^{-1} M_2 x(t) + H M_1^{-1} M_3 R(t+\aleph_y), \tag{2.25}$$

with $H = \begin{bmatrix} 0 \cdots 0 \; I \end{bmatrix}$.

Remark 2.3 Clearly, system (2.20) is of the same form as (2.5) apart from the differences of $\mathcal{K}\left(q^{-1}\right)$ and $\mathcal{A}\left(q^{-1}\right)$, such that the procedure of establishing the IHOFAS prediction model (2.21) is also the same as that of (2.7) with replacing $\mathcal{A}\left(q^{-1}\right)$ by $\mathcal{K}\left(q^{-1}\right)$, which can be omitted for saving the page space. Meanwhile, the adjustment parameters K_η, $\eta = 0, 1, \ldots, n-1$, are also solved by utilizing the same method in Remark 2.2, i.e.,

$$\begin{bmatrix} K_0 \; K_1 \; \cdots \; K_{n-1} \end{bmatrix} = \mathcal{Z}\Lambda^n \begin{bmatrix} \mathcal{Z} \\ \mathcal{Z}\Lambda \\ \vdots \\ \mathcal{Z}\Lambda^{n-1} \end{bmatrix}^{-1},$$

where $\mathcal{Z} \in \mathbb{R}^{\tilde{n} \times \tilde{n}n}$ is an arbitrary parameter matrix and $\Lambda \in \mathbb{R}^{\tilde{n}n \times \tilde{n}n}$ is a Schur matrix satisfying

$$\det\left(\begin{bmatrix} \mathcal{Z} \\ \mathcal{Z}\Lambda \\ \vdots \\ \mathcal{Z}\Lambda^{n-1} \end{bmatrix}\right) \neq 0.$$

2.3.3 Analysis of Bounded Stability and Tracking Performance

In fact, Conditions 1 and 2 in Problem 2.2 can be converted into $\lim_{t\to\infty} \|e(t)\| = 0$, where $e(t) = y(t) - r(t) = Cx(t) - r(t)$ is a tracking error, so that the bounded stability and tracking performance of the closed-loop HOFAS (2.19) can be equivalent to $e(t) \to 0$ with $t \to \infty$. Then, Theorem 2.2 is derived for this problem.

Theorem 2.2 *The closed-loop HOFAS* (2.19) *can achieve the bounded stability and tracking performance if* $\exists W_1 \succ 0$, $\exists W_2 \succ 0$, $\exists \gamma_\eta > 0$, $\eta = 1, 2, \ldots, \aleph_u$, *to guarantee that* $\frac{\partial}{\partial \Delta \hat{V}(t|t)} \mathcal{J}(t) = 0$, *and* Φ *is a Schur stable polynomial matrix in relation to* q, *where*

$$\Phi = I + (q-1)C\Phi_1^{-1}\Phi_2, \tag{2.26}$$

with

$$\begin{aligned} \Phi_1 &= I + \mathcal{K}_c H M_1^{-1}\left(M_2 + M_3 \vec{I}_{\aleph_y} C\right) - q, \\ \Phi_2 &= \mathcal{K}_c H M_1^{-1} M_3 \vec{I}_{\aleph_y}, \; \mathcal{K}_c = \mathcal{K}^{-1}\mathcal{B}, \; \vec{I}_{\aleph_y} = \begin{bmatrix} I \cdots I \end{bmatrix}^{\mathrm{T}}. \end{aligned} \tag{2.27}$$

Proof It is generally assumed that $r(\cdot) = r$, such that $\Delta v(t)$ in (2.25) can be rewritten as

$$\Delta v(t) = HM_1^{-1}M_2 x(t) + HM_1^{-1}M_3 \vec{I}_{\aleph_y}(Cx(t) - e(t)), \tag{2.28}$$

and

$$\begin{aligned}e(t+1) =& y(t+1) - r(t+1)\\ =& e(t) + \Delta y(t+1)\\ =& e(t) + C\Delta x(t+1),\end{aligned}$$

and by using the time operator q, the above can be represented as

$$e(t+1) = e(t) + (q-1)Cx(t). \tag{2.29}$$

Based on (2.20), it is obtained that

$$\Delta x(t+1) = \mathcal{K}_c \Delta v(t),$$

because $\exists W_1 \succ 0$, $\exists W_2 \succ 0$, $\exists \gamma_\eta > 0$, $\eta = 1, 2, \ldots, \aleph_u$, to guarantee that $\frac{\partial}{\partial \Delta \hat{V}(t|t)} \mathcal{J}(t) = 0$, and the optimal tracking control increment $\Delta v(t)$ can be solved in (2.25) and (2.28). By taking (2.28) into the above, it is yielded that

$$\begin{aligned}\Delta x(t+1) =& \mathcal{K}_c \Delta v(t)\\ =& \mathcal{K}_c H M_1^{-1} M_2 x(t) + \mathcal{K}_c H M_1^{-1} M_3 \vec{I}_{\aleph_y}(Cx(t) - e(t)),\end{aligned}$$

which can be derived as

$$x(t) = \Phi_1^{-1}\Phi_2 e(t), \tag{2.30}$$

where Φ_1 and Φ_2 are provided in (2.27). Combined with (2.30), system (2.29) can be further obtained as follows:

$$\begin{aligned}e(t+1) =& e(t) + (q-1)Cx(t),\\ =& e(t) + (q-1)C\Phi_1^{-1}\Phi_2 e(t)\\ =& \Phi e(t),\end{aligned} \tag{2.31}$$

where $\Phi(q)$ is shown in (2.26).

Because $\exists W_1 \succ 0$, $\exists W_2 \succ 0$, $\exists \gamma_\eta > 0$, $\eta = 1, 2, \ldots, \aleph_u$, to guarantee that Φ is a Schur stable polynomial matrix in relation to q, $e(t) \to 0$ with $t \to \infty$. Hence, the closed-loop HOFAS (2.19) can realize the bounded stability and tracking performance.

This completes the proof. □

2.4 With Application to Tracking Control of Air-Bearing Spacecraft Simulator

The air-bearing spacecraft simulator (ABSS) is regarded as a class of widely used simulation device to simulate the attitude joint orbit control of spacecraft under the microgravity environment at ground. The details of the ABSS and its associated experimental platform refer to Appendix A. In this section, two experiments in nonlinear and linear cases by using $1^{\#}$ ABSS are provided here to verify the proposed HOFAS predictive control, i.e., $i = 1$ in (A.2) and (A.4).

2.4.1 Nonlinear Case

When $i = 1$, the nonlinear model of $1^{\#}$ ABSS in the form of (A.2) is provided as

$$m_{1,\text{ABSS}}x_{1,\text{ABSS}}(t+2) = f_{1,x}(\cdot) + F_{I,x_{1,\text{ABSS}}}(t), \tag{2.32a}$$

$$m_{1,\text{ABSS}}y_{1,\text{ABSS}}(t+2) = f_{1,y}(\cdot) + F_{I,y_{1,\text{ABSS}}}(t), \tag{2.32b}$$

$$J_{1,\text{ABSS}}\psi_{1,\text{ABSS}}(t+2) = f_{1,T}(\cdot) + F_{I,T_{1,\text{ABSS}}}(t), \tag{2.32c}$$

with

$$\begin{aligned}
f_{1,x}(\cdot) =& 2m_{1,\text{ABSS}}x_{1,\text{ABSS}}(t+1) - m_{1,\text{ABSS}}x_{1,\text{ABSS}}(t) \\
& + m_{1,\text{ABSS}}(y_{1,\text{ABSS}}(t+1) - y_{1,\text{ABSS}}(t))(\psi_{1,\text{ABSS}}(t+1) - \psi_{1,\text{ABSS}}(t)), \\
f_{1,y}(\cdot) =& 2m_{1,\text{ABSS}}y_{1,\text{ABSS}}(t+1) - m_{1,\text{ABSS}}y_{1,\text{ABSS}}(t) \\
& + m_{1,\text{ABSS}}(x_{1,\text{ABSS}}(t+1) - x_{1,\text{ABSS}}(t))(\psi_{1,\text{ABSS}}(t+1) - \psi_{1,\text{ABSS}}(t)), \\
f_{1,T}(\cdot) =& 2J_{1,\text{ABSS}}\psi_{1,\text{ABSS}}(t+1) - J_{1,\text{ABSS}}\psi_{1,\text{ABSS}}(t).
\end{aligned}$$

Then, a flying-around experiment of $1^{\#}$ ABSS is proposed with $T_s = 0.2$s, where the tracking control for systems (2.32a) and (2.32b) is designed as

$$\begin{aligned}
F_{I,x_{1,\text{ABSS}}}(t) =& - f_{1,x}(\cdot) + \Upsilon(A_{0\sim1}, x_{1,\text{ABSS}}(t)) + v_x(t), \\
F_{I,y_{1,\text{ABSS}}}(t) =& - f_{1,y}(\cdot) + \Upsilon(A_{0\sim1}, y_{1,\text{ABSS}}(t)) + v_y(t),
\end{aligned} \tag{2.33}$$

and a stabilization control for system (2.32c) is designed as

$$F_{I,T_{1,\text{ABSS}}}(t) = -f_{1,T}(\cdot) + \Upsilon(A_{0\sim1}, \psi_{1,\text{ABSS}}(t)). \tag{2.34}$$

For the tracking control (2.33), the design parameters are given as

$$\begin{aligned}\Upsilon(A_{0\sim1}, x_{1,\text{ABSS}}(t)) &=19.4x_{1,\text{ABSS}}(t+1) - 0.3802x_{1,\text{ABSS}}(t),\\ \Upsilon(A_{0\sim1}, y_{1,\text{ABSS}}(t)) &=19.4y_{1,\text{ABSS}}(t+1) - 0.3802y_{1,\text{ABSS}}(t),\end{aligned}$$

and $\aleph_y = 5$, $\aleph_u = 3$, $W_1 = I$, $W_2 = 5I$, $\Gamma = I$. For the stabilization control (2.34), the design parameters are provided as

$$\Upsilon(A_{0\sim1}, \psi_{1,\text{ABSS}}(t)) = 0.2629\psi_{1,\text{ABSS}}(t+1) - 0.0717\psi_{1,\text{ABSS}}(t).$$

By applying (2.33) and (2.34), the experimental results are shown in Figs. 2.2, 2.3, 2.4.

Figure 2.2 implies that the responses of $x_{1,\text{ABSS}}(t)$ and $y_{1,\text{ABSS}}(t)$ can achieve the desired tracking control performance within an allowable error by applying (2.33), and the response of $\psi_{1,\text{ABSS}}(t)$ can also realize the stabilization by applying (2.34), but the vibration still exists during the steady process. The reason is that both the reaction forces of the thrusters and the airflow in the experimental site affect the stabilization control performance of $\psi_{1,\text{ABSS}}(t)$. The control inputs generated by (2.33) and (2.34) are plotted in Fig. 2.3, which shows that there are also the vibrations because of the model uncertainties and external disturbances during the experiment. Figure 2.4 provides the practical trajectory of flying-around of $1^\#$ ABSS, which means that $1^\#$ ABSS can reach the desired orbit and continue to perform the proposed flying-around mission by utilizing (2.33) and (2.34). Through the experimental results, the feasibility and practicability of the HOFAS predictive control can be clearly verified.

2.4.2 *Linear Case*

When $i = 1$, the linear model of $1^\#$ ABSS in the form of (A.4) is provided as

$$m_{1,\text{ABSS}}x_{1,\text{ABSS}}(t+2) = L_{1,x}(\cdot) + F_{I,x_{1,\text{ABSS}}}(t), \tag{2.35a}$$

$$m_{1,\text{ABSS}}y_{1,\text{ABSS}}(t+2) = L_{1,y}(\cdot) + F_{I,y_{1,\text{ABSS}}}(t), \tag{2.35b}$$

$$J_{1,\text{ABSS}}\psi_{1,\text{ABSS}}(t+2) = L_{1,T}(\cdot) + F_{I,T_{1,\text{ABSS}}}(t), \tag{2.35c}$$

with

$$\begin{aligned}L_{1,x}(\cdot) &=2m_{1,\text{ABSS}}x_{1,\text{ABSS}}(t+1) - m_{1,\text{ABSS}}x_{1,\text{ABSS}}(t),\\ L_{1,y}(\cdot) &=2m_{1,\text{ABSS}}y_{1,\text{ABSS}}(t+1) - m_{1,\text{ABSS}}y_{1,\text{ABSS}}(t),\\ L_{1,T}(\cdot) &=2J_{1,\text{ABSS}}\psi_{1,\text{ABSS}}(t+1) - J_{1,\text{ABSS}}\psi_{1,\text{ABSS}}(t).\end{aligned}$$

Then, a tracking control experiment of $1^\#$ ABSS is proposed with $T_s = 0.2\text{s}$, where the tracking control for systems (2.35a) and (2.35b) is designed as

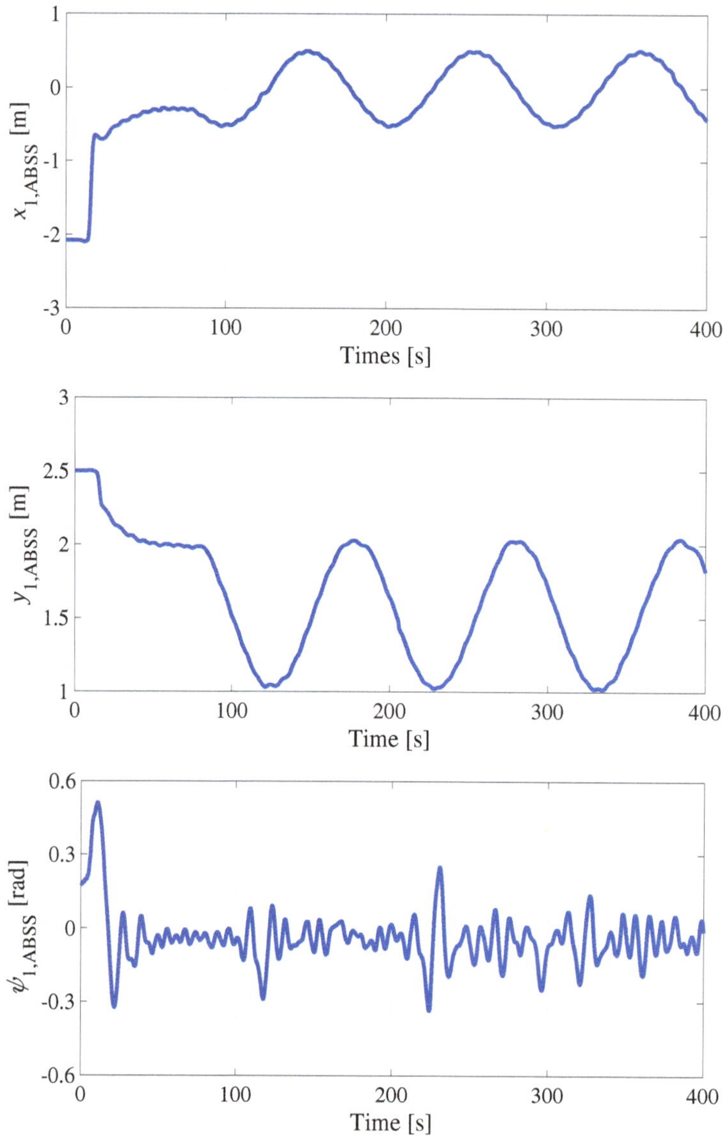

Fig. 2.2 The position and angle responses of flying-around of $1^{\#}$ ABSS by applying (2.33) and (2.34)

$$
\begin{aligned}
F_{I,x_{1,\text{ABSS}}}(t) &= -L_{1,x}(\cdot) + \varUpsilon(K_{0\sim 1}, x_{1,\text{ABSS}}(t)) + v_x(t), \\
F_{I,y_{1,\text{ABSS}}}(t) &= -L_{1,y}(\cdot) + \varUpsilon(K_{0\sim 1}, y_{1,\text{ABSS}}(t)) + v_y(t),
\end{aligned} \tag{2.36}
$$

and a stabilization control for system (2.32c) is designed as

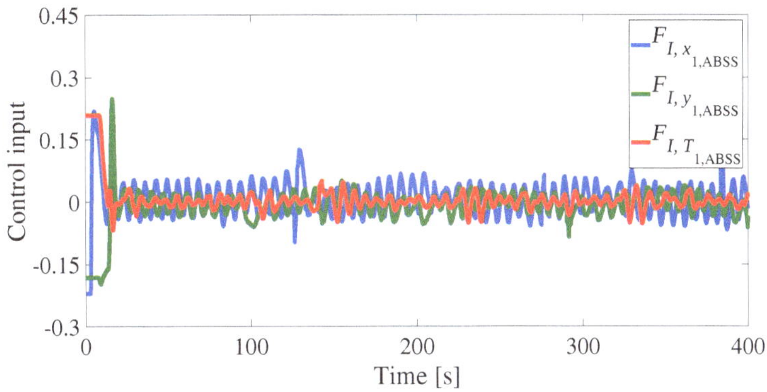

Fig. 2.3 The control inputs of 1# ABSS

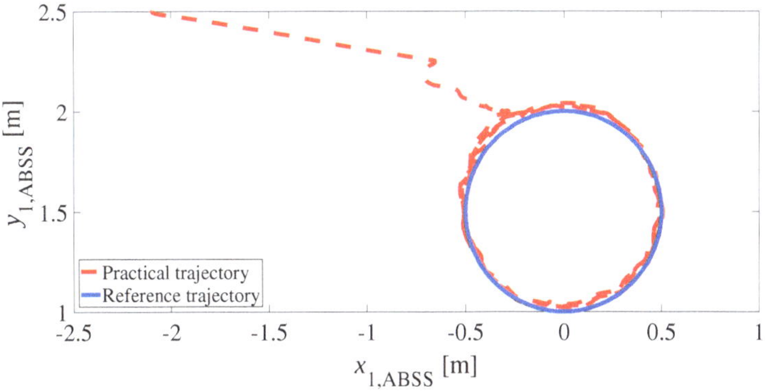

Fig. 2.4 The practical trajectory of 1# ABSS

$$F_{I,T_{1,\mathrm{ABSS}}}(t) = -L_{1,T}(\cdot) + \Upsilon(K_{0\sim1}, \psi_{1,\mathrm{ABSS}}(t)). \tag{2.37}$$

For the tracking control (2.36), the design parameters are given as

$$\begin{aligned}\Upsilon(K_{0\sim1}, x_{1,\mathrm{ABSS}}(t)) =& 19.4x_{1,\mathrm{ABSS}}(t+1) - 0.3802x_{1,\mathrm{ABSS}}(t),\\ \Upsilon(K_{0\sim1}, y_{1,\mathrm{ABSS}}(t)) =& 19.4y_{1,\mathrm{ABSS}}(t+1) - 0.3802y_{1,\mathrm{ABSS}}(t),\end{aligned}$$

and $\aleph_y = 5$, $\aleph_u = 3$, $W_1 = I$, $W_2 = 0.1I$, $\Gamma = \mathrm{diag}\{20, 19, 18, 1\}$. For the stabilization control (2.34), the design parameters are provided as

$$\Upsilon(K_{0\sim1}, \psi_{1,\mathrm{ABSS}}(t)) = 0.2629\psi_{1,\mathrm{ABSS}}(t+1) - 0.0717\psi_{1,\mathrm{ABSS}}(t).$$

By applying (2.36) and (2.37), the experimental results are shown in Figs. 2.5, 2.6, 2.7.

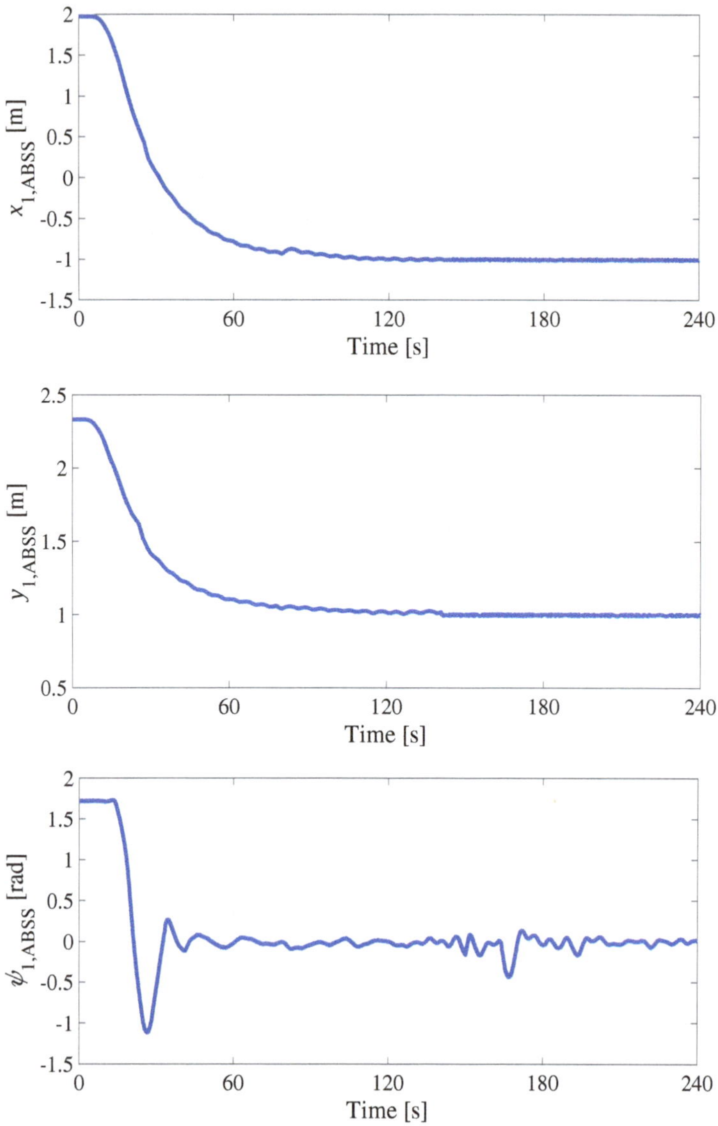

Fig. 2.5 The position and angle responses of flying-around of 1# ABSS by applying (2.36) and (2.37)

Figure 2.5 shows that the responses of $x_{1,\mathrm{ABSS}}(t)$ and $y_{1,\mathrm{ABSS}}(t)$ can achieve the desired tracking control with satisfactory performance by applying (2.36), and the response of $\psi_{1,\mathrm{ABSS}}(t)$ still exhibits the vibration phenomenon by applying (2.37) during the stabilization control; the reason is discussed in Sect. 2.4.1. Figure 2.6 gives the control inputs generated by (2.36) and (2.37), where the reason for the vibrations in the control process is also analyzed in Sect. 2.4.1. The motion

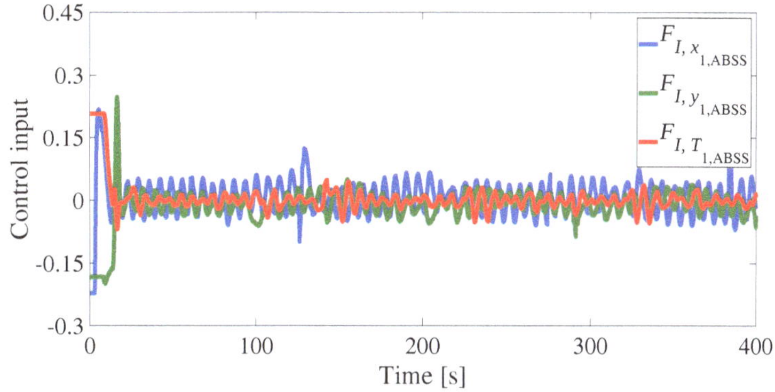

Fig. 2.6 The control inputs of $1^{\#}$ ABSS

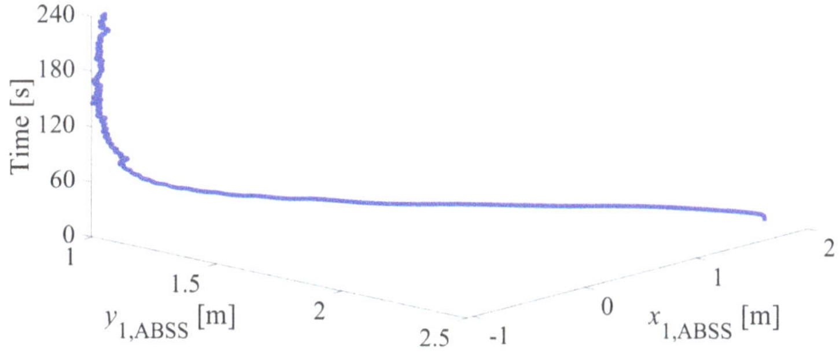

Fig. 2.7 The practical trajectory of $1^{\#}$ ABSS

trajectory is shown in Fig. 2.7, which means that $1^{\#}$ ABSS can successfully arrive at the desired target and then remain at the preset location from any position by applying (2.36). Based on the experimental results, the effectiveness and practicality of the proposed HOFAS predictive control can be clearly demonstrated.

The experiments in Sects. 2.4.1 and 2.4.2 construct the experimental verification for the theoretical results of the proposed HOFAS predictive control, which provides a solid foundation for the large-scale applications of HOFAS predictive control for the attitude joint orbit control of practical spacecraft in the future.

2.5 Notes and References

This chapter has considered the basic design problem of predictive control for the HOFASs in nonlinear and linear cases. A HOFAS predictive control has been proposed with the realization and optimization of the desired tracking control performance in the dynamical and steady processes, where a highlight is that a type of Diophantine Equation has been utilized to develop an IHOFAS prediction model for replacing the first-order one, so that the representation and design of predictive control have been completed by means of the HOFAS theory. A sufficient condition has been presented to analyze the bounded stability and tracking performance of the closed-loop HOFASs. Two experiments of the ABSS have been carried out to demonstrate the feasibility and practicability.

Furthermore, the authors have expanded the proposed HOFAS predictive control to some complex cases in the field of control theory and applications and have obtained a string of representative results, such as tracking control against communication constraints (Zhang and Liu 2023a, 2024b), secure control (Zhang and Liu 2023b, 2024c, 2025), anti-disturbance control (Zhang and Liu 2023a, 2024a; Zhang et al. 2025a), and other fields, such that the study on the theory and application of HOFAS predictive control has been further perfected and completed, which has provided a methodology foundation for the design of predictive cooperative control for MASs based on HOFAS theory.

Chapter 3
Predictive Cooperative Control for HOFAMASs

3.1 Introduction

Because of importantly theoretical value and wide applications, cooperative control for the MASs has attracted the longstanding attention of many scholars (Li et al. 2025; Xiong et al. 2025; Zheng et al. 2025a; Shi et al. 2025). Based on Gu et al. (2020), Gu and Zhang (2020, 2021), the dynamics of most of practical systems are of high order, such that there exist many representative results focusing on the study of cooperative control for high-order MASs. For example, Li et al. (2024c) presented a continuous-discrete-time compensator to design a cooperative control design algorithm with a dynamic event-triggered mechanism, so that the leader-follower consensus of high-order MASs with time delays and disturbances can be realized. In Sui et al. (2024), a fuzzy adaptive control based on fuzzy identification, backstepping approach, and finite-time stability theory was proposed to implement the finite-time consensus for high-order MASs, where a new integral-type Lyapunov function was constructed to ensure the stability and convergence of consensus errors. Li et al. (2024d) firstly used a reduced-order dynamic gain k-filter to reconstruct the states under denial-of-service (DoS) attacks and then established a resilient controller by adopting an event-triggered scheme and a switching control strategy to realize the cooperative control of high-order uncertain MASs under DoS attacks. An et al. (2023) achieved the exponential consensus of high-order fractional-order MASs under mismatched disturbances by utilizing an event-triggered strategy-based anti-disturbance integral sliding-mode control, which designed a finite-time high-order sliding-mode observer to estimate and compensate for the mismatched and matched disturbances. Li et al. (2023e) considered the global output consensus of high-order MASs subject to unknown control directions based on a prescribed-performance control. Meanwhile, Lui et al. (2023), Li et al. (2023c), Wu et al. (2021) and their associated studies also paid close attention to this field.

However, the above results still investigate the cooperative control for high-order MASs in the framework of state-space approach, such that the convenience of

D.-W. Zhang, G.-P. Liu, *Predictive Cooperative Control for High-Order Fully Actuated Multiagent Systems*, https://doi.org/10.1007/978-981-95-1695-7_3

solving the control vector and its physical realizability are ignored because state-space approach is only devoted to the solution of state responses toward the complex high-order form, which is difficult to implement the simplification of cooperative control design and the improvement of cooperative control performance. By introducing the HOFAS theory, the original high-order MASs can be equivalently converted into the HOFAMASs through a mathematical promotion and its relevant equivalent transformations. Then, based on the full actuation characteristic, the cooperative control design can be simplified, and the cooperative control performance can be improved, which is benefit to the development and progress of cooperative control for the MASs.

Following this idea, this chapter is concerned with a cooperative control problem of the HOFAMASs. A corresponding HOFAS predictive control is proposed to address this problem with the implementation and optimization of cooperative control performance, where the main works are concluded as follows. Firstly, a discrete-time HOFAS model is adopted to describe the actual dynamics of the i-th agent, which is called the i-th HOFA agent, such that a better model foundation is provided for the cooperative control design. Then, a kind of Diophantine Equation is used to develop an IHOFAS prediction model, such that the multistep ahead predictions can be generated to minimize an objective function in relation to the cooperative control performance for generating the optimal cooperative controllers. Furthermore, a sufficient condition is constructed to analyze the simultaneous consensus and stability of the closed-loop HOFAMASs. Finally, the HOFAS predictive control provides a solution to the formation control of three ABSSs for verifying the effectiveness and practicability.

3.2 Preliminaries

The information interaction among all agents can be represented by using the Algebraic Graph Theory (Li et al. 2024b; Wang et al. 2023c; Gong and Li 2024), and then a directed graph $\mathcal{G} = \{\mathcal{N}, \mathcal{E}, \mathcal{W}\}$ is adopted to describe the communication topology of HOFAMASs, where the details are provided in Definition 3.1.

Definition 3.1 In the directed graph $\mathcal{G}$, $\mathcal{N} = \{1, 2, \dots, N\}$ is a vertex set including all HOFA agents, $\mathcal{E} \subset \mathcal{N} \times \mathcal{N}$ is an edge set to represent all communication channels among all HOFA agents, and $\mathcal{W} = \{w_{ij}\}$ is an adjacent matrix with $w_{ij} \geq 0$ and $w_{ii} = 0$. The directed edge $(i, j) \in \mathcal{E}$ implies that the i-th HOFA agent can receive the information of the j-th one over the network in terms of the associated adjacent element $w_{ij} > 0$. $\mathcal{N}_i = \{j | j \in \mathcal{N}, j \neq i\}$ is a set of all HOFA agents apart from the i-th one.

Among the study of cooperative control for the MASs, the consensus is investigated as one of the most important problems. Meanwhile, the stability is the prerequisite during the design of control systems. Hence, the consensus and stability should be simultaneously considered in the cooperative control for the HOFAMASs. Based on Liu (2022c), the conditions of simultaneous consensus and stability for the HOFAMASs are provided in Definition 3.2.

Definition 3.2 Let $y_i(t)$ and $u_i(t)$ be the output and control vectors of the i-th HOFA agent and $y_j(t)$ be the output vector of the j-th HOFA agent. $r(t)$ denotes a known desired reference signal. The HOFAMASs can achieve the simultaneous consensus and stability by designing a cooperative control protocol $u_i\left(t, y_i(t), y_j(t), r(t)\right)$ if:

C1 $\forall i \in \mathscr{N}, \forall t \geq 0, \lim\limits_{t\to\infty} \|y_i(t)\| < \infty$ with $\|r(t)\| < \infty$.

C2 $\forall i \in \mathscr{N}, \forall j \in \mathscr{N}_i, \lim_{t\to\infty} \|y_i(t) - y_j(t)\| = 0$.

Remark 3.1 In Definition 3.2, Condition C1 maintains the bounded stability of the closed-loop HOFAMASs, and Condition C2 aims to achieve the output consensus. In summary, the condition on simultaneous consensus and stability of the closed-loop HOFAMASs can be characterized via Conditions C1 and C2.

To ensure the rationality and realizability, there exist some general assumptions during the design of cooperative control for HOFAMASs, which is provided in Assumption 3.1.

Assumption 3.1 *During the design of cooperative control for the HOFAMASs, the following assumptions are satisfied:*

A1 The clocks of all HOFA agents are synchronized.

A2 There exist the timestamps during the process of transmitting the information.

A3 The desired reference signal for each HOFA agent is known.

A4 The topology $\mathscr{G}$ is fixed, and the adjacent matrix $\mathscr{W}$ is constant.

Remark 3.2 Assumption 3.1 provides four basic conditions in the study on cooperative control for the HOFAMASs. Concretely, Assumption 3.1–A1 guarantees that all HOFA agents work under the same time excitation, so that the synchronous transmission of information can be realized. Assumption 3.1–A2 provides a reliable evidence for the generation time of data, which maintains the reliability and traceability of data and avoids the serial number wrapping and data tampering. Assumption 3.1–A3 is a precondition for cooperative tracking control and gives a research foundation for the case that the reference signal is unknown. Assumption 3.1–A4 considers a basic and simple working scenario in theoretical studies and practical applications of cooperative control, which establishes a solid foundation for the solutions to other complex communication topology.

3.3 Problem Statement

Based on Duan (2022c) and system (2.17), the i-th HOFA agent in a type of discrete-time step-forward linear form is investigated as

$$\begin{aligned} x_i(t+n) =& -L_i(A_{i,0\sim n-1}, x_i(t)) + B_i u_i(t), \\ y_i(t) =& C_i x_i(t), \quad i \in \mathscr{N}, \end{aligned} \tag{3.1}$$

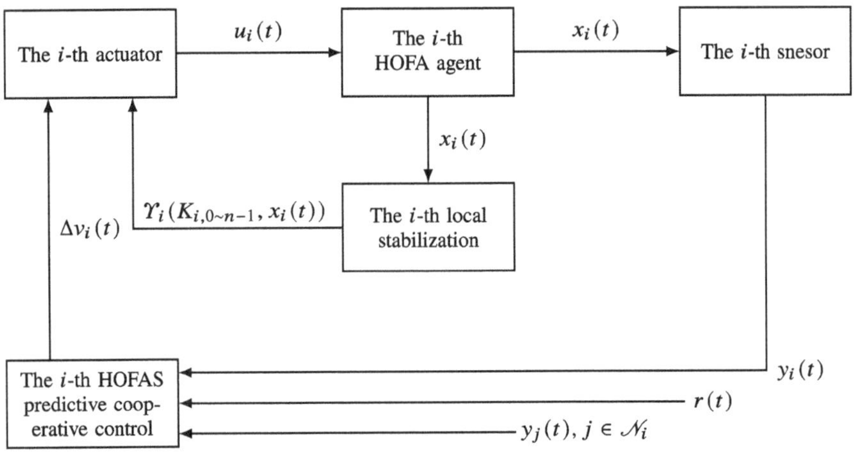

Fig. 3.1 Predictive cooperative control for the HOFAMASs

where $L_i(\cdot) := L_i(A_{i,0\sim n-1}, x_i(t)) = \sum_{\eta=0}^{n-1} A_{i,\eta} x_i(t+\eta) \in \mathbb{R}^{n_i}$ is a linear vector function, and $x_i(t) \in \mathbb{R}^{n_i}$, $u_i(t) \in \mathbb{R}^{n_i}$, $y_i \in \mathbb{R}^m$ are the state, input, and output vectors, respectively. $A_{i,\eta} \in \mathbb{R}^{n_i \times n_i}$, $\eta = 0, 1, \ldots, n-1$, $B_i \in \mathbb{R}^{n_i \times n_i}$, $C_i \in \mathbb{R}^{m \times n_i}$ denote the known coefficient matrices with the corresponding dimensions. Based on Assumption 2.2, the following assumption is proposed for the i-th HOFA agent (3.1).

Assumption 3.2 *A1. $x_i(t)$ is available for the control design. A2.* $\det(B_i) \neq 0$.

To realize the cooperative control for the i-th HOFA agent (3.1), a HOFAS predictive control is presented as

$$u_i(t) = B_i^{-1} \left(L_i(\cdot) + \Upsilon_i(K_{i,0\sim n-1}, x_i(t)) + v_i(t) \right), \tag{3.2}$$

where $L_i(\cdot)$ is used to eliminate the open-loop dynamics, $\Upsilon_i(K_{i,0\sim n-1}, x_i(t)) = \sum_{\eta=0}^{n-1} K_{i,\eta} x_i(t+\eta) \in \mathbb{R}^{n_i}$ is used to adjust the closed-loop performances and $K_{i,\eta} \in \mathbb{R}^{n_i \times n_i}$ denote the feedback gains to be determined, and $v_i(t) \in \mathbb{R}^{n_i}$ is a cooperative control item generated by HOFAS predictive control. The relevant control structure is shown in Fig. 3.1.

By applying (3.2), the closed-loop HOFAMASs can be achieved as

$$\begin{aligned} x_i(t+n) =& \Upsilon_i(K_{i,0\sim n-1}, x_i(t)) + v_i(t) \\ =& \sum_{\eta=0}^{n-1} K_{i,\eta} x_i(t+\eta) + v_i(t), \quad i \in \mathcal{N}. \end{aligned} \tag{3.3}$$

To solve the cooperative control item $v_i(t)$, an objective function $\mathcal{J}(t)$ is given as

$$\mathcal{J}(t) = \sum_{i \in \mathcal{N}} \mathcal{J}_i(t), \tag{3.4}$$

where $\mathcal{J}_i(t)$ is a sub-objective function to measure the cooperative control performance of the i-th HOFA agent and is designed as

$$\begin{aligned} \mathcal{J}_i(t) = \sum_{j \in \mathcal{N}_i} w_{ij} \left\| \hat{Y}_i(t + \aleph_y|t) - \hat{Y}_j(t + \aleph_y|t) \right\|^2 \\ + \alpha_i \left\| \hat{Y}_i(t + \aleph_y|t) - R(t + \aleph_y) \right\|^2 + \beta_i \left\| \Delta \hat{V}_i(t + \aleph_u|t) \right\|^2, \end{aligned} \tag{3.5}$$

with

$$\begin{aligned} \hat{Y}_i(t + \aleph_y|t) &= \left[\hat{y}_i^{\mathrm{T}}(t + \aleph_y|t) \cdots \hat{y}_i^{\mathrm{T}}(t + 1|t) \right]^{\mathrm{T}}, \\ R(t + \aleph_y) &= \left[r^{\mathrm{T}}(t + \aleph_y) \cdots r^{\mathrm{T}}(t + 1) \right]^{\mathrm{T}}, \\ \Delta \hat{V}_i(t + \aleph_u|t) &= \left[\Delta \hat{v}_i^{\mathrm{T}}(t + \aleph_u|t) \cdots \Delta \hat{v}_i^{\mathrm{T}}(t|t) \right]^{\mathrm{T}}, \end{aligned}$$

where $\hat{y}_i(t+\eta|t)$, $\eta = 1, 2, \ldots, \aleph_y$, and $\Delta \hat{v}_i(t+\eta|t)$, $\eta = 1, 2, \cdots, \aleph_u$ are the η-th ahead predictions of output $y_i(t)$ and cooperative control increment $\Delta v_i(t)$ based on time t. $r(t)$ is a known reference signal, and $R(t+\aleph_y)$ denotes the relevant multistep ahead sequence. w_{ij} is the (i, j)-th element of adjacent matrix $\mathscr{W}$, and $\alpha_i > 0$ and $\beta_i > 0$ are two weighting factors.

Remark 3.3 In (3.5), the first item of $\mathcal{J}_i(t)$ aims to consider the cooperative control performance by achieving the approaching of output predictions $\hat{Y}_i(t + \aleph_y|t)$ and $\hat{Y}_j(t + \aleph_y|t)$, $\forall i \in \mathcal{N}$, $\forall j \in \mathcal{N}_i$, the second item is proposed to guarantee the tracking control performance by focusing on the differences between $\hat{Y}_i(t + \aleph_y|t)$ and $R(t + \aleph_y)$, and the third item imposes a constraint on changing the rate and amplitude of $\Delta v_i(t)$ in the view of algorithm design, which ensures the cooperative controller's physical feasibility and reduces the mechanical losses, as well as prolongs the servicing life.

Problem 3.1 For the i-th HOFA agent (3.1) under Assumptions 3.1 and 3.2, a HOFAS predictive control $u_i\left(t, v_i(t, y_i(t), y_j(t), r(t))\right)$ in (3.2) is proposed by minimizing the $\mathcal{J}(t)$ in (3.4) and (3.5), so that the closed-loop HOFAMASs (3.3) can realize the simultaneous consensus and stability, i.e., the following conditions hold:

1. $\forall i \in \mathcal{N}, \forall t \geq 0, \lim\limits_{t \to \infty} \|y_i(t)\| < \infty$ with $\|r(t)\| < \infty$.
2. $\forall i \in \mathcal{N}, \forall j \in \mathcal{N}_i, \lim_{t \to \infty} \|y_i(t) - y_j(t)\| = 0$.

3.4 HOFAS Predictive Cooperative Control Scheme

Based on the time operator q, the closed-loop system (3.3) can be equivalent to the following polynomial one:

$$\mathcal{K}_i\left(q^{-1}\right)x_i(t)=\mathcal{B}_i\left(q^{-1}\right)v_i(t-1), \tag{3.6}$$

where $\mathcal{K}_i\left(q^{-1}\right)=I-\sum_{\eta=0}^{n-1}K_{i,\eta}q^{\eta-n}$ and $\mathcal{B}_i\left(q^{-1}\right)=q^{1-n}$. Based on (2.6), a Diophantine Equation in relation to (3.6) is provided as

$$\mathcal{E}_{i,\eta}\left(q^{-1}\right)\mathcal{A}_i\left(q^{-1}\right)\Delta+q^{-\eta}\mathcal{F}_{i,j}\left(q^{-1}\right)=I, \tag{3.7}$$

where $\mathcal{E}_{i,\eta}\left(q^{-1}\right)=e_{i,\eta,0}+e_{i,\eta,1}q^{-1}+\cdots+e_{i,\eta,\eta-1}q^{-(\eta-1)}$ and $\mathcal{F}_{i,j}\left(q^{-1}\right)=f_{i,\eta,0}+f_{i,\eta,1}q^{-1}+\cdots+f_{i,\eta,n}q^{-n}$ deciding by the prediction horizon η and system polynomial matrix $\mathcal{K}_i\left(q^{-1}\right)$ are two polynomial solutions of Diophantine Equation (3.7). By multiplying $\mathcal{E}_{i,\eta}\Delta q^{\eta}$ on both sides of (3.6), it is obtained that

$$\mathcal{E}_{i,\eta}\mathcal{A}_i\Delta x_i(t+\eta)=\mathcal{E}_{i,\eta}B_i\Delta v_i(t+\eta-1),$$

and then taking (3.7) into the above derives the following IHOFAS prediction model:

$$x_i(t+\eta)=\mathcal{F}_{i,\eta}x(t)+\mathcal{G}_{i,\eta}\Delta v_i(t+\eta-1), \tag{3.8}$$

with $\mathcal{G}_{i,\eta}\left(q^{-1}\right)=\mathcal{E}_{i,\eta}\left(q^{-1}\right)\mathcal{B}_i\left(q^{-1}\right)=g_{i,\eta,0}+g_{i,\eta,1}q^{-1}+\cdots+g_{i,\eta,n+\eta-1}q^{-(n+\eta-2)}$, where its construction process can be repeated from (2.5) to (2.7).

For $\eta=1,2,\ldots,\aleph_y$, the multistep ahead predictions of $x_i(t)$ by applying (3.8) are obtained as

$$\begin{aligned}\hat{x}_i(t+1|t)=&\mathcal{F}_{i,1}x_i(t)+\mathcal{G}_{i,1}\Delta\hat{v}_i(t|t),\\&\vdots\\\hat{x}_i(t+\aleph_y|t)=&\mathcal{F}_{i,\aleph_y}x_i(t)+\mathcal{G}_{i,\aleph_y}\Delta\hat{v}_i(t+\aleph_y-1|t),\end{aligned}$$

and the related output prediction is generated as

$$\hat{y}_i(t+\eta|t)=C_i\hat{x}_i(t+\eta|t),\ \eta=1,2,\ldots,\aleph_y. \tag{3.9}$$

When $\eta=\aleph_u+1,\aleph_u+2,\ldots,\aleph_y$, $\hat{v}_i(t+\eta|t)=\hat{v}_i(t+\aleph_u|t)$ such that $\Delta\hat{v}_i(t+\eta|t)=0$. Hence, the output prediction (3.9) can be compactly summarized as

$$\hat{Y}_i(t+\aleph_y|t) = P_{i,1}x_i(t) + P_{i,2}\Delta\hat{V}_i(t+\aleph_u|t), \tag{3.10}$$

where

$$P_{i,1} = \begin{bmatrix} C_i\mathcal{F}_{i,N_y} \\ \vdots \\ C_i\mathcal{F}_{i,N_u+1} \\ C_i\mathcal{F}_{i,N_u} \\ \vdots \\ C_i\mathcal{F}_{i,1} \end{bmatrix}, \quad P_{i,2} = \begin{bmatrix} C_i\mathcal{G}_{i,\aleph_y} & 0 & \cdots & 0 \\ \vdots & \vdots & \cdots & \vdots \\ C_i\mathcal{G}_{i,\aleph_u+1} & 0 & \cdots & 0 \\ 0 & C_i\mathcal{G}_{i,\aleph_u} & \ddots & \vdots \\ \vdots & \ddots & \ddots & 0 \\ 0 & \cdots & 0 & C_i\mathcal{G}_{i,1} \end{bmatrix}.$$

Based on (2.9), an incremental constraint of cooperative control increment $\Delta v_i(t)$ is provided as

$$\Delta\hat{v}_i(t+\eta|t) = \gamma_{i,\eta}\Delta\hat{v}(t|t),$$

where $\gamma_{i,\eta} > 0$, $\eta = 1, 2, \ldots, \aleph_u$, denotes a weighting factor, such that $P_{i,2}$ can be degenerated as $P_{i,3} = P_{i,2}\Gamma_i$ with $\Gamma_i = \text{Blockdiag}\{\gamma_{i,\aleph_u}I, \ldots, \gamma_{i,1}I, I\}$, and $P_{i,2}\Delta\hat{V}_i(t+\aleph_u|t) = P_{i,3}\Delta\hat{V}_i(t|t)$ with $\Delta\hat{V}_i(t|t) = \left[\Delta\hat{v}_i^{\mathrm{T}}(t|t) \cdots \Delta\hat{v}_i^{\mathrm{T}}(t|t)\right]^{\mathrm{T}}$. Summarizing the above means that (3.10) can be rewritten as

$$\hat{Y}_i(t+\aleph_y|t) = P_{i,1}x_i(t) + P_{i,3}\Delta\hat{V}_i(t|t). \tag{3.11}$$

To solve the optimal cooperative control increment $\Delta v_i(t)$, let

$$\frac{\partial}{\partial\Delta\hat{V}_i(t|t)}\mathcal{J}(t) = 0, \ i \in \mathcal{N}.$$

By applying (3.11), it is derived that

$$\begin{aligned}&\sum_{j\in\mathcal{N}_i} w_{ij}P_{i,3}^{\mathrm{T}}\left(P_{i,1}x_i(t) + P_{i,3}\Delta\hat{V}_i(t|t) - P_{j,1}x_j(t) - P_{j,3}\Delta\hat{V}_j(t|t)\right)\\ &\quad + \alpha_i P_{i,3}^{\mathrm{T}}\left(P_{i,1}x_i(t) + P_{i,3}\Delta\hat{V}_i(t|t) - R(t+\aleph_y)\right) + \beta_i\Gamma_i^{\mathrm{T}}\Gamma_i\Delta\hat{V}_i(t|t) = 0,\end{aligned}$$

which can be converted as

$$\Delta\hat{V}(t|t) = F^{-1}Gx(t) + F^{-1}MR(t+\aleph_y),$$

with $\Delta\hat{V}(t|t) = \left[\Delta\hat{V}_1^{\mathrm{T}}(t|t) \cdots \Delta\hat{V}_N^{\mathrm{T}}(t|t)\right]^{\mathrm{T}}$, $x(t) = \left[x_1^{\mathrm{T}}(t) \cdots x_N^{\mathrm{T}}(t)\right]^{\mathrm{T}}$, and

$$F = \{f_{ij}\}, \ f_{ii} = (w_i + \alpha_i)P_{i,3}^{\mathrm{T}}P_{i,3} + \beta_i\Gamma_i^{\mathrm{T}}\Gamma_i, \ f_{ij} = -w_{ij}P_{i,3}^{\mathrm{T}}P_{j,3},$$

$$
G = \{g_{ij}\},\ g_{ii} = -(w_i + \alpha_i) P_{i,3}^{\mathrm{T}} P_{i,1},\ g_{ij} = w_{ij} P_{i,3}^{\mathrm{T}} P_{j,1},
$$
$$
M = \begin{bmatrix} \alpha_1 P_{1,3} \cdots \alpha_N P_{N,3} \end{bmatrix}^{\mathrm{T}},\ w_i = \sum_{j \in \mathscr{N}_i} w_{ij}.
$$

Then, the i-th optimal cooperative control increment $\Delta v_i(t)$ is solved as $\Delta v_i(t) = \Delta \hat{v}_i(t|t) = H_i \Delta \hat{V}(t|t)$, that is,

$$
\Delta v_i(t) = H_i F^{-1} G x(t) + H_i F^{-1} M R(t + \aleph_y), \tag{3.12}
$$

where $H_i = \begin{bmatrix} H_{i,1} \cdots H_{i,N} \end{bmatrix} \in \mathbb{R}^{n_i \times (\aleph_u + 1)\tilde{n}}$ with $\tilde{n} = \sum_{i=1}^{N} n_i$, $H_{i,i} = \begin{bmatrix} 0 \cdots 0\ I \end{bmatrix}$, $H_{i,j} = 0$, $j \in \mathscr{N}_i$.

Remark 3.4 As reported in Remark 2.3, $\Upsilon_i(K_{i,0\sim n-1}, x_i(t))$ aims to adjust the closed-loop performances and to improve the accuracy of IHOFAS prediction model (3.8) as a feedback correction. Further, the feedback gains $K_{i,\eta}$, $\eta = 0, 1, \ldots, n-1$, can be solved by using the same method in Remark 2.2, i.e.,

$$
\begin{bmatrix} K_{i,0}\ K_{i,1} \cdots K_{i,n-1} \end{bmatrix} = \mathcal{Z}_i \Lambda_i^n \begin{bmatrix} \mathcal{Z}_i \\ \mathcal{Z}_i \Lambda_i \\ \vdots \\ \mathcal{Z}_i \Lambda_i^{n-1} \end{bmatrix}^{-1},
$$

where $\mathcal{Z}_i \in \mathbb{R}^{n_i \times n_i \tilde{n}}$ is an arbitrary parameter matrix and $\Lambda_i \in \mathbb{R}^{n_i \tilde{n} \times n_i \tilde{n}}$ is a Schur matrix satisfying

$$
\det \left(\begin{bmatrix} \mathcal{Z}_i \\ \mathcal{Z}_i \Lambda_i \\ \vdots \\ \mathcal{Z}_i \Lambda_i^{n-1} \end{bmatrix} \right) \neq 0.
$$

3.5 Analysis of Simultaneous Consensus and Stability

Let $e_i(t) = y_i(t) - r(t) = C_i x_i(t) - r(t)$ be the tracking error of the i-th HOFA agent and $\epsilon_{ii}(t) = \epsilon_i(t) = e_i(t)$, $\epsilon_{ij}(t) = y_i(t) - y_j(t)$, $j \in \mathscr{N}_i$, be the consensus error; then the simultaneous consensus and stability of the closed-loop HOFAMAS (3.3) can be equivalent to that $\epsilon_i(t) \to 0$ and $\epsilon_{ij}(t) \to 0$ with $t \to \infty$. In this view, Theorem 3.1 is proposed for this problem.

Theorem 3.1 *The closed-loop HOFAMAS* (3.3) *can achieve the simultaneous consensus and stability if* $\exists w_{ij} \geq 0$, $\sum_{j \in \mathscr{N}_i} w_{ij}^2 \neq 0$, $\exists \alpha_i > 0$, $\exists \beta_i > 0$, $\forall i \in \mathscr{N}$,

$\forall j \in \mathscr{N}_i$, *to guarantee that* $\forall i \in \mathscr{N}$, $\frac{\partial}{\partial \Delta \hat{V}_i(t|t)} \mathcal{J}(t) = 0$, *and* Φ *is a Schur stable polynomial matrix in relation to* q, *where*

$$\Phi = I + (q-1)C\Phi_1^{-1}\Phi_2, \tag{3.13}$$

with

$$\Phi_1 = I - (I + \mathcal{K}_G + \mathcal{K}_M C)q^{-1}, \quad \Phi_2 = -\mathcal{K}_M q^{-1}, \tag{3.14}$$

and

$$\begin{aligned} C =& \text{Blockdiag}\{C_1, \ldots, C_N\}, \\ \mathcal{K}_M =& \text{Blockdiag}\{\mathcal{K}_{1,c} H_1 F^{-1} M \vec{I}_{\aleph_y}, \ldots, \mathcal{K}_{N,c} H_N F^{-1} M \vec{I}_{\aleph_y}\}, \\ \mathcal{K}_G =& \begin{bmatrix} \mathcal{K}_{1,c} H_1 F^{-1} G \\ \vdots \\ \mathcal{K}_{N,c} H_N F^{-1} G \end{bmatrix}, \quad \vec{I}_{\aleph_y} = [\underbrace{I \cdots I}_{\aleph_y}]^{\mathrm{T}}, \quad \mathcal{K}_{i,c} = \mathcal{K}_i^{-1} \mathcal{B}_i. \end{aligned} \tag{3.15}$$

Proof Generally, it is assumed that $r(\cdot) = r$, such that $\Delta v_i(t)$ in (3.12) can be rewritten as

$$\Delta v_i(t) = H_i F^{-1} G x(t) + H_i F^{-1} M \vec{I}_{\aleph_y} \left(C_i x_i(t) - e_i(t) \right), \tag{3.16}$$

and

$$e_i(t+1) = y_i(t+1) - r(t+1) = e_i(t) + C_i \Delta x_i(t+1),$$

and by using the time operator q, the above can be represented as

$$e_i(t+1) = e_i(t) + (q-1) C_i x_i(t),$$

which can be compactly summarized as

$$e(t+1) = e(t) + (q-1) C x(t), \tag{3.17}$$

where C is provided in (3.15), and $e(t) = \left[e_1^{\mathrm{T}}(t) \cdots e_N^{\mathrm{T}}(t) \right]^{\mathrm{T}}$, $x(t) = \left[x_1^{\mathrm{T}}(t) \cdots x_N^{\mathrm{T}}(t) \right]^{\mathrm{T}}$. It is also assumed that $i = 1$, the consensus errors can be defined as $\epsilon_{11}(t) = \epsilon_1(t) = e_1(t)$, and $\forall j \in \mathscr{N}_1$,

$$\epsilon_{1j}(t) = y_1(t) - y_j(t) = e_1(t) - e_j(t);$$

then denote $\epsilon(t) = \left[\epsilon_1^{\mathrm{T}}(t) \cdots \epsilon_{1N}^{\mathrm{T}}(t) \right]^{\mathrm{T}}$, and the above can be concluded as

$$\epsilon(t) = \tilde{\mathbf{I}}e(t), \quad \tilde{\mathbf{I}} = \begin{bmatrix} I & & & \\ I & -I & & \\ \vdots & & \ddots & \\ I & & & -I \end{bmatrix}. \tag{3.18}$$

Based on (3.6), it is obtained that

$$\Delta x_i(t+1) = \mathcal{K}_{i,c}\Delta v_i(t),$$

because $\exists w_{ij} \geq 0, \sum_{j \in \mathcal{N}_i} w_{ij}^2 \neq 0, \exists \alpha_i > 0, \exists \beta_i > 0, \forall i \in \mathcal{N}, \forall j \in \mathcal{N}_i$, to ensure that $\frac{\partial}{\partial \Delta \hat{V}_i(t|t)} \mathcal{J}(t) = 0, \forall i \in \mathcal{N}$, and the optimal cooperative control increment $\Delta v_i(t)$ can be solved by (3.12) and (3.16). By taking (3.16) into the above, it is yielded that

$$\Delta x_i(t+1) = \mathcal{K}_{i,c} H_i F^{-1} G x(t) + \mathcal{K}_{i,c} H_i F^{-1} M \vec{I}_{\aleph_y} \left(C_i x_i(t) - e_i(t) \right),$$

which can be compactly expressed as

$$\Delta x(t+1) = \mathcal{K}_G x(t) + \mathcal{K}_M C x(t) - \mathcal{K}_M e(t),$$

where $\mathcal{K}_G$ and $\mathcal{K}_M$ are given in (3.15). The above is equivalent to

$$x(t) = \Phi_1^{-1} \Phi_2 e(t), \tag{3.19}$$

where Φ_1 and Φ_2 are provided in (3.14). Further, substituting (3.19) into (3.17) can obtain

$$\begin{aligned} e(t+1) =& e(t) + (q-1)Cx(t) \\ =& e(t) + (q-1)C\Phi_1^{-1}\Phi_2 e(t) \\ =& \Phi e(t), \end{aligned} \tag{3.20}$$

where Φ is shown in (3.13). Combining with (3.18), an auxiliary system is given as

$$\begin{cases} e(t+1) =& \Phi e(t), \\ \epsilon(t) =& \tilde{\mathbf{I}} e(t). \end{cases} \tag{3.21}$$

Because $\exists w_{ij} \geq 0, \sum_{j \in \mathcal{N}_i} w_{ij}^2 \neq 0, \exists \alpha_i > 0, \exists \beta_i > 0, \forall i \in \mathcal{N}, \forall j \in \mathcal{N}_i$, to guarantee that Φ is a Schur stable polynomial matrix in relation to q, $e(t) \to 0$ with

$t \to \infty$, such that $\epsilon(t) \to 0$ with $t \to \infty$ because of (3.21). Hence, the closed-loop HOFAMASs (3.3) can achieve the simultaneous consensus and stability.

This completes the proof. □

3.6 With Application to Formation Control of Air-Bearing Spacecraft Simulators

There are three ABSSs to carry out a formation control experiment to demonstrate the effectiveness and practicability of the proposed HOFAS predictive cooperative control, the dynamic models of three ABSSs are provided in (A.4), and other details of three ABSSs and the associated experimental platform have been provided in Appendix A.

3.6.1 Numerical Simulation

Taking system (A.4a) as an example to demonstrate the effectiveness and advantage, a comparison between the proposed HOFAS predictive cooperative control and the classical dynamic matrix control (DMC) in Xi (2013), where the associated design parameters are provided as $T_s = 0.2\text{s}$, $w_{ii} = 0$, $w_{ij} = 1$, $\alpha_i = 1$, $\beta_i = 0.01$, $i, j = 1, 2, 3$, $\aleph_y = 5$, $\aleph_u = 3$, $\Gamma_i = \text{diag}\{25, 24, 23, 1\}$.

Based on (3.2), a HOFAS predictive control for system (A.4a) is designed as

$$F_{I,x_{i,\text{ABSS}}}(t) = -L_{i,x}(\cdot) + \Upsilon(K_{i,0\sim 1}, x_{i,\text{ABSS}}(t)) + v_i(t), \tag{3.22}$$

where $K_{1,0} = -0.3802$, $K_{1,1} = 19.4$, $K_{2,0} = -0.3822$, $K_{2,1} = 19.5$, $K_{3,0} = -0.3763$, $K_{3,1} = 19.2$. For the DMC approach in Xi (2013), system (A.4a) should be firstly transformed into the following first-order state-space one:

$$X_{i,\text{ABSS}}(t+1) = A_{i,\text{ABSS}} X_{i,\text{ABSS}}(t) + B_{i,\text{ABSS}} F_{I,x_{i,\text{ABSS}}}(t), \tag{3.23}$$

with $X_{i,\text{ABSS}}(t) = \begin{bmatrix} x_{i,\text{ABSS}}(t) \\ x_{i,\text{ABSS}}(t+1) \end{bmatrix}$, $A_{i,\text{ABSS}} = \begin{bmatrix} 0 & 1 \\ -1 & 2 \end{bmatrix}$, $B_{i,\text{ABSS}} = \begin{bmatrix} 0 \\ 0.0021 \end{bmatrix}$. Then, $F_{I,x_{i,\text{ABSS}}}(t)$ can be solved by minimizing the objective function $\mathcal{J}_{\text{DMC}}(t) = \sum_{i\in\mathcal{N}} \mathcal{J}_{i,\text{DMC}}(t)$, and $\mathcal{J}_{i,\text{DMC}}(t)$ is designed as

$$\mathcal{J}_{i,\text{DMC}}(t) = \sum_{j\in\mathcal{N}_i} w_{ij} \sum_{\eta=1}^{\aleph_y} \left\| \hat{X}_{i,\text{ABSS}}(t+\eta|t) - \hat{X}_{j,\text{ABSS}}(t+\eta|t) \right\|^2$$

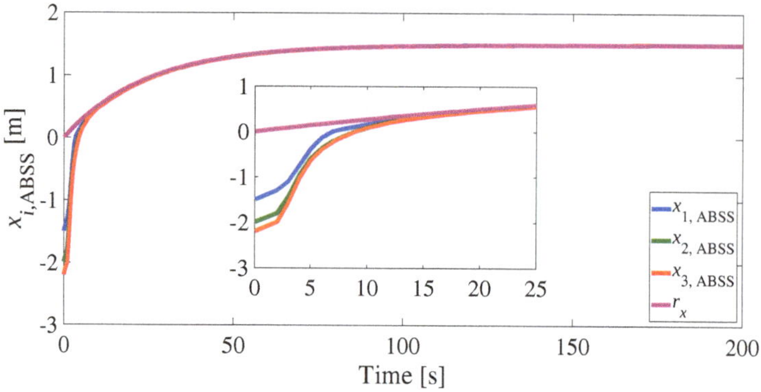

(a) Cooperative control of system (A.4a) by using the control (3.22)

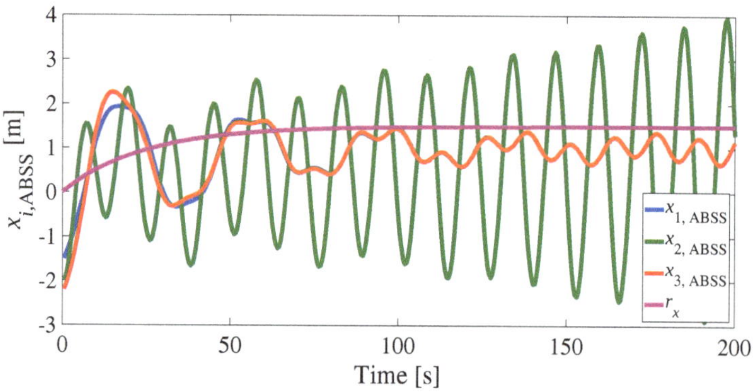

(b) Cooperative control of system (A.4a) via the DMC in Xi (2013)

Fig. 3.2 Comparison between the proposed HOFAS predictive control and the DMC in Xi (2013)

$$+\alpha_i \sum_{\eta=1}^{\aleph_y} \left\| \hat{X}_{i,\text{ABSS}}(t+\eta|t) - R_x(t+\eta) \right\|^2$$

$$+\beta_i \sum_{\eta=1}^{\aleph_u} \left\| \hat{F}_{I,x_{i,\text{ABSS}}}(t+\eta|t) \right\|^2,$$

where $R_x(t+\eta) = \left[r_x(t+\eta)\; r_x(t+\eta+1) \right]^{\text{T}}$, and $r_x(t)$ is a known desired reference signal. The simulated comparison is plotted in Fig. 3.2.

Figure 3.2a shows that the proposed HOFAS predictive control (3.22) can realize the better cooperative tracking control performance during the dynamical and steady processes, but Fig. 3.2b implies that the DMC in Xi (2013) only guarantees the cooperation of $x_{1,\text{ABSS}}(t)$ and $x_{3,\text{ABSS}}(t)$, and it cannot achieve the desired tracking control performance. Meanwhile, there exists the serious oscillation in Fig. 3.2b, where the reason is provided in Remark 3.5. Based on the comparison of Fig. 3.2, the effectiveness and advantage of HOFAS predictive control can be fully illustrated, which provides a better support for the experimental verification.

Remark 3.5 The DMC in Xi (2013) is actually a strategy with "open-loop optimization, closed-loop control," where the corresponding predictions of $\hat{X}_{i,\text{ABSS}}(t+\eta|t)$ are obtained by applying (3.23) without considering the effects of closed-loop feedback, i.e.,

$$\begin{aligned}\hat{X}_{i,\text{ABSS}}(t+\eta|t) =& A_{i,\text{ABSS}}^{\eta} X_{i,\text{ABSS}}(t) \\ &+ \sum_{\epsilon=0}^{\eta-1} A_{i,\text{ABSS}}^{\epsilon} B_{i,\text{ABSS}} \hat{F}_{I,x_{i,\text{ABSS}}}(t+\eta-1-\epsilon|t).\end{aligned}$$

In fact, the eigenvalues of $A_{i,\text{ABSS}}$ are both 1, and the predictions are naturally affected by the unstable open-loop dynamics, such that it is difficult to maintain the desired cooperative control performance because the control inputs solved by these predictions exist the deviations.

The proposed HOFAS predictive control is considered as a strategy with "closed-loop optimization, closed-loop control," which utilizes the full actuation feature to eliminate the unstable open-loop dynamics and then to obtain a desired closed-loop performance based on the HOFAS theory (see Remark 2.2). The predictions are obtained via a prediction model based on a stable closed-loop form to solve the control input, which can implement the desired cooperative control performance.

3.6.2 Experimental Results

A consensus-based formation control experiment of three ABSSs is taken to further demonstrate the availability of the proposed HOFAS predictive control, where the desired formation of three ABSSs is shown in Fig. 3.3.

For systems (A.4a) and (A.4b), the cooperative control protocols are chosen as the same as (3.22) with the same design parameters. For system (A.4c), only a stabilization control is needed to satisfy the requirement of $\psi_{i,\text{ABSS}}(t)$ during the formation control. Thus, the cooperative control items are set as 0, and a stabilization control is designed as

$$F_{I,T_{i,\text{ABSS}}}(t) = -L_{i,T}(\cdot) + \Upsilon(K_{0\sim 1}, \psi_{i,\text{ABSS}}(t)), \tag{3.24}$$

with $K_{1,0} = -0.0717$, $K_{1,1} = 0.2629$, $K_{2,0} = -0.0723$, $K_{2,1} = 0.2651$, $K_{3,0} = -0.0708$, $K_{3,1} = 0.2596$. By applying (3.22) and (3.24), the experimental results are shown in Figs. 3.4, 3.5, 3.6.

Figure 3.5 shows the position and angle responses of formation control for three ABSSs, where the position responses $x_{i,\text{ABSS}}(t)$ and $y_{i,\text{ABSS}}(t)$ can achieve the

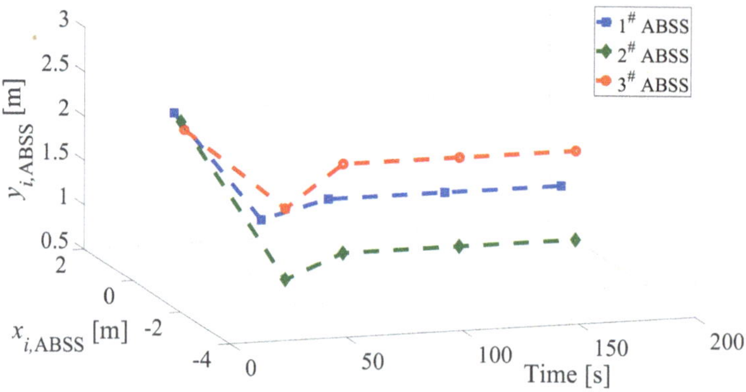

Fig. 3.3 The desired formation of three ABSSs

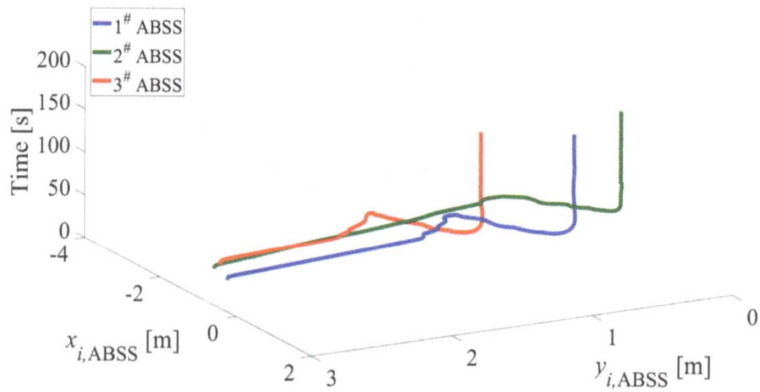

Fig. 3.4 The actual formation of three ABSSs

cooperative control by utilizing (3.22), and they arrive at the pointed locations simultaneously and are changed cooperatively. The angle responses $\psi_{i,\mathrm{ABSS}}(t)$ can realize the stabilization by applying (3.24), but a shortcoming is that there exists the vibration during the steady process. The reason is that both the reaction forces of the thrusters and the airflow in the experimental site affect the stabilization control performance of $\psi_{i,\mathrm{ABSS}}(t)$. The control inputs generated by (3.22) and (3.24) are shown in Fig. 3.6, which is also with some vibrations because of the model uncertainties and external disturbances. Figure 3.4 provides the practical formation of three ABSSs, which shows that the proposed HOFAS predictive control (3.22) can ensure the realization of the desired formation and continue to follow it by comparing with Fig. 3.3.

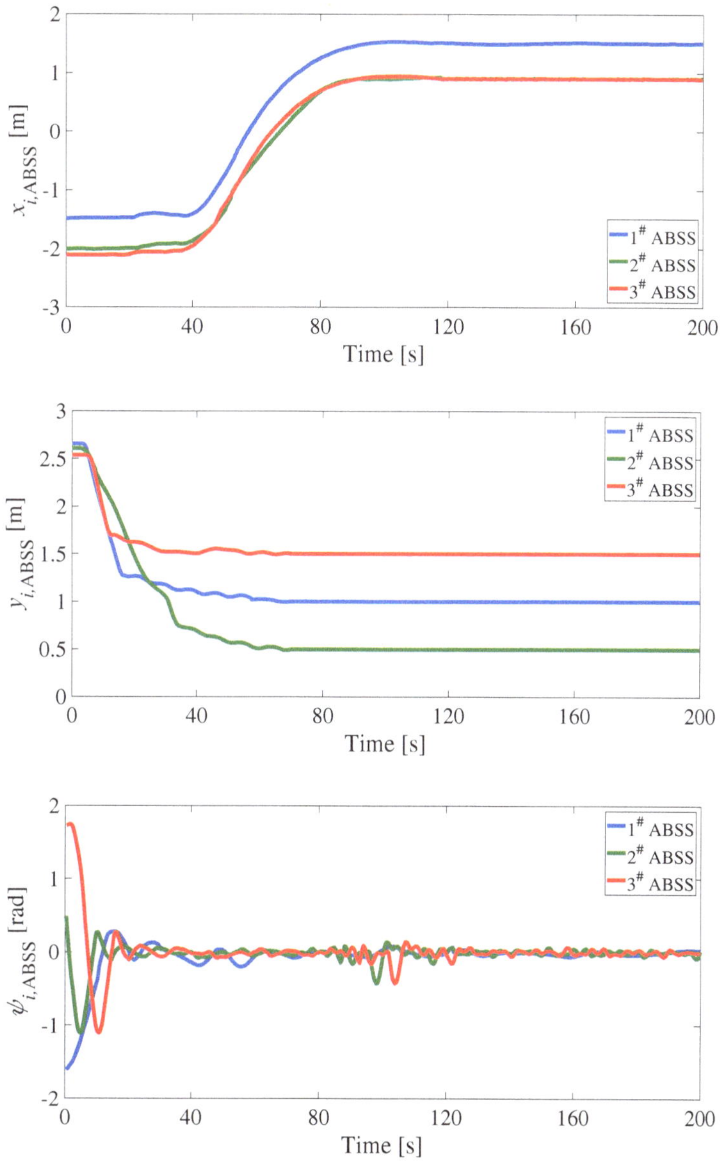

Fig. 3.5 The formation control of three ABSSs by using the controls (3.22) and (3.24)

Based on the results in Figs. 3.4, 3.5, 3.6, the effectiveness and practicability of the HOFAS predictive control can be fully demonstrated, which provides a better foundation for the large-scale applications of practical spacecraft control.

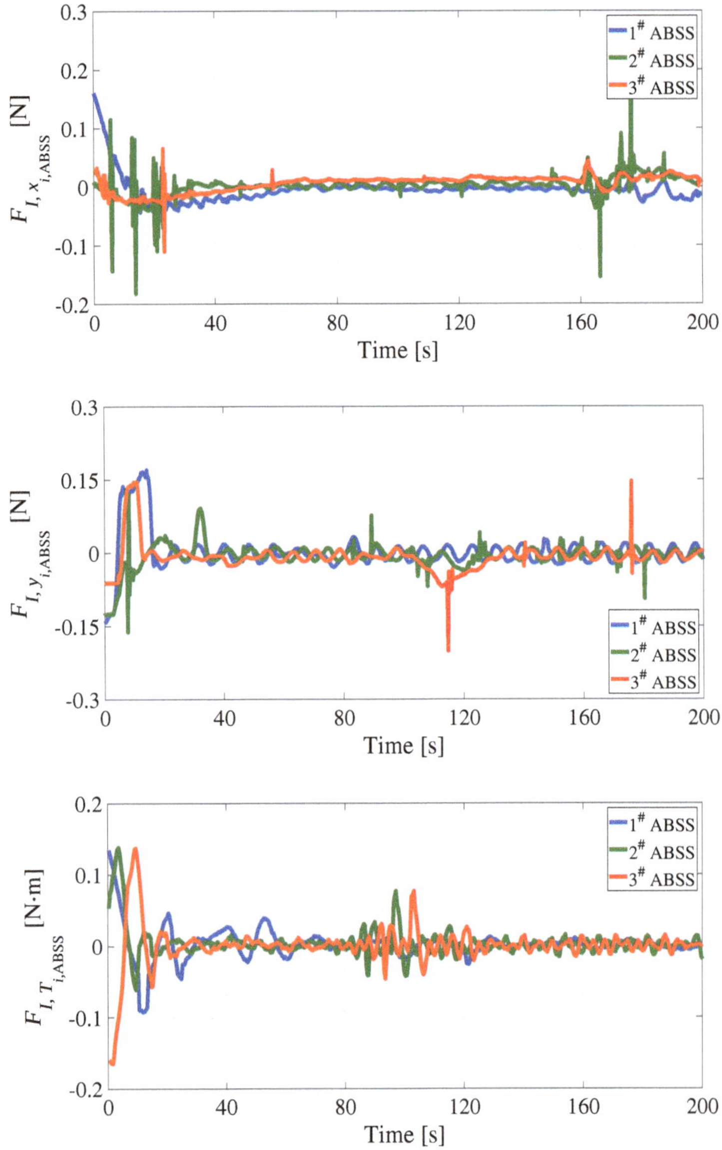

Fig. 3.6 The control inputs generated by the controls (3.22) and (3.24)

3.7 Notes and References

In this chapter, a basic design problem of cooperative control for the HOFAMASs has been investigated. A HOFAS predictive control has been constructed to address this problem with the realization and optimization of cooperative control performance. A sufficient condition has been proposed to analyze the simultaneous consensus and stability of the closed-loop HOFAMASs. A highlight is that an IHOFAS prediction model is established by means of a kind of Diophantine Equation to replace a first-order prediction model, such that the representation and design of predictive control can be completed within the framework of the HOFAS theory. The future work will pay attention to the cooperative control of the HOFAMASs under some complex cases, such as communication constraints, cyberattacks, uncertainties, etc.

Part II
Predictive Cooperative Control for High-Order Fully Actuated Multiagent Systems with Communication Constraints

Chapter 4
Proportional-Integral Predictive Cooperative Control for HOFAMASs with Communication Delays

4.1 Introduction

With the introduction of network into the control systems, it is simple and convenient to achieve the deep integration between cyber space and practical devices for reducing the costs and space constraints when designing and setting up the systems and the information interaction and data sharing for promoting the top-level scheduling and decision-making. However, there are also some negative impacts because of the access of network, where the communication delay is considered as one of the most common network-induced constraints. In the literature, there exist many studies that focus on the cooperative control for the MASs with communication delays.

In the past, Zhao et al. (2020) proposed an event-triggering scheme-based robust control to guarantee the consensus of the MASs under fixed communication delays and input constraints. Chen and Ling (2021) established a bit-rate condition based on a periodic event-triggering strategy and a saturation function to realize the consensus of unstable and scalar MASs with network-induced delays. Qi et al. (2021) used gain margin and analytical interpolation method to design a dynamic output feedback to ensure the consensus of the MASs with fixed communication delays. Jiang et al. (2022) presented an observer to estimate the leader agent under communication delays and then constructed a distributed cooperative controller to achieve the consensus by using a Lyapunov-Krasovskii functional and an LMI approach. Luo et al. (2020) gave a prediction observer to estimate the future states and utilized these state estimations to design a cooperative controller for addressing the bounded communication delays. Wang et al. (2020) combined a reduced-order observer with an event-triggering mechanism to propose a distributed cooperative control to implement the consensus under nonuniform communication delays. Meanwhile, Wang (2022), Wu et al. (2020), and the references therein also considered the cooperative control problem of the MASs with communication delays.

D.-W. Zhang, G.-P. Liu, *Predictive Cooperative Control for High-Order Fully Actuated Multiagent Systems*, https://doi.org/10.1007/978-981-95-1695-7_4

Actually, the above methods can suppress the impacts of communication delays on the cooperative control performance by enhancing the system robustness to raise the tolerance for communication delays, so that the realization of cooperative control under communication delays can be ensured. However, these methods are not with significant effects on improving the cooperative control performance and also construct the consensus conditions with high conservatism and high dependence of communication delays. Compared with the above studies, predictive control can yield the multistep ahead predictions by using historical and current data to actively compensate for communication delays, which improves the cooperative control performance and reduces the conservatism and dependence of simultaneous consensus and stability on the communication delays (Liu 2020a,b). Meanwhile, by introducing the HOFAS theory into the cooperative control design, the complexity and computational load in the design process can be obviously reduced, and the cooperative control performance can be effectively raised.

Following the idea of Liu (2020a), this chapter considers a HOFAS-PI predictive control to address the cooperative control problem of the HOFAMASs with communication delays, where a PI controller is designed to realize the local tracking control of the i-th HOFA agent and a networked predictive controller is established to ensure the cooperative control under communication delays. It is noted that an IHOFAS prediction model with an integral variable can be established, and the communication delays can be actively compensated. The major works are summarized as follows. Firstly, a discrete-time model of the i-th HOFA agent is used to offer a better model foundation for the cooperative control design. Then, an IHOFAS prediction model with an integral variable is constructed by applying a kind of Diophantine Equation, which is utilized to obtain the multistep ahead predictions for actively compensating for communication delays and optimizing the cooperative control performance. Further analysis establishes a sufficient condition about the simultaneous consensus and stability of the closed-loop HOFAMASs under communication delays. Finally, a formation control experiment of three ABSSs is provided to demonstrate the feasibility and practicality.

4.2 Problem Statement

In this chapter, the communication topology is described by Definition 3.1, and the dynamic model of the i-th HOFA agent satisfying Assumptions 3.1 and 3.2 is given in (3.1). Because of the access of network, the communication delays always exist in the i-th forward and feedback channels. Let $\tau_{i,a}$ and $\tau_{i,s}$ be the fixed communication delays in the i-th forward and feedback channels, respectively, and denote $\tau_{ii} = \tau_i = \tau_{i,a} + \tau_{i,s}$, $\tau_{ij} = \tau_{i,a} + \tau_{j,s}$.

Assumption 4.1 (Liu 2020a) *$\forall i \in \mathcal{N}$, $\tau_{i,a}$ and $\tau_{i,s}$ are the known positive integers and also the positively integral multiples of the sampling period.*

Remark 4.1 Assumption 4.1 is regarded as a basic characteristic of communication delays in the discrete-time domain. In fact, Mu et al. (2024), Pang et al. (2023, 2022a), and their associated studies all adopt this assumption to measure the communication delays. Based on Assumption 3.1-A1 and Assumption 3.1-A2, the communication delays can be determined by utilizing the synchronized clocks and the timestamps during the information transmission.

To achieve the cooperative control of the i-th HOFA agent (3.1) with communication delays, a HOFAS-PI predictive control is presented as

$$u_i(t) = B_i^{-1}\left(L_i(\cdot) + \Upsilon_{i,\mathrm{PI}}(K_{i,0\sim n}, x_i(t), z_i(t)) + v_i(t)\right), \tag{4.1}$$

where $L_i(\cdot)$ is used to eliminate the open-loop dynamics, $\Upsilon_{i,\mathrm{PI}}(K_{i,0\sim n}, x_i(t), z_i(t)) = \sum_{\eta=0}^{n-1} K_{i,\eta}x_i(t+\eta) + K_{i,n}z_i(t) \in \mathbb{R}^{n_i}$ aims to implement the local tracking control and $K_{i,\eta} \in \mathbb{R}^{n_i \times n_i}$, $\eta = 0, 1, \ldots, n-1$, $K_{i,n} \in \mathbb{R}^{n_i \times m}$ are the proportional and integral control gains, and $v_i(t) \in \mathbb{R}^{n_i}$ is a cooperative control item designed by HOFAS predictive control. In $\Upsilon_{i,\mathrm{PI}}(K_{i,0\sim n}, x_i(t), z_i(t))$, $z_i(t) \in \mathbb{R}^m$ is an integral variable and is defined as

$$z_i(t+1) = z_i(t) + y_i(t) - r(t) = z_i(t) + e_i(t), \tag{4.2}$$

where $r(t)$ is a known desired reference signal and $e_i(t)$ is a tracking error of the i-th HOFA agent. The related control structure is provided in Fig. 4.1.

By applying (4.1), the closed-loop HOFAMASs can be realized as

$$\begin{aligned} x_i(t+n) =& \Upsilon_{i,\mathrm{PI}}(K_{i,0\sim n}, x_i(t), z_i(t)) + v_i(t) \\ =& \sum_{\eta=0}^{n-1} K_{i,\eta}x_i(t+\eta) + K_{i,n}z_i(t) + v_i(t), \quad i \in \mathscr{N}. \end{aligned} \tag{4.3}$$

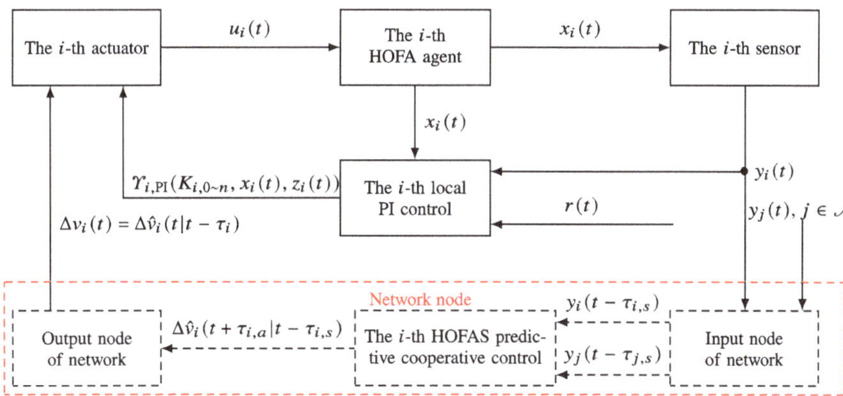

Fig. 4.1 PI predictive cooperative control for the HOFAMASs with communication delays

To solve the cooperative control item $v_i(t)$, an objective function $\mathcal{J}(t)$ is given as

$$\mathcal{J}(t) = \sum_{i \in \mathcal{N}} \mathcal{J}_i(t), \tag{4.4}$$

where $\mathcal{J}_i(t)$ is a sub-objective function in relation to the cooperative control performance of the i-th HOFA agent and is presented as

$$\begin{aligned}\mathcal{J}_i(t) = &\sum_{j \in \mathcal{N}_i} w_{ij} \left\| \hat{Y}_i(t + \tau_{i,a} + \aleph_y | t - \tau_{i,s}) - \hat{Y}_j(t + \tau_{i,a} + \aleph_y | t - \tau_{j,s}) \right\|^2 \\ &+ \beta_i \left\| \Delta \hat{V}_i(t + \tau_{i,a} + \aleph_u | t - \tau_{i,s}) \right\|^2,\end{aligned} \tag{4.5}$$

with

$$\hat{Y}_i(t + \tau_{i,a} + \aleph_y | t - \tau_{i,s}) = \begin{bmatrix} \hat{y}_i(t + \tau_{i,a} + \aleph_y | t - \tau_{i,s}) \\ \vdots \\ \hat{y}_i(t + \tau_{i,a} + 1 | t - \tau_{i,s}) \end{bmatrix},$$

$$\hat{Y}_j(t + \tau_{i,a} + \aleph_y | t - \tau_{j,s}) = \begin{bmatrix} \hat{y}_j(t + \tau_{i,a} + \aleph_y | t - \tau_{j,s}) \\ \vdots \\ \hat{y}_j(t + \tau_{i,a} + 1 | t - \tau_{j,s}) \end{bmatrix},$$

$$\Delta \hat{V}_i(t + \tau_{i,a} + \aleph_u | t - \tau_{i,s}) = \begin{bmatrix} \Delta \hat{v}_i(t + \tau_{i,a} + \aleph_u | t - \tau_{i,s}) \\ \vdots \\ \Delta \hat{v}_i(t + \tau_{i,a} | t - \tau_{i,s}) \end{bmatrix},$$

where $\hat{y}_i(t+\eta|t-\tau_{i,s})$, $\eta = \tau_{i,a}+1, \tau_{i,a}+2, \ldots, \tau_{i,a}+\aleph_y$, and $\Delta\hat{v}_i(t+\eta|t-\tau_{i,s})$, $\eta = \tau_{i,a}, \tau_{i,a}+1, \ldots, \tau_{i,a}+\aleph_u$, are the η-th ahead predictions of output $y_i(t)$ and cooperative control increment $\Delta v_i(t)$ based on $t - \tau_{i,s}$ time. w_{ij} is the (i, j)-th element of adjacent matrix $\mathcal{W}$, and $\beta_i > 0$ is a weighting factor. In (4.5), the first item focuses on the cooperative control performance by implementing the approach between $\hat{Y}_i(t + \tau_{i,a} + \aleph_y | t - \tau_{i,s})$ and $\hat{Y}_j(t + \tau_{i,a} + \aleph_y | t - \tau_{j,s})$, and the second one imposes a constraint on changing the rate and amplitude of $\Delta v_i(t)$ in the view of algorithm design, which ensures the cooperative controller's physical feasibility and reduces the mechanical losses, as well as prolongs the servicing life.

Problem 4.1 Given the i-th HOFA agent (3.1) satisfying Assumptions 3.1, 3.2, and 4.1, a HOFAS-PI predictive control $u_i\big(t, v_i(t, y_i(t), y_j(t))\big)$ in (4.1) is designed via the minimization of $\mathcal{J}(t)$ in (4.4) and (4.5), such that the closed-loop HOFAMASs (4.3) can achieve the simultaneous consensus and stability, i.e., the following conditions are satisfied:

1. $\forall i \in \mathcal{N}, \forall t \geq 0, \lim\limits_{t \to \infty} \|y_i(t)\| < \infty$ with $\|r(t)\| < \infty$.
2. $\forall i \in \mathcal{N}, \forall j \in \mathcal{N}_i, \lim_{t \to \infty} \|y_i(t) - y_j(t)\| = 0$.

4.3 HOFAS Proportional-Integral Predictive Cooperative Control Scheme

By adopting the time operator q, the closed-loop system (4.3) can be equivalent to the following polynomial one:

$$\mathcal{K}_i\left(q^{-1}\right)x_i(t) = \mathcal{B}_i\left(q^{-1}\right)v_i(t-1) + \mathcal{K}_{i,n}\left(q^{-1}\right)z_i(t+1), \tag{4.6}$$

with $\mathcal{K}_i\left(q^{-1}\right) = I + \sum_{\eta=0}^{n-1} K_{i,\eta}q^{\eta-n}$, $\mathcal{B}_i\left(q^{-1}\right) = q^{1-n}$, $\mathcal{K}_{i,n}\left(q^{-1}\right) = K_{i,n}q^{-n-1}$. Based on Diophantine Equation (3.7) with the same process from (3.6) to (3.8), an IHOFAS prediction model with an integral variable is developed as

$$x_i(t+\eta) = \mathcal{F}_{i,\eta}x_i(t) + \mathcal{G}_{i,\eta}\Delta v_i(t+\eta-1) + \mathcal{L}_{i,\eta}\Delta z_i(t+\eta+1), \tag{4.7}$$

where $\mathcal{L}_{i,\eta}\left(q^{-1}\right) = \mathcal{E}_{i,\eta}\left(q^{-1}\right)\mathcal{K}_{i,n}\left(q^{-1}\right) = \ell_{i,\eta,0} + \ell_{i,\eta,1}q^{-1} + \cdots + \ell_{i,\eta,n+\eta}q^{-(n+\eta)}$, and $\mathcal{F}_{i,\eta}$, $\mathcal{G}_{i,\eta}$ are constructed in (3.8). Considering the communication delays in the forward and feedback channels $\tau_{i,a}$ and $\tau_{i,s}$, the IHOFAS prediction model (4.7) can be corrected as

$$\begin{aligned}\hat{x}_i(t-\tau_{i,s}+\eta|t-\tau_{i,s}) =& \mathcal{F}_{i,\eta}x_i(t-\tau_{i,s}) + \mathcal{G}_{i,\eta}\Delta\hat{v}_i(t-\tau_{i,s}+\eta-1|t-\tau_{i,s})\\ &+ \mathcal{L}_{i,\eta}\Delta\hat{z}_i(t-\tau_{i,s}+\eta+1|t-\tau_{i,s}),\end{aligned} \tag{4.8}$$

with $\eta = 1, 2, \ldots, \tau_i + \aleph_y$.

When $\eta = \tau_i + 1, \tau_i + 2, \ldots, \tau_i + \aleph_y$, the multistep ahead predictions of $x_i(t)$ based on (4.8) are derived as

$$\begin{aligned}\hat{x}_i(t+\tau_{i,a}+1|t-\tau_{i,s}) =& \mathcal{F}_{i,\tau_i+1}x_i(t-\tau_{i,s}) + \mathcal{G}_{i,\tau_i+1}\Delta\hat{v}_i(t+\tau_{i,a}|t-\tau_{i,s})\\ &+ \mathcal{L}_{i,\tau_i+1}\Delta\hat{z}_i(t+\tau_{i,a}+2|t-\tau_{i,s}),\\ &\vdots\\ \hat{x}_i(t+\tau_{i,a}+\aleph_y|t-\tau_{i,s}) =& \mathcal{F}_{i,\tau_i+\aleph_y}x_i(t-\tau_{i,s})\\ &+ \mathcal{G}_{i,\tau_i+\aleph_y}\Delta\hat{v}_i(t+\tau_{i,a}+\aleph_y-1|t-\tau_{i,s})\\ &+ \mathcal{L}_{i,\tau_i+\aleph_y}\Delta\hat{z}_i(t+\tau_{i,a}+\aleph_y+1|t-\tau_{i,s});\end{aligned}$$

then the related output predictions are given as

$$\hat{y}_i(t+\tau_{i,a}+\eta|t-\tau_{i,s}) = C_i\hat{x}_i(t+\tau_{i,a}+\eta|t-\tau_{i,s}), \eta = 1, 2, \ldots, \aleph_y. \tag{4.9}$$

For $\eta = \aleph_u + 1, \aleph_u + 2, \ldots, \aleph_y$, $\hat{v}_i(t+\tau_{i,a}+\eta|t-\tau_{i,s}) = \hat{v}_i(t+\tau_{i,a}+\aleph_u|t-\tau_{i,s})$ such that $\Delta\hat{v}_i(t+\tau_{i,a}+\eta|t-\tau_{i,s}) = 0$; thus the output prediction (4.9) can be compactly concluded as

$$\begin{aligned}\hat{Y}_i(t+\tau_{i,a}+\aleph_y|t-\tau_{i,s}) =& P_{i,1}x_i(t-\tau_{i,s}) + P_{i,2}\Delta\hat{Z}_i(t+\tau_{i,a}+\aleph_y+1|t-\tau_{i,s}) \\ &+ P_{i,3}\hat{V}_i(t+\tau_{i,a}+\aleph_u|t-\tau_{i,s}),\end{aligned} \tag{4.10}$$

where $\Delta\hat{Z}_i(t+\tau_{i,a}+\aleph_y+1|t-\tau_{i,s}) = \begin{bmatrix} \Delta\hat{z}_i(t+\tau_{i,a}+\aleph_y+1|t-\tau_{i,s}) \\ \vdots \\ \Delta\hat{z}_i(t+\tau_{i,a}+2|t-\tau_{i,s}) \end{bmatrix}$ and

$$P_{i,1} = \begin{bmatrix} C_i\mathcal{F}_{i,\tau_i+\aleph_y} \\ \vdots \\ C_i\mathcal{F}_{i,\tau_i+1} \end{bmatrix}, \quad P_{i,2} = \begin{bmatrix} C_i\mathcal{L}_{i,\tau_i+\aleph_y} & & \\ & \ddots & \\ & & C_i\mathcal{L}_{i,\tau_i+1} \end{bmatrix},$$

$$P_{i,3} = \begin{bmatrix} C_i\mathcal{G}_{i,\tau_i+\aleph_y} & 0 & \cdots & 0 \\ \vdots & \vdots & \cdots & \vdots \\ C_i\mathcal{G}_{i,\tau_i+\aleph_u+1} & 0 & \cdots & 0 \\ 0 & C_i\mathcal{G}_{i,\tau_i+\aleph_u} & \ddots & \vdots \\ \vdots & \ddots & \ddots & 0 \\ 0 & \cdots & 0 & C_i\mathcal{G}_{i,\tau_i+1} \end{bmatrix}.$$

Because of (4.2), $\Delta z_i(t+1) = y_i(t) - r(t)$. Combining with the communication delays $\tau_{i,a}$ and $\tau_{i,s}$, it is obtained that $\Delta z_i(t-\tau_{i,s}+1) = y_i(t-\tau_{i,s}) - r(t-\tau_{i,s})$, and the related prediction is given as

$$\Delta\hat{z}_i(t-\tau_{i,s}+\eta+1|t-\tau_{i,s}) = \hat{y}_i(t-\tau_{i,s}+\eta|t-\tau_{i,s}) - r(t-\tau_{i,s}+\eta).$$

For $\eta = \tau_i+1, \tau_i+2, \ldots, \tau_i+\aleph_y$, the multistep ahead predictions of $\Delta z_i(t)$ are provided as

$$\begin{aligned}\Delta\hat{z}_i(t+\tau_{i,a}+2|t-\tau_{i,s}) =& \hat{y}_i(t+\tau_{i,a}+1|t-\tau_{i,s}) - r(t+\tau_{i,a}+1), \\ &\vdots \\ \Delta\hat{z}_i(t+\tau_{i,a}+\aleph_y+1|t-\tau_{i,s}) =& \hat{y}_i(t+\tau_{i,a}+\aleph_y|t-\tau_{i,s}) - r(t+\tau_{i,a}+\aleph_y),\end{aligned}$$

that is,

$$\Delta\hat{Z}_i(t+\tau_{i,a}+\aleph_y+1|t-\tau_{i,s}) = \hat{Y}_i(t+\tau_{i,a}+\aleph_y|t-\tau_{i,s}) - R(t+\tau_{i,a}+\aleph_y),$$

with $R(t+\tau_{i,a}+\aleph_y) = \left[r^{\mathrm{T}}(t+\tau_{i,a}+\aleph_y) \cdots r^{\mathrm{T}}(t+\tau_{i,a}+1)\right]^{\mathrm{T}}$, such that the output prediction (4.10) can be represented as

$$\begin{aligned}\hat{Y}_i(t+\tau_{i,a}+\aleph_y|t-\tau_{i,s}) =& Q_{i,1}x_i(t-\tau_{i,s}) + Q_{i,2}R(t+\tau_{i,a}+\aleph_y) \\ &+ Q_{i,3}\Delta\hat{V}_i(t+\tau_{i,a}+\aleph_u|t-\tau_{i,s}),\end{aligned} \tag{4.11}$$

where $Q_{i,1} = (I-P_{i,2})^{-1}P_{i,1}$, $Q_{i,2} = -(I-P_{i,2})^{-1}P_{i,2}$, $Q_{i,3} = (I-P_{i,2})^{-1}P_{i,3}$. Based on (2.9),

$$\Delta\hat{v}_i(t+\tau_{i,a}+\eta|t-\tau_{i,s}) = \gamma_{i,\eta}\Delta\hat{v}_i(t+\tau_{i,a}|t-\tau_{i,s}),$$

where $\gamma_{i,\eta} > 0$, $\eta = 1, 2, \ldots, \aleph_u$, is a weighting factor, so that $Q_{i,3}$ can be degenerated as $Q_{i,4} = Q_{i,3}\Gamma_i$ with $\Gamma_i = \text{Blockdiag}\{\gamma_{i,\aleph_u}I, \ldots, \gamma_{i,1}I, I\}$, and $Q_{i,3}\Delta\hat{V}_i(t+\tau_{i,a}+\aleph_u|t-\tau_{i,s}) = Q_{i,4}\Delta\hat{V}_i(t+\tau_{i,a}|t-\tau_{i,s})$ with

$$\Delta\hat{V}_i(t+\tau_{i,a}|t-\tau_{i,s}) = \left[\,\Delta\hat{v}_i^{\mathrm{T}}(t+\tau_{i,a}|t-\tau_{i,s}) \cdots \Delta\hat{v}_i^{\mathrm{T}}(t+\tau_{i,a}|t-\tau_{i,s})\,\right]^{\mathrm{T}}.$$

Summarizing the above means that (4.11) can be rewritten as

$$\begin{aligned}\hat{Y}_i(t+\tau_{i,a}+\aleph_y|t-\tau_{i,s}) =& Q_{i,1}x_i(t-\tau_{i,s}) + Q_{i,2}R(t+\tau_{i,a}+\aleph_y) \\ &+ Q_{i,4}\Delta\hat{V}_i(t+\tau_{i,a}|t-\tau_{i,s}).\end{aligned} \tag{4.12}$$

$\forall j \in \mathscr{N}_i$, based on (4.8), $x_j(t)$ can be predicted as

$$\begin{aligned}\hat{x}_j(t-\tau_{j,s}+\eta|t-\tau_{j,s}) =& \mathcal{F}_{j,\eta}x_j(t-\tau_{j,s}) + \mathcal{G}_{j,\eta}\Delta\hat{v}_j(t-\tau_{j,s}+\eta-1|t-\tau_{j,s}) \\ &+ \mathcal{L}_{j,\eta}\Delta\hat{z}_j(t-\tau_{j,s}+\eta+1|t-\tau_{j,s}),\end{aligned}$$

with $\eta = 1, 2, \ldots, \tau_{ij}+\aleph_y$. For $\eta = \tau_{ij}+1, \tau_{ij}+2, \ldots, \tau_{ij}+\aleph_y$, the multistep ahead predictions of $x_j(t)$ are given as

$$\begin{aligned}\hat{x}_j(t+\tau_{i,a}+1|t-\tau_{j,s}) =& \mathcal{F}_{j,\tau_{ij}+1}x_j(t-\tau_{j,s}) + \mathcal{G}_{j,\tau_{ij}+1}\Delta\hat{v}_j(t+\tau_{i,a}|t-\tau_{j,s}) \\ &+ \mathcal{L}_{j,\tau_{ij}+1}\Delta\hat{z}_j(t+\tau_{i,a}+2|t-\tau_{j,s}), \\ &\vdots \\ \hat{x}_j(t+\tau_{i,a}+\aleph_y|t-\tau_{j,s}) =& \mathcal{F}_{j,\tau_{ij}+\aleph_y}x_j(t-\tau_{j,s}) \\ &+ \mathcal{G}_{j,\tau_{ij}+\aleph_y}\Delta\hat{v}_j(t+\tau_{i,a}+\aleph_y-1|t-\tau_{j,s}) \\ &+ \mathcal{L}_{j,\tau_{ij}+\aleph_y}\Delta\hat{z}_j(t+\tau_{i,a}+\aleph_y+1|t-\tau_{j,s}),\end{aligned}$$

and the corresponding output prediction is set as $\hat{y}_j(t+\tau_{i,a}+\eta|t-\tau_{j,s}) = C_j\hat{x}_j(t+\tau_{i,a}+\eta|t-\tau_{j,s})$ with $\eta = 1, 2, \ldots, \aleph_y$. Meanwhile, the multistep ahead predictions of $\Delta z_j(t)$ are provided as

$$\begin{aligned}\Delta\hat{z}_j(t+\tau_{i,a}+2|t-\tau_{j,s}) =& \hat{y}_j(t+\tau_{i,a}+1|t-\tau_{j,s})-r(t+\tau_{i,a}+1),\\ &\vdots\\ \Delta\hat{z}_j(t+\tau_{i,a}+\aleph_y+1|t-\tau_{j,s}) =& \hat{y}_i(t+\tau_{i,a}+\aleph_y|t-\tau_{j,s})-r(t+\tau_{i,a}+\aleph_y).\end{aligned}$$

Repeating the process from (4.9) to (4.12), the output prediction of the j-th HOFA agent is derived as

$$\begin{aligned}\hat{Y}_j(t+\tau_{i,a}+\aleph_y|t-\tau_{j,s}) =& Q_{j,1}x_j(t-\tau_{j,s})+Q_{j,2}R(t+\tau_{i,a}+\aleph_y)\\ &+Q_{j,4}\Delta\hat{V}_j(t+\tau_{i,a}|t-\tau_{j,s}),\end{aligned} \tag{4.13}$$

where $\Delta\hat{V}_j(t+\tau_{i,a}|t-\tau_{j,s})=\left[\Delta\hat{v}_j^{\mathrm{T}}(t+\tau_{i,a}|t-\tau_{j,s})\cdots\Delta\hat{v}_j^{\mathrm{T}}(t+\tau_{i,a}|t-\tau_{j,s})\right]^{\mathrm{T}}$, $Q_{j,1}=(I-P_{j,2})^{-1}P_{j,1}$, $Q_{j,2}=-(I-P_{j,2})^{-1}P_{j,2}$, $Q_{j,3}=(I-P_{j,2})^{-1}P_{j,3}$, $Q_{j,4}=Q_{j,3}\Gamma_j$, $\Gamma_j=\mathrm{Blockdiag}\{\gamma_{j,\aleph_u}I,\ldots,\gamma_{j,1}I,I\}$, and

$$P_{j,1}=\begin{bmatrix}C_j\mathcal{F}_{j,\tau_{ij}+\aleph_y}\\ \vdots\\ C_j\mathcal{F}_{j,\tau_{ij}+1}\end{bmatrix},\quad P_{j,2}=\begin{bmatrix}C_j\mathcal{L}_{j,\tau_{ij}+\aleph_y} & & \\ & \ddots & \\ & & C_j\mathcal{L}_{j,\tau_{ij}+1}\end{bmatrix},$$

$$P_{j,3}=\begin{bmatrix}C_j\mathcal{G}_{j,\tau_{ij}+\aleph_y} & 0 & \cdots & 0\\ \vdots & \vdots & \cdots & \vdots\\ C_j\mathcal{G}_{j,\tau_{ij}+\aleph_u+1} & 0 & \cdots & 0\\ 0 & C_j\mathcal{G}_{j,\tau_{ij}+\aleph_u} & \ddots & \vdots\\ \vdots & \ddots & \ddots & 0\\ 0 & \cdots & 0 & C_j\mathcal{G}_{j,\tau_{ij}+1}\end{bmatrix}.$$

To calculate the optimal cooperative cooperative control increment $\Delta v_i(t)$, let

$$\frac{\partial}{\partial\Delta\hat{V}_i(t+\tau_{i,a}|t-\tau_{i,s})}\mathcal{J}(t)=0,\ i\in\mathcal{N}.$$

By utilizing (4.12) and (4.13), it is yielded that

$$\begin{aligned}&\sum_{j\in\mathcal{N}_i}w_{ij}Q_{i,4}^{\mathrm{T}}(Q_{i,1}x_i(t-\tau_{i,s})+Q_{i,2}R(t+\tau_{i,a}+\aleph_y)\\ &\quad+Q_{i4}\Delta\hat{V}_i(t+\tau_{i,a}|t-\tau_{i,s})-Q_{j1}x_j(t-\tau_{j,s})\end{aligned}$$

$$- Q_{j2}R(t+\tau_{i,a}+\aleph_y) - Q_{j4}\Delta\hat{V}_j(t+\tau_{i,a}|t-\tau_{j,s}))$$
$$+ \beta_i\Gamma_i^{\mathrm{T}}\Gamma_i\Delta\hat{V}_i(t+\tau_{i,a}|t-\tau_{i,s}) = 0,$$

which can be summarized as

$$\Delta\hat{V}(t+\tau_{i,a}|t-\tau_s) = F^{-1}Gx(t-\tau_s) + F^{-1}MR(t+\tau_{i,a}+\aleph_y),$$

with $\Delta\hat{V}(t+\tau_{i,a}|t-\tau_s) = \begin{bmatrix} \Delta\hat{V}_1(t+\tau_{i,a}|t-\tau_{1,s}) \\ \vdots \\ \Delta\hat{V}_N(t+\tau_{i,a}|t-\tau_{N,s}) \end{bmatrix}$, $x(t-\tau_s) = \begin{bmatrix} x_1(t-\tau_{1,s}) \\ \vdots \\ x_N(t-\tau_{N,s}) \end{bmatrix}$, and

$$F = \{f_{ij}\},\ \ f_{ii} = w_i Q_{i,4}^{\mathrm{T}}Q_{i,4} + \beta_i\Gamma_i^{\mathrm{T}}\Gamma_i,\ \ f_{ij} = -w_{ij}Q_{i,4}^{\mathrm{T}}Q_{j,4},$$
$$G = \{g_{ij}\},\ \ g_{ii} = -w_i Q_{i,4}^{\mathrm{T}}Q_{i,1},\ \ g_{ij} = w_{ij}Q_{i,4}^{\mathrm{T}}Q_{j,1},$$
$$M = \begin{bmatrix} \sum_{j\in\mathcal{N}_1} w_{1j}Q_{1,4}^{\mathrm{T}}Q_{j,2} - w_1Q_{1,4}^{\mathrm{T}}Q_{1,2} \\ \vdots \\ \sum_{j\in\mathcal{N}_N} w_{Nj}Q_{N,4}^{\mathrm{T}}Q_{j,2} - w_NQ_{N,4}^{\mathrm{T}}Q_{N,2} \end{bmatrix},\ \ w_i = \sum_{j\in\mathcal{N}_i} w_{ij}.$$

Then, the optimal cooperative control increment of the i-th HOFA agent in the network node is designed as $\Delta\hat{v}_i(t+\tau_{i,a}|t-\tau_{i,s}) = H_i\Delta\hat{V}(t+\tau_{i,a}|t-\tau_s)$, i.e.,

$$\Delta\hat{v}_i(t+\tau_{i,a}|t-\tau_{i,s}) = H_iF^{-1}Gx(t-\tau_s) + H_iF^{-1}MR(t+\tau_{i,a}+\aleph_y),$$

where $H_i = \begin{bmatrix} H_{i,1} \cdots H_{i,N} \end{bmatrix} \in \mathbb{R}^{n_i\times(\aleph_u+1)\tilde{n}}$ with $\tilde{n} = \sum_{i\in\mathcal{N}} n_i$, $H_{i,i} = \begin{bmatrix} 0 \cdots 0\ I \end{bmatrix}$, $H_{i,j} = 0$, $j \in \mathcal{N}_i$. On the i-th actuator, the optimal cooperative control increment is set as $\Delta v_i(t) = \Delta\hat{v}_i(t|t-\tau_i)$, i.e.,

$$\Delta v_i(t) = H_iF^{-1}Gx(t-\tau) + H_iF^{-1}MR(t+\aleph_y), \tag{4.14}$$

where $x(t-\tau) = \begin{bmatrix} x_1(t-\tau_{i1}) \\ \vdots \\ x_N(t-\tau_{iN}) \end{bmatrix}$ and $R(t+\aleph_y) = \begin{bmatrix} r(t+\aleph_y) \\ \vdots \\ r(t+1) \end{bmatrix}$.

Remark 4.2 Based on Remark 3.4, $\Upsilon_{i,\mathrm{PI}}(K_{i,0\sim n}, x_i(t), z_i(t))$ is also used to adjust the closed-loop performances and to raise the accuracy of IHOFAS prediction model (4.8) as a feedback correction. Following the idea in Remark 2.2, the proportional and integral control gains $K_{i,\eta}$, $\eta = 0, 1, \ldots, n$, are solved by

$$\left[\, K_{i,0} \cdots K_{i,n-1}\; K_{i,n} \,\right] = \mathcal{Z}_i \Lambda_i^n \begin{bmatrix} \mathcal{Z}_i \\ \mathcal{Z}_i \Lambda_i \\ \vdots \\ \mathcal{Z}_i \Lambda_i^{n-1} \\ C_i \mathcal{Z}_i \left(\Lambda_i - I\right)^{-1} \end{bmatrix}^{-1},$$

where $\mathcal{Z}_i \in \mathbb{R}^{n_i \times n_i(\tilde{n}+m)}$ is an arbitrary parameter matrix and $\Lambda_i \in \mathbb{R}^{n_i(\tilde{n}+m) \times n_i(\tilde{n}+m)}$ is a Schur matrix satisfying

$$\det\left(\begin{bmatrix} \mathcal{Z}_i \\ \mathcal{Z}_i \Lambda_i \\ \vdots \\ \mathcal{Z}_i \Lambda_i^{n-1} \\ C_i \mathcal{Z}_i \left(\Lambda_i - I\right)^{-1} \end{bmatrix}\right) \neq 0.$$

4.4 Analysis of Simultaneous Consensus and Stability Under Communication Delays

Let $e_i(t) = y_i(t) - r(t) = C_i x_i(t) - r(t)$ be the tracking error of the i-th HOFA agent and $\epsilon_{ii}(t) = \epsilon_i(t) = e_i(t)$, $\epsilon_{ij}(t) = y_i(t) - y_j(t)$, $j \in \mathcal{N}_i$, be the consensus error; then the simultaneous consensus and stability of the closed-loop HOFAMAS (4.3) can be transformed into that $\epsilon_i(t) \to 0$ and $\epsilon_{ij}(t) \to 0$ with $t \to \infty$. From this perspective, Theorem 4.1 is proposed to address this problem.

Theorem 4.1 *The closed-loop HOFAMASs* (4.3) *can achieve the simultaneous consensus and stability if* $\exists w_{ij} \geq 0$, $\sum_{j \in \mathcal{N}_i} w_{ij}^2 \neq 0$, $\exists \beta_i > 0$, $\forall i \in \mathcal{N}$, $\forall j \in \mathcal{N}_i$, *to guarantee that* $\forall i \in \mathcal{N}$, $\frac{\partial}{\partial \Delta \hat{V}_i(t|t)} \mathcal{J}(t) = 0$, *and* Φ *is a Schur stable polynomial matrix in relation to* q, *where*

$$\Phi = I + (q-1) C \Phi_1^{-1} \Phi_2, \tag{4.15}$$

with

$$\Phi_1 = I - (I + \mathcal{K}_M C) q^{-1} - \mathcal{K}_G q^{-\tau-1}, \quad \Phi_2 = \mathcal{K}_{nc} - \mathcal{K}_M q^{-1}, \tag{4.16}$$

and

$$
\begin{aligned}
C =& \text{Blockdiag}\{C_1, \ldots, C_N\}, \\
\mathcal{K}_M =& \text{Blockdiag}\{\mathcal{K}_{1,c} H_1 F^{-1} M \vec{I}_{\aleph_y}, \ldots, \mathcal{K}_{N,c} H_N F^{-1} M \vec{I}_{\aleph_y}\}, \\
\mathcal{K}_G =& \begin{bmatrix} \mathcal{K}_{1,c} H_1 F^{-1} G \\ \vdots \\ \mathcal{K}_{N,c} H_N F^{-1} G \end{bmatrix}, \quad \mathcal{K}_{nc} = \text{Blockdiag}\{\mathcal{K}_{1,nc}, \ldots, \mathcal{K}_{N,nc}\}, \\
\vec{I}_{\aleph_y} =& [\underbrace{I \cdots I}_{\aleph_y}]^{\mathrm{T}}, \quad \mathcal{K}_{i,c} = \mathcal{K}_i^{-1} \mathcal{B}_i, \quad \mathcal{K}_{i,nc} = \mathcal{K}_i^{-1} \mathcal{K}_{i,n}.
\end{aligned}
\tag{4.17}
$$

Proof Generally, it is assumed that $r(\cdot) = r$, such that $\Delta v_i(t)$ in (4.14) can be rewritten as

$$
\Delta v_i(t) = H_i F^{-1} G x(t-\tau) + H_i F^{-1} M \vec{I}_{\aleph_y} \left(C_i x_i(t) - e_i(t) \right). \tag{4.18}
$$

Meanwhile, based on the proof of Theorem 3.1, $e(t)$ in this chapter can also be written as (3.17) with $e(t) = \left[e_1^{\mathrm{T}}(t) \cdots e_N^{\mathrm{T}}(t) \right]^{\mathrm{T}}$, $x(t) = \left[x_1^{\mathrm{T}}(t) \cdots x_N^{\mathrm{T}}(t) \right]^{\mathrm{T}}$, i.e.,

$$
e(t+1) = e(t) + (q-1) C x(t), \tag{4.19}
$$

and the consensus error $\epsilon(t)$ in this chapter can also be summarized as (3.18) with $i = 1$ and $\epsilon(t) = \left[\epsilon_1^{\mathrm{T}}(t) \cdots \epsilon_{1N}^{\mathrm{T}}(t) \right]^{\mathrm{T}}$, i.e.,

$$
\epsilon(t) = \tilde{\mathbf{I}} e(t). \tag{4.20}
$$

Based on (4.6), it is obtained that

$$
\Delta x_i(t+1) = \mathcal{K}_{i,c} \Delta v_i(t) + \mathcal{K}_{i,nc} \Delta z_i(t+2),
$$

because $\exists w_{ij} \geq 0$, $\sum_{j \in \mathcal{N}_i} w_{ij}^2 \neq 0$, $\exists \beta_i > 0$, $\forall i \in \mathcal{N}$, $\forall j \in \mathcal{N}_i$, to guarantee that $\frac{\partial}{\partial \Delta \hat{V}_i(t|t)} \mathcal{J}(t) = 0$, $\forall i \in \mathcal{N}$, and the optimal cooperative control increment $\Delta v_i(t)$ can be calculated in (4.14) and (4.18). By taking (4.18) and $\Delta z_i(t+1) = e_i(t)$ into the above, it is yielded that

$$
\begin{aligned}
\Delta x_i(t+1) =& \mathcal{K}_{i,c} H_i F^{-1} G x(t-\tau) + \mathcal{K}_{i,nc} e_i(t+1) \\
&+ \mathcal{K}_{i,c} H_i F^{-1} M \vec{I}_{\aleph_y} \left(C_i x_i(t) - e_i(t) \right),
\end{aligned}
$$

which can be compactly expressed as

$$
\Delta x(t+1) = \mathcal{K}_G x(t-\tau) + \mathcal{K}_M C x(t) - \mathcal{K}_M e(t) + \mathcal{K}_{nc} e(t+1),
$$

where $\mathcal{K}_G$, $\mathcal{K}_M$, and $\mathcal{K}_{nc}$ are given in (4.17). Further, the above can be transformed into

$$x(t) = \Phi_1^{-1}\Phi_2 e(t), \tag{4.21}$$

where Φ_1 and Φ_2 are shown in (4.16). Then, taking (4.21) into (4.19), we obtain

$$\begin{aligned} e(t+1) =& e(t) + (q-1)Cx(t) \\ =& e(t) + (q-1)C\Phi_1^{-1}\Phi_2 e(t) \\ =& \Phi e(t), \end{aligned} \tag{4.22}$$

where Φ is provided in (4.15). Combining with (4.20), an auxiliary system is generated as

$$\begin{cases} e(t+1) =& \Phi e(t), \\ \epsilon(t) =& \tilde{\mathbf{I}} e(t). \end{cases} \tag{4.23}$$

Because $\exists w_{ij} \geq 0$, $\sum_{j\in\mathcal{N}_i} w_{ij}^2 \neq 0$, $\exists \beta_i > 0$, $\forall i \in \mathcal{N}$, $\forall j \in \mathcal{N}_i$, to guarantee that Φ is a Schur stable polynomial matrix in relation to q, $e(t) \to 0$ with $t \to \infty$, so that $\epsilon(t) \to 0$ with $t \to \infty$ because of (4.23). Hence, the closed-loop HOFAMASs (4.3) can achieve the simultaneous consensus and stability.

This completes the proof. □

4.5 With Application to Formation Control of Air-Bearing Spacecraft Simulators

There are three ABSSs to take a formation control experiment to illustrate the feasibility and practicality of the proposed HOFAS-PI predictive control, where the dynamic models of three ABSSs are shown in (A.4) and the details of three ABSSs and its relevant experimental platform are given in Appendix A.

4.5.1 *Numerical Simulation*

By choosing system (A.4a) as an example, a comparison of the proposed HOFAS-PI predictive control and the DMC in Xi (2013) is presented to verify the feasibility and advantage, where the associated design parameters are selected as $T_s = 0.2$s, $w_{ii} = 0$, $w_{ij} = 1$, $\beta_i = 15$, $\Gamma_i = I$, $i, j = 1, 2, 3$, $\aleph_y = 7$, $\aleph_u = 6$. The communication delays in the forward and feedback channels are given as $\tau_{1,a} = 2$, $\tau_{2,a} = 3$, $\tau_{3,a} = 2$, $\tau_{1,s} = 2$, $\tau_{2,s} = 3$, $\tau_{3,s} = 4$.

Based on (4.1), a HOFAS-PI predictive control for system (A.4a) is presented as

$$F_{I,x_{i,\mathrm{ABSS}}}(t) = B_i^{-1}\left(-L_i(\cdot) + \Upsilon_{i,\mathrm{PI}}(K_{i,0\sim 2}, x_{i,\mathrm{ABSS}}(t), z_{i,x_{i,\mathrm{ABSS}}}(t)) + v_i(t)\right), \tag{4.24}$$

where $K_{1,0} = -4.462$, $K_{1,1} = 19.4$, $K_{1,2} = -0.2716$, $K_{2,0} = -4.485$, $K_{2,1} = 19.5$, $K_{2,2} = -0.2730$, $K_{3,0} = -4.416$, $K_{3,1} = 19.2$, $K_{3,2} = -0.2688$. For the DMC in Xi (2013), system (A.4a) should be firstly transformed as (3.23), where $F_{I,x_{i,\mathrm{ABSS}}}(t)$ can be calculated via the minimization of an objective function $\mathcal{J}_{\mathrm{DMC}}(t) = \sum_{i\in\mathcal{N}} \mathcal{J}_{i,\mathrm{DMC}}(t)$, and $\mathcal{J}_{i,\mathrm{DMC}}(t)$ is designed as

$$\begin{aligned}
\mathcal{J}_{i,\mathrm{DMC}}(t) = &\sum_{j\in\mathcal{N}_i} w_{ij} \sum_{\eta=\tau_{i,a}+1}^{\tau_{i,a}+\aleph_y} \left\|\hat{X}_{i,\mathrm{ABSS}}(t+\eta|t-\tau_{i,s}) - \hat{X}_{j,\mathrm{ABSS}}(t+\eta|t-\tau_{j,s})\right\|^2 \\
&+ \alpha_i \sum_{\eta=\tau_{i,a}+1}^{\tau_{i,a}+\aleph_y} \left\|\hat{X}_{i,\mathrm{ABSS}}(t+\eta|t) - R_x(t+\eta)\right\|^2 \\
&+ \beta_i \sum_{\eta=\tau_{i,a}}^{\tau_{i,a}+\aleph_u} \left\|\hat{F}_{I,x_{i,\mathrm{ABSS}}}(t+\eta|t)\right\|^2,
\end{aligned}$$

and $r_x(t)$ is a known desired reference signal, $R_x(t+\eta) = \left[r_x(t+\eta)\ r_x(t+\eta+1)\right]^{\mathrm{T}}$. Then, the simulated comparison is provided in Fig. 4.2.

Figure 4.2a means that the presented HOFAS-PI predictive control (4.24) can actively compensate for the communication delays in the forward and feedback channels, such that the satisfactory cooperative tracking control performance in the dynamic and steady processes can be implemented, but Fig. 4.2b shows that the DMC in Xi (2013) only realizes the cooperation between $x_{1,\mathrm{ABSS}}(t)$ and $x_{3,\mathrm{ABSS}}(t)$, and it cannot ensure the desired tracking control performance. Meanwhile, there exists the serious oscillation in Fig. 4.2b, where the reason is provided in Remark 3.5.

Through the comparison in Fig. 4.2, the feasibility and advantage of HOFAS-PI predictive control can be fully demonstrated, which offers a solid foundation for the experimental verification.

4.5.2 Experimental Results

Based on the above simulation, a formation control experiment for three ABSSs is provided to illustrate the practicality of the presented HOFAS-PI predictive control, where the desired formation is given in Fig. 4.3.

For systems (A.4a) and (A.4b), the cooperative control protocols are chosen as the same as (4.24) with the same design parameters. For system (A.4c), only a tracking control is needed to satisfy the requirement of $\psi_{i,\mathrm{ABSS}}(t)$ during the

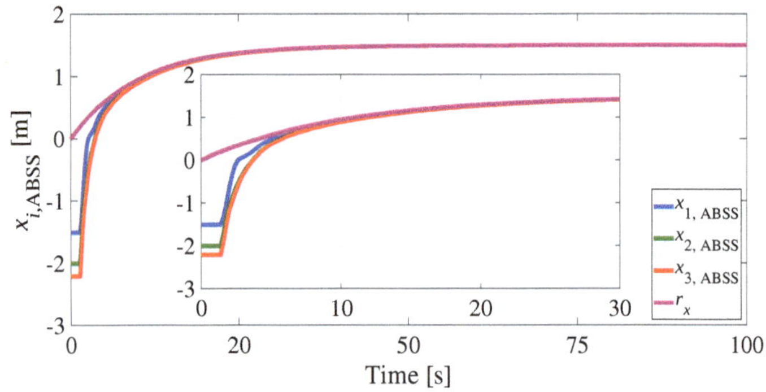

(a) Cooperative control of system (A.4a) by using the control (4.24)

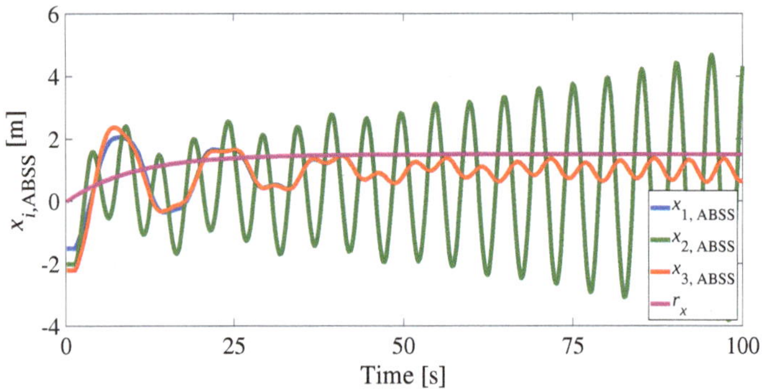

(b) Cooperative control of system (A.4a) via the DMC in Xi (2013)

Fig. 4.2 Comparison of the proposed HOFAS-PI predictive control and the DMC in Xi (2013)

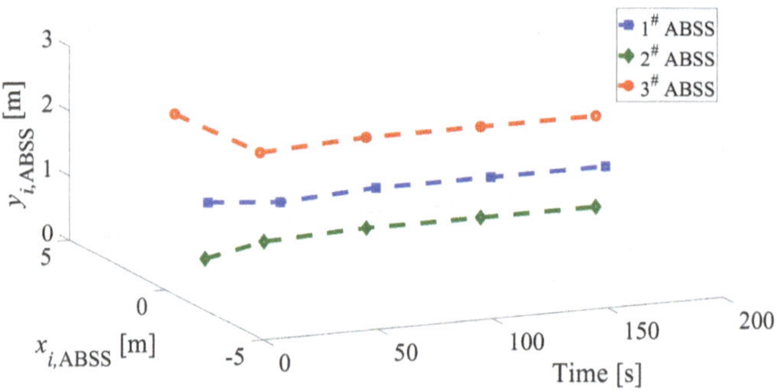

Fig. 4.3 The desired formation of three ABSSs

formation control. Hence, the cooperative control items are set as 0, and a tracking control is designed as

$$F_{I,T_{i,\mathrm{ABSS}}}(t) = -L_{i,T}(\cdot) + \Upsilon_{i,\mathrm{PI}}(K_{0\sim 2}, \psi_{i,\mathrm{ABSS}}(t), z_{i,\psi_{i,\mathrm{ABSS}}}(t)), \tag{4.25}$$

with $K_{1,0} = -0.0693$, $K_{1,1} = 0.2390$, $K_{1,2} = -0.0048$, $K_{2,0} = -0.0699$, $K_{2,1} = 0.2410$, $K_{2,2} = -0.0048$, $K_{3,0} = -0.0684$, $K_{3,1} = 0.2360$, $K_{3,2} = -0.0047$. By applying (4.24) and (4.25), the experimental results are provided in Figs. 4.4, 4.5, 4.6.

Figure 4.4 provides the position and angle responses of formation control of three ABSSs, where the position responses $x_{i,\mathrm{ABSS}}(t)$ and $y_{i,\mathrm{ABSS}}(t)$ can ensure the cooperative control performance by applying (4.24). During the dynamic and steady processes, they can simultaneously reach the desired positions and can be cooperatively changed. The angle responses $\psi_{i,\mathrm{ABSS}}(t)$ can achieve the desired tracking control performance within the tolerant errors by adopting (4.25). The control inputs generated by (4.24) and (4.25) are shown in Fig. 4.5, where there are some vibrations because of the model uncertainties and external disturbances, as well as integral saturation. Figure 4.6 provides the practical formation of three ABSSs, which implies that the presented HOFAS-PI predictive control (4.24) can implement the desired formation and continue to follow it by comparing with Fig. 4.3.

Based on the results in Figs. 4.4, 4.5, 4.6, the feasibility and practicality of HOFAS-PI predictive control can be fully verified, which provides a solid support for the large-scale applications of practical spacecraft control.

4.6 Notes and References

In this chapter, a cooperative control problem of the HOFAMASs with communication delays has been considered. A HOFAS-PI predictive control has been presented to deal with this problem for the optimization of cooperative control performance and the active compensation of communication delays. A sufficient condition has been constructed to discuss the simultaneous consensus of the closed-loop HOFAMASs under communication delays. A highlight is that an IHOFAS prediction model with an integral variable is established with the help of a type of Diophantine Equation. The other is that the communication delays can be actively compensated to improve the cooperative control performance and reduce the conservatism and dependence of simultaneous consensus and stability on the communication delays. Because of the better control performance and simple design process, the proposed HOFAS-PI predictive control can be developed to a number of industrial applications.

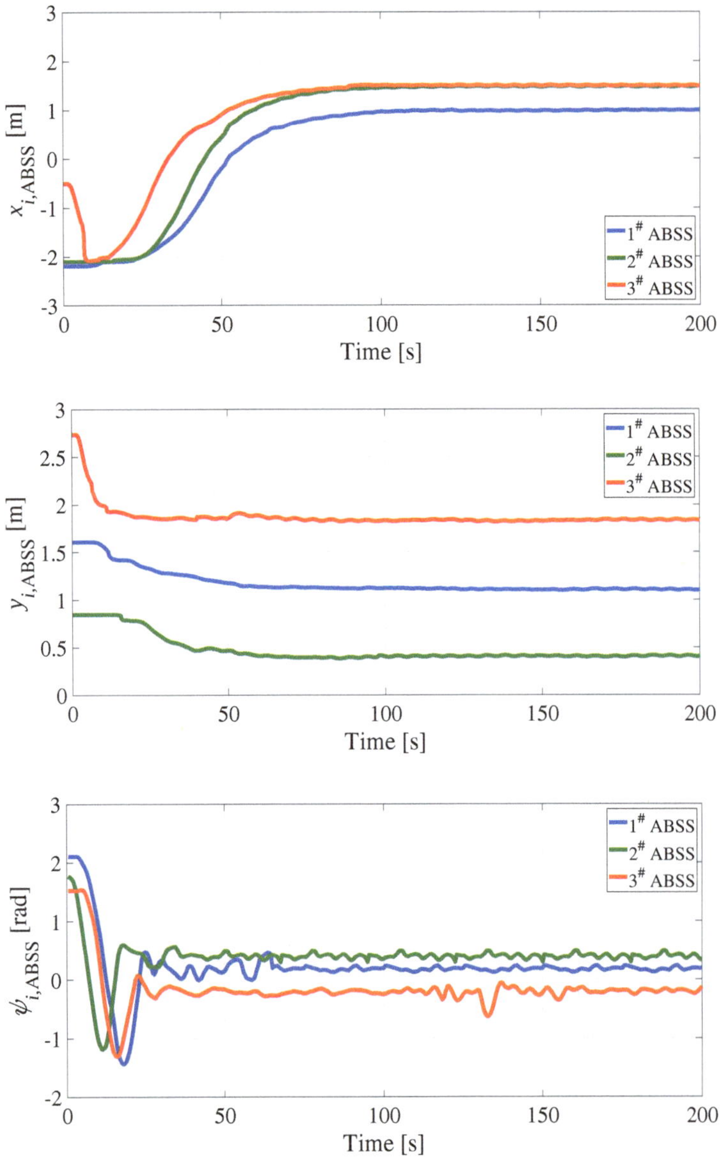

Fig. 4.4 The formation control of three ABSSs by using the controls (4.24) and (4.25)

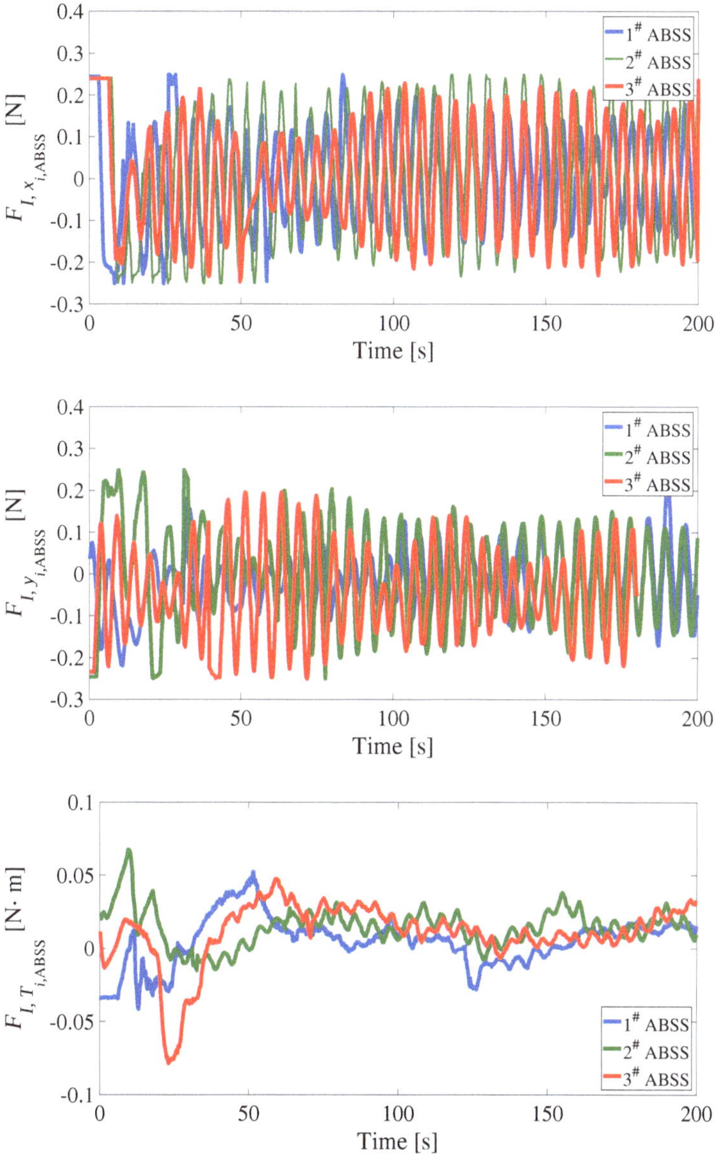

Fig. 4.5 The control inputs generated by the controls (4.24) and (4.25)

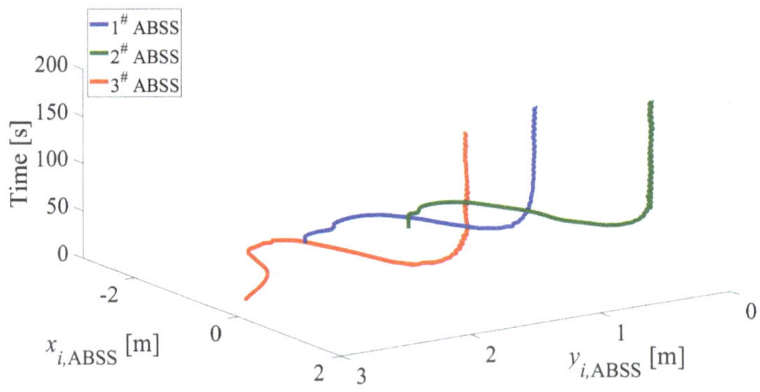

Fig. 4.6 The actual formation of three ABSSs

Chapter 5
Observer-Based Predictive Cooperative Control for HOFAMASs with Time-Varying Communication Constraints

5.1 Introduction

With the growing application scenarios of cooperative control for the MASs, the working conditions have been becoming more and more complex. Due to some limitations in practice, including insufficient accuracy of measuring instruments, complex working conditions in site, and operational difficulties, it is hard to obtain the system states for constructing a cooperative control protocol. Aiming at this problem, observer is considered as an important auxiliary tool to estimate the immeasurable states and then to design an observer-based cooperative control protocol for the MASs. Specifically, Liu (2020a) utilized an observer to estimate an augmented state including an original state and an integral variable and then gave a PI predictive control to realize the cooperative control. Lu et al. (2023b) developed a novel observer to approximate the unknown states by applying the outputs and the state estimations of other agents, so that an adaptive neural inverse optimal controller was established to ensure the cooperative control performance. Cao et al. (2023a) adopted the neural networks to obtain a low-gain observer for estimating the immeasurable states and proposed a dynamic surface control with an event-triggering scheme and the state estimations to achieve the consensus of MASs. Jin et al. (2022b) designed a non-fragile observer to obtain the state estimations that were exploited to construct a novel integral sliding-mode controller for achieving the consensus of T-S fuzzy MASs with the uncertainties and disturbances. Wu and Tong (2023) proposed a fuzzy observer to reconstruct the immeasurable states and used these estimations to develop an adaptive control with prescribed performance for the implementation of formation control. Meanwhile, Wang et al. (2023d), Ding et al. (2023), Zhou and Tong (2023), and the references therein also made contributions to the development on the observer-based cooperative control for MASs.

Due to the uncertainty and complexity of practical network scenarios, there are always the time-varying communication constraints to destroy the stability, security, real time, and other indices and degrade the control qualities and effects. To deal

D.-W. Zhang, G.-P. Liu, *Predictive Cooperative Control for High-Order Fully Actuated Multiagent Systems*, https://doi.org/10.1007/978-981-95-1695-7_5

with this problem, a lot of scholars pay close attention to the cooperative control for the MASs with time-varying communication constraints. For example, Cao et al. (2023a) designed a dynamical switching event-triggering scheme to reduce the negative effects of time-varying input delays and then proposed a dynamic surface controller based on neural networks to ensure the cooperative control performance. Wei et al. (2024) constructed a Lyapunov-Krasovskii functional to address the time-varying delays and provided a prescribed-performance controller to realize the consensus control. Yan et al. (2024) used a Lyapunov-Krasovskii functional and a free-weighting matrix method to design a sliding-mode control for the realization of finite-time consensus under time-varying delays. Liu et al. (2022d) adopted the generalized Halanay inequality and algebraic graph theory to obtain the upper bound of time-varying delays and then presented a state feedback based on this bound to implement the leader-follower formation control. Yang et al. (2023) gave a delay-product-type quadratic to guarantee the consensus of MASs with time-varying communication constraints by utilizing a sampled-data control, where the proposed control was established by using an enhanced memory-based PD-like scheme. Li et al. (2022b) also utilized a Lyapunov-Krasovskii functional to construct an adaptive resilient controller for the containment control of MASs in a non-lower triangular structure under unknown time-varying delays. Fan et al. (2022) proposed a novel distributed switching observer to deal with time-varying communication delays and then established an adaptive cooperative fault-tolerant control to realize the output regulation of heterogeneous MASs. Su et al. (2021a) designed two cooperative control protocols based on adaptive observer to solve the unknown time-varying delays and packet dropouts in the data exchange during the output regulation of MASs.

Based on the idea in Chap. 4, predictive control can actively compensate for the time-varying communication constraints, such that a better cooperative control performance can be obtained and the conservatism and dependence of simultaneous consensus and stability on the time-varying communication constraints. Meanwhile, by introducing the HOFAS theory into the cooperative control design, the complexity and computational load in the design process can be obviously reduced, and the cooperative control performance can be effectively raised. Aiming at the cooperative control for the HOFAMASs with time-varying communication constraints and immeasurable states, an OB-HOFAS predictive control is proposed in this chapter, where the highlight is that a HOFAS observer is constructed to estimate the immeasurable states of HOFASMASs and an observer-based IHOFAS prediction model is developed. The main works are summarized as follows. Firstly, a discrete-time model of the i-th HOFA agent is used to offer a better model foundation for the cooperative control design. Then, a HOFAS observer is designed with the help of time operator to obtain the estimations of immeasurable states. Further, an observer-based IHOFAS prediction model is established by adopting a kind of Diophantine Equation, so that the estimation-based multistep ahead predictions are generated for the active compensation of time-varying communication constraints and the optimization of cooperative control performance. A sufficient condition is derived for the simultaneous consensus and stability of the closed-loop HOFAMASs under time-varying communication constraints and immeasurable states. Finally, a flying-around experiment of three ABSSs is carried out to illustrate the feasibility and practicability.

5.2 Problem Statement

In this chapter, the communication topology is described by Definition 3.1, and the dynamic model of the i-th HOFA agent satisfying Assumptions 3.1 and 3.2 is given in (3.1). Because of the complex working conditions in site, the system states are immeasurable, and then Assumption 3.2 can be replaced by the following one.

Assumption 5.1 *A1. $x_i(t)$ is immeasurable but observable during the control design. A2.* $\det(B_i) \neq 0$.

Meanwhile, the communication constraints, containing the communication delays and packet dropouts, are time varying in the forward and feedback channels due to the uncertainty and complexity of practical network scenarios. Let $\tau_{i,a}(t)$ and $\tau_{i,s}(t)$ be the time-varying communication delays in the i-th forward and feedback channels, respectively, and $\rho_{i,a}(t)$ and $\rho_{i,s}(t)$ be the time-varying packet dropouts in the i-th forward and feedback channels, respectively. Based on Pang et al. (2021a), time-varying packet dropouts can be equivalently considered as time-varying communication delays, such that $\varsigma_{i,a}(t) = \tau_{i,a}(t) + \rho_{i,a}(t)$ and $\varsigma_{i,s}(t) = \tau_{i,s}(t) + \rho_{i,s}(t)$ can be used to represent the total time-varying communication constraints in the i-the forward and feedback channels, and denote $\varsigma_{ii}(t) = \varsigma_i(t) = \varsigma_{i,a}(t) + \varsigma_{i,s}(t)$, $\varsigma_{ij}(t) = \varsigma_{i,a}(t) + \varsigma_{j,s}(t)$.

Assumption 5.2 *A1. $\varsigma_i(t)$ and $\varsigma_{ij}(t)$ are the two known functions with positive integers and are also the positively integral multiples of the sampling period. A2. $\varsigma_i(t)$ and $\varsigma_{ij}(t)$ are with the upper bounds.*

Remark 5.1 The reason of Assumption 5.2–A1 has been provided in Remark 4.1, and Assumption 5.2–A2 is to guarantee the boundedness of time-varying communication constraints; otherwise the system is not controllable.

To implement the cooperative control of the i-th HOFA agent (3.1) with time-varying communication constraints and immeasurable states, an OB-HOFAS predictive control is designed as

$$u_i(t) = B_i^{-1}\left(L_i(A_{i,0\sim n-1}, \hat{x}_i(t|t-1)) + \Upsilon_i(K_{i,0\sim n-1}, \hat{x}_i(t|t-1)) + v_i(t)\right), \tag{5.1}$$

where $L_i(A_{i,0\sim n-1}, \hat{x}_i(t|t-1)) = \sum_{\eta=0}^{n-1} A_{i,\eta}\hat{x}_i(t+\eta|t+\eta-1) \in \mathbb{R}^{n_i}$ is to eliminate the open-loop dynamics, $\Upsilon_i(K_{i,0\sim n-1}, \hat{x}_i(t|t-1)) = \sum_{\eta=0}^{n-1} K_{i,\eta}\hat{x}_i(t+\eta|t+\eta-1) \in \mathbb{R}^{n_i}$ is an observer-based feedback control for adjusting the closed-loop performance and $K_{i,\eta} \in \mathbb{R}^{n_i \times n_i}$ denote the feedback gains to be determined, $\hat{x}_i(t+\eta|t+\eta-1) \in \mathbb{R}^{n_i}$ is the η-th ahead estimation of $x_i(t)$ generated by a

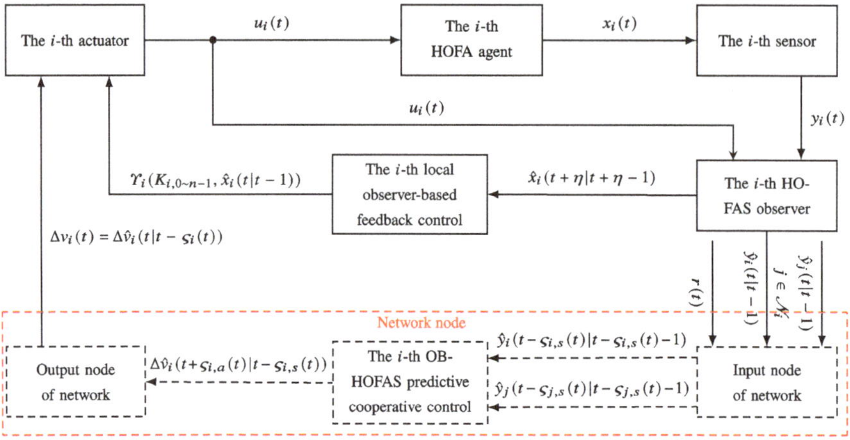

Fig. 5.1 Observer-based predictive cooperative control for the HOFAMASs with time-varying communication constraints and immeasurable states

HOFAS observer, and $v_i(t) \in \mathbb{R}^{n_i}$ indicates a cooperative control item designed by the OB-HOFAS predictive control. The associated control structure is shown in Fig. 5.1.

By substituting (5.1) into (3.1), the closed-loop HOFAMASs can be achieved as

$$\begin{aligned} x_i(t+n) &= -L_i(\cdot) + L_i(A_{i,0\sim n-1}, \hat{x}_i(t|t-1)) + \Upsilon_i(K_{i,0\sim n-1}, \hat{x}_i(t|t-1)) + v_i(t) \\ &= \sum_{\eta=0}^{n-1} K_{i,\eta} x_i(t+\eta) - L_i(A_{i,c,0\sim n-1}, e_{i,x}(t)) + v_i(t) \\ &= \Upsilon_i(K_{i,0\sim n-1}, x_i(t)) - L_i(A_{i,c,0\sim n-1}, e_{i,x}(t)) + v_i(t), \ i \in \mathcal{N}, \end{aligned} \tag{5.2}$$

where $L_i(A_{i,c,0\sim n-1}, e_{i,x}(t)) = \sum_{\eta=0}^{n-1} A_{i,c,\eta} e_{i,x}(t+\eta)$, $A_{i,c,\eta} = A_{i,\eta} + K_{i,\eta}$, and $e_{i,x}(t+\eta) = x_i(t+\eta) - \hat{x}_i(t+\eta|t+\eta-1)$, $\eta = 0, 1, \ldots, n-1$, represent the observation errors. To obtain the cooperative control item $v_i(t)$, an objective function $\mathcal{J}(t)$ is presented as

$$\mathcal{J}(t) = \sum_{i \in \mathcal{N}} \mathcal{J}_i(t), \tag{5.3}$$

where $\mathcal{J}_i(t)$ is a sub-objective function associated with the cooperative control performance of the i-th HOFA agent and is designed as

$$\begin{aligned}\mathcal{J}_i(t) = &\sum_{j\in\mathcal{N}_i} w_{ij} \left\| \hat{Y}_i(t+\varsigma_{i,a}(t)+\aleph_y|t-\varsigma_{i,s}(t)) - \hat{Y}_j(t+\varsigma_{i,a}(t)+\aleph_y|t-\varsigma_{j,s}(t)) \right\|^2 \\ &+ \alpha_i \left\| \hat{Y}_i(t+\varsigma_{i,a}(t)+\aleph_y|t-\varsigma_{i,s}(t)) - R(t+\varsigma_{i,a}(t)+\aleph_y) \right\|^2 \\ &+ \beta_i \left\| \Delta\hat{V}_i(t+\varsigma_{i,a}(t)+\aleph_u|t-\varsigma_{i,s}(t)) \right\|^2,\end{aligned} \tag{5.4}$$

with

$$\hat{Y}_i(t+\varsigma_{i,a}(t)+\aleph_y|t-\varsigma_{i,s}(t)) = \begin{bmatrix} \hat{y}_i(t+\varsigma_{i,a}(t)+\aleph_y|t-\varsigma_{i,s}(t)) \\ \vdots \\ \hat{y}_i(t+\varsigma_{i,a}(t)+1|t-\varsigma_{i,s}(t)) \end{bmatrix},$$

$$\hat{Y}_j(t+\varsigma_{i,a}(t)+\aleph_y|t-\varsigma_{j,s}(t)) = \begin{bmatrix} \hat{y}_j(t+\varsigma_{i,a}(t)+\aleph_y|t-\varsigma_{j,s}(t)) \\ \vdots \\ \hat{y}_j(t+\varsigma_{i,a}(t)+1|t-\varsigma_{j,s}(t)) \end{bmatrix},$$

$$\Delta\hat{V}_i(t+\varsigma_{i,a}(t)+\aleph_u|t-\varsigma_{i,s}(t)) = \begin{bmatrix} \Delta\hat{v}_i(t+\varsigma_{i,a}(t)+\aleph_u|t-\varsigma_{i,s}(t)) \\ \vdots \\ \Delta\hat{v}_i(t+\varsigma_{i,a}(t)|t-\varsigma_{i,s}(t)) \end{bmatrix},$$

$$R(t+\varsigma_{i,a}(t)+\aleph_y) = \begin{bmatrix} r(t+\varsigma_{i,a}(t)+\aleph_y) \\ \vdots \\ r(t+\varsigma_{i,a}(t)+1) \end{bmatrix},$$

where $\hat{y}_i(t+\eta|t-\varsigma_{i,s}(t))$, $\eta = \varsigma_{i,a}(t)+1, \varsigma_{i,a}(t)+2, \ldots, \varsigma_{i,a}(t)+\aleph_y$, and $\Delta\hat{v}_i(t+\eta|t-\varsigma_{i,s}(t))$, $\eta = \varsigma_{i,a}(t), \varsigma_{i,a}(t)+1, \ldots, \varsigma_{i,a}(t)+\aleph_u$, are the η-th ahead predictions of output $y_i(t)$ and cooperative control increment $\Delta v_i(t)$ based on $t - \varsigma_{i,s}(t)$ time. $r(t)$ is a known reference signal, and $R(t+\varsigma_{i,a}(t)+\aleph_y)$ is the related multistep ahead sequence. w_{ij} is the (i, j)-th element of adjacent matrix $\mathcal{W}$, and $\alpha_i > 0$, $\beta_i > 0$ are the two weighting factors. The aim of each item in (5.4) has been provided in Remark 3.3.

Problem 5.1 For the i-th HOFA agent (3.1) satisfying Assumptions 3.1, 5.1, and 5.2, an OB-HOFAS predictive control $u_i\big(t, v_i(t, y_i(t), y_j(t), r(t))\big)$ is proposed in (5.1) by minimizing the $\mathcal{J}(t)$ in (5.3) and (5.4), such that the closed-loop HOFAMASs (5.2) can implement the simultaneous consensus and stability, i.e., the following conditions hold:

1. $\forall i \in \mathcal{N}, \forall t \geq 0, \lim\limits_{t\to\infty} \|y_i(t)\| < \infty$ with $\|r(t)\| < \infty$.
2. $\forall i \in \mathcal{N}, \forall j \in \mathcal{N}_i, \lim_{t\to\infty} \|y_i(t) - y_j(t)\| = 0$.

5.3 Observer-Based HOFAS Predictive Cooperative Control Scheme

5.3.1 Design of HOFAS Observer

With the help of time operator q, the i-th HOFA agent (3.1) can be equivalent to the following polynomial system:

$$\begin{aligned} x_i(t+1) =& -\mathcal{A}_{i,o}(q^{-1})x_i(t) + \mathcal{B}_{i,o}(q^{-1})u_i(t), \\ y_i(t) =& C_i x_i(t), \quad i \in \mathcal{N}, \end{aligned} \tag{5.5}$$

with $\mathcal{A}_{i,o}(q^{-1}) = \sum_{\eta=0}^{n-1} A_{i,\eta} q^{\eta+1-n}$ and $\mathcal{B}_{i,o}(q^{-1}) = B_i q^{1-n}$. To estimate the immeasurable states of (3.1) with the guarantee of full actuation characteristic, a HOFAS observer based on an equivalent system (5.5) is designed as

$$\begin{aligned} \hat{x}_i(t+1|t) =& -\mathcal{A}_{i,o}(q^{-1})\hat{x}_i(t|t-1) + \mathcal{B}_{i,o}(q^{-1})u_i(t) \\ &+ \mathcal{K}_{i,o}(q^{-1})\left(y_i(t) - \hat{y}_i(t|t-1)\right), \\ \hat{y}_i(t|t-1) =& C_i \hat{x}_i(t|t-1), \quad i \in \mathcal{N}, \end{aligned} \tag{5.6}$$

where $\mathcal{K}_{i,o}(q^{-1}) = \sum_{\eta=0}^{n-1} K_{i,o,\eta} q^{\eta+1-n}$ and $K_{i,o,\eta} \in \mathbb{R}^{n_i \times m}$, $\eta = 0, 1, \ldots, n-1$, denote the observer gains to be determined. Then, Theorem 5.1 is proposed for the existence of (5.6) and for the solutions to the observer gains $K_{i,o,\eta}$, $\eta = 0, 1, \ldots, n-1$.

Theorem 5.1 *The existence of HOFAS observer* (5.6) *and* $e_{i,x}(t) \to 0$ *with* $t \to \infty$ *can be guaranteed if there exists a group of observer gains* $K_{i,o,\eta}$, $\eta = 0, 1, \ldots, n-1$, *to ensure that* $\mathcal{A}_{i,oc}(q^{-1}) = \mathcal{A}_{i,o}(q^{-1}) + \mathcal{K}_{i,o}(q^{-1})C_i$ *is a Schur stable polynomial matrix in relation to* q, *where the observer gains* $K_{i,o,\eta}$, $\eta = 0, 1, \ldots, n-1$, *are solved as*

$$\left[K_{i,o,0}^{\mathrm{T}} \cdots K_{i,o,n-1}^{\mathrm{T}}\right] = \left(C_i C_i^{\mathrm{T}}\right)^{-1} C_i \left(\mathcal{Z}_i \Lambda_i^n + \sum_{\eta=0}^{n-1} A_{i,\eta}^{\mathrm{T}} \mathcal{Z}_i \Lambda^\eta\right) \begin{bmatrix} \mathcal{Z}_i \\ \mathcal{Z}_i \Lambda_i \\ \vdots \\ \mathcal{Z}_i \Lambda_i^{n-1} \end{bmatrix}^{-1}, \tag{5.7}$$

$\mathcal{Z}_i$ *is an arbitrary matrix, and* Λ_i *is a Schur matrix.*

Proof From (5.2), the observation error of the i-th HOFAS observer (5.6) is defined as $e_{i,x}(t) = x_i(t) - \hat{x}_i(t|t-1)$, and then $e_{i,x}(t+1) = x_i(t+1) - \hat{x}_i(t+1|t)$, which can be further expressed as

$$e_{i,x}(t+1) = x_i(t+1) - \hat{x}_i(t+1|t)$$

$$
\begin{aligned}
&= - \mathcal{A}_{i,o}(q^{-1})x_i(t) + \mathcal{B}_{i,o}(q^{-1})u_i(t) + \mathcal{A}_{i,o}(q^{-1})\hat{x}_i(t|t-1) \\
&\quad - \mathcal{B}_{i,o}(q^{-1})u_i(t) - \mathcal{K}_{i,o}(q^{-1})\left(y_i(t) - \hat{y}_i(t|t-1)\right) \\
&= - \left(\mathcal{A}_{i,o}(q^{-1}) + \mathcal{K}_{i,o}(q^{-1})C_i\right) e_{i,x}(t) \\
&= - \mathcal{A}_{i,oc}(q^{-1})e_{i,x}(t).
\end{aligned}
$$

Because there is a group of observer gains $K_{i,o,\eta}$, $\eta = 0, 1, \ldots, n-1$, to ensure that $\mathcal{A}_{i,oc}(q^{-1})$ is a Schur stable polynomial matrix, the error system $e_{i,x}(t+1) = -\mathcal{A}_{i,oc}(q^{-1})e_{i,x}(t)$ is stable, i.e., $e_{i,x}(t) \to 0$ with $t \to \infty$. Hence, the i-th HOFAS observer (5.6) is held.

Meanwhile, $\mathcal{A}_{i,oc}(q^{-1}) = \mathcal{A}_{i,o}(q^{-1}) + \mathcal{K}_{i,o}(q^{-1})C_i$ can be expanded as

$$
\begin{aligned}
\mathcal{A}_{i,oc}(q^{-1}) =& \sum_{\eta=0}^{n-1} \left(A_{i,\eta} + K_{i,o,\eta}C_i\right) q^{\eta+1-n} \\
=& A_{i,n-1} + K_{i,o,n-1}C_i + \cdots + (A_{i,1} + K_{i,o,1}C_i)q^{-(n-2)} \\
& + (A_{i,0} + K_{i,o,0}C_i)q^{-(n-1)},
\end{aligned}
$$

so that the error system $e_{i,x}(t+1) = -\mathcal{A}_{i,oc}(q^{-1})e_{i,x}(t)$ can be correspondingly represented as

$$
\begin{aligned}
e_{i,x}(t+1) =& - (A_{i,n-1} + K_{i,o,n-1}C_i)e_{i,x}(t) \\
& - \cdots - (A_{i,1} + K_{i,o,1}C_i)e_{i,x}(t-n+2) \\
& - (A_{i,0} + K_{i,o,0}C_i)e_{i,x}(t-n+1).
\end{aligned}
$$

Thus, the following facts are equivalent:

1. Solve the observer gains $K_{i,o,\eta}$, $\eta = 0, 1, \ldots, n-1$, to ensure that $\mathcal{A}_{i,oc}(q^{-1})$ is a Schur polynomial matrix.
2. Solve the observer gains $K_{i,o,\eta}$, $\eta = 0, 1, \ldots, n-1$, to construct a Schur matrix $\Phi(A_{i,oc,0\sim n-1})$, where

$$
\Phi(A_{i,oc,0\sim n-1}) = \begin{bmatrix} 0 & I & & \\ \vdots & & \ddots & \\ 0 & & & I \\ -A_{i,0} - K_{i,o,0}C_i & -A_{i,1} - K_{i,o,1}C_i & \cdots & -A_{i,n-1} - K_{i,o,n-1}C_i \end{bmatrix}.
$$

Based on Remark 3.4, the solutions of $K_{i,o,\eta}$, $\eta = 0, 1, \ldots, n-1$, are given in (5.7).

This completes the proof. □

5.3.2 Design of OB-HOFAS Predictive Cooperative Control

For the simple representation, the closed-loop system (5.2) can be expressed as

$$\begin{aligned} x_i(t+n) &= -L_i(\cdot) + L_i(A_{i,0\sim 1}, \hat{x}_i(t|t-1)) + \Upsilon_i(K_{i,0\sim n-1}, \hat{x}_i(t|t-1)) + v_i(t) \\ &= -\sum_{\eta=0}^{n-1} A_{i,\eta} x_i(t+\eta) + u_{i,o}(t) + v_i(t), \end{aligned}$$

where $u_{i,o}(t) = L_i(A_{i,0\sim n-1}, \hat{x}_i(t|t-1)) + \Upsilon_i(K_{i,0\sim n-1}, \hat{x}_i(t|t-1)) = L_i(A_{i,c,0\sim n-1}, \hat{x}_i(t|t-1))$. With the help of time operator q, the above system can be equivalently converted into the following polynomial one:

$$\mathcal{A}_i(q^{-1})x_i(t) = \mathcal{B}_i(q^{-1})v_i(t-1) + \mathcal{B}_i(q^{-1})u_{i,o}(t-1), \tag{5.8}$$

with $\mathcal{A}_i(q^{-1}) = I + \sum_{\eta=0}^{n-1} A_{i,\eta} q^{-n+\eta}$ and $\mathcal{B}_i(q^{-1}) = q^{-n+1}$. Based on Diophantine Equation (3.7) with the same process from (3.6) to (3.8), an IHOFAS prediction model is established as

$$x_i(t+\eta) = \mathcal{F}_{i,\eta} x_i(t) + \mathcal{G}_{i,\eta} \Delta v_i(t+\eta-1) + \mathcal{L}_{i,\eta} \Delta u_{i,o}(t), \tag{5.9}$$

where $\mathcal{L}_{i,\eta}(q^{-1}) = q^{\eta-1}\mathcal{E}_{i,\eta}(q^{-1})\mathcal{B}_i(q^{-1}) = \ell_{i,\eta,0} + \ell_{i,\eta,1}q^{-1} + \cdots + \ell_{i,\eta,n-1}q^{-(n-1)}$, and $\mathcal{F}_{i,\eta}$, $\mathcal{G}_{i,\eta}$ are constructed in (3.8). Combining with time-varying communication constraints and immeasurable states, the IHOFAS prediction model (5.9) can be corrected as

$$\begin{aligned} \hat{x}_i(t-\varsigma_{i,s}(t)+\eta|t-\varsigma_{i,s}(t)) =& \mathcal{F}_{i,\eta}\hat{x}_i(t-\varsigma_{i,s}(t)|t-\varsigma_{i,s}(t)-1) \\ &+ \mathcal{G}_{i,\eta}\Delta\hat{v}_i(t-\varsigma_{i,s}(t)+\eta-1|t-\varsigma_{i,s}(t)) \\ &+ \mathcal{L}_{i,\eta}\Delta u_{i,o}(t-\varsigma_{i,s}(t)), \end{aligned} \tag{5.10}$$

where $\eta = 1, 2, \ldots, \varsigma_i(t) + \aleph_y$, and $\hat{x}_i(t-\varsigma_{i,s}(t)|t-\varsigma_{i,s}(t)-1)$ is an estimation generated by HOFAS observer (5.6).

In the observer-based IHOFAS prediction model (5.10), the first step is to obtain the $\hat{x}_i(t-\varsigma_{i,s}(t)|t-\varsigma_{i,s}(t)-1)$ for yielding the multistep ahead predictions. By using $u_i(t-\varsigma_{i,s}(t)-1)$ and $y_i(t-\varsigma_{i,s}(t)-1)$, $\hat{x}_i(t-\varsigma_{i,s}(t)|t-\varsigma_{i,s}(t)-1)$ based on HOFAS observer, (5.6) can be estimated as

$$\begin{aligned} &\hat{x}_i(t-\varsigma_{i,s}(t)|t-\varsigma_{i,s}(t)-1) \\ &\quad= -\mathcal{A}_{i,o}(q^{-1})\hat{x}_i(t-\varsigma_{i,s}(t)-1|t-\varsigma_{i,s}(t)-2) + \mathcal{B}_{i,o}(q^{-1})u_i(t-\varsigma_{i,s}(t)-1) \\ &\qquad+ \mathcal{K}_{i,o}(q^{-1})\left(y_i(t-\varsigma_{i,s}(t)-1) - \hat{y}_i(t-\varsigma_{i,s}(t-1)|t-\varsigma_{i,s}(t)-2)\right), \\ &\hat{y}_i(t-\varsigma_{i,s}(t-1)|t-\varsigma_{i,s}(t)-2) = C_i\hat{x}_i(t-\varsigma_{i,s}(t-1)|t-\varsigma_{i,s}(t)-2). \end{aligned}$$

When $\eta = 1, 2, \ldots, \varsigma_i(t)$, the multistep ahead predictions of $x_i(t)$ by applying the observer-based IHOFAS prediction model (5.10) are given as

$$\begin{aligned}\hat{x}_i(t - \varsigma_{i,s}(t) + 1|t - \varsigma_{i,s}(t)) =& \mathcal{F}_{i,1}\hat{x}_i(t - \varsigma_{i,s}(t)|t - \varsigma_{i,s}(t) - 1)\\ &+ \mathcal{G}_{i,1}\Delta\hat{v}_i(t - \varsigma_{i,s}(t)|t - \varsigma_{i,s}(t)\\ &+ \mathcal{L}_{i,1}\Delta u_{i,o}(t - \varsigma_{i,s}(t)),\\ &\vdots\\ \hat{x}_i(t + \varsigma_{i,a}(t)|t - \varsigma_{i,s}(t)) =& \mathcal{F}_{i,\varsigma_i(t)}\hat{x}_i(t - \varsigma_{i,s}(t)|t - \varsigma_{i,s}(t) - 1)\\ &+ \mathcal{G}_{i,\varsigma_i(t)}\Delta\hat{v}_i(t+\varsigma_{i,a}(t) - 1|t-\varsigma_{i,s}(t))\\ &+ \mathcal{L}_{i,\varsigma_i(t)}\Delta u_{i,o}(t - \varsigma_{i,s}(t)),\end{aligned}$$

such that the relevant output predictions are given as

$$\hat{y}_i(t + \eta|t - \varsigma_{i,s}(t)) = C_i\hat{x}_i(t + \eta|t - \varsigma_{i,s}(t)),$$

with $\eta = -\varsigma_{i,s}(t) + 1, -\varsigma_{i,s}(t) + 2, \ldots, \varsigma_i(t)$. To avoid the negative impacts of packet dropouts, the following output sequence

$$\left[\, \hat{y}_i^{\mathrm{T}}(t + \varsigma_{i,a}(t)|t - \varsigma_{i,s}(t)) \cdots \hat{y}_i^{\mathrm{T}}(t - \varsigma_{i,s}(t) + 1|t - \varsigma_{i,s}(t)) \,\right]^{\mathrm{T}}$$

is put into a packet each time when transmitting the data over network.

When $\eta = \varsigma_i(t) + 1, \varsigma_i(t) + 2, \ldots, \varsigma_i(t) + \aleph_y$, the multistep ahead predictions of $x_i(t)$ are provided as

$$\begin{aligned}\hat{x}_i(t + \varsigma_{i,a}(t) + 1|t - \varsigma_{i,s}(t)) =& \mathcal{F}_{i,\varsigma_i(t)+1}\hat{x}_i(t - \varsigma_{i,s}(t)|t - \varsigma_{i,s}(t) - 1)\\ &+ \mathcal{G}_{i,\varsigma_i(t)+1}\Delta\hat{v}_i(t + \varsigma_{i,a}(t)|t - \varsigma_{i,s}(t))\\ &+ \mathcal{L}_{i,\varsigma_i(t)+1}\Delta u_{i,o}(t - \varsigma_{i,s}(t)),\\ &\vdots\\ \hat{x}_i(t + \varsigma_{i,a}(t) + \aleph_y|t - \varsigma_{i,s}(t)) =& \mathcal{F}_{i,\varsigma_i(t)+\aleph_y}\hat{x}_i(t - \varsigma_{i,s}(t)|t - \varsigma_{i,s}(t) - 1)\\ &+ \mathcal{G}_{i,\varsigma_i(t)+\aleph_y}\Delta\hat{v}_i(t+\varsigma_{i,a}(t)+\aleph_y - 1|t-\varsigma_{i,s}(t))\\ &+ \mathcal{L}_{i,\varsigma_i(t)+\aleph_y}\Delta u_{i,o}(t - \varsigma_{i,s}(t));\end{aligned}$$

then the relevant output predictions are shown as

$$\hat{y}_i(t + \varsigma_{i,a}(t) + \eta|t - \varsigma_{i,s}(t)) = C_i\hat{x}_i(t + \varsigma_{i,a}(t) + \eta|t - \varsigma_{i,s}(t)), \tag{5.11}$$

with $\eta = 1, 2, \ldots, \aleph_y$. When $\eta = \aleph_u + 1, \aleph_u + 2, \ldots, \aleph_y$, $\hat{v}_i(t + \varsigma_{i,a}(t) + \eta|t - \varsigma_{i,s}(t)) = \hat{v}_i(t+\varsigma_{i,a}(t)+\aleph_u|t-\varsigma_{i,s}(t))$, such that $\Delta\hat{v}_i(t+\varsigma_{i,a}(t)+\eta|t-\varsigma_{i,s}(t)) = 0$. Hence, the output predictions (5.11) can be compactly written as

$$\begin{aligned}
&\hat{Y}_i(t + \varsigma_{i,a}(t) + \aleph_y|t - \varsigma_{i,s}(t)) \\
&\quad = P_{i,1}\hat{x}_i(t - \varsigma_{i,s}(t)|t - \varsigma_{i,s}(t) - 1) + P_{i,2}\Delta u_{i,o}(t - \varsigma_{i,s}(t)) \\
&\qquad + P_{i,3}\Delta\hat{V}_i(t + \varsigma_{i,a}(t) + \aleph_u|t - \varsigma_{i,s}(t)),
\end{aligned} \tag{5.12}$$

with

$$P_{i,1} = \begin{bmatrix} C_i\mathcal{F}_{i,\varsigma_i(t)+\aleph_y} \\ \vdots \\ C_i\mathcal{F}_{i,\varsigma_i(t)+1} \end{bmatrix}, \quad P_{i,2} = \begin{bmatrix} C_i\mathcal{L}_{i,\varsigma_i(t)+\aleph_y} \\ \vdots \\ C_i\mathcal{L}_{i,\varsigma_i(t)+1} \end{bmatrix},$$

$$P_{i,3} = \begin{bmatrix} C_i\mathcal{G}_{i,\varsigma_i(t)+\aleph_y} & 0 & \cdots & 0 \\ \vdots & \vdots & \cdots & \vdots \\ C_i\mathcal{G}_{i,\varsigma_i(t)+\aleph_u+1} & 0 & \cdots & 0 \\ 0 & C_i\mathcal{G}_{i,\varsigma_i(t)+\aleph_u} & \ddots & \vdots \\ \vdots & \ddots & \ddots & 0 \\ 0 & \cdots & 0 & C_i\mathcal{G}_{i,\varsigma_i(t)+1} \end{bmatrix}.$$

Based on (2.9), the incremental constraint of cooperative control increment is defined as

$$\Delta\hat{v}_i(t + \varsigma_{i,a}(t) + \eta|t - \varsigma_{i,s}(t)) = \gamma_{i,\eta}\Delta\hat{v}_i(t + \varsigma_{i,a}(t)|t - \varsigma_{i,s}(t)),$$

where $\gamma_{i,\eta} > 0$, $\eta = 1, 2, \ldots, \aleph_u$, is a weighting factor, such that $P_{i,3}$ can be degenerated as $P_{i,4} = P_{i,3}\Gamma_i$ with $\Gamma_i = \text{Blockdiag}\{\gamma_{i,\aleph_u}I, \ldots, \gamma_{i,1}I, I\}$, and $P_{i,3}\Delta\hat{V}_i(t + \varsigma_{i,a}(t) + \aleph_u|t - \varsigma_{i,s}(t)) = P_{i,4}\Delta\hat{V}_i(t + \varsigma_{i,a}(t)|t - \varsigma_{i,s}(t))$ with

$$\begin{aligned}
&\Delta\hat{V}_i(t + \varsigma_{i,a}(t)|t - \varsigma_{i,s}(t)) \\
&\quad = \left[\, \Delta\hat{v}_i^{\mathrm{T}}(t + \varsigma_{i,a}(t)|t - \varsigma_{i,s}(t)) \cdots \Delta\hat{v}_i^{\mathrm{T}}(t + \varsigma_{i,a}(t)|t - \varsigma_{i,s}(t)) \,\right]^{\mathrm{T}}.
\end{aligned}$$

Summarizing the above means that (5.12) can be rewritten as

$$\begin{aligned}
&\hat{Y}_i(t + \varsigma_{i,a}(t) + \aleph_y|t - \varsigma_{i,s}(t)) \\
&\quad = P_{i,1}\hat{x}_i(t - \varsigma_{i,s}(t)|t - \varsigma_{i,s}(t) - 1) + P_{i,2}\Delta u_{i,o}(t - \varsigma_{i,s}(t)) \\
&\qquad + P_{i,4}\Delta\hat{V}_i(t + \varsigma_{i,a}(t)|t - \varsigma_{i,s}(t)).
\end{aligned} \tag{5.13}$$

$\forall j \in \mathcal{N}_i$, based on the observer-based IHOFAS prediction model (5.10), $x_j(t)$ can be predicted as

$$\begin{aligned}\hat{x}_j(t-\varsigma_{j,s}(t)+\eta|t-\varsigma_{j,s}(t)) =&\mathcal{F}_{j,\eta}\hat{x}_j(t-\varsigma_{j,s}(t)|t-\varsigma_{j,s}(t)-1)\\&+\mathcal{G}_{j,\eta}\Delta\hat{v}_j(t-\varsigma_{j,s}(t)+\eta-1|t-\varsigma_{j,s}(t))\\&+\mathcal{L}_{j,\eta}\Delta u_{j,o}(t-\varsigma_{j,s}(t)),\end{aligned}$$

where $\eta = 1, 2, \ldots, \varsigma_{ij}(t)+\aleph_y$, and $\hat{x}_j(t-\varsigma_{j,s}(t)|t-\varsigma_{j,s}(t)-1)$ is also obtained on the basis of (5.6), i.e.,

$$\begin{aligned}&\hat{x}_j(t-\varsigma_{j,s}(t)|t-\varsigma_{j,s}(t)-1)\\&\quad=-\mathcal{A}_{j,o}(q^{-1})\hat{x}_j(t-\varsigma_{j,s}(t)-1|t-\varsigma_{j,s}(t)-2)+\mathcal{B}_{j,o}(q^{-1})u_j(t-\varsigma_{j,s}(t)-1)\\&\qquad+\mathcal{K}_{j,o}(q^{-1})\left(y_j(t-\varsigma_{j,s}(t)-1)-\hat{y}_j(t-\varsigma_{j,s}(t-1)|t-\varsigma_{j,s}(t)-2)\right),\\&\hat{y}_j(t-\varsigma_{j,s}(t-1)|t-\varsigma_{j,s}(t)-2)=C_j\hat{x}_j(t-\varsigma_{j,s}(t-1)|t-\varsigma_{j,s}(t)-2).\end{aligned}$$

When $\eta = \varsigma_{ij}(t)+1, \varsigma_{ij}(t)+2, \ldots, \varsigma_{ij}(t)+\aleph_y$, the multistep ahead predictions of $x_j(t)$ are derived as

$$\begin{aligned}\hat{x}_j(t+\varsigma_{i,a}(t)+1|t-\varsigma_{j,s}(t)) =&\mathcal{F}_{j,\varsigma_{ij}(t)+1}\hat{x}_j(t-\varsigma_{j,s}(t)|t-\varsigma_{j,s}(t)-1)\\&+\mathcal{G}_{j,\varsigma_{ij}(t)+1}\Delta\hat{v}_j(t+\varsigma_{i,a}(t)|t-\varsigma_{j,s}(t))\\&+\mathcal{L}_{j,\varsigma_{ij}(t)+1}\Delta u_{j,o}(t-\varsigma_{j,s}(t)),\\&\vdots\\\hat{x}_j(t+\varsigma_{i,a}(t)+\aleph_y|t-\varsigma_{j,s}(t)) =&\mathcal{F}_{j,\varsigma_{ij}(t)+\aleph_y}\hat{x}_j(t-\varsigma_{j,s}(t)|t-\varsigma_{j,s}(t)-1)\\&+\mathcal{G}_{j,\varsigma_{ij}(t)+\aleph_y}\Delta\hat{v}_l(t+\varsigma_{i,a}(t)+\aleph_y-1|t-\varsigma_{j,s}(t))\\&+\mathcal{L}_{j,\varsigma_{ij}(t)+\aleph_y}\Delta u_{j,o}(t-\varsigma_{j,s}(t)).\end{aligned}$$

Repeating the process from (5.11)–(5.13), the output prediction of the j-th HOFA agent is generated as

$$\begin{aligned}&\hat{Y}_j(t+\varsigma_{i,a}(t)+\aleph_y|t-\varsigma_{j,s}(t))\\&\quad=P_{j,1}\hat{x}_j(t-\varsigma_{j,s}(t)|t-\varsigma_{j,s}(t)-1)+P_{j,2}\Delta u_{j,o}(t-\varsigma_{j,s}(t))\\&\qquad+P_{j,4}\Delta\hat{V}_j(t+\varsigma_{i,a}(t)|t-\varsigma_{j,s}(t)),\end{aligned}\tag{5.14}$$

with $\Delta\hat{V}_j(t+\varsigma_{i,a}(t)|t-\varsigma_{j,s}(t)) = \begin{bmatrix}\Delta\hat{v}_j(t+\varsigma_{i,a}(t)|t-\varsigma_{j,s}(t))\\\vdots\\\Delta\hat{v}_j(t+\varsigma_{i,a}(t)|t-\varsigma_{j,s}(t))\end{bmatrix}$, and

$$P_{j,1} = \begin{bmatrix} C_j \mathcal{F}_{j,\varsigma_{ij}(t)+\aleph_y} \\ \vdots \\ C_j \mathcal{F}_{j,\varsigma_{ij}(t)+1} \end{bmatrix}, \quad P_{j,2} = \begin{bmatrix} C_j \mathcal{L}_{j,\varsigma_{ij}(t)+\aleph_y} \\ \vdots \\ C_i \mathcal{L}_{j,\varsigma_{ij}(t)+1} \end{bmatrix},$$

$$P_{j,3} = \begin{bmatrix} C_j \mathcal{G}_{j,\varsigma_{ij}(t)+\aleph_y} & 0 & \cdots & 0 \\ \vdots & \vdots & \cdots & \vdots \\ C_j \mathcal{G}_{j,\varsigma_{ij}(t)+\aleph_u+1} & 0 & \cdots & 0 \\ 0 & C_j \mathcal{G}_{j,\varsigma_{ij}(t)+\aleph_u} & \ddots & \vdots \\ \vdots & \ddots & \ddots & 0 \\ 0 & \cdots & 0 & C_j \mathcal{G}_{j,\varsigma_{ij}(t)+1} \end{bmatrix},$$

$$P_{j,4} = P_{j,3}\Gamma_j, \quad \Gamma_j = \text{Blockdiag}\{\gamma_{j,\aleph_u} I, \ldots, \gamma_{j,1} I, I\}.$$

To generate the optimal cooperative control increment $\Delta v_i(t)$, let

$$\frac{\partial}{\partial \Delta \hat{V}_i(t+\varsigma_{i,a}(t)|t-\varsigma_{i,s}(t))} \mathcal{J}(t) = 0, \ i \in \mathcal{N},$$

and by utilizing (5.13) and (5.14), it is obtained that

$$\begin{aligned} &\sum_{j\in\mathcal{N}_i} w_{ij} P_{i,4}^{\mathrm{T}} \big(P_{i,1}\hat{x}_i(t-\varsigma_{i,s}(t)|t-\varsigma_{i,s}(t)-1) + P_{i,2}\Delta u_{i,o}(t-\varsigma_{i,s}(t)) \\ &\quad + P_{i,4}\Delta\hat{V}_i(t+\varsigma_{i,a}(t)|t-\varsigma_{i,s}(t)) - P_{j,1}\hat{x}_j(t-\varsigma_{j,s}(t)|t-\varsigma_{j,s}(t)-1) \\ &\quad - P_{j,2}\Delta u_{j,o}(t-\varsigma_{j,s}(t)) - P_{j,4}\Delta\hat{V}_j(t+\varsigma_{i,a}(t)|t-\varsigma_{j,s}(t))\big) \\ &\quad + \alpha_i P_{i,4}^{\mathrm{T}} \big(P_{i,1}\hat{x}_i(t-\varsigma_{i,s}(t)|t-\varsigma_{i,s}(t)-1) + P_{i,2}\Delta u_{i,o}(t-\varsigma_{i,s}(t)) \\ &\quad + P_{i,4}\Delta\hat{V}_i(t+\varsigma_{i,a}(t)|t-\varsigma_{i,s}(t)) - R(t+\varsigma_{i,a}(t)+\aleph_y)\big) \\ &\quad + \beta_i \Gamma_i^{\mathrm{T}}\Gamma_i \hat{V}_i(t+\varsigma_{i,a}(t)|t-\varsigma_{i,s}(t)) = 0, \end{aligned}$$

which can be concluded as

$$\begin{aligned} \Delta\hat{V}(t+\varsigma_{i,a}(t)|t-\varsigma_s(t)) =& F^{-1}G\hat{x}(t-\varsigma_s(t)|t-\varsigma_s(t)-1) \\ &+ F^{-1}L\Delta u_o(t-\varsigma_s(t)) + F^{-1}MR(t+\varsigma_{i,a}(t)+\aleph_y), \end{aligned}$$

with $\Delta\hat{V}(t+\varsigma_{i,a}(t)|t-\varsigma_s(t)) = \begin{bmatrix} \Delta\hat{V}_1(t+\varsigma_{i,a}(t)|t-\varsigma_{1,s}(t)) \\ \vdots \\ \Delta\hat{V}_N(t+\varsigma_{i,a}(t)|t-\varsigma_{N,s}(t)) \end{bmatrix}$, $\hat{x}(t-\varsigma_s(t)|t-\varsigma_s(t)-1) = \begin{bmatrix} \hat{x}_1(t-\varsigma_{1,s}(t)|t-\varsigma_{1,s}(t)-1) \\ \vdots \\ \hat{x}_N(t-\varsigma_{N,s}(t)|t-\varsigma_{N,s}(t)-1) \end{bmatrix}$, $\Delta u_o(t-\varsigma_s(t)) = \begin{bmatrix} \Delta u_{1,o}(t-\varsigma_{1,s}(t)) \\ \vdots \\ \Delta u_{N,o}(t-\varsigma_{N,s}(t)) \end{bmatrix}$, and

$$
\begin{aligned}
F =&\{f_{ij}\},\ \ f_{ii} = (w_i+\alpha_i)P_{i,4}^{\mathrm{T}}P_{i,4} + \beta_i\Gamma_i^{\mathrm{T}}\Gamma_i,\ \ f_{ij} = -w_{ij}P_{i,4}^{\mathrm{T}}P_{j,4},\\
G =&\{g_{ij}\},\ \ g_{ii} = -(w_i+\alpha_i)P_{i,4}^{\mathrm{T}}P_{i,1},\ \ g_{ij} = w_{ij}P_{i,4}^{\mathrm{T}}P_{j,1},\\
L =&\{l_{ij}\},\ \ l_{ii} = -(w_i+\alpha_i)P_{i,4}^{\mathrm{T}}P_{i,2},\ \ l_{ij} = w_{ij}P_{i,4}^{\mathrm{T}}P_{j,4},\\
M =&\begin{bmatrix}\alpha_1 P_{1,4} & \cdots & \alpha_N P_{N,4}\end{bmatrix}^{\mathrm{T}},\ \ w_i = \sum_{j\in\mathcal{N}_i} w_{ij}.
\end{aligned}
$$

Then, the optimal cooperative control increment of the i-th HOFA agent in the network node is set as $\Delta\hat{v}_i(t+\varsigma_{i,a}(t)|t-\varsigma_s(t)) = H_i\Delta\hat{V}(t+\varsigma_{i,a}(t)|t-\varsigma_s(t))$, i.e.,

$$
\begin{aligned}
\Delta\hat{v}_i(t+\varsigma_{i,a}(t)|t-\varsigma_s(t)) =& H_iF^{-1}G\hat{x}(t-\varsigma_s(t)|t-\varsigma_s(t)-1)\\
&+ H_iF^{-1}L\Delta u_o(t-\varsigma_s(t)) + H_iF^{-1}MR(t+\varsigma_{i,a}(t)+\aleph_y),
\end{aligned}
$$

where $H_i = \begin{bmatrix} H_{i,1} & \cdots & H_{i,N}\end{bmatrix} \in \mathbb{R}^{n_i\times(\aleph_u+1)\tilde{n}}$ with $\tilde{n} = \sum_{i\in\mathcal{N}} n_i$, $H_{i,i} = \begin{bmatrix} 0 & \cdots & 0 & I\end{bmatrix}$, $H_{i,j} = 0$, $j\in\mathcal{N}_i$. On the i-th actuator, the optimal cooperative control increment is proposed as $\Delta v_i(t) = \Delta\hat{v}_i(t|t-\varsigma_i(t))$, i.e.,

$$
\begin{aligned}
\Delta v_i(t) =& H_iF^{-1}G\hat{x}(t-\varsigma(t)|t-\varsigma(t)-1)\\
&+ H_iF^{-1}L\Delta u_o(t-\varsigma(t)) + H_iF^{-1}MR(t+\aleph_y),
\end{aligned}
\tag{5.15}
$$

where $\hat{x}(t-\varsigma(t)|t-\varsigma(t)-1) = \begin{bmatrix} \hat{x}_1(t-\varsigma_{i1}(t)|t-\varsigma_{i1}(t)-1) \\ \vdots \\ \hat{x}_N(t-\varsigma_{iN}(t)|t-\varsigma_{iN}(t)-1) \end{bmatrix}$, $\Delta u_o(t-\varsigma(t)) = \begin{bmatrix} \Delta u_{1,o}(t-\varsigma_{i1}(t)) \\ \vdots \\ \Delta u_{N,o}(t-\varsigma_{iN}(t)) \end{bmatrix}$, $R(t+\aleph_y) = \begin{bmatrix} r(t+\aleph_y) \\ \vdots \\ r(t+1) \end{bmatrix}$. In (5.15), because of $u_{i,o}(t) = L_i(A_{i,c,0\sim n-1}, \hat{x}_i(t|t-1))$,

$$\Delta u_o(t-\varsigma(t)) = \begin{bmatrix} L_1(A_{1,c,0\sim n-1}, \Delta\hat{x}_1(t-\varsigma_{i1}(t)+\eta|t-\varsigma_{i1}(t)+\eta-1)) \\ \vdots \\ L_N(A_{N,c,0\sim n-1}, \Delta\hat{x}_N(t-\varsigma_{iN}(t)+\eta|t-\varsigma_{iN}(t)+\eta-1)) \end{bmatrix}$$
$$= \begin{bmatrix} \sum_{\eta=0}^{n-1} A_{1,c,\eta}\Delta\hat{x}_1(t-\varsigma_{i1}(t)+\eta|t-\varsigma_{i1}(t)+\eta-1) \\ \vdots \\ \sum_{\eta=0}^{n-1} A_{N,c,\eta}\Delta\hat{x}_N(t-\varsigma_{iN}(t)+\eta|t-\varsigma_{iN}(t)+\eta-1) \end{bmatrix}$$
$$=A_c(q)\Delta\hat{x}(t-\varsigma(t)|t-\varsigma(t)-1),$$
$$A_c(q) = \text{Blockdiag}\left\{\sum_{\eta=0}^{n-1} A_{1,c,\eta}q^{\eta}, \ldots, \sum_{\eta=0}^{n-1} A_{N,c,\eta}q^{\eta}\right\}.$$

Hence, $\Delta v_i(t)$ in (5.15) can be further represented as

$$\Delta v_i(t) = H_iF^{-1}G\hat{x}(t-\varsigma(t)|t-\varsigma(t)-1) + H_iF^{-1}LA_c(q)\Delta\hat{x}(t-\varsigma(t)|t-\varsigma(t)-1) + H_iF^{-1}MR(t+\aleph_y). \tag{5.16}$$

5.4 Analysis of Simultaneous Consensus and Stability Under Time-Varying Communication Constraints

Let $e_i(t) = y_i(t) - r(t) = C_ix_i(t) - r(t)$ be the tracking error of the i-th HOFA agent and $\epsilon_{ii}(t) = \epsilon_i(t) = e_i(t)$, $\epsilon_{ij}(t) = y_i(t) - y_j(t)$, $j \in \mathcal{N}_i$, be the consensus error; then the simultaneous consensus and stability of the closed-loop HOFAMAS (5.2) can be transformed into that $\epsilon_i(t) \to 0$ and $\epsilon_{ij}(t) \to 0$ with $t \to \infty$. From this perspective, Theorem 5.2 is proposed to address this problem.

Theorem 5.2 *The closed-loop HOFAMASs* (5.2) *can implement the simultaneous consensus and stability if the following conditions are simultaneously held:*

1. $\exists w_{ij} \geq 0$, $\sum_{j\in\mathcal{N}_i} w_{ij}^2 \neq 0$, $\exists \beta_i > 0$, $\forall i \in \mathcal{N}$, $\forall j \in \mathcal{N}_i$, *to guarantee that* $\frac{\partial}{\partial \Delta\hat{V}_i(t|t)}\mathcal{J}(t) = 0$, *and* Φ *is a Schur stable polynomial matrix in relation to* q, *where*

$$\Phi = I + (q-1)C\Phi_1^{-1}\Phi_2, \tag{5.17}$$

with

$$\begin{aligned}\Phi_1 =& I - (I - \mathcal{A}_M C - \mathcal{A}_C A_c(q))\, q^{-1} + \mathcal{A}_C A_c(q) q^{-2} \\ & - (\mathcal{A}_G + \mathcal{A}_L)\, q^{-\varsigma(t)-1} + \mathcal{A}_L q^{-\varsigma(t)-2}, \\ \Phi_2 =& - \mathcal{A}_M q^{-1},\end{aligned} \tag{5.18}$$

and

$$\begin{aligned} C =& \text{Blockdiag}\{C_1, \ldots, C_N\}, \\ \mathcal{A}_M =& \text{Blockdiag}\{\mathcal{A}_{1,c} H_1 F^{-1} M \vec{I}_{\aleph_y}, \ldots, \mathcal{A}_{N,c} H_N F^{-1} M \vec{I}_{\aleph_y}\}, \\ \mathcal{A}_G =& \begin{bmatrix} \mathcal{A}_{1,c} H_1 F^{-1} G \\ \vdots \\ \mathcal{A}_{N,c} H_N F^{-1} G \end{bmatrix}, \ \mathcal{A}_L = \begin{bmatrix} \mathcal{A}_{1,c} H_1 F^{-1} L A_c(q) \\ \vdots \\ \mathcal{A}_{N,c} H_N F^{-1} L A_c(q) \end{bmatrix}, \\ \mathcal{A}_C =& \text{Blockdiag}\{\mathcal{A}_{1,c}, \ldots, \mathcal{A}_{N,c}\}, \ \vec{I}_{\aleph_y} = [\underbrace{I \cdots I}_{\aleph_y}]^{\mathrm{T}}, \ \mathcal{A}_{i,c} = \mathcal{A}_i^{-1} \mathcal{B}_i, \end{aligned} \tag{5.19}$$

and $C = \text{Blockdiag}\{C_1, \ldots, C_N\}$, $\mathcal{A}_M = \text{Blockdiag}\{\mathcal{A}_{1,c} H_1 F^{-1} M \vec{I}_{\aleph_y}, \ldots,$ $\mathcal{A}_{N,c} H_N F^{-1} M \vec{I}_{\aleph_y}\}$, $\mathcal{A}_G = \begin{bmatrix} \mathcal{A}_{1,c} H_1 F^{-1} G \\ \vdots \\ \mathcal{A}_{N,c} H_N F^{-1} G \end{bmatrix}$, $\mathcal{A}_L = \begin{bmatrix} \mathcal{A}_{1,c} H_1 F^{-1} L A_c(q) \\ \vdots \\ \mathcal{A}_{N,c} H_N F^{-1} L A_c(q) \end{bmatrix}$, $\mathcal{A}_C = \text{Blockdiag}\{\mathcal{A}_{1,c}, \ldots, \mathcal{A}_{N,c}\}$, $\vec{I}_{\aleph_y} = [\underbrace{I \cdots I}_{\aleph_y}]^{\mathrm{T}}$, *and* $\mathcal{A}_{i,c} = \mathcal{A}_i^{-1} \mathcal{B}_i$.

2. *The observer gains* $K_{i,o,\eta}$, $\eta = 0, 1, \ldots, n-1$, *are solved in* (5.7).

Proof It is generally assumed that $r(\cdot) = r$, such that $\Delta v_i(t)$ in (5.16) can be rewritten as

$$\begin{aligned}\Delta v_i(t) =& H_i F^{-1} G \hat{x}(t - \varsigma(t) | t - \varsigma(t) - 1) + H_i F^{-1} L A_c(q) \\ & \times \Delta \hat{x}(t - \varsigma(t) | t - \varsigma(t) - 1) + H_i F^{-1} M \vec{I}_{\aleph_y} \left(C_i x_i(t) - e_i(t) \right).\end{aligned} \tag{5.20}$$

Meanwhile, by means of the proof of Theorem 3.1, $e(t)$ in this chapter can also be written as (3.17) with $e(t) = \left[e_1^{\mathrm{T}}(t) \cdots e_N^{\mathrm{T}}(t) \right]^{\mathrm{T}}$, $x(t) = \left[x_1^{\mathrm{T}}(t) \cdots x_N^{\mathrm{T}}(t) \right]^{\mathrm{T}}$, i.e.,

$$e(t+1) = e(t) + (q-1) C x(t), \tag{5.21}$$

and the consensus error $\epsilon(t)$ in this chapter can also be summarized as (3.18) with $i = 1$ and $\epsilon(t) = \left[\epsilon_1^{\mathrm{T}}(t) \cdots \epsilon_{1N}^{\mathrm{T}}(t) \right]^{\mathrm{T}}$, i.e.,

$$\epsilon(t) = \tilde{\mathbf{I}} e(t). \tag{5.22}$$

Based on (5.8), it is derived that

$$\Delta x_i(t+1) = \mathcal{A}_{i,c}\Delta v_i(t) + \mathcal{A}_{i,c}\Delta u_{i,o}(t),$$

because $\exists w_{ij} \geq 0$, $\sum_{j\in\mathcal{N}_i} w_{ij}^2 \neq 0$, $\exists \beta_i > 0$, $\forall i \in \mathcal{N}$, $\forall j \in \mathcal{N}_i$, to guarantee that $\frac{\partial}{\partial \Delta \hat{V}_i(t|t)}\mathcal{J}(t) = 0$, $\forall i \in \mathcal{N}$, and the optimal cooperative control increment $\Delta v_i(t)$ can be calculated in (5.15)–(5.20). By substituting (5.20) into the above, it is obtained that

$$\begin{aligned}
&\Delta x_i(t+1)\\
&= \mathcal{A}_{i,c}\Delta v_i(t) + \mathcal{A}_{i,c}\Delta u_{i,osc}(t)\\
&= \mathcal{A}_{i,c}H_i F^{-1}G\hat{x}(t-\varsigma(t)|t-\varsigma(t)-1)\\
&+ \mathcal{A}_{i,c}H_i F^{-1}M\vec{I}_{\aleph_y}\left(C_i x_i(t) - e_i(t)\right)\\
&+ \mathcal{A}_{i,c}H_i F^{-1}LA_c(q)\Delta\hat{x}(t-\varsigma(t)|t-\varsigma(t)-1) + \mathcal{A}_{i,c}\Delta u_{i,o}(t)\\
&= \mathcal{A}_{i,c}H_i F^{-1}G\left(x(t-\varsigma(t)) - e_x(t-\varsigma(t))\right) + \mathcal{A}_{i,c}H_i F^{-1}M\vec{I}_{\aleph_y}\left(C_i x_i(t) - e_i(t)\right)\\
&+ \mathcal{A}_{i,c}H_i F^{-1}LA_c(q)\left(\Delta x(t-\varsigma(t)) - \Delta e_x(t-\varsigma(t))\right) + \mathcal{A}_{i,c}\Delta u_{i,o}(t),
\end{aligned}$$

with

$$x(t-\varsigma(t)) = \begin{bmatrix} x_1(t-\varsigma_{i1}(t)) \\ \vdots \\ x_N(t-\varsigma_{iN}(t)) \end{bmatrix}, \quad e_x(t-\varsigma(t)) = \begin{bmatrix} e_{1,x}(t-\varsigma_{i1}(t)) \\ \vdots \\ e_{N,x}(t-\varsigma_{iN}(t)) \end{bmatrix},$$

$$\Delta x(t-\varsigma(t)) = \begin{bmatrix} \Delta x_1(t-\varsigma_{i1}(t)) \\ \vdots \\ \Delta x_N(t-\varsigma_{iN}(t)) \end{bmatrix}, \quad \Delta e_x(t-\varsigma(t)) = \begin{bmatrix} \Delta e_{1,x}(t-\varsigma_{i1}(t)) \\ \vdots \\ \Delta e_{N,x}(t-\varsigma_{iN}(t)) \end{bmatrix}.$$

Summarizing the above can be compactly represented as

$$\begin{aligned}
\Delta x(t+1) =& \mathcal{A}_G x(t-\varsigma(t)) - \mathcal{A}_G e_x(t-\varsigma(t)) + \mathcal{A}_L \Delta x(t-\varsigma(t))\\
&- \mathcal{A}_L \Delta e_x(t-\varsigma(t)) + \mathcal{A}_M (Cx(t) - e(t)) + \mathcal{A}_C \Delta u_o(t),
\end{aligned} \tag{5.23}$$

where $\mathcal{A}_G$, $\mathcal{A}_L$, $\mathcal{A}_M$, and $\mathcal{A}_C$ are defined in (5.19). Because $\Delta u_o(t-\varsigma(t)) = A_c(q)\Delta\hat{x}(t-\varsigma(t)|t-\varsigma(t)-1)$, $\Delta u_o(t)$ in (5.23) can be written as

$$\Delta u_o(t) = A_c(q)\Delta\hat{x}(t|t-1) = A_c(q)\Delta x(t) - A_c(q)\Delta e_x(t).$$

Then, system (5.23) can be rewritten as

$$
\begin{aligned}
\Delta x(t+1) =& \mathcal{A}_G x(t-\varsigma(t)) + \mathcal{A}_L \Delta x(t-\varsigma(t)) + \mathcal{A}_M C x(t) - \mathcal{A}_M e(t) \\
& - \mathcal{A}_G e_x(t-\varsigma(t)) - \mathcal{A}_L \Delta e_x(t-\varsigma(t)) + \mathcal{A}_C \left(A_c(q)\Delta x(t)\right. \\
& \left. - A_c(q)\Delta e_x(t)\right),
\end{aligned}
$$

which can be equivalently expressed as

$$
x(t) = \Phi_1^{-1}\Phi_2 e(t) + \Phi_1^{-1}\Phi_3 e_x(t), \tag{5.24}
$$

where Φ_1 and Φ_2 are given in (5.18), and

$$
\Phi_3 = -\mathcal{A}_C A_c(q) q^{-1} + \mathcal{A}_C A_c(q) q^{-2} - (\mathcal{A}_G + \mathcal{A}_L) q^{-\varsigma(t)-1} - \mathcal{A}_L q^{-\varsigma(t)-2}.
$$

By substituting (5.24) into (5.21), it is obtained that

$$
\begin{aligned}
e(t+1) =& e(t) + (q-1)Cx(t) \\
=& e(t) + (q-1)C\Phi_1^{-1}\Phi_2 e(t) + (q-1)C\Phi_1^{-1}\Phi_3 e_x(t) \\
=& \Phi e(t) + (q-1)C\Phi_1^{-1}\Phi_3 e_x(t),
\end{aligned} \tag{5.25}
$$

where Φ is defined in (5.17). Combining with (5.22), an auxiliary system is generated as

$$
\begin{cases}
e(t+1) = \Phi e(t) + (q-1)C\Phi_1^{-1}\Phi_3 e_x(t), \\
\epsilon(t) = \tilde{\mathbf{I}} e(t).
\end{cases} \tag{5.26}
$$

Because the observer gains $K_{i,o,\eta}$, $\eta = 0, 1, \ldots, n-1$, are solved in (5.7), $e_{i,x}(t) \to 0$ with $t \to \infty$ on the basis of Theorem 5.1, such that $e_x(t) \to 0$ with $t \to \infty$, which implies that system (5.26) can be degenerated as

$$
\begin{cases}
e(t+1) = \Phi e(t), \\
\epsilon(t) = \tilde{\mathbf{I}} e(t).
\end{cases} \tag{5.27}
$$

Because $\exists w_{ij} \geq 0$, $\sum_{j\in\mathcal{N}_i} w_{ij}^2 \neq 0$, $\exists \beta_i > 0$, $\forall i \in \mathcal{N}$, $\forall j \in \mathcal{N}_i$, to guarantee that Φ is a Schur stable polynomial matrix in relation to q, system (5.27) is stable, such that $e(t) \to 0$ with $t \to \infty$, which derives that $\epsilon(t) \to 0$ with $t \to \infty$. Hence, the closed-loop HOFAMASs (5.2) can implement the simultaneous consensus and stability.

This completes the proof. □

5.5 With Application to Flying-Around of Air-Bearing Spacecraft Simulators

There are three ABSSs to carry out a flying-around experiment to demonstrate the feasibility and practicability of the proposed OB-HOFAS predictive control, where the dynamic models of three ABSSs are shown in (A.4) and the details of three ABSSs and its relevant experimental platform are given in Appendix A.

5.5.1 Numerical Simulation

By selecting system (A.4a) as an example, a comparison between the proposed OB-HOFAS predictive control and a distributed model predictive control (DMPC) in Su et al. (2021b) is provided to verify the feasibility and superiority, where the relevant design parameters are chosen as $T_s = 0.2$s, $w_{ii} = 0$, $w_{ij} = 1$, $\alpha_i = 20$, $\beta_i = 0.01$, $\Gamma_i = I$, $i, j = 1, 2, 3$, $\aleph_y = 5$, $\aleph_u = 3$. The time-varying communication constraints in the forward and feedback channels are provided as $\tau_{1,a}(t) \in [2, 4]$, $\tau_{2,a}(t) \in [3, 8]$, $\tau_{3,a}(t) \in [1, 5]$, $\tau_{1,s}(t) \in [3, 4]$, $\tau_{2,s}(t) \in [1, 4]$, $\tau_{3,s}(t) \in [2, 3]$, and $\rho_{1,a}(t) \in [2, 3]$, $\rho_{2,a}(t) \in [4, 7]$, $\rho_{3,a}(t) \in [3, 5]$, $\rho_{1,s}(t) \in [3, 7]$, $\rho_{2,s}(t) \in [2, 4]$, $\rho_{3,s}(t) \in [2, 5]$.

Based on (5.1), an OB-HOFAS predictive control for system (A.4a) is constructed as

$$
\begin{aligned}
F_{I,x_{i,\mathrm{ABSS}}}(t) = B_i^{-1}\left(-L_i(A_{i,0\sim 1}, \hat{x}_{i,\mathrm{ABSS}}(t|t-1)) + \Upsilon_i(K_{i,0\sim 1}, \hat{x}_{i,\mathrm{ABSS}}(t|t-1))\right. \\
\left. + v_i(t)\right),
\end{aligned}
\tag{5.28}
$$

where $K_{1,0} = -0.3802$, $K_{1,1} = 19.4$, $K_{2,0} = -0.3822$, $K_{2,1} = 19.5$, $K_{3,0} = -0.3763$, $K_{3,1} = 19.2$, and the associated HOFAS observer is designed as

$$
\begin{aligned}
\hat{x}_{i,\mathrm{ABSS}}(t+1|t) = & -\mathcal{A}_{i,o,x}(q^{-1})\hat{x}_{i,\mathrm{ABSS}}(t|t-1) + \mathcal{B}_{i,o,x}(q^{-1})F_{I,x_{i,\mathrm{ABSS}}}(t) \\
& + \mathcal{K}_{i,o,x}(q^{-1})(x_{i,\mathrm{ABSS}}(t) - \hat{x}_{i,\mathrm{ABSS}}(t|t-1)),
\end{aligned}
\tag{5.29}
$$

where $\mathcal{A}_{i,o,x}(q^{-1}) = -2 + q^{-1}$, $\mathcal{B}_{i,o,x}(q^{-1}) = 0.0021q^{-1}$, and $\mathcal{K}_{i,o,x}(q^{-1}) = 0.0199q^{-1} - 0.0200$. For the DMPC method in Su et al. (2021b), system (A.4a) should be firstly transformed as (3.23), where $F_{I,x_{i,\mathrm{ABSS}}}(t)$ can be obtained by minimizing an objective function $\mathcal{J}_{\mathrm{DMPC}}(t) = \sum_{i\in\mathcal{N}} \mathcal{J}_{i,\mathrm{DMPC}}(t)$, and $\mathcal{J}_{i,\mathrm{DMPC}}(t)$ is presented as

$$
\mathcal{J}_{i,\mathrm{DMPC}}(t) = \sum_{\eta=0}^{\aleph_y-1}\left(\left\|\sum_{j\in\mathcal{N}_i} w_{ij}\left(\hat{X}_{i,\mathrm{ABSS}}(t+\eta|t) - X_{j,\mathrm{ABSS}}(t-\varsigma_{j,s}(t))\right)\right\|_{Q_i}^2\right.
$$

$$+ \left\| \hat{X}_{i,\text{ABSS}}(t+\eta|t) - R_x(t+\eta) \right\|_{Q_i}^2 + \left\| \hat{F}_{I,x_{i,\text{ABSS}}}(t+\eta|t) \right\|_{R_i}^2 \Bigg)$$

$$+ \left\| \hat{X}_i(t+\aleph_y|t) - R_x(t+\aleph_y) \right\|_{P_i}^2,$$

where $Q_i \succ 0$, $P_i \succ 0$, $R_i \succ 0$ are weighting matrices and $r_x(t)$ is a known desired reference signal with $R_x(t+\eta) = \left[r_x(t+\eta) \; r_x(t+\eta+1) \right]^{\mathrm{T}}$. Then, the simulated comparison is plotted in Fig. 5.2.

Figure 5.2a shows that the observation errors of HOFAS observer (5.29) can converge to 0, i.e., the immeasurable states of system (A.4a) can be estimated and reconstructed by using the HOFAS observer (5.29), which demonstrates the feasibility of HOFAS observer (5.29). Figure 5.2b means that the proposed OB-HOFAS predictive control (5.28) can achieve the active compensation of time-varying communication constraints in the forward and feedback channels, so that the desired cooperative tracking control in the dynamical and steady processes can be realized. However, Fig. 5.2c presents that the DMPC method in Su et al. (2021b) is hard to ensure the cooperative control performance under time-varying communication constraints and there exists the serious oscillation, where the reason has been provided in Remark 3.5.

Based on the comparison in Fig. 5.2, the feasibility and superiority of the proposed OB-HOFAS predictive control can be fully illustrated, which provides a strong support for the experimental verification.

5.5.2 *Experimental Results*

Based on the above simulation, a cooperative flying-around experiment of three ABSSs is given to verify the practicability of the proposed OB-HOFAS predictive control, where the desired circular orbit is shown in Fig. 5.3.

For systems (A.4a) and (A.4b), the cooperative control protocols are chosen as the same as (5.28) with the same design parameters. For system (A.4c), only a stabilization control is needed to satisfy the requirement of $\psi_{i,\text{ABSS}}(t)$ during the cooperative flying-around. Hence, the cooperative control items are set as 0, and a stabilization control is designed as

$$F_{I,T_{i,\text{ABSS}}}(t) = -L_i(A_{i,0\sim1}, \hat{\psi}_{i,\text{ABSS}}(t|t-1)) + \Upsilon_i(K_{i,0\sim n-1}, \hat{\psi}_{i,\text{ABSS}}(t|t-1)), \tag{5.30}$$

with $K_{1,0} = -0.0717$, $K_{1,1} = 0.2629$, $K_{2,0} = -0.0723$, $K_{2,1} = 0.2651$, $K_{3,0} = -0.0708$, $K_{3,1} = 0.2596$. The HOFAS observers for systems (A.4b) and (A.4c) are proposed as

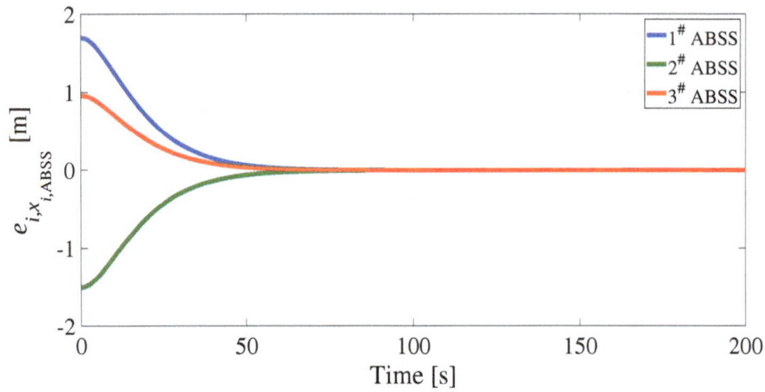

(a) The observation errors generated by the observer (5.29)

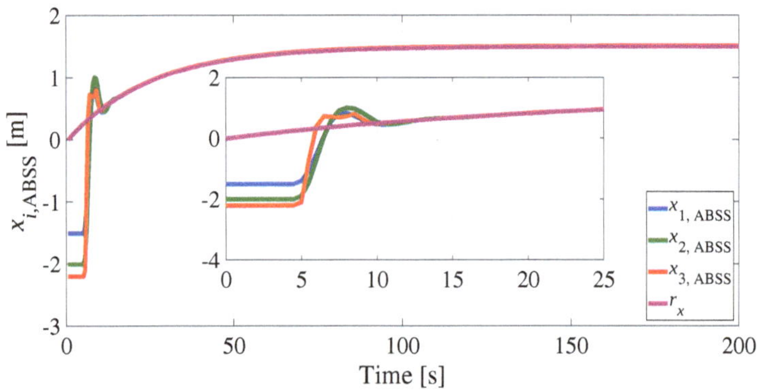

(b) Cooperative control of system (A.4a) by using the control (5.28)

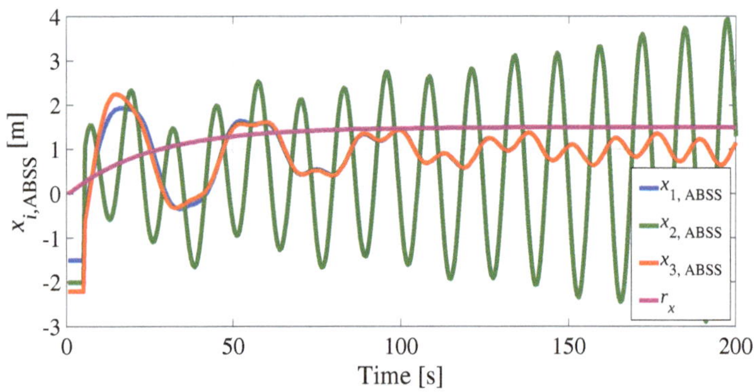

(c) Cooperative control of system (A.4a) via the DMPC in Su et al. (2021b)

Fig. 5.2 Comparison between the OB-HOFAS predictive control and the DMPC in Su et al. (2021b)

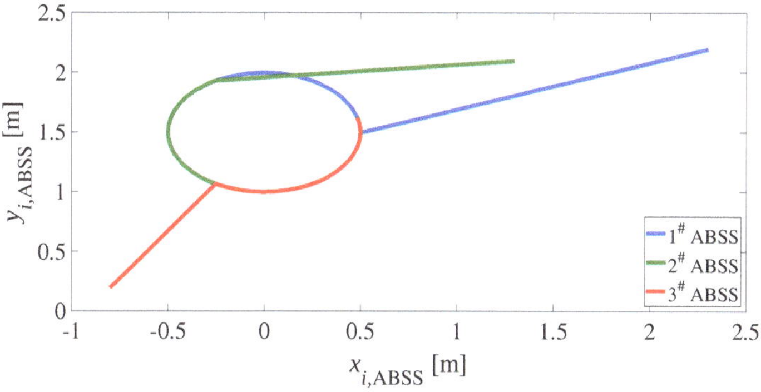

Fig. 5.3 The desired trajectory of three ABSSs

$$\begin{aligned}\hat{y}_{i,\mathrm{ABSS}}(t+1|t) =& -\mathcal{A}_{i,o,y}(q^{-1})\hat{y}_{i,\mathrm{ABSS}}(t|t-1) + \mathcal{B}_{i,o,i}(q^{-1})F_{I,y_{i,\mathrm{ABSS}}}(t)\\ &+ \mathcal{K}_{i,o,y}(q^{-1})(y_{i,\mathrm{ABSS}}(t) - \hat{y}_{i,\mathrm{ABSS}}(t|t-1)),\\ \hat{\psi}_{i,\mathrm{ABSS}}(t+1|t) =& -\mathcal{A}_{i,o,\psi}(q^{-1})\hat{\psi}_{i,\mathrm{ABSS}}(t|t-1) + \mathcal{B}_{i,o,\psi}(q^{-1})F_{I,T_{i,\mathrm{ABSS}}}(t)\\ &+ \mathcal{K}_{i,o,\psi}(q^{-1})(\psi_{i,\mathrm{ABSS}}(t) - \hat{\psi}_{i,\mathrm{ABSS}}(t|t-1)),\end{aligned} \tag{5.31}$$

with $\mathcal{A}_{i,o,y}(q^{-1}) = \mathcal{A}_{o,\psi,i}(q^{-1}) = -2 + q^{-1}$, $\mathcal{B}_{o,y,i}(q^{-1}) = 0.0021q^{-1}$, and $\mathcal{B}_{o,\psi,i}(q^{-1}) = 0.1674q^{-1}$. The associated observer gains computing by Theorem 5.1 are provided as $\mathcal{K}_{i,o,y}(q^{-1}) = \mathcal{K}_{i,o,\psi}(q^{-1}) = 0.0199q^{-1} - 0.0200$. By utilizing (5.28) and (5.30), the experimental results are provided in Figs. 5.4, 5.5, 5.6, 5.7.

The observation errors of $y_{i,\mathrm{ABSS}}(t)$ and $\psi_{i,\mathrm{ABSS}}(t)$ obtained by HOFAS observer (5.31) are plotted in Fig. 5.4, which shows that the observation errors can converge to 0, such that the effectiveness of HOFAS observer (5.31) can be illustrated. Figure 5.5 gives the position and angle responses of cooperative flying-around of three ABSSs, which implies that the position responses $x_{i,\mathrm{ABSS}}(t)$ and $y_{i,\mathrm{ABSS}}(t)$ can achieve the dynamical cooperative control under time-varying communication constraints and immeasurable states within the tolerant errors and their amplitudes and phases can be changed cooperatively. The angle responses $\psi_{i,\mathrm{ABSS}}(t)$ can realize the stabilization control with the allowable errors by adopting (5.30), but a shortcoming is that there exists the vibration during the steady process. The reason is that both the reaction forces of the thrusters and the airflow in the experimental site affect the stabilization control performance of $\psi_{i,\mathrm{ABSS}}(t)$. The control inputs generated by (5.28) and (5.30) are shown in Fig. 5.6, where there are some vibrations because of the model uncertainties and external disturbances. Figure 5.7 provides the practical trajectory of cooperative flying-around of three ABSSs, which means that the proposed OB-HOFAS predictive control (5.28) can implement the desired flying-around mission and continue to carry out it by comparing with Fig. 5.3.

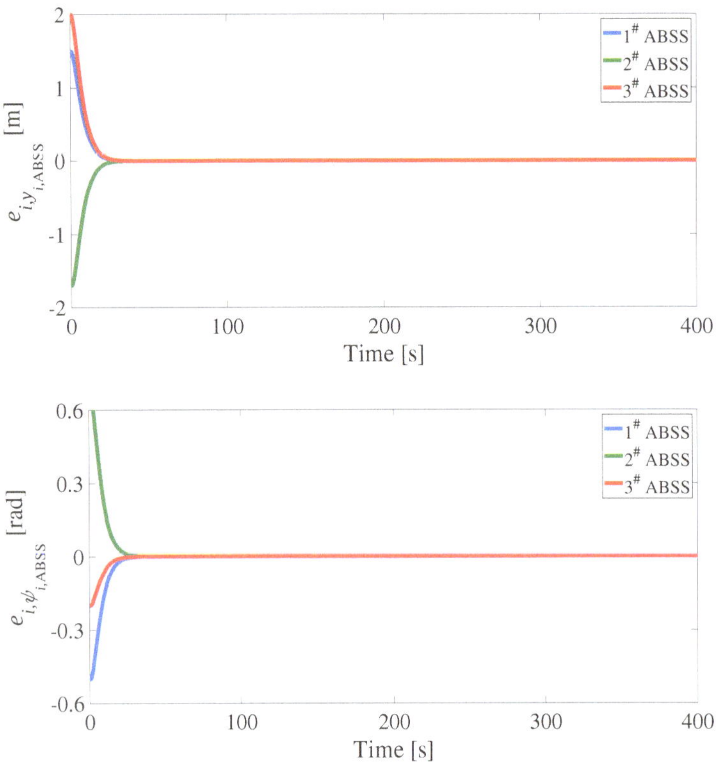

Fig. 5.4 The observation errors generated by the observer (5.31)

Based on the results in Figs. 5.4, 5.5, 5.6, 5.7, the feasibility and practicability of OB-HOFAS predictive control can be fully demonstrated, which gives a powerful basis for the large-scale applications of practical spacecraft control.

5.6 Notes and References

This chapter has investigated a design problem of cooperative control for the HOFAMASs with time-varying communication constraints and immeasurable states. An OB-HOFAS predictive control has been provided to compensate for time-varying communication constraints and estimate the immeasurable states for the optimization of cooperative control performance. A sufficient condition has been constructed to analyze the simultaneous consensus and stability of the closed-loop HOFAMASs. One of the highlights is that an observer is designed in a HOFAS form with the help of time operator and an observer-based IHOFAS prediction model is developed by using a kind of Diophantine Equation, which avoids the

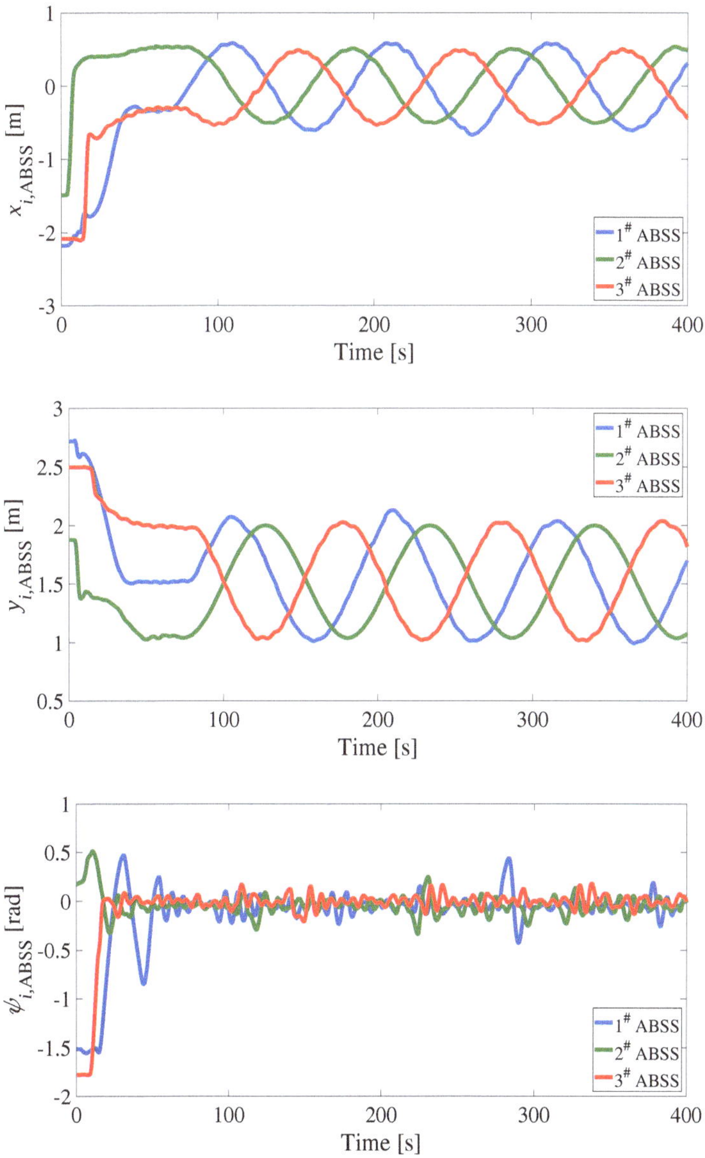

Fig. 5.5 The cooperative flying-around of three ABSSs by using the controls (5.28) and (5.30)

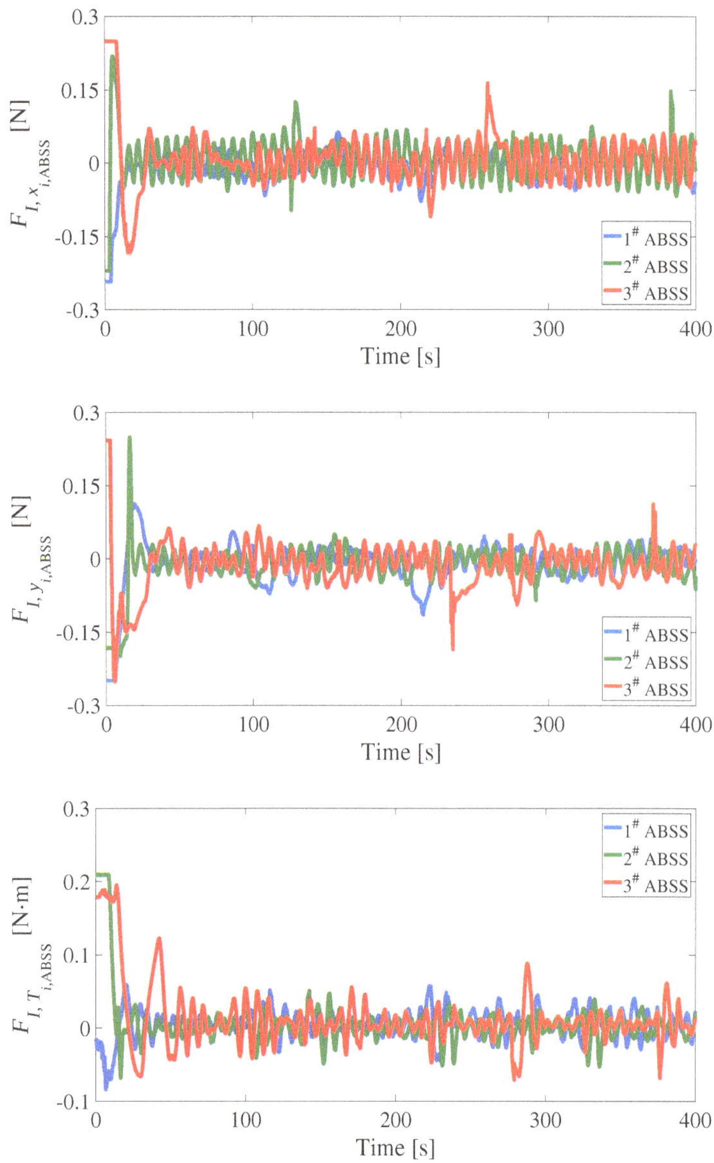

Fig. 5.6 The control inputs generated by the controls (5.28) and (5.30)

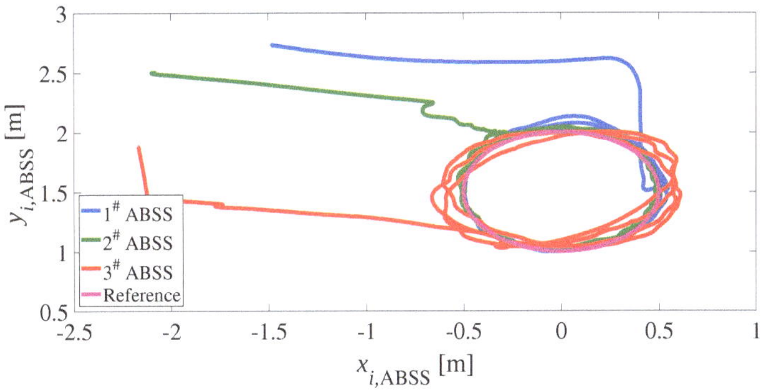

Fig. 5.7 The actual trajectory of three ABSSs

model reduction during the whole design process. The other is that the time-varying communication constraints can be actively compensated to improve the cooperative control performance and reduce the conservatism and dependence of simultaneous consensus and stability on time-varying communication constraints. Because of its advantages, the proposed OB-HOFAS predictive control can be expanded to the practical application of numerous fields.

Part III
Predictive Cooperative Control for High-Order Fully Actuated Multiagent Systems Under Cyberattacks and Uncertainties

Chapter 6
Packet-Based Predictive Cooperative Control for HOFAMASs Under Random DoS Attacks

6.1 Introduction

Apart from the communication constraints, cyberattack is also regarded as one of the most general network-induced constraints when introducing the network into the control loop, which has received the longstanding attention of scholars and has been deeply considered in the literature. In the analysis and control of the MASs, cyberattack can cause the mistakes, even failures, during the information transmission, which will result in the degradation of cooperative control performance, even instability, and out of control. Among them, DoS attack is one of the most common cyberattacks because of its simple principle, low cost, and large negative impacts. It utilizes the security vulnerabilities of network protocols to reduce or lose the availability of data transmission, such that many serious consequences will be occurred. Hence, secure cooperative control against DoS attacks is investigated as an important study hotspot, which has attracted the great attention of a number of scholars.

In the previous work, Yang and Ye (2022) designed a distributed fixed-time observer to estimate the leader for handling two classes of DoS attacks and then proposed a fixed-time control based on a power integrator method to achieve the fixed-time consensus tracking control. Du et al. (2023) gave the distributed self-triggering and event-triggering schemes to implement the exponential synchronization of heterogeneous MASs with aperiodic DoS attacks, where an explicit relationship of synchronous control performance and the properties of DoS attacks was constructed. For the connection edges attacked by the DoS attacks with different intensities, Zhang et al. (2023c) constructed an adaptive output feedback by applying a backstepping approach and Lyapunov stability theory to ensure that the consensus error can converge to a small interval of the origin. In Azarbahram and Amini (2022), a resilient control protocol was provided to guarantee the secure consensus of nonlinear MASs under DoS attacks, where an event-triggering strategy with a local auxiliary system was exploited to reduce the frequency of

D.-W. Zhang, G.-P. Liu, *Predictive Cooperative Control for High-Order Fully Actuated Multiagent Systems*, https://doi.org/10.1007/978-981-95-1695-7_6

DoS attacks and the pressure of information transmission. Further, Amini et al. (2022a) also developed a dynamical event-triggering mechanism to cope with the communication channels blocked by the DoS attacks and then presented a novel convex optimization strategy to maintain the resilient consensus. On the basis of an adaptive memory observer with an event-triggering scheme, Guo et al. (2021) proposed a reliable control based on the idea of anti-disturbance control to deal with the DoS attacks. Wang et al. (2022b) established a novel hybrid distributed control to enhance the secure consensus of MASs under DoS attacks, where a problem that the controller is ineffective in the attack interval was solved and a sufficient condition in relation to the attack parameters and the coupled strengths was derived. Amini et al. (2022b) designed a periodic event-triggering control to ensure the exponential mean-square bounded consensus via a delay-dependent Lyapunov-Krasovskii functional, where the gains of consensus control are associated with the expected levels of DoS attacks. In Yang et al. (2021c), an event-triggering strategy with dual terminations was presented to handle the DoS attacks, which was used to construct a leader-follower tracking control for the realization of distributed secure consensus. Sakthivel et al. (2023) provided an event-triggering scheme to handle random DoS attacks in the process of data transmission and then designed a H_∞ control based on a Lyapunov- Krasovskii functional to implement the secure mean-square consensus. In addition, the results in Fang et al. (2023), Feng and Ishii (2022), Amini et al. (2021), and their associated studies also made contributions to the progress of secure cooperative control against DoS attacks.

Summarizing the above implies that secure cooperative control for the MASs with DoS attacks can guarantee the system security and reliable operation for enhancing the cooperative control performance, which is benefit to the application and expansion in DC motors (Cheng et al. 2024), power systems (Wu et al. 2025), robotic systems (Liang et al. 2024), unmanned vehicles (Hong et al. 2024), and other fields. Meanwhile, by introducing the HOFAS theory into the secure cooperative control, the design complexity and computational load can be effectively simplified, and the cooperative control performance can be obviously improved.

Following this idea, this chapter considers a secure cooperative control problem of HOFAMASs under random DoS attacks. A PB-HOFAS predictive control is proposed to address this problem, where an IHOFA prediction model is developed by means of a kind of Diophantine Equation, and then a packet-based compensation scheme to compensate for random data dropout and disorders caused by random DoS attacks. The main works are summarized as follows. Firstly, a discrete-time model of the i-th HOFA agent is used to offer a better model foundation for the cooperative control design. Then, an IHOFAS prediction model is constructed by applying a type of Diophantine Equation, so that the multistep ahead predictions are generated to develop a packet-based compensation scheme for random DoS attacks and optimize the cooperative control performance. Further analysis presents a sufficient condition on the simultaneous consensus and stability of the closed-loop HOFAMASs. Finally, the effectiveness and practicality of the proposed method can be illustrated via a formation control experiment for three ABSSs.

6.2 Problem Statement

In this chapter, the communication topology is described by Definition 3.1, and the dynamic model of the i-th HOFA agent satisfying Assumptions 3.1 and 3.2 is given in (3.1). Let $\tau_{i,a}$ and $\tau_{i,s}$ be the upper bounds of time-varying communication delays in the i-th forward and feedback channels, respectively, where $\tau_{i,a}$ and $\tau_{i,s}$ satisfy Assumption 4.1.

Because of the uncertainties and complexity of network scenarios, the behaviors of cyberattackers are without regularity and predictability, so that the stochastic processes are usually adopted to describe the characteristics of behaviors of cyberattackers (He et al. 2020; Liu et al. 2024a; Wu et al. 2024; Wen et al. 2020), where the Bernoulli process is one of the most common ways to describe the mode of cyberattacks because it can well represent the randomness of cyberattacks and is of generality and practicality to some degree (He et al. 2020; Wen et al. 2020). In this chapter, $\delta_{i,a}(t)$ and $\delta_{i,s}(t)$ are random variables to denote whether the DoS attacks in the i-th forward and feedback channels are successful or not, where $\delta_{i,a}(t) = 1$ and $\delta_{i,s}(t) = 1$ denote that the DoS attacks are successful in the i-th forward and feedback channels, respectively, and $\delta_{i,a}(t) = 0$ and $\delta_{i,s}(t) = 0$ denote that the DoS attacks are failed in the i-th forward and feedback channels, respectively. $\delta_{i,a}(t)$ and $\delta_{i,s}(t)$ can be described by a Bernoulli process with the following probabilities:

$$\begin{aligned} &\text{Prob}\{\delta_{i,a}(t) = 1\} = \nu_i, \quad \text{Prob}\{\delta_{i,a}(t) = 0\} = 1 - \nu_i, \\ &\text{Prob}\{\delta_{i,s}(t) = 1\} = \mu_i, \quad \text{Prob}\{\delta_{i,s}(t) = 0\} = 1 - \mu_i, \end{aligned} \tag{6.1}$$

where $\nu_i \in [0, 1]$ and $\mu_i \in [0, 1]$ are two known constants to indicate the successful rates of the initial random DoS attacks in the i-th the forward and feedback channels, respectively.

As reported in Yang et al. (2021a), Yang and Zheng (2020), and the related studies, this work also considers that random data dropouts and disorders can be caused by random DoS attacks. Let $\rho_{i,a}(t)$ and $\rho_{i,s}(t)$ be the random data dropouts and disorders in the i-th forward and feedback channels, respectively, and denote $\varsigma_{i,a}(t) = \tau_{i,a} + \rho_{i,a}(t)$, $\varsigma_{i,s}(t) = \tau_{i,s} + \rho_{i,s}(t)$, $\varsigma_{ii}(t) = \varsigma_i(t) = \varsigma_{i,a}(t) + \varsigma_{i,s}(t)$, $\varsigma_{ij}(t) = \varsigma_{i,a}(t) + \varsigma_{j,s}(t)$, where $\varsigma_i(t)$ and $\varsigma_{ij}(t)$ satisfy Assumption 5.2.

Assumption 6.1 *$\bar{\rho}_{i,a}$ and $\bar{\rho}_{i,s}$ are the upper bounds of $\rho_{i,a}(t)$ and $\rho_{i,s}(t)$, respectively, such that $\bar{\varsigma}_{i,a} = \tau_{i,a} + \bar{\rho}_{i,a}$ and $\bar{\varsigma}_{i,s} = \tau_{i,s} + \bar{\rho}_{i,s}$ can be regarded as the upper bounds of $\varsigma_{i,a}(t)$ and $\varsigma_{i,s}(t)$. Then, let $\bar{\varsigma}_i(t) = \bar{\varsigma}_{i,a} + \varsigma_{i,s}(t)$, $\bar{\varsigma}_{ij}(t) = \bar{\varsigma}_{i,a} + \varsigma_{j,s}(t)$.*

To consider the secure cooperative control for the i-th HOFA agent (3.1) under random DoS attacks, a PB-HOFAS predictive control is proposed as

$$u_i(t) = B_i^{-1}\left(L_i(\cdot) + \Upsilon_i(K_{i,0\sim n-1}, x_i(t)) + v_i(t)\right), \tag{6.2}$$

where $L_i(\cdot)$ is exploited to eliminate the open-loop dynamics, $\Upsilon_i(K_{i,0\sim n-1}, x_i(t)) = \sum_{\eta=0}^{n-1} K_{i,\eta} x_i(t+\eta) \in \mathbb{R}^{n_i}$ is used to adjust the closed-loop performances and

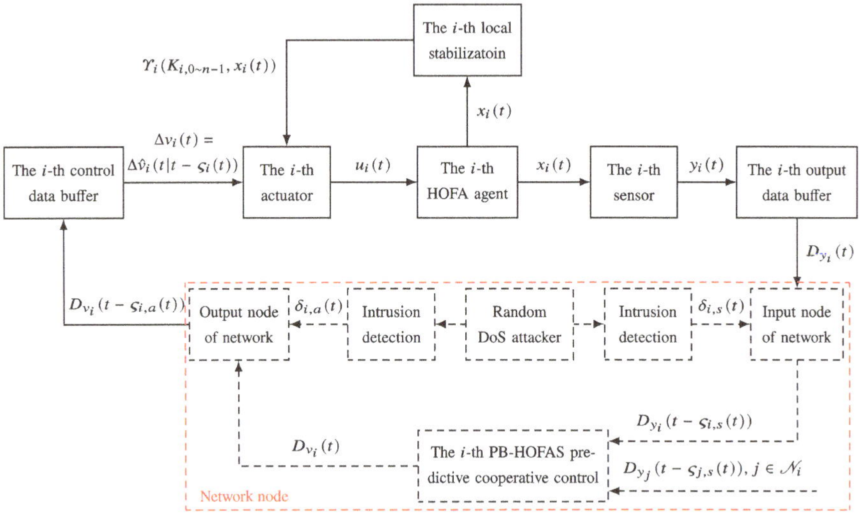

Fig. 6.1 Packet-based predictive cooperative control for the HOFAMASs under random DoS attacks

$K_{i,\eta} \in \mathbb{R}^{n_i \times n_i}$ denote the feedback gains to be determined, and $v_i(t) \in \mathbb{R}^{n_i}$ is a secure cooperative control item designed by PB-HOFAS predictive control. The related control structure is shown in Fig. 6.1, where $D_{y_i}(t) = \{Y_{i,\bar{\varsigma}_{i,s}}(t), t\}$ with $Y_{i,\bar{\varsigma}_{i,s}}(t) = \{y_i(t), \ldots, y_i(t-\bar{\varsigma}_{i,s})\}$ and $D_{y_i}(t-\varsigma_{i,s}(t)) = \{Y_{i,\bar{\varsigma}_{i,s}}(t-\varsigma_{i,s}(t)), t-\varsigma_{i,s}(t)\}$ with $Y_{i,\bar{\varsigma}_{i,s}}(t-\varsigma_{i,s}(t)) = \{y_i(t-\varsigma_{i,s}(t)), \ldots, y_i(t-\bar{\varsigma}_{i,s}-\varsigma_{i,s}(t))\}$ are the data packets of outputs and their corresponding timestamps before and after passing the network, respectively, and $D_{v_i}(t) = \{\Delta\hat{V}_{i,\bar{\varsigma}_{i,a}}(t+\varsigma_{i,a}(t)), t\}$ with $\Delta\hat{V}_{i,\bar{\varsigma}_{i,a}}(t+\varsigma_{i,a}(t)) = \{\Delta\hat{v}_i(t+\tau_{i,a}|t-\varsigma_{i,s}(t)), \ldots, \Delta\hat{v}_i(t+\bar{\varsigma}_{i,a}|t-\varsigma_{i,s}(t))\}$ and $D_{v_i}(t-\varsigma_{i,a}(t)) = \{\Delta\hat{V}_{i,\bar{\varsigma}_{i,a}}(t), t-\varsigma_{i,a}(t)\}$ with $\Delta\hat{V}_{i,\bar{\varsigma}_{i,a}}(t) = \{\Delta\hat{v}_i(t-\varsigma_{i,a}(t)+\tau_{i,a}|t-\varsigma_i(t)), \ldots, \Delta\hat{v}_i(t-\varsigma_{i,a}(t)+\bar{\varsigma}_{i,a}|t-\varsigma_i(t))\}$ are the data packets of secure cooperative control increments and their corresponding timestamps before and after passing the network, respectively.

By applying (6.2), the closed-loop HOFAMASs can be implemented as

$$x_i(t+n) = \Upsilon_i(K_{i,0\sim n-1}, x_i(t)) + v_i(t) = \sum_{\eta=0}^{n-1} K_{i,\eta} x_i(t+\eta) + v_i(t), \; i \in \mathcal{N}. \tag{6.3}$$

To calculate the secure cooperative control item $v_i(t)$, an objective function $\mathcal{J}(t)$ is given as

$$\mathcal{J}(t) = \sum_{i \in \mathcal{N}} \mathcal{J}_i(t), \tag{6.4}$$

where $\mathcal{J}_i(t)$ is a sub-objective function about the secure cooperative control performance of the i-th HOFA agent and is constructed as

$$\begin{aligned}\mathcal{J}_i(t) = \sum_{j\in\mathcal{N}_i} w_{ij} &\left\|\hat{Y}_i(t+\bar{\varsigma}_{i,a}+\aleph_y|t-\varsigma_{i,s}(t)) - \hat{Y}_j(t+\bar{\varsigma}_{i,a}+\aleph_y|t-\varsigma_{j,s}(t))\right\|^2 \\ &+ \alpha_i \left\|\hat{Y}_i(t+\bar{\varsigma}_{i,a}+\aleph_y|t-\varsigma_{i,s}(t)) - R(t+\bar{\varsigma}_{i,a}+\aleph_y)\right\|^2 \\ &+ \beta_i \left\|\Delta\hat{V}_i(t+\bar{\varsigma}_{i,a}+\aleph_u|t-\varsigma_{i,s}(t))\right\|^2,\end{aligned} \tag{6.5}$$

with

$$\hat{Y}_i(t+\bar{\varsigma}_{i,a}+\aleph_y|t-\varsigma_{i,s}(t)) = \begin{bmatrix} \hat{y}_i(t+\bar{\varsigma}_{i,a}+\aleph_y|t-\varsigma_{i,s}(t)) \\ \vdots \\ \hat{y}_i(t+\tau_{i,a}+1|t-\varsigma_{i,s}(t)) \end{bmatrix},$$

$$\hat{Y}_j(t+\bar{\varsigma}_{i,a}+\aleph_y|t-\varsigma_{j,s}(t)) = \begin{bmatrix} \hat{y}_j(t+\bar{\varsigma}_{i,a}+\aleph_y|t-\varsigma_{j,s}(t)) \\ \vdots \\ \hat{y}_j(t+\tau_{i,a}+1|t-\varsigma_{j,s}(t)) \end{bmatrix},$$

$$\Delta\hat{V}_i(t+\bar{\varsigma}_{i,a}+\aleph_u|t-\varsigma_{i,s}(t)) = \begin{bmatrix} \Delta\hat{v}_i(t+\bar{\varsigma}_{i,a}+\aleph_u|t-\varsigma_{i,s}(t)) \\ \vdots \\ \Delta\hat{v}_i(t+\tau_{i,a}|t-\varsigma_{i,s}(t)) \end{bmatrix},$$

$$R(t+\bar{\varsigma}_{i,a}+\aleph_y) = \begin{bmatrix} r(t+\bar{\varsigma}_{i,a}+\aleph_y) \\ \vdots \\ r(t+\tau_{i,a}+1) \end{bmatrix},$$

where $\hat{y}_i(t+\eta|t-\varsigma_{i,s}(t))$, $\eta = \tau_{i,a}+1, \tau_{i,a}+2, \ldots, \bar{\varsigma}_{i,a}+\aleph_y$, and $\Delta\hat{v}_i(t+\eta|t-\varsigma_{i,s}(t))$, $\eta = \tau_{i,a}, \tau_{i,a}+1, \ldots, \bar{\varsigma}_{i,a}+\aleph_u$ are the η-th ahead predictions of output $y_i(t)$ and cooperative control increment $\Delta v_i(t)$ based on $t-\varsigma_{i,s}(t)$ time. $r(t)$ is a known reference signal, and $R(t+\bar{\varsigma}_{i,a}+\aleph_y)$ denotes the relevant multistep ahead sequence. w_{ij} is the (i,j)-th element of adjacent matrix $\mathcal{W}$, and $\alpha_i > 0$ and $\beta_i > 0$ are two weighting factors. The aim of each item in (6.5) has been provided in Remark 3.3.

Problem 6.1 Given the i-th HOFA agent (3.1) under Assumptions 3.1, 3.2, 4.1, 5.2, and 6.1, a PB-HOFAS predictive control $u_i\left(t, v_i(t, y_i(t), y_j(t), r(t))\right)$ is designed in (6.2) by minimizing the objective function $\mathcal{J}(t)$ in (6.4) and (6.5), such that the closed-loop HOFAMASs (6.3) can realize the simultaneous consensus and stability, i.e., the following conditions are satisfied:

1. $\forall i \in \mathcal{N}, \forall t \geq 0, \lim_{t \to \infty} \|y_i(t)\| < \infty$ with $\|r(t)\| < \infty$.
2. $\forall i \in \mathcal{N}, \forall j \in \mathcal{N}_i, \lim_{t \to \infty} \|y_i(t) - y_j(t)\| = 0$.

6.3 Packet-Based HOFAS Predictive Cooperative Control Scheme

6.3.1 A Packet-Based Compensation Scheme for Random DoS Attacks

Based on Liu et al. (2006), Liu (2022d), the networked predictive control can break through the point-to-point single data transmission mode by using the feature that the network can transmit the vector data streams, such that the active compensation of communication delays and data dropouts can be achieved. Concretely, the multiple output data are stored in an output data buffer and packed as an output data packet to send to the networked predictive controller over the network. Based on this output data packet and historical control data, the multiple control sequence can be solved by the networked predictive controller and packed as a control data packet to send to a control data buffer over the network. Then, the latest control can be selected by the control data buffer from the control data packet.

On the basis of the networked predictive control, a packet-based compensation scheme is developed to cope with random data dropouts and disorders caused by random DoS attacks in the forward and feedback channels, so that the similar or the same cooperative control performance as that of a case without DoS attacks can be realized. The details are provided as follows.

On the local node, the i-th output data buffer transmits the $D_{y_i}(t)$ instead of $y_i(t)$ to the i-th PB-HOFAS predictive cooperative controller, such that random data dropouts and disorders caused by random DoS attacks and the communication delays in the i-th feedback channel can be effectively addressed. Because the latest output data sequence with $\varsigma_{i,s}(t)$ is available for the i-th PB-HOFAS predictive cooperative controller at time t, the $D_{y_i}(t - \varsigma_{i,s}(t))$ can be exploited to establish the multistep ahead predictions, which can be used to compute the $\Delta \hat{V}_{i,\bar{\varsigma}_{i,a}}(t + \varsigma_{i,a}(t))$ on the network node. Then, the $\Delta \hat{V}_{i,\bar{\varsigma}_{i,a}}(t + \varsigma_{i,a}(t))$ and its timestamp t can be encapsulated into a control data packet $D_{v_i}(t)$ to send to the i-th control data buffer at time t through the i-th forward channel, which can effectively cope with random data dropouts and disorders caused by random DoS attacks and the communication delays in the i-th forward channel. Finally, the i-th control data buffer is used to provide an appropriately secure predictive control increment $\Delta v_i(t)$ from the $D_{v_i}(t - \varsigma_{i,a}(t))$, i.e., $\Delta v_i(t) = \Delta \hat{v}_i(t|t - \varsigma_i(t))$. Meanwhile, the $D_{y_j}(t - \varsigma_{j,s}(t))$, $j \in \mathcal{N}_i$, can also be transmitted to the i-th PB-HOFAS predictive cooperative controller by following this scheme for computing the $\Delta v_i(t)$.

By utilizing this scheme, random data dropouts and disorders caused by random DoS attacks and the communication delays can be actively compensated in the real time, which is benefit to enhance the secure cooperative control performance and reduce the conservatism for constructing the simultaneous consensus and stability condition. Meanwhile, it also provides a reasonable basis for designing the $\mathcal{J}(t)$ in (6.4) and (6.5), which constructed a feasible foundation for the subsequent design of secure cooperative control.

6.3.2 Design of PB-HOFAS Predictive Cooperative Control

By means of the time operator q, the closed-loop system (6.3) can be equivalent to the following polynomial one:

$$\mathcal{K}_i\left(q^{-1}\right)x_i(t) = \mathcal{B}_i\left(q^{-1}\right)v_i(t-1), \tag{6.6}$$

where $\mathcal{K}_i\left(q^{-1}\right) = I - \sum_{\eta=0}^{n-1} K_{i,\eta}q^{\eta-n}$ and $\mathcal{B}_i\left(q^{-1}\right) = q^{1-n}$. Based on Diophantine Equation (3.7) with the same process from (3.6) to (3.8), an IHOFAS prediction model based on (6.6) is established as (3.8), i.e.,

$$x_i(t+\eta) = \mathcal{F}_{i,\eta}x_i(t) + \mathcal{G}_{i,\eta}\Delta v_i(t+\eta-1),$$

where $\mathcal{F}_{i,\eta}$ and $\mathcal{G}_{i,\eta}$ are constructed in (3.8). Combining with the $D_{y_i}(t-\varsigma_{i,s}(t))$ and $D_{v_i}(t)$, the above IHOFAS prediction model can be corrected as

$$\begin{aligned}\hat{x}_i(t-\varsigma_{i,s}(t)+\eta|t-\varsigma_{i,s}(t)) =& \mathcal{F}_{i,\eta}x_i(t-\varsigma_{i,s}(t)) \\ &+ \mathcal{G}_{i,\eta}\Delta\hat{v}_i(t-\varsigma_{i,s}(t)+\eta-1|t-\varsigma_{i,s}(t)),\end{aligned} \tag{6.7}$$

with $\eta = 1, 2, \ldots, \bar{\varsigma}_i(t) + \aleph_y$.

When $\eta = \varsigma_{i,s}(t) + \tau_{i,a} + 1, \varsigma_{i,s}(t) + \tau_{i,a} + 2, \ldots, \bar{\varsigma}_i(t) + \aleph_y$, the multistep ahead predictions of $x_i(t)$ on the basis of (6.7) are yielded as

$$\begin{aligned}\hat{x}_i(t+\tau_{i,a}+1|t-\varsigma_{i,s}(t)) =& \mathcal{F}_{i,\varsigma_{i,s}(t)+\tau_{i,a}+1}x_i(t-\varsigma_{i,s}(t)) \\ &+ \mathcal{G}_{i,\varsigma_{i,s}(t)+\tau_{i,a}+1}\Delta\hat{v}_i(t+\tau_{i,a}|t-\varsigma_{i,s}(t)), \\ &\vdots \\ \hat{x}_i(t+\bar{\varsigma}_{i,a}+\aleph_y|t-\varsigma_{i,s}(t)) =& \mathcal{F}_{i,\bar{\varsigma}_i(t)+\aleph_y}x_i(t-\varsigma_{i,s}(t)) \\ &+ \mathcal{G}_{i,\bar{\varsigma}_i(t)+\aleph_y}\Delta\hat{v}_i(t+\bar{\varsigma}_{i,a}+\aleph_y-1|t-\varsigma_{i,s}(t)),\end{aligned}$$

so that the associated output predictions are given as

$$\hat{y}_i(t+\tau_{i,a}+\eta|t-\varsigma_{i,s}(t)) = C_i\hat{x}_i(t+\tau_{i,a}+\eta|t-\varsigma_{i,s}(t), \tag{6.8}$$

with $\eta = 1, 2, \ldots, \bar{\rho}_{i,a} + \aleph_y$. When $\eta = \bar{\rho}_{i,a} + \aleph_u + 1, \bar{\rho}_{i,a} + \aleph_u + 2, \ldots, \bar{\rho}_{i,a} + \aleph_y$, $\hat{\upsilon}_i(t + \tau_{i,a} + \eta | t - \varsigma_{i,s}(t)) = \hat{\upsilon}_i(t + \tau_{i,a} + \bar{\rho}_{i,a} + \aleph_u | t - \varsigma_{i,s}(t)) = \hat{\upsilon}_i(t + \bar{\varsigma}_{i,a} + \aleph_u | t - \varsigma_{i,s}(t))$, such that $\Delta\hat{\upsilon}_i(t + \tau_{i,a} + \eta | t - \varsigma_{i,s}(t)) = 0$. Hence, the output prediction (6.8) can be compactly written as

$$\begin{aligned} \hat{Y}_i(t + \bar{\varsigma}_{i,a} + \aleph_y | t - \varsigma_{i,s}(t)) = & P_{i,1} x_i(t - \varsigma_{i,s}(t)) \\ & + P_{i,2} \Delta\hat{V}_i(t + \bar{\varsigma}_{i,a} + \aleph_u | t - \varsigma_{i,s}(t)), \end{aligned} \tag{6.9}$$

with

$$P_{i,1} = \left[\mathcal{F}^{\mathrm{T}}_{i,\bar{\varsigma}_i(t)+\aleph_y} C_i^{\mathrm{T}} \cdots \mathcal{F}^{\mathrm{T}}_{i,\bar{\varsigma}_i(t)+\aleph_u} C_i^{\mathrm{T}} \cdots \mathcal{F}^{\mathrm{T}}_{i,\varsigma_{i,s}(t)+\tau_{i,a}+1} C_i^{\mathrm{T}} \right]^{\mathrm{T}},$$

$$P_{i,2} = \begin{bmatrix} C_i \mathcal{G}_{i,\bar{\varsigma}_i(t)+\aleph_y} & 0 & \cdots & 0 \\ \vdots & \vdots & \cdots & \vdots \\ C_i \mathcal{G}_{i,\bar{\varsigma}_i(t)+\aleph_u+1} & 0 & \cdots & 0 \\ 0 & C_i \mathcal{G}_{i,\bar{\varsigma}_i(t)+\aleph_u} & \ddots & \vdots \\ \vdots & \ddots & \ddots & 0 \\ 0 & \cdots & 0 & C_i \mathcal{G}_{i,\varsigma_{i,s}(t)+\tau_{i,a}+1} \end{bmatrix}.$$

Because of (2.9), the incremental constraint of cooperative control increment is defined as

$$\Delta\hat{\upsilon}_i(t + \tau_{i,a} + \eta | t - \varsigma_{i,s}(t)) = \gamma_{i,\eta} \Delta\hat{\upsilon}_i(t + \tau_{i,a} | t - \varsigma_{i,s}(t)),$$

where $\gamma_{i,\eta} > 0$, $\eta = 1, 2, \ldots, \bar{\rho}_{i,a} + \aleph_u$, is a weighting factor, such that $P_{i,2}$ can be degenerated as $P_{i,3} = P_{i,2} \Gamma_i$ with $\Gamma_i = \text{Blockdiag}\{\gamma_{i,\bar{\rho}_{i,a}+\aleph_u} I, \ldots, \gamma_{i,1} I, I\}$, and $P_{i,2} \Delta\hat{V}_i(t + \bar{\varsigma}_{i,a} + \aleph_u | t - \varsigma_{i,s}(t)) = P_{i,3} \Delta\hat{V}_i(t + \tau_{i,a} | t - \varsigma_{i,s}(t))$ with

$$\begin{aligned} & \Delta\hat{V}_i(t + \tau_{i,a} | t - \varsigma_{i,s}(t)) \\ & = \left[\Delta\hat{\upsilon}_i^{\mathrm{T}}(t + \tau_{i,a} | t - \varsigma_{i,s}(t)) \cdots \Delta\hat{\upsilon}_i^{\mathrm{T}}(t + \tau_{i,a} | t - \varsigma_{i,s}(t)) \right]^{\mathrm{T}}. \end{aligned}$$

Thus, the output prediction (6.9) can be transformed as

$$\hat{Y}_i(t + \bar{\varsigma}_{i,a} + \aleph_y | t - \varsigma_{i,s}(t)) = P_{i,1} x_i(t - \varsigma_{i,s}(t)) + P_{i,3} \Delta\hat{V}_i(t + \tau_{i,a} | t - \varsigma_{i,s}(t)). \tag{6.10}$$

$\forall j \in \mathcal{N}_i$, based on IHOFAS prediction model (6.7), $x_j(t)$ can be predicted as

$$\begin{aligned} \hat{x}_j(t - \varsigma_{j,s}(t) + \eta | t - \varsigma_{j,s}(t)) = & \mathcal{F}_{j,\eta} x_j(t - \varsigma_{j,s}(t)) \\ & + \mathcal{G}_{j,\eta} \Delta\hat{\upsilon}_j(t - \varsigma_{j,s}(t) + \eta - 1 | t - \varsigma_{j,s}(t)), \end{aligned}$$

with $\eta = 1, 2, \ldots, \bar{\varsigma}_{ij}(t) + \aleph_y$. When $\eta = \varsigma_{j,s}(t) + \tau_{i,a} + 1, \varsigma_{j,s}(t) + \tau_{i,a} + 2, \ldots, \bar{\varsigma}_{ij}(t) + \aleph_y$, the multistep ahead predictions of $x_j(t)$ are generated as

$$\begin{aligned}
\hat{x}_j(t + \tau_{i,a} + 1|t - \varsigma_{j,s}(t)) =& \mathcal{F}_{j,\varsigma_{j,s}(t)+\tau_{i,a}+1} x_j(t - \varsigma_{j,s}(t)) \\
&+ \mathcal{G}_{j,\varsigma_{j,s}(t)+\tau_{i,a}+1} \Delta\hat{v}_j(t + \tau_{i,a}|t - \varsigma_{j,s}(t)), \\
&\vdots \\
\hat{x}_j(t + \bar{\varsigma}_{i,a} + \aleph_y|t - \varsigma_{j,s}(t)) =& \mathcal{F}_{j,\bar{\varsigma}_{ij}(t)+\aleph_y} x_j(t - \varsigma_{j,s}(t)) \\
&+ \mathcal{G}_{j,\bar{\varsigma}_{ij}(t)+\aleph_y} \Delta\hat{v}_j(t + \bar{\varsigma}_{i,a} + \aleph_y - 1|t - \varsigma_{j,s}(t)).
\end{aligned}$$

Repeating the process from (6.8)–(6.10), the output prediction of the j-th HOFA agent is obtained as

$$\begin{aligned}
&\hat{Y}_j(t + \bar{\varsigma}_{i,a} + \aleph_y|t - \varsigma_{j,s}(t)) \\
&= P_{j,1} x_j(t - \varsigma_{j,s}(t)) + P_{j,3} \Delta\hat{V}_j(t + \tau_{i,a}|t - \varsigma_{j,s}(t)),
\end{aligned} \tag{6.11}$$

with $\Delta\hat{V}_j(t + \tau_{i,a}|t - \varsigma_{j,s}(t)) = \begin{bmatrix} \Delta\hat{v}_j(t + \tau_{i,a}|t - \varsigma_{j,s}(t)) \\ \vdots \\ \Delta\hat{v}_j(t + \tau_{i,a}|t - \varsigma_{j,s}(t)) \end{bmatrix}$, and

$$P_{j,1} = \left[\mathcal{F}^{\mathrm{T}}_{j,\bar{\varsigma}_{ij}(t)+\aleph_y} C_j^{\mathrm{T}} \cdots \mathcal{F}^{\mathrm{T}}_{j,\bar{\varsigma}_{ij}(t)+\aleph_u} C_j^{\mathrm{T}} \cdots \mathcal{F}^{\mathrm{T}}_{j,\varsigma_{j,s}(t)+\tau_{i,a}+1} C_j^{\mathrm{T}} \right]^{\mathrm{T}},$$

$$P_{j,2} = \begin{bmatrix}
C_j \mathcal{G}_{j,\bar{\varsigma}_{ij}(t)+\aleph_y} & 0 & \cdots & 0 \\
\vdots & \vdots & \cdots & \vdots \\
C_j \mathcal{G}_{j,\bar{\varsigma}_{ij}(t)+\aleph_u+1} & 0 & \cdots & 0 \\
0 & C_j \mathcal{G}_{j,\bar{\varsigma}_{ij}(t)+\aleph_u} & \ddots & \vdots \\
\vdots & \ddots & \ddots & 0 \\
0 & \cdots & 0 & C_j \mathcal{G}_{j,\varsigma_{j,s}(t)+\tau_{i,a}+1}
\end{bmatrix},$$

$$P_{j,3} = P_{j,2} \Gamma_j, \quad \Gamma_j = \mathrm{Blockdiag}\{\gamma_{j,\bar{\rho}_{j,a}+\aleph_u} I, \ldots, \gamma_{j,1} I, I\}.$$

To obtain the optimal secure cooperative control increment $\Delta v_i(t)$, let

$$\frac{\partial}{\partial \Delta\hat{V}_i(t + \tau_{i,a}|t - \varsigma_{i,s}(t))} \mathcal{J}(t) = 0, \ i \in \mathcal{N},$$

and by applying (6.10) and (6.11), it is derived that

$$\begin{aligned}
&\sum_{j\in\mathcal{N}_i} w_{ij}P_{i,3}^{\mathrm{T}}\Big(P_{i,1}x_i(t-\varsigma_{i,s}(t))+P_{i,3}\Delta\hat{V}_i(t+\tau_{i,a}|t-\varsigma_{i,s}(t))\\
&\quad -P_{j,1}x_j(t-\varsigma_{j,s}(t))-P_{j,3}\Delta\hat{V}_j(t+\tau_{i,a}|t-\varsigma_{j,s}(t))\Big)\\
&\quad +\alpha_i P_{i,3}^{\mathrm{T}}\big(P_{i,1}x_i(t-\varsigma_{i,s}(t))+P_{i,3}\Delta\hat{V}_i(t+\tau_{i,a}|t-\varsigma_{i,s}(t))\\
&\quad -R(t+\bar{\varsigma}_{i,a}+\aleph_y)\big)+\beta_i\Gamma_i^{\mathrm{T}}\Gamma_i\Delta\hat{V}_i(t+\tau_{i,a}|t-\varsigma_{i,s}(t))=0,
\end{aligned}$$

which can be concluded as

$$\Delta\hat{V}(t+\tau_{i,a}|t-\varsigma_s(t))=F^{-1}Gx(t-\varsigma_s(t))+F^{-1}MR(t+\bar{\varsigma}_{i,a}+\aleph_y),$$

with $\Delta\hat{V}(t+\tau_{i,a}|t-\varsigma_s(t))=\begin{bmatrix}\Delta\hat{V}_1(t+\tau_{i,a}|t-\varsigma_{1,s}(t))\\ \vdots\\ \Delta\hat{V}_N(t+\tau_{i,a}t-\varsigma_{N,s}(t))\end{bmatrix}$, $x(t-\varsigma_s(t))=\begin{bmatrix}x_1(t-\varsigma_{1,s}(t))\\ \vdots\\ x_N(t-\varsigma_{N,s}(t))\end{bmatrix}$, and

$$\begin{aligned}
F&=\{f_{ij}\},\quad f_{ii}=(w_i+\alpha_i)P_{i,3}^{\mathrm{T}}P_{i,3}+\beta_i\Gamma_i^{\mathrm{T}}\Gamma_i,\quad f_{ij}=-w_{ij}P_{i,3}^{\mathrm{T}}P_{j,3},\\
G&=\{g_{ij}\},\quad g_{ii}=-(w_i+\alpha_i)P_{i,3}^{\mathrm{T}}P_{i,1},\quad g_{ij}=w_{ij}P_{i,3}^{\mathrm{T}}P_{j,1},\\
M&=\big[\alpha_1P_{1,4}\cdots\alpha_NP_{N,4}\big]^{\mathrm{T}},\quad w_i=\sum_{j\in\mathcal{N}_i}w_{ij}.
\end{aligned}$$

Because $\tau_{i,a}$, $\tau_{i,s}$, $\rho_{i,a}(t)$, and $\rho_{i,s}(t)$ are known at time t, F, G, and M are the known coefficient matrices at time t. However, in the whole time domain, $\rho_{i,a}(t)$ and $\rho_{i,s}(t)$ are random, such that F, G, and M are also correspondingly random. On the network node, the i-th secure cooperative control increment sequence $\Delta\hat{V}_{i,\bar{\varsigma}_{i,a}}(t+\varsigma_{i,a}(t))$ in the i-th packet $D_{v_i}(t)$ are designed as $\Delta\hat{v}_i(t+\tau_{i,a}+\eta|t-\varsigma_s(t))=H_{\eta,i}\Delta\hat{V}(t+\tau_{i,a}|t-\varsigma_s(t))$ with $\eta=1,2,\ldots,\bar{\rho}_{i,a}$, i.e.,

$$\begin{aligned}
&\Delta\hat{v}_i(t+\tau_{i,a}+\eta|t-\varsigma_s(t))\\
&\quad=H_{\eta,i}F^{-1}Gx(t-\varsigma_s(t))+H_{\eta,i}F^{-1}MR(t+\bar{\varsigma}_{i,a}+\aleph_y),
\end{aligned}$$

where $H_{\eta,i}=\big[H_{\eta,i,1}\cdots H_{\eta,i,N}\big]\in\mathbb{R}^{n_i\times(\bar{\rho}_{i,a}+\aleph_u+1)\tilde{n}}$ with $\tilde{n}=\sum_{i\in\mathcal{N}}n_i$, $H_{\eta,i,i}=\big[H_{\eta,i,i,\bar{\rho}_{i,a}+\aleph_u+1}\cdots H_{\eta,i,i,1}\big]$, $H_{\eta,i,j}=0$, $j\in\mathcal{N}_i$. For the $H_{\eta,i,i,\iota}$, $\iota=1,2,\ldots,\bar{\rho}_{i,a}+\aleph_u+1$, when $\iota=\eta+1$, $H_{\eta,i,i,\iota}=I$ and the others in the $H_{\eta,i,i}$ are zeros. When $\eta = \rho_{i,a}(t)$, on the i-th actuator, the i-th optimal secure cooperative control increment from the i-th control data buffer is designed as $\Delta v_i(t) = \Delta \hat{v}_i(t|t - \varsigma_i(t))$, i.e.,

$$\Delta v_i(t) = H_{\rho_{i,a}(t),i} F^{-1} G x(t - \varsigma(t)) + H_{\rho_{i,a}(t),i} F^{-1} M R(t + \bar{\varsigma}_{i,a} - \varsigma_{i,a}(t) + \aleph_y), \tag{6.12}$$

with $x(t - \varsigma(t)) = \begin{bmatrix} x_1(t - \varsigma_{i1}(t)) \\ \vdots \\ x_N(t - \varsigma_{iN}(t)) \end{bmatrix}$ and $R(t + \bar{\varsigma}_{i,a} - \varsigma_{i,a}(t) + \aleph_y) = \begin{bmatrix} r(t + \bar{\varsigma}_{i,a} - \varsigma_{i,a}(t) + \aleph_y) \\ \vdots \\ r(t + \bar{\varsigma}_{i,a} - \varsigma_{i,a}(t) + 1) \end{bmatrix}$.

6.4 Analysis of Simultaneous Consensus and Stability Under Random DoS Attacks

Let $e_i(t) = y_i(t) - r(t) = C_i x_i(t) - r(t)$ be the tracking error of the i-th HOFA agent and $\epsilon_{ii}(t) = \epsilon_i(t) = e_i(t)$, $\epsilon_{ij}(t) = y_i(t) - y_j(t)$, $j \in \mathscr{N}_i$, be the consensus error, such that the simultaneous consensus and stability of the closed-loop HOFAMASs (6.3) can be converted into that $\epsilon_i(t) \to 0$ and $\epsilon_{ij}(t) \to 0$ with $t \to \infty$. In this perspective, Theorem 6.1 is proposed to cope with this problem.

Theorem 6.1 *The closed-loop HOFAMASs* (6.3) *can realize the simultaneous consensus and stability if* $\exists w_{ij} \geq 0$, $\sum_{j \in \mathscr{N}_i} w_{ij}^2 \neq 0$, $\exists \alpha_i > 0$, $\exists \beta_i > 0$, $\forall i \in \mathscr{N}$, $\forall j \in \mathscr{N}_i$, *to maintain that* $\forall i \in \mathscr{N}$, $\frac{\partial}{\partial \Delta \hat{V}_i(t + \tau_{i,a}|t - \varsigma_{i,s}(t))} \mathcal{J}(t) = 0$, *and* Φ *is a Schur stable polynomial matrix in relation to* q, *where*

$$\Phi = I + (q - 1) C \Phi_1^{-1} \Phi_2, \tag{6.13}$$

with

$$\Phi_1 = I - (I + \mathcal{K}_M C) q^{-1} - \mathcal{K}_G q^{-\varsigma(t) - 1}, \quad \Phi_2 = -\mathcal{K}_M q^{-1}, \tag{6.14}$$

and

$$\begin{aligned} C =& \text{Blockdiag}\{C_1, \ldots, C_N\}, \\ \mathcal{K}_M =& \text{Blockdiag}\{\mathcal{K}_{1,c} H_{\rho_{1,a}(t),n} F^{-1} M \vec{I}_{\aleph_y}, \ldots, \mathcal{K}_{N,c} H_{\rho_{N,a}(t),N} F^{-1} M \vec{I}_{\aleph_y}\}, \\ \mathcal{K}_G =& \begin{bmatrix} \mathcal{K}_{1,c} H_{\rho_{1,a}(t),1} F^{-1} G \\ \vdots \\ \mathcal{K}_{N,c} H_{\rho_{N,a}(t),N} F^{-1} G \end{bmatrix}, \quad \vec{I}_{\aleph_y} = [\underbrace{I \cdots I}_{\aleph_y}]^{\mathrm{T}}, \quad \mathcal{K}_{i,c} = \mathcal{K}_i^{-1} \mathcal{B}_i. \end{aligned} \tag{6.15}$$

Proof It is generally assumed that $r(\cdot) = r$, such that $\Delta v_i(t)$ in (6.12) can be rewritten as

$$\Delta v_i(t) = H_{\rho_{i,a}(t),i} F^{-1} G x(t - \varsigma(t)) + H_{\rho_{i,a}(t),i} F^{-1} M \vec{I}_{\aleph_y} \left(C_i x_i(t) - e_i(t)\right). \tag{6.16}$$

Meanwhile, by means of the proof of Theorem 3.1, $e(t)$ in this chapter can also be written as (3.17) with $e(t) = \left[e_1^{\mathrm{T}}(t) \cdots e_N^{\mathrm{T}}(t)\right]^{\mathrm{T}}$, $x(t) = \left[x_1^{\mathrm{T}}(t) \cdots x_N^{\mathrm{T}}(t)\right]^{\mathrm{T}}$, i.e.,

$$e(t+1) = e(t) + (q-1) C x(t), \tag{6.17}$$

and the consensus error $\epsilon(t)$ in this chapter can also be summarized as (3.18) with $i = 1$ and $\epsilon(t) = \left[\epsilon_1^{\mathrm{T}}(t) \cdots \epsilon_{1N}^{\mathrm{T}}(t)\right]^{\mathrm{T}}$, i.e.,

$$\epsilon(t) = \tilde{\mathbf{I}} e(t). \tag{6.18}$$

On the basis of (6.6), it is derived that

$$\Delta x_i(t+1) = \mathcal{K}_{i,c} \Delta v_i(t),$$

because $\exists w_{ij} \geq 0$, $\sum_{j \in \mathcal{N}_i} w_{ij}^2 \neq 0$, $\exists \alpha_i > 0$, $\exists \beta_i > 0$, $\forall i \in \mathcal{N}$, $\forall j \in \mathcal{N}_i$, to maintain that $\frac{\partial}{\partial \Delta \hat{V}_i(t+\tau_{i,a}|t-\varsigma_{i,s}(t))} \mathcal{J}(t) = 0$, $\forall i \in \mathcal{N}$, and the optimal secure cooperative control increment $\Delta v_i(t)$ can be calculated in (6.12) and (6.16). By taking (6.16) into the above, it is yielded that

$$\begin{aligned} \Delta x_i(t+1) =& \mathcal{K}_{i,c} H_{\rho_{i,a}(t),i} F^{-1} G x(t - \varsigma(t)) \\ &+ \mathcal{K}_{i,c} H_{\rho_{i,a}(t),i} F^{-1} M \vec{I}_{\aleph_y} \left(C_i x_i(t) - e_i(t)\right), \end{aligned}$$

which can be compactly represented as

$$\Delta x(t+1) = \mathcal{K}_G x(t - \varsigma(t)) + \mathcal{K}_M C x(t) - \mathcal{K}_M e(t),$$

where $\mathcal{K}_G$ and $\mathcal{K}_M$ are provided in (6.15). Then, the above can be equivalently converted into that

$$x(t) = \Phi_1^{-1} \Phi_2 e(t), \tag{6.19}$$

where Φ_1 and Φ_2 are provided in (6.14). Further, taking (6.19) into (6.17) can be obtained that

$$\begin{aligned} e(t+1) =& e(t) + (q-1) C x(t) \\ =& e(t) + (q-1) C \Phi_1^{-1} \Phi_2 e(t) \\ =& \Phi e(t), \end{aligned} \tag{6.20}$$

where Φ is shown in (6.13). Combining with (6.18), an auxiliary system is given as

$$\begin{cases} e(t+1) = \Phi e(t), \\ \epsilon(t) = \tilde{\mathbf{I}} e(t). \end{cases} \tag{6.21}$$

Because $\exists w_{ij} \geq 0$, $\sum_{j \in \mathcal{N}_i} w_{ij}^2 \neq 0$, $\exists \alpha_i > 0$, $\exists \beta_i > 0$, $\forall i \in \mathcal{N}$, $\forall j \in \mathcal{N}_i$, to maintain that Φ is a Schur stable polynomial matrix in relation to q, $e(t) \to 0$ with $t \to \infty$, such that $\epsilon(t) \to 0$ with $t \to \infty$ because of (6.21). Hence, the closed-loop HOFAMASs (6.3) can achieve the simultaneous consensus and stability.

This completes the proof. □

6.5 With Application to Formation Control of Air-Bearing Spacecraft Simulators

A formation control experiment of three ABSSs is provided here to demonstrate the effectiveness and practicality of the proposed PB-HOFAS predictive control, where the dynamic models of three ABSSs are given in (A.4) and the details of three ABSSs and its associated experimental platform are provided in Appendix A.

6.5.1 *Numerical Simulation*

By taking system (A.4a) as an example, a comparison of the proposed PB-HOFAS predictive control and a cloud predictive control (CPC) method in Yang et al. (2021a) is presented to illustrate the effectiveness and superiority, where the relevant design parameters are given as $T_s = 0.2$s, $w_{ii} = 0$, $w_{ij} = 1$, $\alpha_i = 1$, $\beta_i = 200$, $\Gamma_i = I$, $i, j = 1, 2, 3$, $\aleph_y = 5$, $\aleph_u = 3$. The upper communication delays in the forward and feedback channels are set as $\tau_{1,a} = 2$, $\tau_{2,a} = 3$, $\tau_{3,a} = 3$, $\tau_{1,s} = 2$, $\tau_{2,s} = 3$, $\tau_{3,s} = 2$. The parameters of random DoS attacks in the forward and feedback channels are provided as $\nu_1 = 0.05$, $\nu = 0.07$, $\nu_3 = 0.09$, $\mu_1 = 0.04$, $\mu_2 = 0.06$, $\mu_3 = 0.08$, and then the active times of random DoS attacks in the forward and feedback channels are shown in Fig. 6.2. When $\delta_{i,a}(t) = 1$ and $\delta_{i,s}(t) = 1$, random data dropouts and disorders caused by random DoS attacks in the forward and feedback channels are given in Fig. 6.3, where $\rho_{1,a}(t) \in [3, 4]$, $\rho_{2,a}(t) \in [2, 6]$, $\rho_{3,a}(t) \in [3, 5]$, $\rho_{1,s}(t) \in [4, 6]$, $\rho_{2,s}(t) \in [3, 4]$, $\rho_{3,s}(t) \in [2, 5]$.

Based on (6.2), a PB-HOFAS predictive control for system (A.4a) is constructed as

$$F_{I,x_{i,\mathrm{ABSS}}}(t) = B_i^{-1}\left(-L_i(A_{i,0\sim 1}, x_{i,\mathrm{ABSS}}(t) + \Upsilon_i(K_{i,0\sim 1}, x_{i,\mathrm{ABSS}}(t)) + v_i(t)\right), \tag{6.22}$$

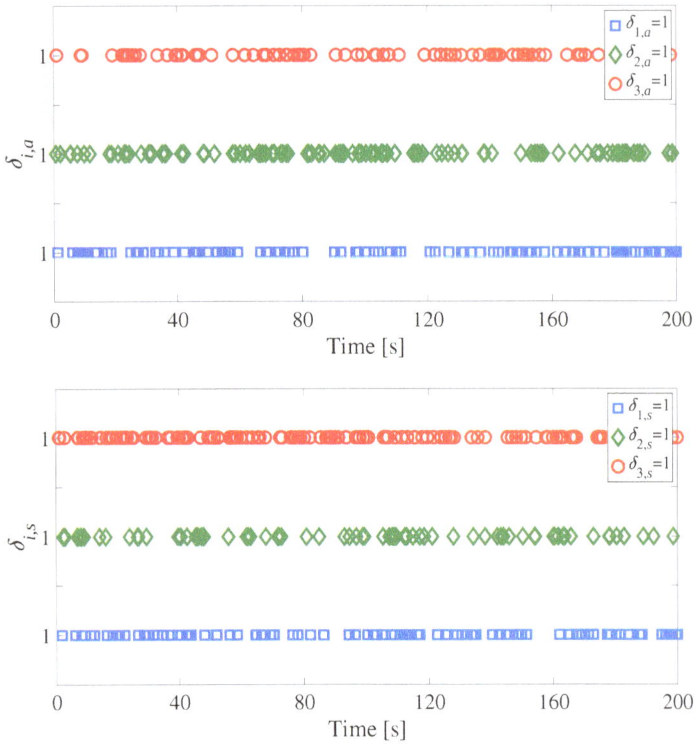

Fig. 6.2 The active times of random DoS attacks in the forward and feedback channels

where $K_{1,0} = -0.3802$, $K_{1,1} = 19.4$, $K_{2,0} = -0.3822$, $K_{2,1} = 19.5$, $K_{3,0} = -0.3763$, $K_{3,1} = 19.2$. For the CPC method in Yang et al. (2021a), system (A.4a) should be firstly transformed as (3.23). Then, denote $e_{i,rx}(t) = x_{i,\mathrm{ABSS}}(t) - r_x(t)$ and $X_{e,i}(t) = \left[\Delta X_{i,\mathrm{ABSS}}^{\mathrm{T}}(t)\ e_{i,rx}^{\mathrm{T}}(t) \right]^{\mathrm{T}}$, where $r_x(t)$ is the known desired reference signal, such that system (3.23) can be further transformed as

$$X_{e,i}(t+1) = A_{xe,i} X_{e,i}(t) + B_{xe,i} \Delta F_{I,x_{i,\mathrm{ABSS}}}(t) - E_e \Delta r_x(t+1), \tag{6.23}$$

with $A_{xe,i} = \begin{bmatrix} A_{i,\mathrm{ABSS}} & 0 \\ \begin{bmatrix} 1 & 0 \end{bmatrix} A_{i,\mathrm{ABSS}} & 1 \end{bmatrix}$, $B_{xe,i} = \begin{bmatrix} B_{i,\mathrm{ABSS}} \\ \begin{bmatrix} 1 & 0 \end{bmatrix} B_{i,\mathrm{ABSS}} \end{bmatrix}$, $E_e = \begin{bmatrix} 0 \\ 1 \end{bmatrix}$, which implies that the cooperative tracking control problem of system (3.23) can be equivalent to a cooperative stabilization one of system (6.23). It is generally assumed that $\Delta r_x(t+1) = 0$, and $\Delta F_{I,x_{i,\mathrm{ABSS}}}(t)$ can be proposed as

$$\Delta F_{I,x_{i,\mathrm{ABSS}}}(t) = K_i \sum_{j \in \mathcal{N}} w_{ij} \left(\hat{X}_{e,j}(t|t - \varsigma_{ij}(t)) - \hat{X}_{e,i}(t|t - \varsigma_i(t)) \right),$$

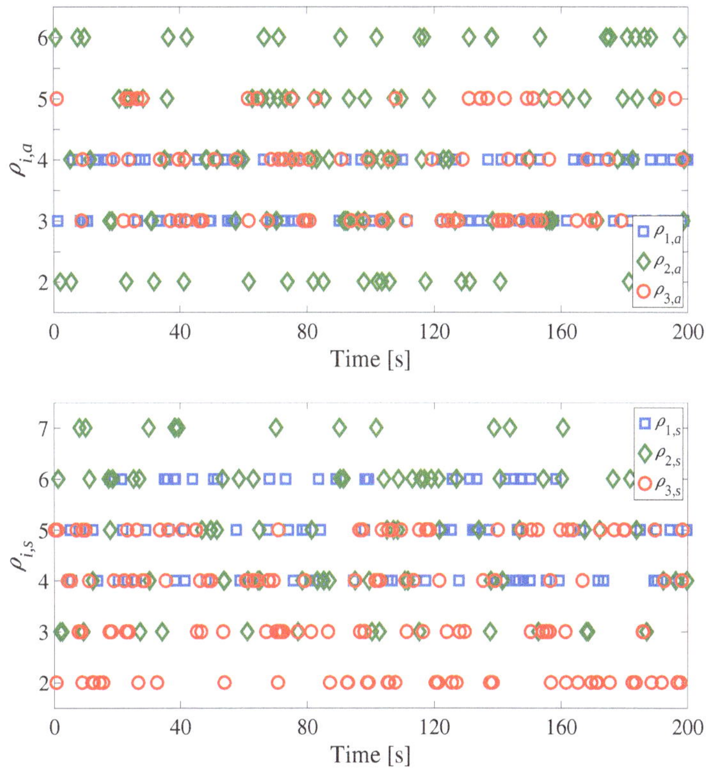

Fig. 6.3 The random data losses and disorders in the forward and feedback channels

where K_i, $i = 1, 2, 3$, denote the feedback gain to be determined for ensuring the stabilization of system $X_e(t+1) = A_{ex,c} X_e(t)$ with $X_e(t) = \left[X_{e,1}^{\mathrm{T}}(t)\ X_{e,2}^{\mathrm{T}}(t)\ X_{e,3}^{\mathrm{T}}(t) \right]^{\mathrm{T}}$, and

$$
\begin{aligned}
&A_{xe,c} \\
&= \begin{bmatrix}
A_{xe,1} - \sum\limits_{j \in \mathscr{N}_1} w_{1j} B_{xe,1} K_1 & w_{12} B_{xe,1} K_1 & w_{13} B_{xe,1} K_1 \\
w_{21} B_{xe,2} K_2 & A_{xe,2} - \sum\limits_{j \in \mathscr{N}_2} w_{2j} B_{xe,1} K_2 & w_{23} B_{xe,2} K_2 \\
w_{31} B_{xe,3} K_3 & w_{32} B_{xe,3} K_3 & A_{xe,3} - \sum\limits_{j \in \mathscr{N}_3} w_{3j} B_{xe,3} K_3
\end{bmatrix}.
\end{aligned}
$$

Then, the simulated comparison is plotted in Fig. 6.4.

Figure 6.4a means that the proposed PB-HOFAS predictive control (6.22) can actively compensate for random data dropouts and disorders caused by random DoS attacks in the forward and feedback channels, such that the desired secure cooperative tracking control during the dynamic and steady processes can be

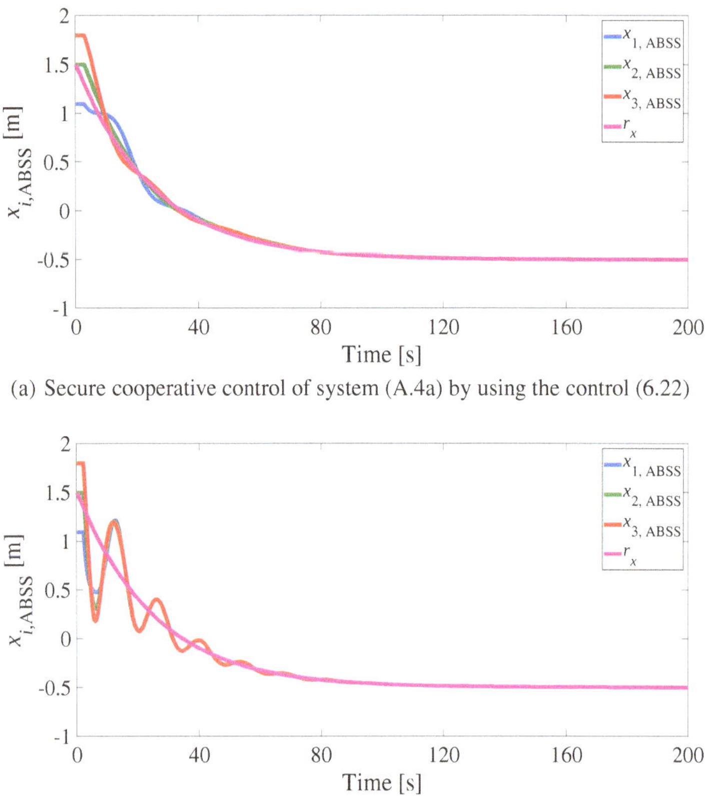

(a) Secure cooperative control of system (A.4a) by using the control (6.22)

(b) Secure cooperative control of system (A.4a) via the CPC method

Fig. 6.4 Comparison between the PB-HOFAS predictive control and the CPC in Yang et al. (2021a)

implemented. However, Fig. 6.4b shows that the CPC method in Yang et al. (2021a) can only achieve the secure cooperative tracking control of steady process, and it cannot realize the same performance as that in Fig. 6.4a during the dynamic process. The reason is that the PB-HOFAS predictive control adopts the rolling-horizon optimization to improve the dynamic control performance.

Based on the numerical comparison in Fig. 6.4, the effectiveness and superiority of the proposed PB-HOFAS predictive control can be fully demonstrated, which gives a solid basis for the experimental verification.

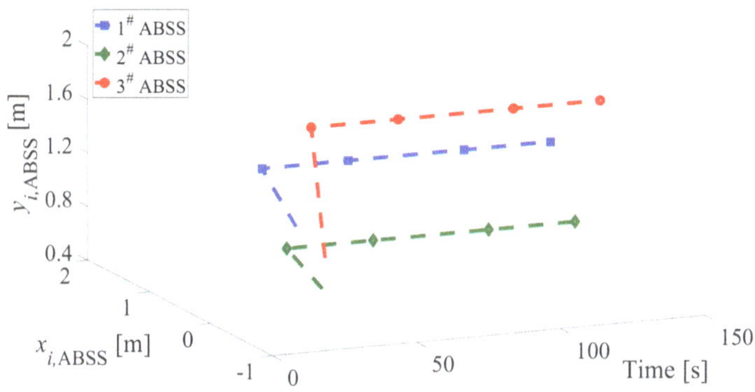

Fig. 6.5 The desired formation of three ABSSs

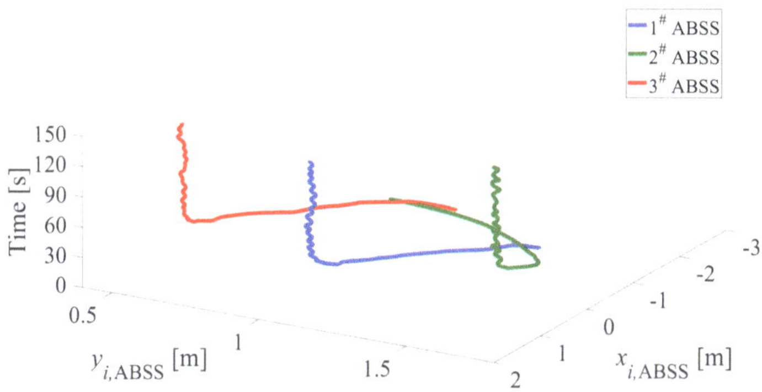

Fig. 6.6 The actual formation of three ABSSs

6.5.2 Experimental Results

On the basis of the above simulation, a formation control experiment for three ABSSs is provided here to verify the practicality of the proposed PB-HOFAS predictive control, where the desired formation is shown in Fig. 6.5.

For systems (A.4a) and (A.4b), the cooperative control protocols are chosen as the same as (6.22) with the same design parameters. For system (A.4c), only a stabilization control is needed to satisfy the requirement of $\psi_{i,\mathrm{ABSS}}(t)$ during the formation control. Hence, the cooperative control items are set as 0, and a stabilization control is designed in (3.24) with the same design parameters. By applying (6.22) and (3.24), the experimental results are provided in Figs. 6.6, 6.7, 6.8.

Figure 6.7 provides the position and angle responses of formation control for three ABSSs, which means that the position responses $x_{i,\mathrm{ABSS}}(t)$ and $y_{i,\mathrm{ABSS}}(t)$ can implement the secure cooperative control under random DoS attacks by utilizing the proposed PB-HOFAS predictive control (6.22), and they can reach the desired

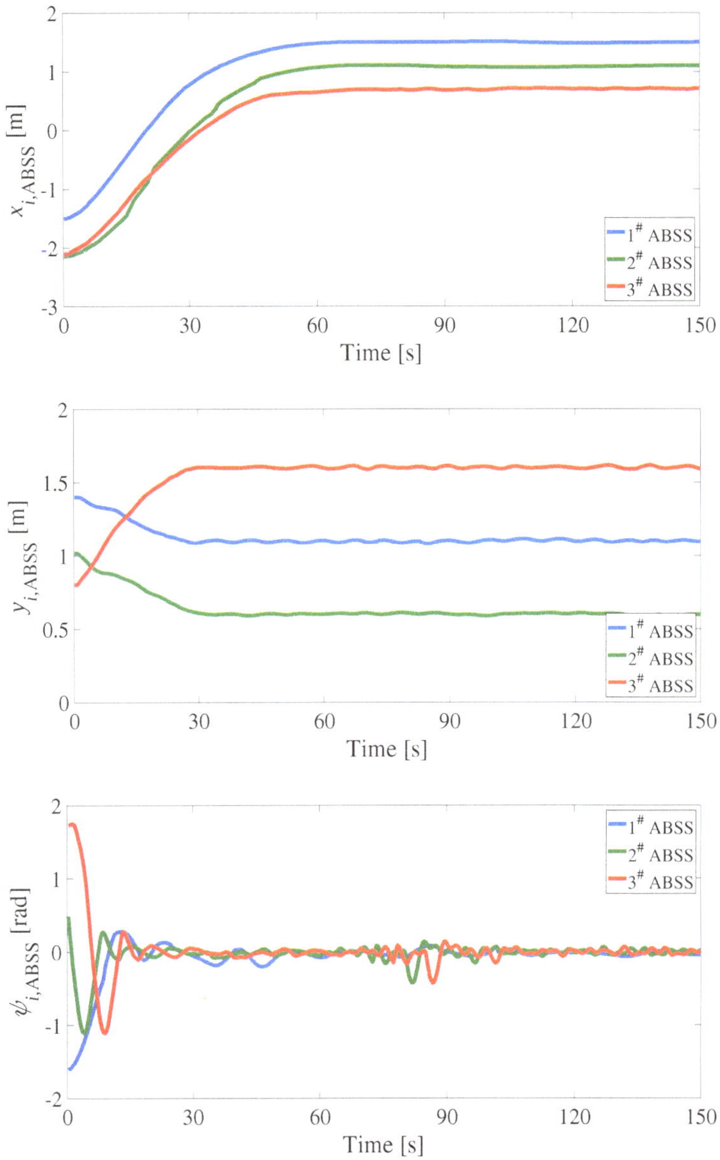

Fig. 6.7 The formation control of three ABSSs by using the controls (6.22) and (3.24)

positions cooperatively. The angle responses $\psi_{i,\mathrm{ABSS}}(t)$ can realize the stabilization by applying (3.24), but a shortcoming is that there exists the vibration during the steady process. The reason is that both the reaction forces of the thrusters and the airflow in the experimental site affect the stabilization control performance of $\psi_{i,\mathrm{ABSS}}(t)$. The control inputs generated by (6.22) and (3.24) are plotted in Fig. 6.8,

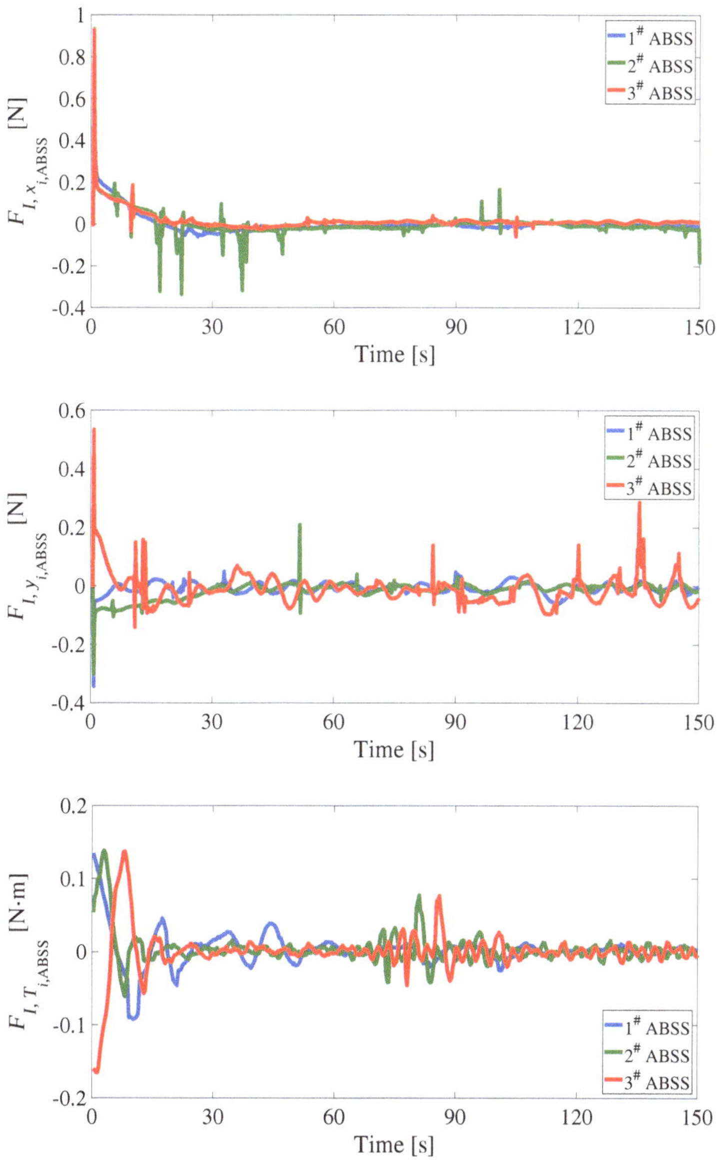

Fig. 6.8 The control inputs generated by the controls (6.22) and (3.24)

where there are some vibrations because of the model uncertainties and external disturbances. Figure 6.6 gives the practical formation of formation control for three ABSSs, which implies that the proposed OB-HOFAS predictive control (6.22) can realize the expected formation control task and continue to remain it by comparing with the desired formation in Fig. 6.5.

According to the results in Figs. 6.6, 6.7, 6.8, the effectiveness and practicality of the PB-HOFAS predictive control can be fully verified, which provides a solid basis for the large-scale applications of practical spacecraft control.

6.6 Notes and References

In this chapter, a secure cooperative control problem of the HOFASMASs under random DoS attacks has been investigated, where random data dropouts and disorders are caused by random DoS attacks in the forward and feedback channels. A PB-HOFAS predictive control has been constructed to cope with this problem, such that random data dropouts and disorders can be actively compensated and the secure cooperative control performance can be optimized. A sufficient condition on the simultaneous consensus and stability of the closed-loop HOFAMASs has been developed in the following analysis. A highlight is that a packet-based compensation scheme is presented to address random DoS attacks, and the other is that an IHOFAS prediction model is established via a type of Diophantine Equation. Because of the better control performance, the proposed PB-HOFAS predictive control can be applied to practical applications in various fields.

Chapter 7
Sliding-Mode Predictive Cooperative Control for HOFAMASs Under Random Deception Attacks

7.1 Introduction

During the research on secure cooperative control for the MASs under cyberattacks, the deception attack is also regarded as one of the most general study hotspots, which can utilize the vulnerabilities of data detection systems to maliciously tamper with the output and input data, such that the consensus, security, and reliability can be seriously affected or even destroyed. To achieve the secure cooperative control under deception attacks, a lot of scholars have provided a string of representative achievements to consider this problem in the previous studies.

For instance, Liu et al. (2021) presented a definition of the quasi-consensus to address the secure consensus control of the MASs under stochastic deception attacks, where a sufficient condition was established by utilizing a recursive LMI approach and a stochastic analysis method to ensure that the consensus errors can converge to a desired interval. Cui et al. (2021) utilized the eigenvectors of Laplacian matrix to design a new Lyapunov function for constructing a decoupled condition, such that the mean-square consensus under deception attacks in each sampling period can be ensured. Based on a pining scheme, He et al. (2020) proposed a novel distributed impulsive controller to realize the mean-square synchronization of the MASs with random deception attacks, which derived a sufficient condition to guarantee the convergence of the synchronization errors. Li et al. (2020) also adopted a recursive LMI method to calculate the control gains for implementing the H_∞ consensus under random false data injection attack and parameter uncertainties, where an event-triggering scheme was proposed to save the communication resources. Zhong et al. (2022) provided an aperiodic switched control to enhance the anti-attack ability and reduce the actions of the actuators when existing the abnormal deception attacks, such that a Lyapunov-Krasovskii functional with low conservatism was constructed to achieve the secure consensus of the MASs. Zhao and Yang (2020) developed a distributed adaptive fault-tolerant control to consider the deception attacks in physical layer, which realized the synchronization of the

D.-W. Zhang, G.-P. Liu, *Predictive Cooperative Control for High-Order Fully Actuated Multiagent Systems*, https://doi.org/10.1007/978-981-95-1695-7_7

MASs under deception attacks and actuator failures. Zhang et al. (2021) constructed a distributed edge-based event-triggering mechanism to cope with the deception attacks, which realize the formation control of nonlinear MASs. Fu et al. (2021) adopted a particle swarm optimization algorithm to design a resilient cooperative control protocol for addressing a kind of d-local deception attacks occurred in the double-integrator multi-robots. Wen et al. (2020) established a distributed impulsive control to achieve the mean-square consensus of the MASs under random deception attacks modeled by a Bernoulli process and yielded an analytical relation among the deception attacks, the actuator failures, and the bounds of mean-square consensus errors. Li et al. (2023c) proposed a model-free adaptive control to investigate the consensus of the MASs with the deception attacks, where a consensus control protocol based on a dynamical linearized model with the deception attacks was designed by applying the input and output data and its boundedness of all distributed outputs can be proved by using the contraction mapping principle. Meanwhile, Liu et al. (2023d), Zhang et al. (2023a), Ahmed et al. (2023), and the references therein also had contributions to the study on the secure cooperative control of the MASs under the deception attacks.

Summarizing the above means that secure cooperative control for the MASs under deception attacks can ensure the safe and stable operation of control systems, which provides a reliable support for practical applications, including the unmanned vehicles (Han et al. 2024), DC microgrids (Abianeh et al. 2022), and robot manipulators (Jahangiri-Heidari et al. 2025). Meanwhile, by introducing the HOFAS theory into the secure cooperative control, the complexity and its related computational load can be effectively reduced during the design process, which can obviously improve the secure cooperative control performance.

To further consider the secure cooperative control for the HOFAMASs under random deception attacks, this chapter proposes an SM-HOFAS predictive control to address this problem, where a linear sliding-mode variable is adopted to enhance the defense performance by improving the robustness and an IHOFAS prediction model of linear sliding-mode variable is constructed by means of a type of Diophantine Equation. The main works are concluded as follows. Firstly, a discrete-time model of the i-th HOFA agent is utilized to provide a better model foundation for the cooperative control design. Then, a linear sliding-mode variable is introduced to defend random deception attacks by enhancing the robustness, and an IHOFAS prediction model of linear sliding-mode variable is established by utilizing a kind of Diophantine Equation, such that the multistep ahead predictions of linear sliding-mode variable can be obtained to develop an optimal sliding-mode predictive controller for the secure cooperative control. Further, a sufficient condition on the simultaneous consensus and stability of the closed-loop HOFAMASs is derived by means of the Lyapunov stability theory and an LMI method. Finally, the proposed SM-HOFAS predictive control provides a solution to the formation control of three ABSSs for demonstrating the feasibility and availability.

7.2 Problem Statement

In this chapter, the communication topology is described by Definition 3.1, and the dynamic model of the i-th HOFA agent satisfying Assumptions 3.1 and 3.2 is given in (3.1). Let $\varsigma_{i,a}$ and $\varsigma_{i,s}$ be the upper bounds of time-varying communication constraints in the i-th forward and feedback channels, respectively, where $\varsigma_{i,a}$ and $\varsigma_{i,s}$ satisfy Assumption 4.1, and $\varsigma_{ii} = \varsigma_i = \varsigma_{i,a} + \varsigma_{i,s}$, $\varsigma_{ij} = \varsigma_{i,a} + \varsigma_{j,s}$.

This chapter further investigates a secure cooperative control problem of HOFAMASs under random deception attacks, where random variables $\delta_{i,a}(t)$ and $\delta_{i,s}(t)$ are also adopted to indicate whether the deception attacks in the i-th forward and feedback channels are successful or not. Concretely, $\delta_{i,a}(t) = 1$ and $\delta_{i,s}(t) = 1$ denote that the deception attacks are successful in the i-th the forward and feedback channels, respectively, and $\delta_{i,a}(t) = 0$ and $\delta_{i,s}(t) = 0$ denote that the deception attacks are failed in the i-th the forward and feedback channels, respectively. Meanwhile, $\delta_{i,a}(t)$ and $\delta_{i,s}(t)$ are also described by a Bernoulli process in (6.1), i.e.,

$$\text{Prob}\{\delta_{i,a}(t) = 1\} = \nu_i, \quad \text{Prob}\{\delta_{i,a}(t) = 0\} = 1 - \nu_i,$$

$$\text{Prob}\{\delta_{i,s}(t) = 1\} = \mu_i, \quad \text{Prob}\{\delta_{i,s}(t) = 0\} = 1 - \mu_i,$$

where $\nu_i \in [0, 1]$ and $\mu_i \in [0, 1]$ are two known constants to represent the successful rates of the initial random deception attacks in the i-th forward and feedback channels, respectively.

When $\delta_{i,a}(t) = 1$ and $\delta_{i,s}(t) = 1$, the false data $\zeta_{i,a}(t)$ and $\zeta_{i,s}(t)$ can be injected into the i-th forward and feedback channels to tamper the control and output signals, respectively, i.e.,

$$y_{i,c}(t) = y_i(t) + \delta_{i,s}(t)\zeta_{i,s}(t), \tag{7.1a}$$

$$u_i(t) = u_{i,c}(t) + \delta_{i,a}(t)\zeta_{i,a}(t), \tag{7.1b}$$

where $y_i(t)$ and $u_i(t)$ denote the actual signals of the output and input sent by the i-th sensor and received by the i-th actuator, respectively, and $y_{i,c}(t)$ and $u_{i,c}(t)$ are the signals of output and input received and generated by the i-th networked secure cooperative controller.

Assumption 7.1 (Chattopadhyay and Mitra 2020) $\zeta_{i,a}(t)$ *and* $\zeta_{i,s}(t)$ *are bounded in relation to time* t.

To investigate the secure cooperative control for the i-th HOFA agent (3.1) under random deception attacks, an SM-HOFAS predictive control is proposed as

$$u_i(t) = B_i^{-1}\left(L_i(\cdot) + \Upsilon_i(K_{i,0\sim n-1}, x_i(t)) + v_i(t)\right), \tag{7.2}$$

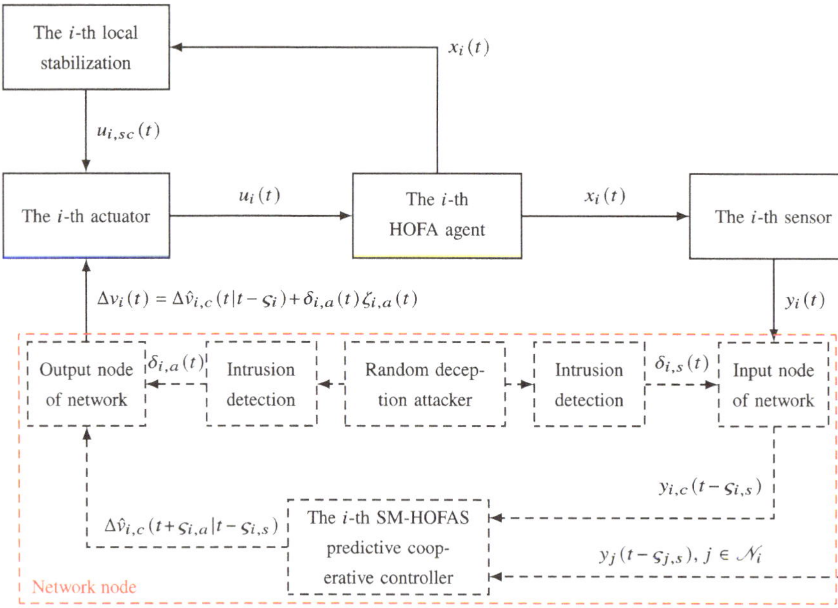

Fig. 7.1 Sliding-mode predictive cooperative control for the HOFAMASs under random deception attacks

where $L_i(\cdot)$ is exploited to eliminate the open-loop dynamics, $\Upsilon_i(K_{i,0\sim n-1}, x_i(t)) = \sum_{\eta=0}^{n-1} K_{i,\eta}x_i(t+\eta) \in \mathbb{R}^{n_i}$ is used to adjust the closed-loop performances and $K_{i,\eta} \in \mathbb{R}^{n_i\times n_i}$ denote the feedback gains to be determined, and $v_i(t) \in \mathbb{R}^{n_i}$ is a secure cooperative control item designed by SM-HOFAS predictive control. The related control structure is shown in Fig. 7.1. Combining (7.2) with Fig. 7.1, the control signal tampered with the false data in (7.1b) is redefined as

$$\begin{aligned}\Delta v_i(t) =&\Delta v_{i,c}(t) + \delta_{i,a}(t)\zeta_{i,a}(t),\\ v_{i,c}(t) =&\Delta v_{i,c}(t) + v_i(t-1),\\ v_i(t) =&v_{i,c}(t) + \delta_{i,a}(t)\zeta_{i,a}(t),\end{aligned} \tag{7.3}$$

where $v_i(t)$ and $\Delta v_i(t)$ denote the secure cooperative control item and its relevant increment received by the i-th actuator, and $v_{i,c}(t)$ and $\Delta v_{i,c}(t)$ denote the secure cooperative control item and its relevant increment generated by the i-th SM-HOFAS predictive cooperative controller. By taking (7.2), (7.1a), and (7.3) into (3.1), the closed-loop HOFAMAS can be achieved as

$$
\begin{aligned}
x_i(t+n) =& \Upsilon_i(K_{i,0\sim n-1}, x_i(t)) + v_{i,c}(t) + \delta_{i,a}(t)\zeta_{i,a}(t) \\
=& \sum_{\eta=0}^{n-1} K_{i,\eta} x_i(t+\eta) + v_{i,c}(t) + \delta_{i,a}(t)\zeta_{i,a}(t), \\
y_{i,c}(t) =& y_i(t) + \delta_{i,s}(t)\zeta_{i,s}(t), \\
y_i(t) =& C_i x_i(t), \quad i \in \mathcal{N}.
\end{aligned}
\tag{7.4}
$$

To compute the secure cooperative control item $v_i(t)$, an objective function $\mathcal{J}(t)$ is presented as

$$
\mathcal{J}(t) = \sum_{i \in \mathcal{N}} \mathcal{J}_i(t), \tag{7.5}
$$

where $\mathcal{J}_i(t)$ is a sub-objective function on the secure cooperative control performance of the i-th HOFA agent and is designed as

$$
\begin{aligned}
\mathcal{J}_i(t) =& \sum_{j \in \mathcal{N}_i} w_{ij} \left\| \hat{S}_i(t+\varsigma_{i,a}+\aleph_y|t-\varsigma_{i,s}) - \hat{S}_j(t+\varsigma_{i,a}+\aleph_y|t-\varsigma_{j,s}) \right\|^2 \\
&+ \alpha_i \left\| \hat{S}_i(t+\varsigma_{i,a}+\aleph_y|t-\varsigma_{i,s}) - S_{i,\mathrm{ref}}(t+\varsigma_{i,a}+\aleph_y) \right\|^2 \\
&+ \beta_i \left\| \Delta\hat{V}_{i,c}(t+\varsigma_{i,a}+\aleph_u|t-\varsigma_{i,s}) \right\|^2,
\end{aligned}
\tag{7.6}
$$

with

$$
\hat{S}_i(t+\varsigma_{i,a}+\aleph_y|t-\varsigma_{i,s}) = \begin{bmatrix} \hat{s}_i(t+\varsigma_{i,a}+\aleph_y|t-\varsigma_{i,s}) \\ \vdots \\ \hat{s}_i(t+\varsigma_{i,a}+1|t-\varsigma_{i,s}) \end{bmatrix},
$$

$$
\hat{S}_j(t+\varsigma_{i,a}+\aleph_y|t-\varsigma_{j,s}) = \begin{bmatrix} \hat{s}_j(t+\varsigma_{i,a}+\aleph_y|t-\varsigma_{j,s}) \\ \vdots \\ \hat{s}_j(t+\varsigma_{i,a}+1|t-\varsigma_{j,s}) \end{bmatrix},
$$

$$
\Delta\hat{V}_{i,c}(t+\varsigma_{i,a}+\aleph_u|t-\varsigma_{i,s}) = \begin{bmatrix} \Delta\hat{v}_{i,c}(t+\varsigma_{i,a}+\aleph_u|t-\varsigma_{i,s}) \\ \vdots \\ \Delta\hat{v}_{i,c}(t+\varsigma_{i,a}|t-\varsigma_{i,s}) \end{bmatrix},
$$

$$
S_{i,\mathrm{ref}}(t+\varsigma_{i,a}+\aleph_y) = \begin{bmatrix} s_{i,\mathrm{ref}}(t+\varsigma_{i,a}+\aleph_y) \\ \vdots \\ s_{i,\mathrm{ref}}(t+\varsigma_{i,a}+1) \end{bmatrix},
$$

where $s_i(t)$ is a linear sliding-mode variable of the i-th HOFA agent (3.1) and $s_{i,\text{ref}}(t)$ is a reference sliding-mode variable. Then, $\hat{s}_i(t+\eta|t-\varsigma_{i,s})$, $\eta = \varsigma_{i,a}+1, \varsigma_{i,a}+2, \ldots, \varsigma_{i,a}+\aleph_y$, and $\Delta\hat{v}_{i,c}(t+\eta|t-\varsigma_{i,s})$, $\eta = \eta = \varsigma_{i,a}, \varsigma_{i,a}+1, \ldots, \varsigma_{i,a}+\aleph_u$, denote the η-th ahead predictions of linear sliding-mode variable $s(t)$ and cooperative control increment $\Delta v_{i,c}(t)$ based on $t-\varsigma_{i,s}$ time. $S_{i,\text{ref}}(t+\varsigma_{i,a}+\aleph_y)$ indicates the relevant multistep ahead sequence of $s_{i,\text{ref}}(t)$. w_{ij} is the (i,j)-th element of adjacent matrix $\mathscr{W}$, and $\alpha_i > 0$ and $\beta_i > 0$ are two weighting factors.

Remark 7.1 In (7.6), the first item of $\mathcal{J}_i(t)$ is concerned with the secure cooperative control performance by realizing the approaching of sliding-mode predictions $\hat{S}_i(t+\varsigma_{i,a}+\aleph_y|t-\varsigma_{i,s})$ and $\hat{S}_j(t+\varsigma_{i,a}+\aleph_y|t-\varsigma_{j,s})$ $\forall i \in \mathcal{N}, \forall j \in \mathcal{N}_i$, the second item is to maintain the tracking control performance by considering the differences of $\hat{S}_i(t+\varsigma_{i,a}+\aleph_y|t-\varsigma_{i,s})$ and $S_{i,\text{ref}}(t+\varsigma_{i,a}+\aleph_y)$, and the third item imposes a constraint on changing the rate and amplitude of $\Delta v_i(t)$ in the view of algorithm design, which ensures the cooperative controller's physical feasibility and reduces the mechanical losses, as well as prolongs the servicing life.

Problem 7.1 For the i-th HOFA agent (3.1) under Assumptions 3.1, 3.2, 4.1, and 7.1, an SM-HOFAS predictive control $u_i\left(t, v_i(t, y_i(t), y_j(t), r(t))\right)$ is developed in (7.2) by minimizing the objective function $\mathcal{J}(t)$ in (7.5) and (7.6), such that the closed-loop HOFAMASs (7.4) can achieve the simultaneous consensus and stability, i.e., the following conditions hold:

1. $\forall i \in \mathcal{N}, \forall t \geq 0, \lim\limits_{t\to\infty} \|y_i(t)\| < \infty$ with $\|r(t)\| < \infty$.
2. $\forall i \in \mathcal{N}, \forall j \in \mathcal{N}_i, \lim_{t\to\infty}\|y_i(t) - y_j(t)\| = 0$.

7.3 HOFAS Sliding-Mode Predictive Cooperative Control Scheme

7.3.1 *Design of Linear Sliding-Mode Variable*

From the closed-loop system (7.4), the successful launch of random deception attacks in (7.1) and (7.3) can be equivalent to that two disturbances are introduced into the forward and feedback channels. As we know, sliding-mode control is regarded as an effective method to cope with the uncertainties and external disturbances, such that it is naturally utilized to achieve the defense of random deception attacks (see Cao et al. 2023d; Qi et al. 2022; Xing et al. 2023, and their related studies).

Following this idea, a linear sliding-mode variable is designed to cope with random deception attacks in (7.1) and (7.3) for the secure cooperative control. Firstly, let $e_i(t) = y_i(t) - r(t)$ be the tracking error of the i-th HOFA agent, which means that Conditions 1 and 2 of Problem 7.1 can be transformed into

$\lim_{t\to\infty}\|e_i(t)\| = 0$. Then, a linear sliding-mode variable $s_i(t) \in \mathbb{R}^m$ is proposed as

$$s_i(t) = \Xi_i(q^{-1})e_i(t), \tag{7.7}$$

where $\Xi_i(q^{-1}) = \sum_{\eta=0}^{n_{i,\xi}} \xi_{i,\eta}q^{-\eta}$ is chosen as a Schur polynomial matrix, $\xi_{i,\eta} \in \mathbb{R}^{m\times m}$, $\eta = 0, 1, \ldots, n_{i,\xi}$, denote the corresponding coefficient matrices, and $n_{i,\xi}$ is a given positive integer. Based on (7.7), $s_i(0) = 0$ with $t = 0$.

$\forall t$, $s_i(t) = 0$ can be derived as

$$\begin{aligned} s_i(t) =&\Xi_i(q^{-1})e_i(t) = \sum_{\eta=0}^{n_{i,\xi}} \xi_{i,\eta}q^{-\eta}e_i(t) \\ =&\xi_{i,0}e_i(t) + \xi_{i,1}e_i(t-1) + \cdots + \xi_{i,n_{i,\xi}}e_i(t-n_{i,\xi}) = 0. \end{aligned}$$

When $\xi_{i,\eta}$, $\eta = 0, 1, \ldots, n_{i,\xi}$, are not all zeros, $\Xi_i(q^{-1})$ is a nonzero Schur polynomial matrix in relation to q^{-1}, such that $s_i(t) = 0 \Longrightarrow e_i(t) = 0$ with $t \to \infty$, i.e., $s(t) = 0 \Longrightarrow e(t) = 0$ with $t \to \infty$, where $e(t) = \left[e_1^{\mathrm{T}}(t) \cdots e_N^{\mathrm{T}}(t)\right]^{\mathrm{T}}$ and $s(t) = \left[s_1^{\mathrm{T}}(t) \cdots s_N^{\mathrm{T}}(t)\right]^{\mathrm{T}}$.

7.3.2 Design of SM-HOFAS Predictive Cooperative Control

Based on the closed-loop system (7.4), its nominal expression without random deception attacks is provided as

$$\begin{aligned} x_i(t+n) =&\sum_{\eta=0}^{n-1} K_{i,\eta}x_i(t+\eta) + v_{i,c}(t), \\ y_{i,c}(t) =&y_i(t) = C_ix_i(t). \end{aligned} \tag{7.8}$$

By means of the time operator q, system (7.8) can be equivalently converted as a polynomial one, i.e.,

$$\mathcal{K}_i\left(q^{-1}\right)x_i(t) = \mathcal{B}_i\left(q^{-1}\right)v_{i,c}(t-1), \tag{7.9}$$

where $\mathcal{K}_i\left(q^{-1}\right) = I - \sum_{\eta=0}^{n-1} K_{i,\eta}q^{\eta-n}$ and $\mathcal{B}_i\left(q^{-1}\right) = q^{1-n}$. Based on Diophantine Equation (3.7) with the same process from (3.6) to (3.8), an IHOFAS prediction model based on (7.9) can be developed as (3.8), i.e.,

$$x_i(t+\eta) = \mathcal{F}_{i,\eta}x_i(t) + \mathcal{G}_{i,\eta}\Delta v_i(t+\eta-1),$$

where $\mathcal{F}_{i,\eta}$ and $\mathcal{G}_{i,\eta}$ are constructed in (3.8). Considering the upper bounds of time-varying communication constraints $\varsigma_{i,a}$ and $\varsigma_{i,s}$ in the i-th forward and feedback channels, the above IHOFAS prediction model can be corrected as

$$\hat{x}_i(t-\varsigma_{i,s}+\eta|t-\varsigma_{i,s}) = \mathcal{F}_{i,\eta}x_i(t-\varsigma_{i,s}) + \mathcal{G}_{i,\eta}\Delta\hat{\upsilon}_{i,c}(t-\varsigma_{i,s}+\eta-1|t-\varsigma_{i,s}), \tag{7.10}$$

with $\eta = 1, 2, \ldots, \varsigma_i + \aleph_y$, and the relevant output prediction is generated as

$$\hat{y}_i(t-\varsigma_{i,s}+\eta|t-\varsigma_{i,s}) = C_i\hat{x}_i(t-\varsigma_{i,s}+\eta|t-\varsigma_{i,s}). \tag{7.11}$$

Combining (7.7) with (7.10) and (7.11), an IHOFAS prediction model of linear sliding-mode variable is constructed as

$$\begin{aligned}\hat{s}_i(t-\varsigma_{i,s}+\eta|t-\varsigma_{i,s}) =& \mathcal{D}_{i,\eta}x_i(t-\varsigma_{i,s}) + \mathcal{L}_{i,\eta}\Delta\hat{\upsilon}_{i,c}(t-\varsigma_{i,s}+\eta-1|t-\varsigma_{i,s}) \\ &- \Xi_i r(t-\varsigma_{i,s}+\eta),\end{aligned} \tag{7.12}$$

with $\mathcal{D}_{i,\eta}(q^{-1}) = \Xi_i(q^{-1})C_i\mathcal{F}_{i,\eta}(q^{-1})$ and $\mathcal{L}_{i,\eta}(q^{-1}) = \Xi_i(q^{-1})C_i\mathcal{G}_{i,\eta}(q^{-1})$.

For $\eta = \varsigma_i + 1, \varsigma_i + 2, \ldots, \varsigma_i + \aleph_y$, the multistep ahead predictions of $s_i(t)$ by using (7.12) are provided as

$$\begin{aligned}\hat{s}_i(t+\varsigma_{i,a}+1|t-\varsigma_{i,s}) =& \mathcal{D}_{i,\varsigma_i+1}x_i(t-\varsigma_{i,s}) - \Xi_i r(t+\varsigma_{i,a}+1) \\ &+ \mathcal{L}_{i,\varsigma_i+1}\Delta\hat{\upsilon}_{i,c}(t+\varsigma_{i,a}|t-\varsigma_{i,s}), \\ &\vdots \\ \hat{s}_i(t+\varsigma_{i,a}+\aleph_y|t-\varsigma_{i,s}) =& \mathcal{D}_{i,\varsigma_i+\aleph_y}x_i(t-\varsigma_{i,s}) - \Xi_i r(t+\varsigma_{i,a}+\aleph_y) \\ &+ \mathcal{L}_{i,\varsigma+\aleph_y}\Delta\hat{\upsilon}_{i,c}(t+\varsigma_{i,a}+\aleph_y-1|t-\varsigma_{i,s}).\end{aligned}$$

When $\eta = \varsigma_i + \aleph_u + 1, \varsigma_i + \aleph_u + 2, \ldots, \varsigma_i + \aleph_y$, $\hat{\upsilon}_{i,c}(t-\varsigma_{i,s}+\eta|t-\varsigma_{i,s}) = \hat{\upsilon}_{i,c}(t+\varsigma_{i,a}+\aleph_u|t-\varsigma_{i,s})$, such that $\Delta\hat{\upsilon}_{i,c}(t-\varsigma_{i,s}+\eta|t-\varsigma_{i,s}) = 0$. Thus, the above multistep ahead predictions of sliding-mode variable can be compactly summarized as

$$\begin{aligned}\hat{S}_i(t+\varsigma_{i,a}+\aleph_y|t-\varsigma_{i,s}) =& P_{i,1}x_i(t-\varsigma_{i,s}) + P_{i,2}\Delta\hat{V}_{i,c}(t+\varsigma_{i,a}+\aleph_u|t-\varsigma_{i,s}) \\ &- \Xi_{i,d}R(t+\varsigma_{i,a}+\aleph_y),\end{aligned} \tag{7.13}$$

with $R(t+\varsigma_{i,a}+\aleph_y) = \begin{bmatrix} r(t+\varsigma_{i,a}+\aleph_y) \\ \vdots \\ r(t+\varsigma_{i,a}+1) \end{bmatrix}$, and

$$P_{i,1} = \begin{bmatrix} \mathcal{D}_{i,\varsigma_i+N_y} \\ \vdots \\ \mathcal{D}_{i,\varsigma_i+N_u+1} \\ \mathcal{D}_{i,\varsigma_i+N_u} \\ \vdots \\ \mathcal{D}_{i,\varsigma_i+1} \end{bmatrix}, \quad P_{i,2} = \begin{bmatrix} \mathcal{L}_{i,\varsigma_i+\aleph_y} & 0 & \cdots & 0 \\ \vdots & \vdots & \cdots & \vdots \\ \mathcal{L}_{i,\varsigma_i+\aleph_u+1} & 0 & \cdots & 0 \\ 0 & \mathcal{L}_{i,\varsigma_i+\aleph_u} & \ddots & \vdots \\ \vdots & \ddots & \ddots & 0 \\ 0 & \cdots & 0 & \mathcal{L}_{i,\varsigma_i+1} \end{bmatrix},$$

$$\Xi_{i,d} = \text{Blockdiag}\{\Xi_i, \ldots, \Xi_i\}.$$

Based on (2.9), an incremental constraint of cooperative control increment is presented as

$$\Delta\hat{v}_{i,c}(t+\varsigma_{i,a}+\eta|t-\varsigma_{i,s}) = \gamma_{i,\eta}\Delta\hat{v}_{i,c}(t+\varsigma_{i,a}|t-\varsigma_{i,s}),$$

where $\gamma_{i,\eta} > 0$, $\eta = 1, 2, \ldots, \aleph_u$, is a weighting factor, such that $P_{i,2}$ can be degenerated as $P_{i,3} = P_{i,2}\Gamma_i$ with $\Gamma_i = \text{Blockdiag}\{\gamma_{i,\aleph_u}I, \ldots, \gamma_{i,1}I, I\}$, and $P_{i,2}\Delta\hat{V}_{i,c}(t+\varsigma_{i,a}+\aleph_u|t-\varsigma_{i,s}) = P_{i,3}\Delta\hat{V}_{i,c}(t+\varsigma_{i,a}|t-\varsigma_{i,s})$ with

$$\Delta\hat{V}_{i,c}(t+\varsigma_{i,a}|t-\varsigma_{i,s}) = \left[\Delta\hat{v}_{i,c}^{\mathrm{T}}(t+\varsigma_{i,a}|t-\varsigma_{i,s}) \cdots \Delta\hat{v}_{i,c}^{\mathrm{T}}(t+\varsigma_{i,a}|t-\varsigma_{i,s})\right]^{\mathrm{T}}.$$

Hence, the sliding-mode prediction (7.13) can be converted as

$$\begin{aligned}\hat{S}_i(t+\varsigma_{i,a}+\aleph_y|t-\varsigma_{i,s}) =& P_{i,1}x_i(t-\varsigma_{i,s}) + P_{i,3}\Delta\hat{V}_{i,c}(t+\varsigma_{i,a}|t-\varsigma_{i,s}) \\ &- \Xi_{i,d}R(t+\varsigma_{i,a}+\aleph_y).\end{aligned} \tag{7.14}$$

$\forall j \in \mathcal{N}_i$, based on the IHOFAS prediction model of sliding-mode variable (7.12), $s_j(t)$ can be predicted as

$$\begin{aligned}&\hat{s}_j(t-\varsigma_{j,s}+\eta|t-\varsigma_{j,s}) \\ &\quad = \mathcal{D}_{j,\eta}x_j(t-\varsigma_{j,s}) + \mathcal{L}_{j,\eta}\Delta\hat{v}_{j,c}(t-\varsigma_{j,s}+\eta-1|t-\varsigma_{j,s}) \\ &\quad\quad - \Xi_j r(t-\varsigma_{j,s}+\eta),\end{aligned}$$

with $\eta = 1, 2, \ldots, \varsigma_{ij}+\aleph_y$. For $\eta = \varsigma_{ij}+1, \varsigma_{ij}+2, \ldots, \varsigma_{ij}+\aleph_y$, the multistep ahead predictions of $s_j(t)$ can be obtained as

$$\begin{aligned}\hat{s}_j(t+\varsigma_{i,a}+1|t-\varsigma_{j,s}) =& \mathcal{D}_{j,\varsigma_{ij}+1}x_j(t-\varsigma_{j,s}) - \Xi_j r(t+\varsigma_{i,a}+1) \\ &+ \mathcal{L}_{j,\varsigma_{ij}+1}\Delta\hat{v}_{j,c}(t+\varsigma_{i,a}|t-\varsigma_{j,s}), \\ &\vdots\end{aligned}$$

$$\hat{s}_j(t+\varsigma_{i,a}+\aleph_y|t-\varsigma_{j,s}) = \mathcal{D}_{j,\varsigma_{ij}+\aleph_y}x_j(t-\varsigma_{j,s}) - \Xi_j r(t+\varsigma_{i,a}+\aleph_y) + \mathcal{L}_{j,\varsigma_{ij}+\aleph_y}\Delta\hat{v}_{j,c}(t+\varsigma_{i,a}+\aleph_y-1|t-\varsigma_{j,s}).$$

Repeating the process from (7.13)–(7.14), the above multistep sliding-mode predictions for the j-th HOFA agent can be summarized as

$$\begin{aligned}\hat{S}_j(t+\varsigma_{i,a}+\aleph_y|t-\varsigma_{j,s}) =& P_{j,1}x_j(t-\varsigma_{j,s}) + P_{j,3}\Delta\hat{V}_{j,c}(t+\varsigma_{i,a}|t-\varsigma_{j,s}) \\ &- \Xi_{j,d}R(t+\varsigma_{i,a}+\aleph_y),\end{aligned} \tag{7.15}$$

with $\Delta\hat{V}_{j,c}(t+\varsigma_{i,a}|t-\varsigma_{j,s}) = \begin{bmatrix}\Delta\hat{v}_{j,c}(t+\varsigma_{i,a}|t-\varsigma_{j,s})\\ \vdots \\ \Delta\hat{v}_{j,c}(t+\varsigma_{i,a}|t-\varsigma_{j,s})\end{bmatrix}$, and

$$P_{j,1} = \begin{bmatrix}\mathcal{D}_{j,\varsigma_{ij}+\aleph_y}\\ \vdots \\ \mathcal{D}_{j,\varsigma_{ij}+\aleph_u+1}\\ \mathcal{D}_{j,\varsigma_{ij}+\aleph_u}\\ \vdots \\ \mathcal{D}_{j,\varsigma_{ij}+1}\end{bmatrix},\quad P_{j,2} = \begin{bmatrix}\mathcal{L}_{j,\varsigma_{ij}+\aleph_y} & 0 & \cdots & 0\\ \vdots & \vdots & \cdots & \vdots\\ \mathcal{L}_{j,\varsigma_{ij}+\aleph_u+1} & 0 & \cdots & 0\\ 0 & \mathcal{L}_{j,\varsigma_{ij}+\aleph_u} & \ddots & \vdots\\ \vdots & \ddots & \ddots & 0\\ 0 & \cdots & 0 & \mathcal{L}_{j,\varsigma_{ij}+1}\end{bmatrix},$$

$$P_{j,3} = P_{j,2}\Gamma_j,\quad \Gamma_j = \text{Blockdiag}\{\gamma_{j,\aleph_u}I,\ldots,\gamma_{j,1}I,I\},$$
$$\Xi_{j,d} = \text{Blockdiag}\{\Xi_j,\ldots,\Xi_j\}.$$

To solve the optimal secure cooperative control increment $\Delta v_{i,c}(t)$, let

$$\frac{\partial}{\partial\Delta\hat{V}_{i,c}(t+\varsigma_{i,a}|t-\varsigma_{i,s})}\mathcal{J}(t) = 0,\ i\in\mathcal{N},$$

and by utilizing (7.14) and (7.15), it is obtained that

$$\begin{aligned}&\sum_{j\in\mathcal{N}_i} w_{ij}P_{i,3}^{\mathrm{T}}\Big(P_{i,1}x_i(t-\varsigma_{i,s}) + P_{i,3}\Delta\hat{V}_{i,c}(t+\varsigma_{i,a}|t-\varsigma_{i,s}) - \Xi_{i,d}R(t+\varsigma_{i,a}+\aleph_y)\\ &-P_{j,1}x_j(t-\varsigma_{j,s}) - P_{j,3}\Delta\hat{V}_{j,c}(t+\varsigma_{i,a}|t-\varsigma_{j,s}) + \Xi_{j,d}R(t+\varsigma_{i,a}+\aleph_y)\Big)\\ &+\alpha_i P_{i,3}^{\mathrm{T}}\Big(P_{i,1}x_i(t-\varsigma_{i,s}) + P_{i,3}\Delta\hat{V}_{i,c}(t+\varsigma_{i,a}|t-\varsigma_{i,s}) - \Xi_{i,d}R(t+\varsigma_{i,a}+\aleph_y)\\ &-S_{i,\text{ref}}(t+\varsigma_{i,a}+\aleph_y)\Big) + \beta_i\Gamma_i^{\mathrm{T}}\Gamma_i\Delta\hat{V}_{i,c}(t+\varsigma_{i,a}|t-\varsigma_{i,s}) = 0,\end{aligned}$$

which can be represented as

$$\begin{aligned}\Delta\hat{V}_c(t+\varsigma_{i,a}|t-\varsigma_s) =&F^{-1}Gx(t-\varsigma_s)+F^{-1}MR(t+\varsigma_{i,a}+\aleph_y)\\&+F^{-1}LS_{i,\mathrm{ref}}(t+\varsigma_{i,a}+\aleph_y),\end{aligned}$$

with $\Delta\hat{V}_c(t+\varsigma_{i,a}|t-\varsigma_s)=\begin{bmatrix}\Delta\hat{V}_{1,c}(t+\varsigma_{i,a}|t-\varsigma_{1,s})\\ \vdots\\ \Delta\hat{V}_{N,c}(t+\varsigma_{i,a}t-\varsigma_{N,s})\end{bmatrix}$, $x(t-\varsigma_s)=\begin{bmatrix}x_1(t-\varsigma_{1,s})\\ \vdots\\ x_N(t-\varsigma_{N,s})\end{bmatrix}$, and

$$\begin{aligned}F=&\{f_{ij}\},\quad f_{ii}=(w_i+\alpha_i)P_{i,3}^{\mathrm{T}}P_{i,3}+\beta_i\Gamma_i^{\mathrm{T}}\Gamma_i,\quad f_{ij}=-w_{ij}P_{i,3}^{\mathrm{T}}P_{j,3},\\ G=&\{g_{ij}\},\quad g_{ii}=-(w_i+\alpha_i)P_{i,3}^{\mathrm{T}}P_{i,1},\quad g_{ij}=w_{ij}P_{i,3}^{\mathrm{T}}P_{j,1},\\ M=&\begin{bmatrix}(\alpha_1+w_1)P_{1,3}^{\mathrm{T}}\Xi_{1,d}-\sum_{j\in\mathcal{N}_1}w_{ij}P_{1,3}^{\mathrm{T}}\Xi_{j,d}\\ \vdots\\ (\alpha_N+w_N)P_{N,3}^{\mathrm{T}}\Xi_{N,d}-\sum_{j\in\mathcal{N}_N}w_{ij}P_{N,3}^{\mathrm{T}}\Xi_{j,d}\end{bmatrix},\\ L=&\begin{bmatrix}\alpha_1P_{1,3}\cdots\alpha_NP_{N,3}\end{bmatrix}^{\mathrm{T}},\quad w_i=\sum_{j\in\mathcal{N}_i}w_{ij}.\end{aligned}$$

Then, the optimal secure cooperative control increment of the i-th HOFA agent in the network node is solved as $\Delta\hat{v}_{i,c}(t+\varsigma_{i,a}|t-\varsigma_s)=H_i\Delta\hat{V}_c(t+\varsigma_{i,a}|t-\varsigma_s)$, i.e.,

$$\begin{aligned}\Delta\hat{v}_{i,c}(t+\varsigma_{i,a}|t-\varsigma_s) =&H_iF^{-1}Gx(t-\varsigma_s)+H_iF^{-1}MR(t+\varsigma_{i,a}+\aleph_y)\\&+H_iF^{-1}LS_{i,\mathrm{ref}}(t+\varsigma_{i,a}+\aleph_y),\end{aligned}$$

where $H_i=\begin{bmatrix}H_{i,1}\cdots H_{i,N}\end{bmatrix}\in\mathbb{R}^{n_i\times(\aleph_u+1)\tilde{n}}$ with $\tilde{n}=\sum_{i\in\mathcal{N}}n_i$, $H_{i,i}=\begin{bmatrix}0\cdots0\ I\end{bmatrix}$, $H_{i,j}=0$, $j\in\mathcal{N}_i$. On the i-th actuator, the optimal secure cooperative control increment is proposed as $\Delta v_{i,c}(t)=\Delta\hat{v}_{i,c}(t|t-\varsigma_i)$, i.e.,

$$\Delta v_{i,c}(t)=H_iF^{-1}Gx(t-\varsigma)+H_iF^{-1}MR(t+\aleph_y)+H_iF^{-1}LS_{i,\mathrm{ref}}(t+\aleph_y),\tag{7.16}$$

with $x(t-\varsigma)=\begin{bmatrix}x_1(t-\varsigma_{i1})\\ \vdots\\ x_N(t-\varsigma_{iN})\end{bmatrix}$ and $S_{i,\mathrm{ref}}(t+\aleph_y)=\begin{bmatrix}s_{i,\mathrm{ref}}(t+\aleph_y)\\ \vdots\\ s_{i,\mathrm{ref}}(t+1)\end{bmatrix}$.

Based on (7.16), it clearly shows that the reference sliding-mode $s_{i,\text{ref}}(t)$ plays a critical role in the solution of $\Delta v_{i,c}(t)$. In this study, $s_{i,\text{ref}}(t)$ is chosen as a power function-based sliding-mode reaching law and is designed as

$$s_{i,\text{ref}}(t+1) = (1-\lambda_1 T_s)s_i(t) - \lambda_2 T_s \hbar_i(t), \quad s_{i,\text{ref}}(t) = s_i(t), \tag{7.17}$$

where $0 < \lambda_1 T_s, \lambda_2 T_s < 1$, T_s denotes the sampling period, and $\hbar_i(t)$ is a power function in relation to $s_i(t)$ and is provided as

$$\hbar_i(t) = \begin{cases} |s_i|^{\eth} \operatorname{sgn}(s_i), & |s_i| \geq \sigma, \\ \frac{s_i}{\sigma^{1-\eth}}, & |s_i| < \sigma, \end{cases}$$

where $\sigma > \left(\frac{\lambda_2 T_s}{1-\lambda_1 T_s}\right)^{\frac{1}{1-\eth}}, \frac{\lambda_2 T_s}{1-\lambda_1 T_s}$, $\eth, \sigma \in (0, 1)$ are constants, and $\operatorname{sgn}(s_i)$ is the symbolic function in relation to $s_i(t)$, i.e.,

$$\operatorname{sgn}(s_i) = \begin{cases} 1, & s_i > 0, \\ 0, & s_i = 0, \\ -1, & s_i < 0. \end{cases} \tag{7.18}$$

7.4 Analysis of Simultaneous Consensus and Stability Under Random Deception Attacks

Because $e_i(t) = y_i(t) - r(t)$ is the tracking error of the i-th HOFA agent, let $\epsilon_{ii}(t) = \epsilon_i(t) = e_i(t)$, $\epsilon_{ij}(t) = y_i(t) - y_j(t) = e_i(t) - e_j(t)$, $j \in \mathcal{N}_i$, be the consensus error, such that the simultaneous consensus and stability of the closed-loop HOFAMASs (7.4) can be equivalent to $\epsilon_i(t) \to 0$ and $\epsilon_{ij}(t) \to 0$ with $t \to \infty$. Further, because of the proof of Theorem 3.1, the consensus error $\epsilon(t)$ in this chapter can also be summarized as (3.18) with $i = 1$ and $\epsilon(t) = \left[\epsilon_1^{\text{T}}(t) \cdots \epsilon_{1N}^{\text{T}}(t)\right]^{\text{T}}$, i.e.,

$$\epsilon(t) = \tilde{\mathbf{I}} e(t),$$

which implies that $e(t) = 0 \Longrightarrow \epsilon(t) = 0$ with $t \to \infty$. On the basis of the analysis in Subsection 7.3.1, $s(t) = 0 \Longrightarrow e(t) = 0$ with $t \to \infty$, such that $s(t) = 0 \Longrightarrow \epsilon(t) = 0$ with $t \to \infty$. It implies that the simultaneous consensus and stability of the closed-loop HOFAMASs (7.4) can be transformed into the asymptotic stability of $s(t)$, that is, Problem 7.1 is solvable if $s(t)$ is asymptotically stable, i.e., $\lim_{t\to\infty} \|s(t)\| = 0$.

Actually, $\Delta v_{i,c}(t)$ in (7.16) is designed for the closed-loop nominal system (7.8). For the complete form of the closed system (7.4), the IHOFAS prediction model for linear sliding-mode variable $s_i(t)$ in (7.12) can be corrected as

$$\begin{aligned}
&\hat{s}_i(t+\varsigma_{i,a}+\eta|t-\varsigma_{i,s}) \\
&\quad = \mathcal{D}_{i,\varsigma_i+\eta}x_i(t-\varsigma_{i,s}) + \mathcal{L}_{i,\varsigma_i+\eta}\Delta\hat{v}_{i,c}(t+\varsigma_{i,a}+\eta-1|t-\varsigma_{i,s}) \\
&\quad\quad + \mathcal{N}_{i,\varsigma_i+\eta}\varpi_i(t+\varsigma_{i,a}) - \Xi_i r(t-\varsigma_{i,s}+\eta),
\end{aligned}$$

where $\varpi_i(t+\varsigma_{i,a}) = \begin{bmatrix} \delta_{i,a}(t+\varsigma_{i,a}-1)\zeta_{i,a}(t+\varsigma_{i,a}-1) \\ \delta_{i,s}(t+\varsigma_{i,a})\zeta_{i,s}(t+\varsigma_{i,a}) \end{bmatrix}$ and $\mathcal{N}_{i,\varsigma_i+\eta} = \begin{bmatrix} \mathcal{L}_{i,\varsigma_i+\eta} & \Xi_i \end{bmatrix}$. Hence, the sliding-mode predictions in (7.14) and (7.15) can be rewritten as

$$\begin{aligned}
\hat{S}_i(t+\varsigma_{i,a}+\aleph_y|t-\varsigma_{i,s}) =& P_{i,1}x_i(t-\varsigma_{i,s}) + P_{i,3}\Delta\hat{V}_{i,c}(t+\varsigma_{i,a}|t-\varsigma_{i,s}) \\
&+ P_{i,4}\varpi_i(t+\varsigma_{i,a}) - \Xi_{i,d}R(t+\varsigma_{i,a}+\aleph_y), \\
\hat{S}_j(t+\varsigma_{i,a}+\aleph_y|t-\varsigma_{j,s}) =& P_{j,1}x_j(t-\varsigma_{j,s}) + P_{j,3}\Delta\hat{V}_{j,c}(t+\varsigma_{i,a}|t-\varsigma_{j,s}) \\
&+ P_{j,4}\varpi_j(t+\varsigma_{i,a}) - \Xi_{j,d}R(t+\varsigma_{i,a}+\aleph_y),
\end{aligned} \tag{7.19}$$

with $P_{i,4} = \begin{bmatrix} \mathcal{N}_{i,\varsigma_i+\aleph_y} \\ \vdots \\ \mathcal{N}_{i,\varsigma_i+1} \end{bmatrix}$ and $P_{j,4} = \begin{bmatrix} \mathcal{N}_{j,\varsigma_{ij}+\aleph_y} \\ \vdots \\ \mathcal{N}_{j,\varsigma_{ij}+1} \end{bmatrix}$.

Further, $\Delta v_{i,c}(t)$ in (7.16) is obtained by minimizing the objective function $\mathcal{J}(t)$ in (7.5) and (7.6), which can be equivalent to adjusting the weighting factors w_{ij}, α_i, and β_i for satisfying the following relationship:

$$\begin{aligned}
&S_{i,\text{ref}}(t+\varsigma_{i,a}+\aleph_y) \\
&\quad = P_{i,1}x_i(t-\varsigma_{i,s}) + P_{i,3}\Delta\hat{V}_{i,c}(t+\varsigma_{i,a}|t-\varsigma_{i,s}) - \Xi_{i,d}R(t+\varsigma_{i,a}+\aleph_y) \\
&\quad = P_{j,1}x_j(t-\varsigma_{j,s}) + P_{j,3}\Delta\hat{V}_{j,c}(t+\varsigma_{i,a}|t-\varsigma_{j,s}) - \Xi_{j,d}R(t+\varsigma_{i,a}+\aleph_y).
\end{aligned} \tag{7.20}$$

By taking (7.19) into (7.20), it is derived that

$$\begin{aligned}
\hat{S}_i(t+\varsigma_{i,a}+\aleph_y|t-\varsigma_{i,s}) =& S_{i,\text{ref}}(t+\varsigma_{i,a}+\aleph_y) + P_{i,4}\varpi_i(t+\varsigma_{i,a}), \\
\hat{S}_j(t+\varsigma_{i,a}+\aleph_y|t-\varsigma_{j,s}) =& S_{i,\text{ref}}(t+\varsigma_{i,a}+\aleph_y) + P_{j,4}\varpi_j(t+\varsigma_{i,a}),
\end{aligned}$$

which can be equivalent to

$$\begin{aligned}
\hat{S}_i(t+\aleph_y|t-\varsigma_i) =& S_{i,\text{ref}}(t+\aleph_y) + P_{i,4}\varpi_i(t), \\
\hat{S}_j(t+\aleph_y|t-\varsigma_{ij}) =& S_{i,\text{ref}}(t+\aleph_y) + P_{j,4}\varpi_j(t),
\end{aligned}$$

where the last row is provided as

$$\begin{aligned} s_i(t+1) =& s_{i,\mathrm{ref}}(t+1) + \mathcal{N}_{i,\varsigma_i+1}\varpi_i(t) \\ =& (1-\lambda_1 T_s)s_i(t) - \lambda_2 T_s \hbar_i(t) + \mathcal{N}_{i,\varsigma_i+1}\varpi_i(t), \\ s_j(t+1) =& s_{i,\mathrm{ref}}(t+1) + \mathcal{N}_{j,\varsigma_{ij}+1}\varpi_i(t) \\ =& (1-\lambda_1 T_s)s_i(t) - \lambda_2 T_s \hbar_i(t) + \mathcal{N}_{j,\varsigma_{ij}+1}\varpi_j(t). \end{aligned} \tag{7.21}$$

Then, Theorem 7.1 is proposed here to discuss the asymptotic stability of sliding-mode variable $s(t)$ in (7.21).

Theorem 7.1 *System* (7.21) *can implement the asymptotic stability if*

$$\Omega_{i,j,1} < 0, \quad \Omega_{i,j,3} - \Omega_{i,j,2}^{\mathrm{T}}\Omega_{i,j,1}^{-1}\Omega_{i,j,2} < 0, \tag{7.22}$$

where

$$\begin{aligned} \Omega_{i,j,1} =& 2(1-\lambda_1 T_s)^2 - 1, \\ \Omega_{i,j,2} =& \Big[-2(1-\lambda_1 T_s)\lambda_2 T_s \;\; (1-\lambda_1 T_s)\mathcal{N}_{i,\varsigma_i+1} \;\; (1-\lambda_1 T_s)\mathcal{N}_{j,\varsigma_{ij}+1} \Big], \\ \Omega_{i,j,3} =& \begin{bmatrix} 2\lambda_2^2 T_s^2 & -\lambda_2 T_s \mathcal{N}_{i,\varsigma_i+1} & -\lambda_2 T_s \mathcal{N}_{j,\varsigma_{ij}+1} \\ -\lambda_2 T_s \mathcal{N}_{i,\varsigma_i+1}^{\mathrm{T}} & \mathcal{N}_{i,\varsigma_i+1}^{\mathrm{T}}\mathcal{N}_{i,\varsigma_i+1} & 0 \\ -\lambda_2 T_s \mathcal{N}_{j,\varsigma_{ij}+1}^{\mathrm{T}} & 0 & \mathcal{N}_{j,\varsigma_{ij}+1}^{\mathrm{T}}\mathcal{N}_{j,\varsigma_{ij}+1} \end{bmatrix}. \end{aligned} \tag{7.23}$$

Proof Considering the Lyapunov stability theory, a definite Lyapunov function for system (7.21) is designed as

$$\mathscr{V}_{i,j}(t) = s_i^{\mathrm{T}}(t)s_i(t) + s_j^{\mathrm{T}}(t)s_j(t) \succ 0,$$

so that system (7.21) can implement the asymptotic stability if $\Delta\mathscr{V}_{i,j}(t+1) < 0$, i.e.,

$$\begin{aligned} &\Delta\mathscr{V}_{i,j}(t+1) \\ &= \mathscr{V}_{i,j}(t+1) - \mathscr{V}_{i,j}(t) \\ &= 2(1-\lambda_1 T_s)^2 s_i^{\mathrm{T}}(t)s_i(t) - 2(1-\lambda_1 T_s)\lambda_2 T_s s_i^{\mathrm{T}}(t)\hbar_i(t) + 2\lambda_2^2 T_s^2 \hbar_i^{\mathrm{T}}(t)\hbar_i(t) \\ &- 2(1-\lambda_1 T_s)\lambda_2 T_s \hbar_i^{\mathrm{T}}(t)s_i(t) + (1-\lambda_1 T_s)s_i^{\mathrm{T}}(t)\mathcal{N}_{i,\varsigma_i+1}\varpi_i(t) - \lambda_2 T_s \hbar_i^{\mathrm{T}}(t) \\ &\times \mathcal{N}_{i,\varsigma_i+1}\varpi_i(t) + (1-\lambda_1 T_s)\varpi_i^{\mathrm{T}}(t)\mathcal{N}_{i,\varsigma_i+1}^{\mathrm{T}}s_i(t) - \lambda_2 T_s \varpi_i^{\mathrm{T}}(t)\mathcal{N}_{i,\varsigma_i+1}^{\mathrm{T}}\hbar_i(t) \\ &+ \varpi_i^{\mathrm{T}}(t)\mathcal{N}_{i,\varsigma_i+1}^{\mathrm{T}}\mathcal{N}_{i,\varsigma_i+1}\varpi_i(t) - s_i^{\mathrm{T}}(t)s_i(t) + (1-\lambda_1 T_s)s_i^{\mathrm{T}}(t)\mathcal{N}_{j,\varsigma_{ij}+1}\varpi_j(t) \\ &- \lambda_2 T_s \hbar_i^{\mathrm{T}}(t)\mathcal{N}_{j,\varsigma_{ij}+1}\varpi_j(t) + (1-\lambda_1 T_s)\varpi_j^{\mathrm{T}}(t)\mathcal{N}_{j,\varsigma_{ij}+1}^{\mathrm{T}}s_i(t) - \lambda_2 T_s \varpi_j^{\mathrm{T}}(t) \end{aligned}$$

$$
\times \mathcal{N}_{j,\varsigma_{ij}+1}^{\mathrm{T}} \hbar_i(t) + \varpi_j^{\mathrm{T}}(t) \mathcal{N}_{j,\varsigma_{ij}+1}^{\mathrm{T}} \mathcal{N}_{j,\varsigma_{ij}+1} \varpi_j(t) - s_j^{\mathrm{T}}(t) s_j(t)
$$

$$
= \begin{bmatrix} s_i(t) \\ \hbar_i(t) \\ \varpi_i(t) \\ \varpi_j(t) \\ s_j(t) \end{bmatrix}^{\mathrm{T}} \begin{bmatrix} \Omega_{i,j} & 0 \\ 0 & -1 \end{bmatrix} \begin{bmatrix} s_i(t) \\ \hbar_i(t) \\ \varpi_i(t) \\ \varpi_j(t) \\ s_j(t) \end{bmatrix} < 0,
$$

with $\Omega_{i,j} = \begin{bmatrix} \Omega_{i,j,1} & \Omega_{i,j,2} \\ \Omega_{i,j,2}^{\mathrm{T}} & \Omega_{i,j,3} \end{bmatrix}$, where $\Omega_{i,j,1}$, $\Omega_{i,j,2}$, and $\Omega_{i,j,3}$ are provided in (7.23). Based on the Schur complement, $\begin{bmatrix} \Omega_{i,j} & 0 \\ 0 & -1 \end{bmatrix} < 0 \Longleftrightarrow \Omega_{i,j} = \begin{bmatrix} \Omega_{i,j,1} & \Omega_{i,j,2} \\ \Omega_{i,j,2}^{\mathrm{T}} & \Omega_{i,j,3} \end{bmatrix} < 0$, which can be further derived that

$$
\Omega_{i,j} < 0 \Longleftrightarrow \Omega_{i,j,1} < 0, \quad \Omega_{i,j,3} - \Omega_{i,j,2}^{\mathrm{T}} \Omega_{i,j,1}^{-1} \Omega_{i,j,2} < 0,
$$

such that condition (7.22) is satisfied, which implies that system (7.21) can implement the asymptotic stability.

This completes the proof. □

Remark 7.2 Theorem 7.1 provides a guiding principle for the parameter design of linear sliding-mode variable $s_i(t)$ and reference sliding-mode $s_{i,\mathrm{ref}}(t)$, which implies that the simultaneous consensus and stability of the closed-loop HOFAMASs (7.4) are in final dependent on the $s_i(t)$ and $s_{i,\mathrm{ref}}(t)$. Concretely, $\Omega_{i,j,1} < 0$ in (7.22) further presents a constraint on the $0 < \lambda_1 T_s, \lambda_2 T_s < 1$ of $s_{i,\mathrm{ref}}(t)$ in (7.17). Meanwhile, $\Omega_{i,j,2}$ and $\Omega_{i,j,3}$ are in relation to $\mathcal{L}_{i,\varsigma_i+\eta}$ and Ξ_i, which means that the selection of parameters $s_i(t)$ and $s_{i,\mathrm{ref}}(t)$ is also affected by the $\Omega_{i,j,3} - \Omega_{i,j,2}^{\mathrm{T}} \Omega_{i,j,1}^{-1} \Omega_{i,j,2} < 0$ in (7.22). By introducing the linear sliding-mode variable $s_i(t)$ in (7.7), the proposed design problem can be transformed into the design of $s_i(t)$ and $s_{i,\mathrm{ref}}(t)$, and Theorem 7.1 can be considered as a design rule to achieve the desired secure cooperative control performance.

7.5 With Application to Formation Control of Air-Bearing Spacecraft Simulators

A formation control experiment of three ABSSs is taken here to illustrate the feasibility and availability of the proposed SM-HOFAS predictive control, where the dynamic models of three ABSSs are given in (A.4) and the details of three ABSSs and its associated experimental platform are provided in Appendix A.

7.5.1 *Numerical Simulation*

By choosing system (A.4a) as an example, a comparison between the proposed SM-HOFAS predictive control and H_∞ output fault-tolerant consensus (OFTC) control in Chen et al. (2023) is presented to demonstrate the feasibility and advantages, where the related design parameters are provided as $T_s = 0.2$s, $w_{ii} = 0$, $w_{ij} = 1$, $\alpha_i = 1$, $\beta_i = 15$, $\Gamma_i = I$, $i, j = 1, 2, 3$, $\aleph_y = 5$, $\aleph_u = 3$. The communication constraints in the forward and feedback channels are set as $\varsigma_{1,a} = 2$, $\varsigma_{2,a} = 3$, $\varsigma_{3,a} = 3$, $\varsigma_{1,s} = 2$, $\varsigma_{2,s} = 3$, $\varsigma_{3,s} = 2$. The parameters of random deception attacks are given as $\nu_1 = 0.05$, $\nu = 0.07$, $\nu_3 = 0.09$, $\mu_1 = 0.04$, $\mu_2 = 0.06$, $\mu_3 = 0.08$; then the active times of random deception attacks are shown in Fig. 7.2. When $\delta_{i,a}(t) = 1$ and $\delta_{i,s}(t) = 1$, the false data $\zeta_{i,a}(t)$ and $\zeta_{i,s}(t)$ caused by random deception attacks are injected into the forward and feedback channels, where the false data $\zeta_{i,a}(t)$ and $\zeta_{i,s}(t)$ are plotted in Fig. 7.3.

Fig. 7.2 The active times of random deception attacks in the forward and feedback channels

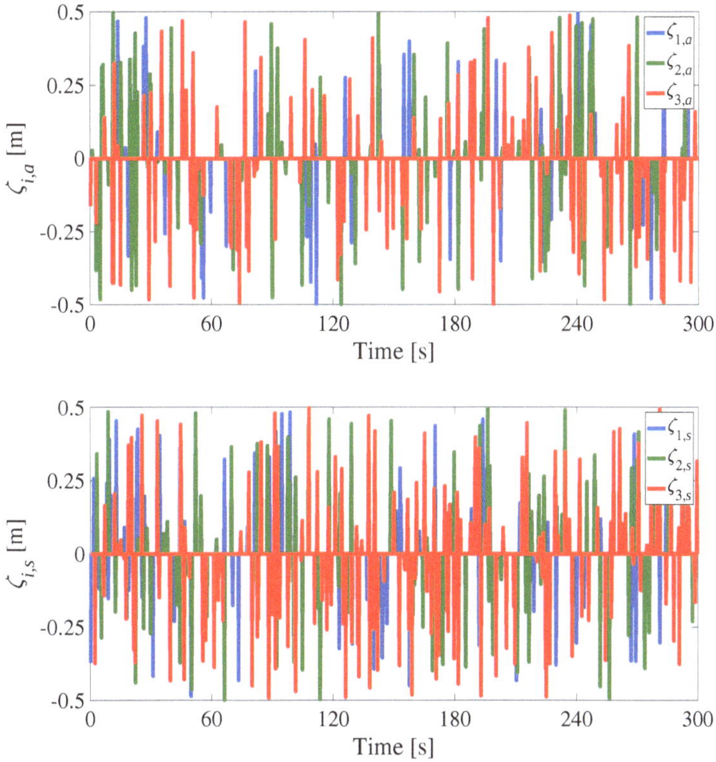

Fig. 7.3 The false data injected in the forward and feedback channels

Based on (7.2), an SM-HOFAS predictive control for system (A.4a) is designed as

$$F_{I,x_{i,\mathrm{ABSS}}}(t) = B_i^{-1}\left(-L_i(A_{i,0\sim1}, x_{i,\mathrm{ABSS}}(t) + \Upsilon_i(K_{i,0\sim1}, x_{i,\mathrm{ABSS}}(t)) + v_i(t)\right), \tag{7.24}$$

where $K_{1,0} = -0.3802$, $K_{1,1} = 19.4$, $K_{2,0} = -0.3822$, $K_{2,1} = 19.5$, $K_{3,0} = -0.3763$, $K_{3,1} = 19.2$. Based on (7.7), the sliding-mode variable for system (A.4a) is presented as $s_{i,x}(t) = \Xi_{i,x}\left(x_{i,\mathrm{ABSS}}(t) - r_x(t)\right)$, where $\Xi_{i,x}(q^{-1}) = 0.05 - 0.03q^{-1} - 0.01q^{-2}$ and $r_x(t)$ is a known reference signal. For the reference sliding-mode $s_{i,\mathrm{ref}}(t)$, the associated parameters are given as $\lambda_1 = 0.1$, $\lambda_2 = 0.05$, $\eth = 0.5$, $\sigma = \left(\frac{\lambda_2 T_s}{1-\lambda_1 T_s}\right)^{\frac{1}{1-\eth}} + 0.1$.

For the H_∞ OFTC control in Chen et al. (2023), system (A.4a) with random deception attacks should be firstly converted into the following first-order form:

$$
\begin{aligned}
X_{i,\mathrm{ABSS}}(t+1) =& A_{i,\mathrm{ABSS}} X_{i,\mathrm{ABSS}}(t) + B_{i,\mathrm{ABSS}} F_{I,x_{i,\mathrm{ABSS}}}(t) \\
& + \delta_{i,a}(t) B_{i,\mathrm{ABSS}} \zeta_{i,a}(t), \\
\mathcal{Y}_{i,\mathrm{ABSS}}(t) =& C_{i,\mathrm{ABSS}} X_{i,\mathrm{ABSS}}(t), \\
\mathcal{Y}_{i,c,\mathrm{ABSS}}(t) =& \mathcal{Y}_{i,\mathrm{ABSS}}(t) + \delta_{i,s}(t) \zeta_{i,s}(t),
\end{aligned}
\tag{7.25}
$$

where $C_{i,\mathrm{ABSS}} = \begin{bmatrix} 1 & 0 \end{bmatrix}$ and other coefficient matrices are as the same as (3.23). Let $e_{i,rx}(t) = \mathcal{Y}_{i,\mathrm{ABSS}}(t) - r_x(t)$ and $X_{e,i}(t) = \begin{bmatrix} \Delta X_{i,\mathrm{ABSS}}^{\mathrm{T}}(t) & e_{i,rx}^{\mathrm{T}}(t) \end{bmatrix}^{\mathrm{T}}$, and system (7.25) can be further transformed as

$$
\begin{aligned}
X_{e,i}(t+1) =& A_{xe,i} X_{e,i}(t) + B_{xe,i} \Delta F_{I,x_{i,\mathrm{ABSS}}}(t) \\
& + \delta_{i,s}(t) B_{xe,i} \Delta \zeta_{i,a}(t) - E_e \Delta r_x(t+1), \\
\Delta \mathcal{Y}_{i,\mathrm{ABSS}}(t) =& C_{i,\mathrm{ABSS}} \Delta X_{i,\mathrm{ABSS}}(t), \\
\Delta \mathcal{Y}_{i,c,\mathrm{ABSS}}(t) =& \Delta \mathcal{Y}_{i,\mathrm{ABSS}}(t) + \delta_{i,s}(t) \Delta \zeta_{i,s}(t),
\end{aligned}
$$

with $A_{xe,i} = \begin{bmatrix} A_{i,\mathrm{ABSS}} & 0 \\ C_{i,\mathrm{ABSS}} A_{i,\mathrm{ABSS}} & 1 \end{bmatrix}$, $B_{xe,i} = \begin{bmatrix} B_{i,\mathrm{ABSS}} \\ C_{i,\mathrm{ABSS}} B_{i,\mathrm{ABSS}} \end{bmatrix}$, $E_e = \begin{bmatrix} 0 \\ 1 \end{bmatrix}$. It is generally assumed that $\Delta r_x(t+1) = 0$, $\Delta F_{I,x_{i,\mathrm{ABSS}}}(t)$ can be designed as $\Delta F_{I,x_{i,\mathrm{ABSS}}}(t) = K_i(t) \sum_{j \in \mathcal{N}_i} w_{ij} \left(\Delta \mathcal{Y}_{j,c,\mathrm{ABSS}}(t) - \Delta \mathcal{Y}_{i,\mathrm{ABSS}}(t) \right)$, where $K_i(t)$ denotes the time-varying gain of H_∞ OFTC control to guarantee the mathematical expectation of $\mathcal{J}_{i,\mathrm{OFTC}}(t)$, denoted as $\mathbb{E}\{\mathcal{J}_{i,\mathrm{OFTC}}(t)\}$, satisfying $\mathbb{E}\{\mathcal{J}_{i,\mathrm{OFTC}}(t)\} < 0$ with

$$
\begin{aligned}
\mathcal{J}_{i,\mathrm{OFTC}}(t) =& \sum_{t=0}^{\aleph_y - 1} \left(\Delta \mathcal{Y}_{i,\mathrm{ABSS}}^{\mathrm{T}}(t) \Delta \mathcal{Y}_{i,\mathrm{ABSS}}(t) - \omega_i^2 \Delta \zeta_{i,a}^{\mathrm{T}}(t) \Delta \zeta_{i,a}(t) \right) \\
& - \omega_i^2 \sum_{t=0}^{\aleph_y - 1} \left(\Delta \mathcal{Y}_{i,\mathrm{ABSS}}^{\mathrm{T}}(0) W_i \Delta \mathcal{Y}_{i,\mathrm{ABSS}}^{\mathrm{T}}(0) \right), \quad \forall \Delta \mathcal{Y}_{i,\mathrm{ABSS}}(0) \neq 0.
\end{aligned}
$$

In the above, $W_i \succ 0$ is a weighting matrix, and ω_i is a given upper bound of H_∞ form to measure the level of noise attenuation. Then, the simulated comparison is plotted in Fig. 7.4.

Figure 7.4a shows that the proposed SM-HOFAS predictive control can achieve the desired cooperative tracking control performance within the tolerant errors during the steady and dynamic processes, which implies that the negative impacts of random deception attacks in the forward and feedback channels can be overcome. The trends of sliding-mode variables $s_{i,x}(t)$ are plotted in Fig. 7.4b, which means that $s_{i,x}(t)$ can converge to 0 with the allowable errors and the related errors are less than 1.5‰. Figure 7.4c means that H_∞ OFTC control can only ensure the

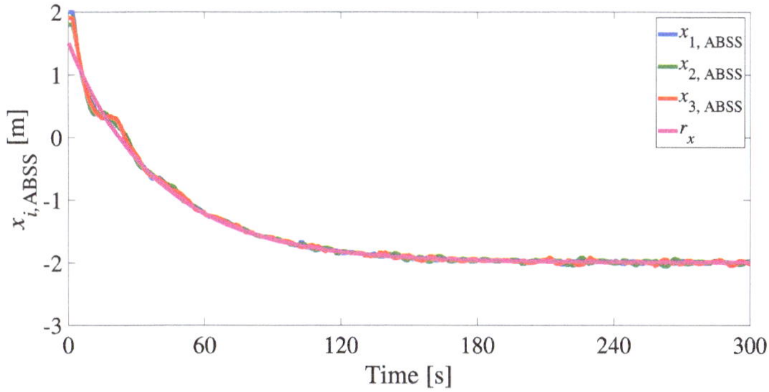

(a) Cooperative control of system (A.4a) by using the control (7.24)

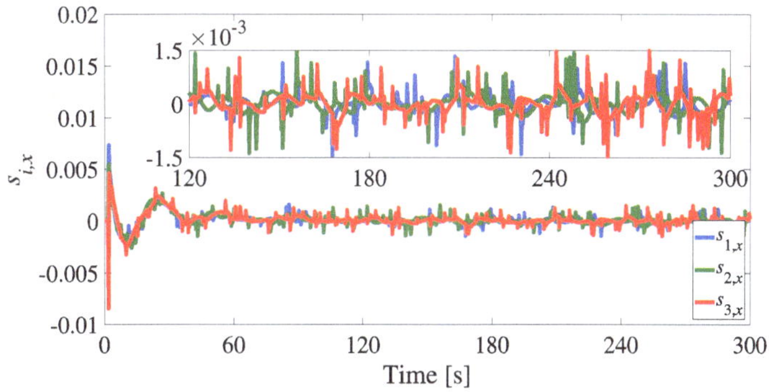

(b) The trends of sliding-mode variables $s_{i,x}(t)$

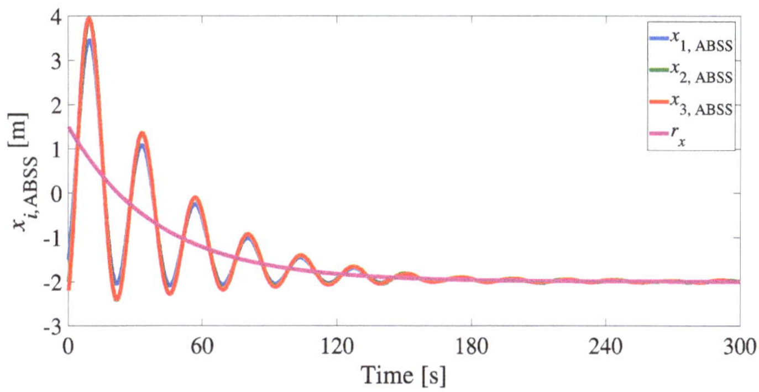

(c) Cooperative control of system (A.4a) via the H_∞ OFTC control

Fig. 7.4 Comparison between the SM-HOFAS predictive control and the H_∞ OFTC control in Chen et al. (2023)

cooperative tracking control performance in the steady process, and it does worse in dynamical cooperative tracking control.

Based on the simulated results in Fig. 7.4, the feasibility and advantages of the proposed SM-HOFAS predictive control can be fully illustrated, which provides a better foundation for the experimental verification.

7.5.2 Experimental Results

Based on the above simulation, a formation control experiment for three ABSSs is carried out to illustrate the availability of the proposed SM-HOFAS predictive control, where the desired formation is provided in Fig. 7.5.

For systems (A.4a) and (A.4b), the cooperative control protocols are designed as the same as (7.24) with the same design parameters. For system (A.4c), only a stabilization control is needed to satisfy the requirement of $\psi_{i,\mathrm{ABSS}}(t)$ during the formation control. Hence, the cooperative control items are set as 0, and a stabilization control is designed in (3.24) with the same design parameters. By applying (7.24) and (3.24), the experimental results are provided in Figs. 7.6, 7.7, 7.8, 7.9.

Figure 7.7 shows the position and angle responses of formation control for three ABSSs, which implies that the position responses $x_{i,\mathrm{ABSS}}(t)$ and $y_{i,\mathrm{ABSS}}(t)$ can realize the secure cooperative control performance under random deception attacks by applying the proposed SM-HOFAS predictive control (7.24), and they can cooperatively arrive at the desired positions. The angle responses $\psi_{i,\mathrm{ABSS}}(t)$ can implement the stabilization by adopting (3.24); however, a drawback is that there still exists the vibration in the steady process. The reason is that both the reaction forces of the thrusters and the airflow in the experimental site affect the stabilization control performance of $\psi_{i,\mathrm{ABSS}}(t)$. The control inputs generated by (7.24) and (3.24) are plotted in Fig. 7.8, where there exist some vibrations

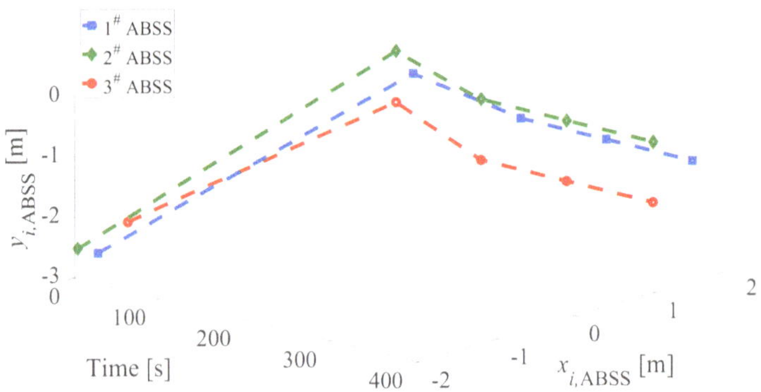

Fig. 7.5 The desired formation of three ABSSs

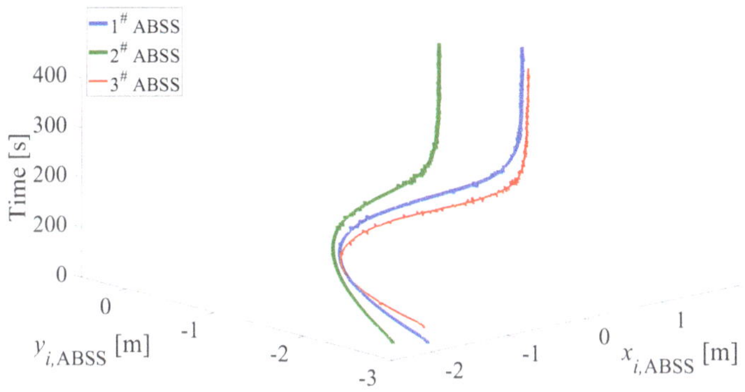

Fig. 7.6 The actual formation of three ABSSs

because of the false data injected in the forward and feedback channels and other uncertain cases including the model uncertainties and external disturbances, etc. Figure 7.6 provides the practical implementation of formation control for three ABSSs, which means that the proposed SM-HOFAS predictive control (7.24) can ensure the implementation of the desired formation control task under random deception attacks as shown in Fig. 7.5. Figure 7.9 gives the variation trends of $s_{i,x}(t)$ and $s_{i,y}(t)$, which implies that $s_{i,x}(t)$ and $s_{i,y}(t)$ can converge to 0 with the tolerant errors, and the range of error is from 0.3% to 1%.

On the basis of the results in Figs. 7.6, 7.7, 7.8, 7.9, the feasibility and availability of the proposed SM-HOFAS predictive control can be fully demonstrated, which gives a better foundation for the large-scale applications of practical spacecraft control.

7.6 Notes and References

This chapter has investigated a secure cooperative control of the HOFAMASs under random deception attacks, where the false data are injected in the forward and feedback channels because of random deception attacks. An SM-HOFAS predictive control has been proposed to address this problem, such that the secure cooperative control performance can be ensured and optimized. A sufficient condition has been derived to analyze the simultaneous consensus and stability of the closed-loop HOFAMASs by utilizing the Lyapunov stability theory and an LMI method. A highlight of this study is that a linear sliding-mode variable is introduced to improve the defense performance by enhancing the robustness and a related IHOFAS prediction model of sliding-mode variable is constructed by using a type of Diophantine Equation, such that the HOFAS theory can be further enriched. The other is that a new idea is provided to develop the sliding-mode control in the discrete-time domain by combining with the predictive control. Because of the

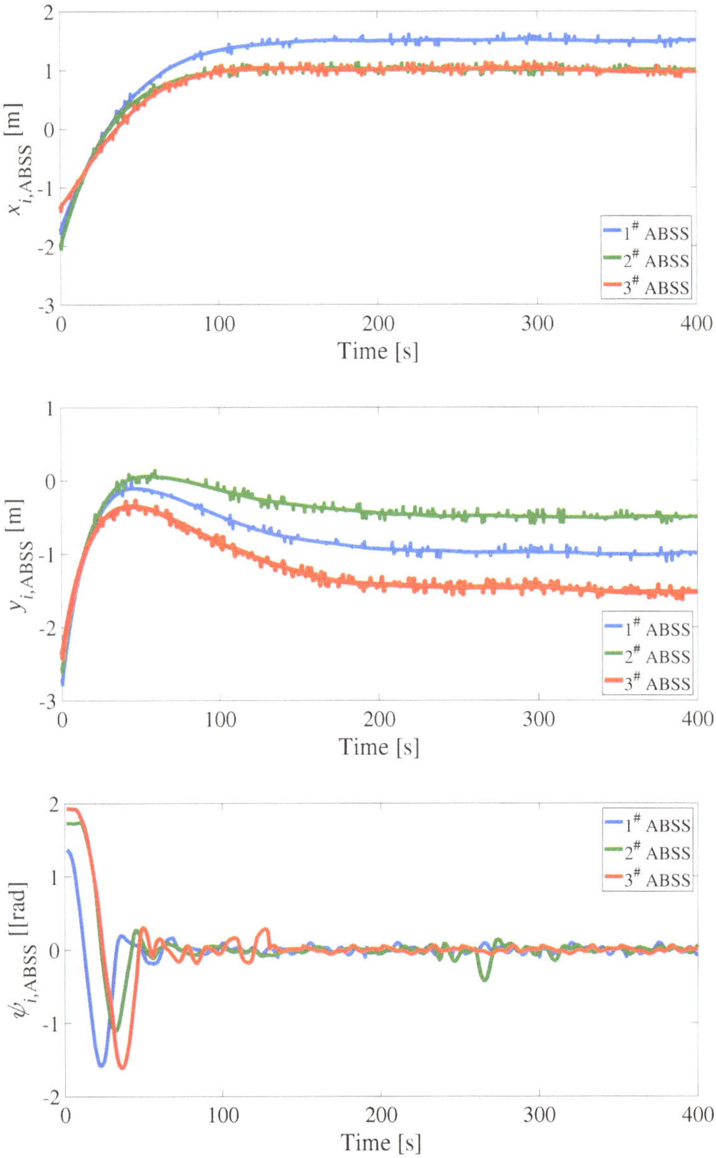

Fig. 7.7 The formation control of three ABSSs by using the controls (7.24) and (3.24)

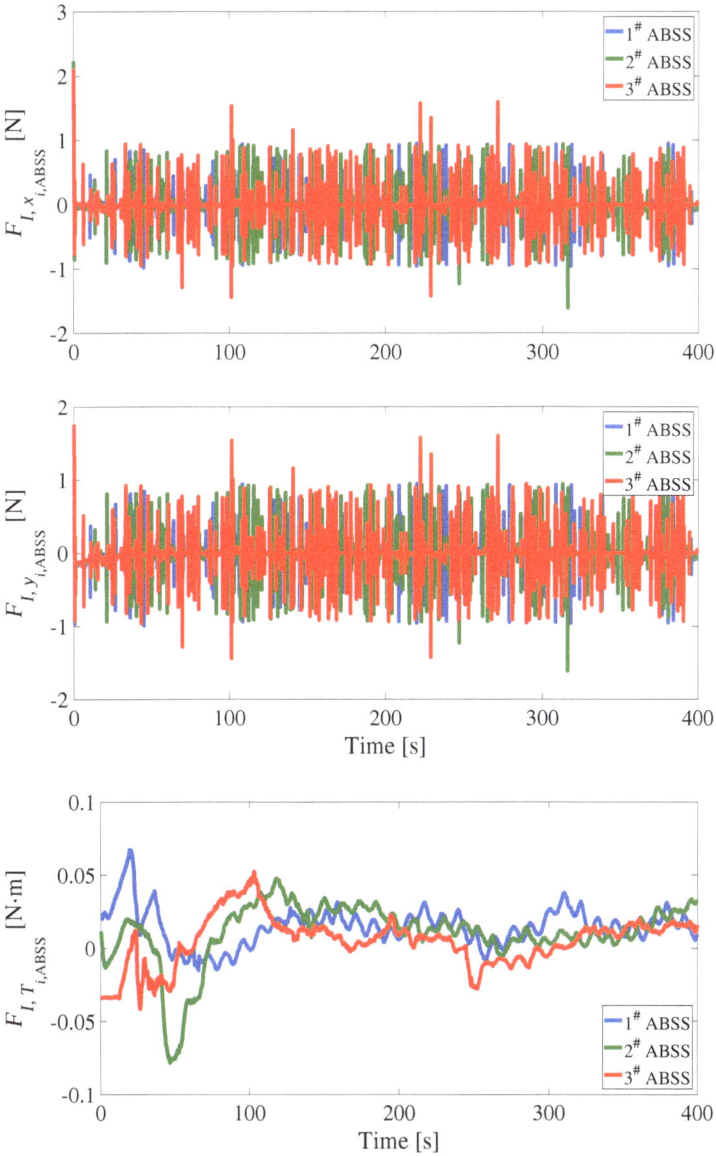

Fig. 7.8 The control inputs generated by the controls (7.24) and (3.24)

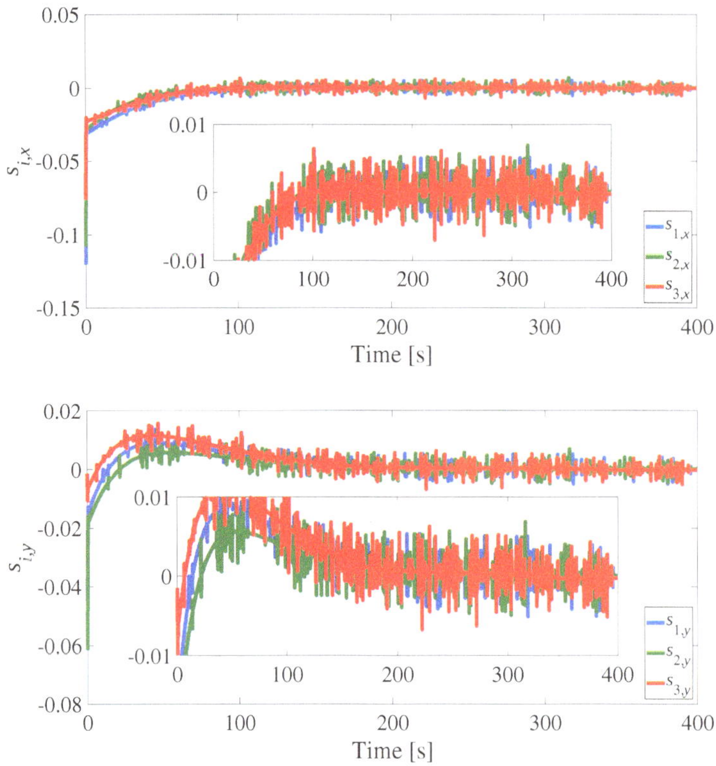

Fig. 7.9 The trends of sliding-mode variables $s_{i,x}(t)$ and $s_{i,y}(t)$

better control performance, the proposed SM-HOFAS predictive control will make the great contributions to practical applications of various fields.

Chapter 8
Terminal Sliding-Mode Predictive Cooperative Control for HUN-HOFAMASs

8.1 Introduction

Because of the complex application scenarios of cooperative control for the MASs, the cooperative control tasks have become more and more complex, such that the dynamic model of each agent is with the complex nonlinearities and uncertainties, and even their dynamics are different from each other. Considering the above status, the HUN-MAS is more general and more practical to describe the actual dynamics of the agent in the complex cooperative control tasks, such that the cooperative control for the HUN-MASs, as a longstanding concern, has attracted great attention of a string of scholars and engineers.

In the previous, Guo et al. (2022) provided an internal model-based adaptive distributed regulator to consider the cooperative output regulation problem of HUN-MASs. Lu and Liu (2021) also adopted the internal model principle to construct a distributed nonlinear dynamical controller for the consensus of second-order HUN-MASs. Aiming at strict-feedback HUN-MASs with quantization constraint, Choi and Yoo (2022) proposed a weighting adjusting law based on quantized signals for a neural network function approximator, such that a distributed adaptive control was obtained to realize the adaptive consensus tracking performance. Li et al. (2022a) applied the high-order neural network to construct a nonlinear regulator with unknown dynamics, which established an adaptive controller with a forward compensation for the approximate output regulation. Dong et al. (2022) designed a T-S fuzzy cooperative control to achieve the output synchronization of HUN-MASs with external disturbances and quantization constraint. Katsoukis and Rovithakis (2022) proposed a prescribed performance control method to achieve the robust output synchronization of MIMO high-order HUN-MASs with low complexities and computations. Combining a parameter updating law with distributed observer, Dong and Xu (2021) presented an adaptive output feedback control to enhance the robustness for handling the heterogeneous strong nonlinear dynamics, which realized the cooperative output regulation with external disturbances. Parsa and

D.-W. Zhang, G.-P. Liu, *Predictive Cooperative Control for High-Order Fully Actuated Multiagent Systems*, https://doi.org/10.1007/978-981-95-1695-7_8

Danesh (2021) used a Lyapunov-Krasovskii functional and an LMI method to design a smooth control for Lipschitz HUN-MASs, such that the states of follower agents can be converged to a convex set of leader agents with a desired exponential rate. In Zhang and Yang (2022), a fully distributed output feedback control based on a fuzzy logic and an input filter was developed to realize the output synchronization of the HUN-MASs. Jiang et al. (2023) presented a neural network backstepping control to construct a distributed controller for the synchronization control of the HUN-MASs under the input quantization. Meanwhile, Xiao and Dong (2022), Tang and Wang (2021), Yan et al. (2022), Tan et al. (2022), and the references therein also had contributions to the progress of this field.

Among the above studies, sliding-mode control plays an import role in the cooperative control for HUN-MASs with a better control performance and has obtained some representative achievements. Concretely, Liu et al. (2024d) presented an integral sliding mode based on Gudermannian function to realize the fixed-time consensus of first- and second-order HUN-MASs. Li et al. (2023d) designed a fuzzy adaptive terminal sliding-mode control to maintain the predefined-time consensus of third-order HUN-MASs with dead zone and its application in vehicular platoon. You et al. (2022) provided an advanced sliding-mode control to implement the formation control for multiple heterogeneous ships under uncertain dynamics. Cheng et al. (2021) proposed a robust finite-time fast terminal sliding-mode control to guarantee the cooperative formation control of multiple unmanned ground vehicle-unmanned aerial vehicle under heterogeneous unmodeled dynamics. Further, by introducing the HOFAS theory into the cooperative control for HUN-MASs, the complexity and its related computational load can be effectively reduced during the design process, which can obviously raise the cooperative control performance.

To further investigate the robust cooperative control for the HUN-HOFAMASs, this chapter proposes a TSM-HOFAS predictive control to address this problem, where a terminal sliding-mode variable is introduced to enhance the robustness and accelerate the convergence rate, and an IHOFAS prediction model of terminal sliding-mode variable is constructed with the help of a type of Diophantine Equation. The major works are summarized as follows. Firstly, a discrete-time model of the i-th HOFA agent with HUN dynamics is adopted to provide a better model foundation for the cooperative control design. Then, a terminal sliding-mode variable is utilized to enhance the robustness and accelerate the convergence rate, and an IHOFAS prediction model of terminal sliding-mode variable is established by applying a kind of Diophantine Equation. Based on this prediction model, the multistep ahead predictions of terminal sliding-mode variable can be developed to construct an optimal terminal sliding-mode predictive controller for the cooperative control. Further, a sufficient condition for the simultaneous consensus and stability of the closed-loop HOFAMASs can be proposed by using the Lypaunov stability theory and an LMLI method. Finally, the proposed TSM-HOFAS predictive control provides a solution to the cooperative flying-around of three ABSSs for illustrating the effectiveness and availability.

8.2 Problem Statement

Based on Duan (2022c) and system (2.1), the i-th HOFA agent with HUN dynamics in a type of discrete-time step-forward form is considered as

$$\begin{aligned} y_i(t+n_i) =& f_i\left(y_i^{\lfloor 0,n_i-1\rfloor}(t), u_i^{\lceil p_i,1\rceil}(t)\right) + g_i\left(y_i^{\lfloor 0,n_i-1\rfloor}(t), u_i^{\lceil p_i,1\rceil}(t)\right)u_i(t) \\ &+ \phi_i\left(y_i^{\lfloor 0,n_i-1\rfloor}(t), u_i^{\lceil p_i,1\rceil}(t), t\right), \\ y_i(t) =& y_{i0}(t), \quad u_i(t) = u_{i0}(t), \quad \forall t \leq 0, \end{aligned} \tag{8.1}$$

with

$$\begin{aligned} y_i^{\lfloor 0,n_i-1\rfloor}(y) &:= \{y_i(t), y_i(t+1), \ldots, y_i(t+n_i-1)\}, \\ u_i^{\lceil p_i,1\rceil}(t) &:= \{u_i(t-p_i), u(t-p_i+1), \ldots, u_i(t-1)\}, \end{aligned}$$

where $y_i(t) \in \mathbb{R}^m$ and $u_i(t) \in \mathbb{R}^m$ are the output and input vectors, $y_{i0}(t) \in \mathbb{R}^m$ and $u_{i0}(t) \in \mathbb{R}^m$ are the related initial values of $y_i(t)$ and $u_i(t)$, and n_i and p_i are two positive integers. $f_i(\cdot) := f_i\left(y_i^{\lfloor 0,n_i-1\rfloor}(t), u_i^{\lceil p_i,1\rceil}(t)\right) \in \mathbb{R}^m$ and $g_i(\cdot) := g_i\left(y_i^{\lfloor 0,n_i-1\rfloor}(t), u_i^{\lceil p_i,1\rceil}(t)\right) \in \mathbb{R}^{m\times m}$ represent the given vector and matrix functions, respectively. $\phi_i(\cdot, t) := \phi_i\left(y_i^{\lfloor 0,n_i-1\rfloor}(t), u_i^{\lceil p_i,1\rceil}(t), t\right) \in \mathbb{R}^m$ is a high-order HUN function.

Assumption 8.1 *A1.* $\forall t \geq 0$, $\det(g_i(\cdot)) \neq 0$ *or* ∞. *A2.* $y(t)$ *is available in the control design. A3.* $\phi_i(\cdot, t)$ *is unknown but is bounded in relation to time t (Katsoukis and Rovithakis 2022).*

Meanwhile, the communication topology is described by Definition 3.1, and Assumption 3.1 is satisfied during the cooperative control design. Let $\varsigma_{i,a}$ and $\varsigma_{i,s}$ be the upper bounds of time-varying communication constraints in the i-th forward and feedback channels, respectively, where $\varsigma_{i,a}$ and $\varsigma_{i,s}$ satisfy Assumption 4.1, and $\varsigma_{ii} = \varsigma_i = \varsigma_{i,a} + \varsigma_{i,s}$, $\varsigma_{ij} = \varsigma_{i,a} + \varsigma_{j,s}$.

To consider the robust cooperative control for the i-th HOFA agent (8.1), a TSM-HOFAS predictive control is proposed as

$$u_i(t) = g_i^{-1}(\cdot)\left(-f_i(\cdot) + \Upsilon_i(A_{i,0\sim n_i-1}, y_i(t)) + v_i(t)\right), \tag{8.2}$$

where $-f_i(\cdot)$ is used to eliminate the original nonlinearities, $\Upsilon_i(A_{i,0\sim n_i-1}, y_i(t)) = \sum_{\eta=0}^{n_i-1} A_{i,\eta} y_i(t+\eta) \in \mathbb{R}^m$ aims to adjust the closed-loop performances and $A_{i,\eta} \in \mathbb{R}^{m\times m}$ are the adjustment parameters to be determined, and $v_i(t) \in \mathbb{R}^m$ is a robust cooperative control item designed by the proposed TSM-HOFAS predictive control. The related control structure is shown in Fig. 8.1.

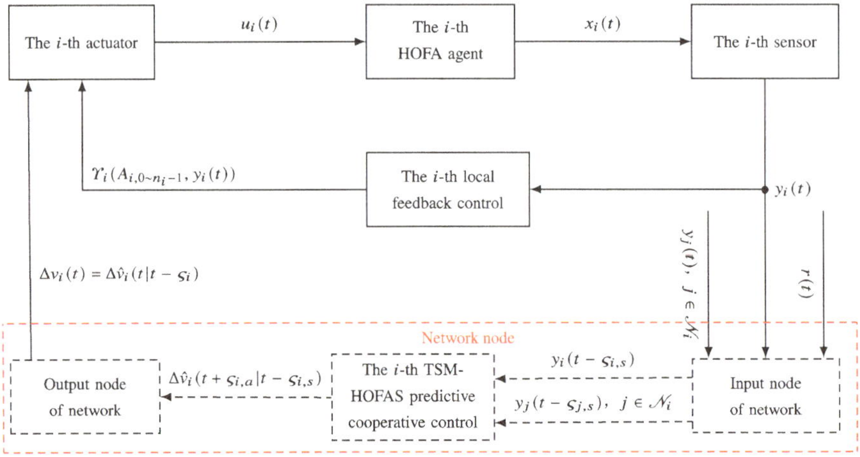

Fig. 8.1 Terminal sliding-mode predictive cooperative control for the HUN-HOFAMASs

By using (8.2), the closed-loop HOFAMASs can be achieved as

$$\begin{aligned} y_i(t+n_i) =& \Upsilon_i(A_{i,0\sim n_i-1}, y_i(t)) + v_i(t) + \phi_i(\cdot,t) \\ =& \sum_{\eta=0}^{n_i-1} A_{i,\eta} y_i(t+\eta) + v_i(t) + \phi_i(\cdot,t), \quad i \in \mathscr{N}. \end{aligned} \tag{8.3}$$

To obtain the optimal robust cooperative control item $v_i(t)$, an objective function is presented as

$$\mathcal{J}(t) = \sum_{i\in\mathscr{N}} \mathcal{J}_i(t), \tag{8.4}$$

where $\mathcal{J}_i(t)$ is a sub-objective function for the robust cooperative control performance of the i-th HOFA agent and is provided as

$$\begin{aligned} \mathcal{J}_i(t) =& \sum_{j\in\mathscr{N}_i} w_{ij} \left\| \hat{S}_i(t+\varsigma_{i,a}+\aleph_y|t-\varsigma_{i,s}) - \hat{S}_j(t+\varsigma_{i,a}+\aleph_y|t-\varsigma_{j,s}) \right\|^2 \\ &+ \alpha_i \left\| \hat{S}_i(t+\varsigma_{i,a}+\aleph_y|t-\varsigma_{i,s}) - S_{i,\mathrm{ref}}(t+\varsigma_{i,a}+\aleph_y) \right\|^2 \\ &+ \beta_i \left\| \Delta\hat{V}_i(t+\varsigma_{i,a}+\aleph_u|t-\varsigma_{i,s}) \right\|^2, \end{aligned} \tag{8.5}$$

with

$$\hat{S}_i(t+\varsigma_{i,a}+\aleph_y|t-\varsigma_{i,s}) = \begin{bmatrix} \hat{s}_i(t+\varsigma_{i,a}+\aleph_y|t-\varsigma_{i,s}) \\ \vdots \\ \hat{s}_i(t+\varsigma_{i,a}+1|t-\varsigma_{i,s}) \end{bmatrix},$$

$$\hat{S}_j(t+\varsigma_{i,a}+\aleph_y|t-\varsigma_{j,s}) = \begin{bmatrix} \hat{s}_j(t+\varsigma_{i,a}+\aleph_y|t-\varsigma_{j,s}) \\ \vdots \\ \hat{s}_j(t+\varsigma_{i,a}+1|t-\varsigma_{j,s}) \end{bmatrix},$$

$$\Delta\hat{V}_i(t+\varsigma_{i,a}+\aleph_u|t-\varsigma_{i,s}) = \begin{bmatrix} \Delta\hat{v}_i(t+\varsigma_{i,a}+\aleph_u|t-\varsigma_{i,s}) \\ \vdots \\ \Delta\hat{v}_i(t+\varsigma_{i,a}|t-\varsigma_{i,s}) \end{bmatrix},$$

$$S_{i,\mathrm{ref}}(t+\varsigma_{i,a}+\aleph_y) = \begin{bmatrix} s_{i,\mathrm{ref}}(t+\varsigma_{i,a}+\aleph_y) \\ \vdots \\ s_{i,\mathrm{ref}}(t+\varsigma_{i,a}+1) \end{bmatrix},$$

where $s_i(t)$ is a terminal sliding-mode variable of the i-th HOFA agent (8.1) and $s_{i,\mathrm{ref}}(t)$ is a reference sliding-mode variable. Then, $\hat{s}_i(t+\eta|t-\varsigma_{i,s})$, $\eta = \varsigma_{i,a}+1, \varsigma_{i,a}+2, \ldots, \varsigma_{i,a}+\aleph_y$, and $\Delta\hat{v}_i(t+\eta|t-\varsigma_{i,s})$, $\eta = \eta = \varsigma_{i,a}, \varsigma_{i,a}+1, \ldots, \varsigma_{i,a}+\aleph_u$, denote the η-th ahead predictions of terminal sliding-mode variable $s(t)$ and robust cooperative control increment $\Delta v_i(t)$ based on time $t-\varsigma_{i,s}$. $S_{i,\mathrm{ref}}(t+\varsigma_{i,a}+\aleph_y)$ indicates the relevant multistep ahead sequence of $s_{i,\mathrm{ref}}(t)$. w_{ij} is the (i, j)-th element of adjacent matrix $\mathscr{W}$, and $\alpha_i > 0$ and $\beta_i > 0$ are the two weighting factors. The aim of each item in (8.5) has been summarized in Remark 7.1.

Problem 8.1 For the i-th HOFA agent (8.1) under Assumptions 3.1, 4.1, and 8.1, a TSM-HOFAS predictive control $u_i\left(t, v_i(t, y_i(t), y_j(t), r(t))\right)$ is constructed in (8.2) by minimizing the objective function $\mathcal{J}(t)$ in (8.4) and (8.5), such that the closed-loop HOFAMASs (8.3) can implement the simultaneous consensus and stability, i.e., the following conditions hold:

1. $\forall i \in \mathcal{N}, \forall t \geq 0, \lim\limits_{t\to\infty} \|y_i(t)\| < \infty$ with $\|r(t)\| < \infty$.
2. $\forall i \in \mathcal{N}, \forall j \in \mathcal{N}_i, \lim_{t\to\infty}\|y_i(t) - y_j(t)\| = 0$.

8.3 HOFAS Terminal Sliding-Mode Predictive Cooperative Control Scheme

8.3.1 *Design of Terminal Sliding-Mode Variable*

Actually, sliding-mode control is considered as one of the most common strategies to overcome the negative impacts of the uncertainties. To enhance the robustness and accelerate the convergence rate, the terminal sliding-mode control scheme is always used in the related literature (see Yang et al. 2021b; Wang et al. 2022a; Fei et al. 2022, and the references therein). Following this idea, a terminal sliding-mode variable is constructed to handle the HUN dynamics for the robust cooperative control. Firstly, let $e_i(t) = y_i(t) - r(t)$ be the tracking error of the i-th HOFA agent, which means that Conditions 1 and 2 of Problem 8.1 can be transformed into $\lim_{t\to\infty}\|e_i(t)\| = 0$. Then, a terminal sliding-mode variable $s_i(t) \in \mathbb{R}^m$ is proposed as

$$s_i(t) = \Xi_i(q^{-1})e_i(t) - \vartheta_i^t \Xi_i(q^{-1})e_i(0), \quad 0 < \vartheta_i < 1, \tag{8.6}$$

where $\Xi_i(q^{-1}) = \sum_{\eta=0}^{n_{i,\xi}} \xi_{i,\eta} q^{-\eta}$ is chosen as a Schur polynomial matrix, $\xi_{i,\eta} \in \mathbb{R}^{m\times m}$, $\eta = 0, 1, \ldots, n_{i,\xi}$, denote the corresponding coefficient matrices, $n_{i,\xi}$ is a given positive integer, and $e_i(0)$ is the initial value of $e_i(t)$. Based on (8.6), $s_i(0) = 0$ with $t = 0$, which means that all initial values of tracking errors $e_i(0)$ can be located at the terminal sliding-mode surface.

In (8.6), $\vartheta_i^t \Xi_i(q^{-1})e_i(0) \to 0$ with $t \to \infty$, such that $\forall t$, $s_i(t) = 0$ can be derived as

$$\begin{aligned} s_i(t) =& \Xi_i(q^{-1})e_i(t) = \sum_{\eta=0}^{n_{i,\xi}} \xi_{i,\eta} q^{-\eta} e_i(t) \\ =& \xi_{i,0}e_i(t) + \xi_{i,1}e_i(t-1) + \cdots + \xi_{i,n_{i,\xi}} e_i(t - n_{i,\xi}) = 0. \end{aligned}$$

When $\xi_{i,\eta}$, $\eta = 0, 1, \ldots, n_{i,\xi}$, are not all zeros, $\Xi_i(q^{-1})$ is a nonzero Schur polynomial matrix in relation to q^{-1}, such that $s_i(t) = 0 \Longrightarrow e_i(t) = 0$ with $t \to \infty$, i.e., $s(t) = 0 \Longrightarrow e(t) = 0$ with $t \to \infty$, where $e(t) = \begin{bmatrix} e_1^{\mathrm{T}}(t) & \cdots & e_N^{\mathrm{T}}(t) \end{bmatrix}^{\mathrm{T}}$ and $s(t) = \begin{bmatrix} s_1^{\mathrm{T}}(t) & \cdots & s_N^{\mathrm{T}}(t) \end{bmatrix}^{\mathrm{T}}$.

8.3.2 Design of TSM-HOFAS Predictive Cooperative Control

Based on the closed-loop system (8.3), its nominal expression without HUN dynamics $\phi_i(\cdot, t)$ is provided as

$$y_i(t + n_i) = \sum_{\eta=0}^{n_i - 1} A_{i,\eta} y_i(t + \eta) + v_i(t), \tag{8.7}$$

and by using the time operator q, system (8.7) can be equivalently transformed as a polynomial one, i.e.,

$$\mathcal{A}_i(q^{-1})y_i(t) = \mathcal{B}_i(q^{-1})v_i(t-1), \tag{8.8}$$

with $\mathcal{A}_i(q^{-1}) = I - \sum_{\eta=0}^{n_i-1} A_{i,\eta} q^{-n+\eta}$ and $\mathcal{B}_i(q^{-1}) = q^{1-n_i}$. Based on Diophantine Equation (3.7) with the same process from (2.5) to (2.7), an IHOFAS prediction model based on (8.8) can be developed as (2.7), i.e.,

$$y_i(t+\eta) = \mathcal{F}_{i,\eta} y_i(t) + \mathcal{G}_{i,\eta} \Delta v_i(t+\eta-1),$$

where $\mathcal{F}_{i,\eta}$ and $\mathcal{G}_{i,\eta}$ are constructed in (3.8). Considering the upper bounds of time-varying communication constraints $\varsigma_{i,a}$ and $\varsigma_{i,s}$ in the i-th forward and feedback channels, the above IHOFAS prediction model can be corrected as

$$\hat{y}_i(t-\varsigma_{i,s}+\eta|t-\varsigma_{i,s}) = \mathcal{F}_{i,\eta} y_i(t-\varsigma_{i,s}) + \mathcal{G}_{i,\eta} \Delta \hat{v}_i(t-\varsigma_{i,s}+\eta-1|t-\varsigma_{i,s}), \quad (8.9)$$

with $\eta = 1, 2, \ldots, \varsigma_i + \aleph_y$. Combining the terminal sliding-mode variable (8.6) with the IHOFAS prediction model (8.9), an IHOFAS prediction model of terminal sliding-mode variable can be established as

$$\begin{aligned} \hat{s}_i(t-\varsigma_{i,s}+\eta|t-\varsigma_{i,s}) = & \mathcal{D}_{i,\eta} y_i(t-\varsigma_{i,s}) + \mathcal{L}_{i,\eta} \Delta \hat{v}_i(t-\varsigma_{i,s}+\eta-1|t-\varsigma_{i,s}) \\ & - \Xi_i r(t-\varsigma_{i,s}+\eta) - \vartheta_i^{t-\varsigma_{i,s}+\eta} \Xi_i e_i(0), \end{aligned} \quad (8.10)$$

with $\mathcal{D}_{i,\eta}(q^{-1}) = \Xi_i(q^{-1})\mathcal{F}_{i,\eta}(q^{-1})$ and $\mathcal{L}_{i,\eta}(q^{-1}) = \Xi_i(q^{-1})\mathcal{G}_{i,\eta}(q^{-1})$.

When $\eta = \varsigma_i+1, \varsigma_i+2, \ldots, \varsigma_i+\aleph_y$, the multistep ahead predictions of terminal sliding-mode variable $s_i(t)$ can be obtained as

$$\begin{aligned} \hat{s}_i(t+\varsigma_{i,a}+1|t-\varsigma_{i,s}) = & \mathcal{D}_{i,\varsigma_i+1} y_i(t-\varsigma_{i,s}) + \mathcal{L}_{i,\varsigma_i+1} \Delta \hat{v}_i(t+\varsigma_{i,a}|t-\varsigma_{i,s}) \\ & - \Xi_i r(t+\varsigma_{i,a}+1) - \vartheta_i^{t+\varsigma_{i,a}+1} \Xi_i e_i(0), \\ & \vdots \\ \hat{s}_i(t+\varsigma_{i,a}+\aleph_y|t-\varsigma_{i,s}) = & \mathcal{D}_{i,\varsigma_i+\aleph_y} y_i(t-\varsigma_{i,s}) + \mathcal{L}_{i,\varsigma+\aleph_y} \Delta \hat{v}_i \\ & \times (t+\varsigma_{i,a}+\aleph_y-1|t-\varsigma_{i,s}) \\ & - \Xi_i r(t+\varsigma_{i,a}+\aleph_y) - \vartheta_i^{t+\varsigma_{i,a}+\aleph_y} \Xi_i e_i(0). \end{aligned}$$

When $\eta = \varsigma_i+\aleph_u+1, \varsigma_i+\aleph_u+2, \ldots, \varsigma_i+\aleph_y$, $\hat{v}_i(t-\varsigma_{i,s}+\eta|t-\varsigma_{i,s}) = \hat{v}_i(t+\varsigma_{i,a}+\aleph_u|t-\varsigma_{i,s})$ such that $\Delta\hat{v}_i(t-\varsigma_{i,s}+\eta|t-\varsigma_{i,s}) = 0$. Hence, the above multistep ahead predictions of terminal sliding-mode variable can be compactly rewritten as

$$\begin{aligned} \hat{S}_i(t+\varsigma_{i,a}+\aleph_y|t-\varsigma_{i,s}) = & P_{i,1} y_i(t-\varsigma_{i,s}) + P_{i,2} \Delta \hat{V}_i(t+\varsigma_{i,a}+\aleph_u|t-\varsigma_{i,s}) \\ & - \Xi_{i,d} R(t+\varsigma_{i,a}+\aleph_y) - \Theta_i(t+\varsigma_{i,a}+\aleph_y) \Xi_i e_i(0), \end{aligned} \quad (8.11)$$

where $R(t+\varsigma_{i,a}+\aleph_y) = \begin{bmatrix} r(t+\varsigma_{i,a}+\aleph_y) \\ \vdots \\ r(t+\varsigma_{i,a}+1) \end{bmatrix}$, $\Theta_i(t+\varsigma_{i,a}+\aleph_y) = \begin{bmatrix} \vartheta_i^{t+\varsigma_{i,a}+\aleph_y} \\ \vdots \\ \vartheta_i^{t+\varsigma_{i,a}+1} \end{bmatrix}$, $\Xi_{i,d} = \text{Blockdiag}\{\Xi_i, \ldots, \Xi_i\}$, and

$$P_{i,1} = \begin{bmatrix} \mathcal{D}_{i,\varsigma_i+N_y} \\ \vdots \\ \vdots \\ \mathcal{D}_{i,\varsigma_i+1} \end{bmatrix}, \quad P_{i,2} = \begin{bmatrix} \mathcal{L}_{i,\varsigma_i+\aleph_y} & 0 & \cdots & 0 \\ \vdots & \vdots & \cdots & \vdots \\ \mathcal{L}_{i,\varsigma_i+\aleph_u+1} & 0 & \cdots & 0 \\ 0 & \mathcal{L}_{i,\varsigma_i+\aleph_u} & \ddots & \vdots \\ \vdots & \ddots & \ddots & 0 \\ 0 & \cdots & 0 & \mathcal{L}_{i,\varsigma_i+1} \end{bmatrix}.$$

Based on (2.9), an incremental constraint of cooperative control increment is defined as

$$\Delta\hat{v}_i(t+\varsigma_{i,a}+\eta|t-\varsigma_{i,s}) = \gamma_{i,\eta}\Delta\hat{v}_i(t+\varsigma_{i,a}|t-\varsigma_{i,s}),$$

where $\gamma_{i,\eta} > 0$, $\eta = 1, 2, \ldots, \aleph_u$, is a weighting factor, such that $P_{i,2}$ can be degenerated as $P_{i,3} = P_{i,2}\Gamma_i$ with $\Gamma_i = \text{Blockdiag}\{\gamma_{i,\aleph_u}I, \ldots, \gamma_{i,1}I, I\}$, and $P_{i,2}\Delta\hat{V}_i(t+\varsigma_{i,a}+\aleph_u|t-\varsigma_{i,s}) = P_{i,3}\Delta\hat{V}_i(t+\varsigma_{i,a}|t-\varsigma_{i,s})$ with

$$\Delta\hat{V}_i(t+\varsigma_{i,a}|t-\varsigma_{i,s}) = \left[\, \Delta\hat{v}_i^{\mathrm{T}}(t+\varsigma_{i,a}|t-\varsigma_{i,s}) \cdots \Delta\hat{v}_i^{\mathrm{T}}(t+\varsigma_{i,a}|t-\varsigma_{i,s}) \,\right]^{\mathrm{T}}.$$

Thus, the prediction of terminal sliding-mode variable (8.11) can be transformed as

$$\begin{aligned} \hat{S}_i(t+\varsigma_{i,a}+\aleph_y|t-\varsigma_{i,s}) =& P_{i,1}y_i(t-\varsigma_{i,s}) + P_{i,3}\Delta\hat{V}_i(t+\varsigma_{i,a}|t-\varsigma_{i,s}) \\ &- \Xi_{i,d}R(t+\varsigma_{i,a}+\aleph_y) - \Theta_i(t+\varsigma_{i,a}+\aleph_y)\Xi_i e_i(0). \end{aligned} \tag{8.12}$$

$\forall j \in \mathcal{N}_i$, based on the IHOFAS prediction model of terminal sliding-mode variable (8.10), $s_j(t)$ can be predicted as

$$\begin{aligned} \hat{s}_j(t-\varsigma_{j,s}+\eta|t-\varsigma_{j,s}) =& \mathcal{D}_{j,\eta}y_j(t-\varsigma_{j,s}) + \mathcal{L}_{j,\eta}\Delta\hat{v}_j(t-\varsigma_{j,s}+\eta-1|t-\varsigma_{j,s}) \\ &- \Xi_j r(t-\varsigma_{j,s}+\eta) - \vartheta_j^{t-\varsigma_{j,s}+\eta}\Xi_j e_j(0), \end{aligned}$$

with $\eta = 1, 2, \ldots, \varsigma_{ij}+\aleph_y$. When $\eta = \varsigma_{ij}+1, \varsigma_{ij}+2, \ldots, \varsigma_{ij}+\aleph_y$, the multistep ahead predictions of terminal sliding-mode variable $s_j(t)$ can be derived as

$$\begin{aligned} \hat{s}_j(t+\varsigma_{i,a}+1|t-\varsigma_{j,s}) =& \mathcal{D}_{j,\varsigma_{ij}+1}y_j(t-\varsigma_{j,s}) + \mathcal{L}_{j,\varsigma_{ij}+1}\Delta\hat{v}_j(t+\varsigma_{i,a}|t-\varsigma_{j,s}) \\ &- \Xi_j r(t+\varsigma_{i,a}+1) - \vartheta_j^{t+\varsigma_{i,a}+1}\Xi_j e_j(0), \end{aligned}$$

$$
\begin{aligned}
&\vdots \\
\hat{s}_j(t+\varsigma_{i,a}+\aleph_y|t-\varsigma_{j,s}) =& \mathcal{D}_{j,\varsigma_{ij}+\aleph_y} y_j(t-\varsigma_{j,s}) \\
&+ \mathcal{L}_{j,\varsigma_{ij}+\aleph_y} \Delta\hat{\upsilon}_j(t+\varsigma_{i,a}+\aleph_y-1|t-\varsigma_{j,s}) \\
&- \Xi_j r(t+\varsigma_{i,a}+\aleph_y) - \vartheta_j^{t+\varsigma_{i,a}+\aleph_y} \Xi_j e_j(0).
\end{aligned}
$$

Repeating the process from (8.11)–(8.12), the above multistep terminal sliding-mode predictions for the j-th HOFA agent can be summarized as

$$
\begin{aligned}
\hat{S}_j(t+\varsigma_{i,a}+\aleph_y|t-\varsigma_{j,s}) =& P_{j,1} y_j(t-\varsigma_{j,s}) + P_{j,3}\Delta\hat{V}_j(t+\varsigma_{i,a}|t-\varsigma_{j,s}) \\
&- \Xi_{j,d} R(t+\varsigma_{i,a}+\aleph_y) - \Theta_j \\
&\times (t+\varsigma_{i,a}+\aleph_y)\Xi_j e_{j,r}(0),
\end{aligned}
\tag{8.13}
$$

where $\Delta\hat{V}_j(t+\varsigma_{i,a}|t-\varsigma_{j,s}) = \begin{bmatrix} \Delta\hat{\upsilon}_j(t+\varsigma_{i,a}|t-\varsigma_{j,s}) \\ \vdots \\ \Delta\hat{\upsilon}_j(t+\varsigma_{i,a}|t-\varsigma_{j,s}) \end{bmatrix}$, $\Theta_j(t+\varsigma_{i,a}+\aleph_y) = \begin{bmatrix} \vartheta_j^{t+\varsigma_{i,a}+\aleph_y} \\ \vdots \\ \vartheta_j^{t+\varsigma_{i,a}+1} \end{bmatrix}$, $\Xi_{j,d} = \text{Blockdiag}\{\Xi_j, \ldots, \Xi_j\}$, and

$$
P_{j,1} = \begin{bmatrix} \mathcal{D}_{j,\varsigma_{ij}+\aleph_y}^{\mathrm{T}} & \cdots\cdots & \mathcal{D}_{j,\varsigma_{ij}+1}^{\mathrm{T}} \end{bmatrix}^{\mathrm{T}},
$$

$$
P_{j,2} = \begin{bmatrix}
\mathcal{L}_{j,\varsigma_{ij}+\aleph_y} & 0 & \cdots & 0 \\
\vdots & \vdots & \cdots & \vdots \\
\mathcal{L}_{j,\varsigma_{ij}+\aleph_u+1} & 0 & \cdots & 0 \\
0 & \mathcal{L}_{j,\varsigma_{ij}+\aleph_u} & \ddots & \vdots \\
\vdots & \ddots & \ddots & 0 \\
0 & \cdots & 0 & \mathcal{L}_{j,\varsigma_{ij}+1}
\end{bmatrix},
$$

$$
P_{j,3} = P_{j,2}\Gamma_j, \quad \Gamma_j = \text{Blockdiag}\{\gamma_{j,\aleph_u} I, \ldots, \gamma_{j,1} I, I\}.
$$

To solve the optimal robust cooperative control increment $\Delta\upsilon_i(t)$, let

$$
\frac{\partial}{\partial \Delta\hat{V}_i(t+\varsigma_{i,a}|t-\varsigma_{i,s})} \mathcal{J}(t) = 0, \; i \in \mathcal{N},
$$

and by using (8.12) and (8.13), it is yielded that

$$
\begin{aligned}
\Delta\hat{V}(t+\varsigma_{i,a}|t-\varsigma_s) =& F^{-1}Gy(t-\varsigma_s)+F^{-1}MR(t+\varsigma_{i,a}+\aleph_y) \\
&+F^{-1}L\tilde{\Theta}(t+\varsigma_{i,a}+\aleph_y)+F^{-1}WS_{i,\mathrm{ref}}(t+\varsigma_{i,a}+\aleph_y),
\end{aligned}
$$

where $\Delta\hat{V}(t+\varsigma_{i,a}|t-\varsigma_s) = \begin{bmatrix} \Delta\hat{V}_1(t+\varsigma_{i,a}|t-\varsigma_{1,s}) \\ \vdots \\ \Delta\hat{V}_N(t+\varsigma_{i,a}t-\varsigma_{N,s}) \end{bmatrix}$, $y(t-\varsigma_s) = \begin{bmatrix} y_1(t-\varsigma_{1,s}) \\ \vdots \\ y_N(t-\varsigma_{N,s}) \end{bmatrix}$, $\tilde{\Theta}(t+\varsigma_{i,a}+\aleph_y) = \begin{bmatrix} \Theta_1(t+\varsigma_{i,a}+\aleph_y)\Xi_1 e_1(0) \\ \vdots \\ \Theta_N(t+\varsigma_{i,a}+\aleph_y)\Xi_N e_N(0) \end{bmatrix}$, and

$$
\begin{aligned}
F =& \{f_{ij}\},\ \ f_{ii} = (w_i+\alpha_i)P_{i,3}^{\mathrm{T}}P_{i,3}+\beta_i\Gamma_i^{\mathrm{T}}\Gamma_i,\ \ f_{ij} = -w_{ij}P_{i,3}^{\mathrm{T}}P_{j,3}, \\
G =& \{g_{ij}\},\ \ g_{ii} = -(w_i+\alpha_i)P_{i,3}^{\mathrm{T}}P_{i,1},\ \ g_{ij} = w_{ij}P_{i,3}^{\mathrm{T}}P_{j,1}, \\
M =& \begin{bmatrix} (\alpha_1+w_1)P_{1,3}^{\mathrm{T}}\Xi_{1,d}-\sum_{j\in\mathcal{N}_1}w_{ij}P_{1,3}^{\mathrm{T}}\Xi_{j,d} \\ \vdots \\ (\alpha_N+w_N)P_{N,3}^{\mathrm{T}}\Xi_{N,d}-\sum_{j\in\mathcal{N}_N}w_{ij}P_{N,3}^{\mathrm{T}}\Xi_{j,d} \end{bmatrix}, \\
L =& \{l_{ij}\},\ \ l_{ii} = (w_i+\alpha_i)P_{i,3}^{\mathrm{T}},\ \ l_{ij} = -w_{ij}P_{i,3}^{\mathrm{T}}, \\
W =& \begin{bmatrix}\alpha_1 P_{1,3} \cdots \alpha_N P_{N,3}\end{bmatrix}^{\mathrm{T}},\ \ w_i = \sum_{j\in\mathcal{N}_i} w_{ij}.
\end{aligned}
$$

Then, the optimal robust cooperative control increment of the i-th HOFA agent in the network node is solved as $\Delta\hat{v}_i(t+\varsigma_{i,a}|t-\varsigma_s) = H_i\Delta\hat{V}(t+\varsigma_{i,a}|t-\varsigma_s)$, i.e.,

$$
\begin{aligned}
\Delta\hat{v}_i(t+\varsigma_{i,a}|t-\varsigma_s) =& H_iF^{-1}Gy(t-\varsigma_s)+H_iF^{-1}MR(t+\varsigma_{i,a}+\aleph_y) \\
&+H_iF^{-1}L\tilde{\Theta}(t+\varsigma_{i,a}+\aleph_y) \\
&+H_iF^{-1}WS_{i,\mathrm{ref}}(t+\varsigma_{i,a}+\aleph_y),
\end{aligned}
$$

where $H_i = \begin{bmatrix} H_{i,1} \cdots H_{i,N}\end{bmatrix} \in \mathbb{R}^{m\times(\aleph_u+1)Nm}$ with $H_{i,i} = \begin{bmatrix}0\cdots 0\ I\end{bmatrix}$, $H_{i,j} = 0$, $j\in\mathcal{N}_i$. On the i-th actuator, the optimal robust cooperative control increment is proposed as $\Delta v_i(t) = \Delta\hat{v}_i(t|t-\varsigma_i)$, i.e.,

$$
\begin{aligned}
\Delta v_i(t) =& H_iF^{-1}Gy(t-\varsigma)+H_iF^{-1}MR(t+\aleph_y) \\
&+H_iF^{-1}L\tilde{\Theta}(t+\aleph_y)+H_iF^{-1}WS_{i,\mathrm{ref}}(t+\aleph_y),
\end{aligned} \tag{8.14}
$$

where $y(t-\varsigma)=\begin{bmatrix} y_1(t-\varsigma_{i1}) \\ \vdots \\ y_N(t-\varsigma_{iN}) \end{bmatrix}$ and $\tilde{\Theta}(t+\aleph_y)=\begin{bmatrix} \Theta_1(t+\aleph_y)\Xi_1 e_1(0) \\ \vdots \\ \Theta_N(t+\aleph_y)\Xi_N e_N(0) \end{bmatrix}$.

Based on (8.14), it obviously means that the reference sliding-mode $s_{i,\mathrm{ref}}(t)$ plays a critical role in the solution of $\Delta v_i(t)$. In this study, $s_{i,\mathrm{ref}}(t)$ is selected as an improved sliding-mode reaching law and is presented as

$$s_{i,\mathrm{ref}}(t+1)=(1-\lambda_1 T)s_i(t)-\lambda_2 T\hbar_i(t),\quad s_{i,\mathrm{ref}}(t)=s_i(t),$$

where $0<\lambda_1 T_s,\lambda_2 T_s<1$, T_s denotes the sampling period, and $\hbar_i(t)=|s_i|^{\eth}\operatorname{sgn}(s_i)$ with $0<\eth<1$, where $\operatorname{sgn}(s_i)$ is the symbolic function in relation to $s_i(t)$ and is also given in (7.18).

8.4 Analysis of Simultaneous Consensus and Stability Under Heterogeneous Uncertainties

Because $e_i(t)=y_i(t)-r(t)$ is the tracking error of the i-th HOFA agent, let $\epsilon_{ii}(t)=\epsilon_i(t)=e_i(t)$, $\epsilon_{ij}(t)=y_i(t)-y_j(t)=e_i(t)-e_j(t)$, $j\in\mathcal{N}_i$, be the consensus error, so that the simultaneous consensus and stability of the closed-loop HOFAMASs (8.3) can be equivalently transformed into $\epsilon_i(t)\to 0$ and $\epsilon_{ij}(t)\to 0$ with $t\to\infty$. Furthermore, because of the proof of Theorem 3.1, the consensus error $\epsilon(t)$ in this chapter can also be converted as (3.18) with $i=1$ and $\epsilon(t)=\left[\epsilon_1^{\mathrm{T}}(t)\ \cdots\ \epsilon_{1N}^{\mathrm{T}}(t)\right]^{\mathrm{T}}$, i.e.,

$$\epsilon(t)=\tilde{\mathbf{I}}e(t),$$

which implies that $e(t)=0\Longrightarrow\epsilon(t)=0$ with $t\to\infty$. Based on the discussion in Subsection 8.3.1, $s(t)=0\Longrightarrow e(t)=0$ with $t\to\infty$, such that $s(t)=0\Longrightarrow\epsilon(t)=0$ with $t\to\infty$. It means that the simultaneous consensus and stability of the closed-loop HOFAMASs (8.3) can be equivalent to the asymptotic stability of $s(t)$, that is, Problem 8.1 is solvable if $s(t)$ is asymptotically stable, i.e., $\lim_{t\to\infty}\|s(t)\|=0$.

In fact, $\Delta v_i(t)$ in (8.14) is designed for the closed-loop nominal system (8.7). For the complete form of the closed system (8.3), the IHOFAS prediction model for terminal sliding-mode variable $s_i(t)$ in (8.10) can be corrected as

$$\begin{aligned}\hat{s}_i(t+\varsigma_{i,a}+\eta|t-\varsigma_{i,s})=&\mathcal{D}_{i,\varsigma_i+\eta}y_i(t-\varsigma_{i,s})+\mathcal{L}_{i,\varsigma_i+\eta}\Delta\hat{v}_i\\&\times(t+\varsigma_{i,a}+\eta-1|t-\varsigma_{i,s})\\&+\mathcal{L}_{i,\varsigma_i+\eta}\Delta\phi_i(\cdot,t-\varsigma_{i,s})\\&-\Xi_i r(t-\varsigma_{i,s}+\eta)-\vartheta_i^{t-\varsigma_{i,s}+\eta}\Xi_i e_i(0),\end{aligned}$$

such that the predictions in (8.12) and (8.13) can be rewritten as

$$\begin{aligned}\hat{S}_i(t+\varsigma_{i,a}+\aleph_y|t-\varsigma_{i,s}) =& P_{i,1}y_i(t-\varsigma_{i,s})+P_{i,3}\Delta\hat{V}_i(t+\varsigma_{i,a}|t-\varsigma_{i,s})\\ &+P_{i,4}\Delta\phi_i(\cdot,t-\varsigma_{i,s})-\Xi_{i,d}R(t+\varsigma_{i,a}+\aleph_y)\\ &-\Theta_i(t+\varsigma_{i,a}+\aleph_y)\Xi_i e_i(0),\\ \hat{S}_j(t+\varsigma_{i,a}+\aleph_y|t-\varsigma_{j,s}) =& P_{j,1}y_j(t-\varsigma_{j,s})+P_{j,3}\Delta\hat{V}_j(t+\varsigma_{i,a}|t-\varsigma_{j,s})\\ &+P_{j,4}\Delta\phi_j(\cdot,t-\varsigma_{j,s})-\Xi_{j,d}R(t+\varsigma_{i,a}+\aleph_y)\\ &-\Theta_j(t+\varsigma_{i,a}+\aleph_y)\Xi_j e_j(0),\end{aligned}\tag{8.15}$$

with $P_{i,4}=\begin{bmatrix}\mathcal{L}_{i,\varsigma_i+\aleph_y}\\ \vdots\\ \mathcal{L}_{i,\varsigma_i+1}\end{bmatrix}$ and $P_{j,4}=\begin{bmatrix}\mathcal{L}_{j,\varsigma_{ij}+\aleph_y}\\ \vdots\\ \mathcal{L}_{j,\varsigma_{ij}+1}\end{bmatrix}$.

Actually, $\Delta v_i(t)$ in (8.14) is calculated by minimizing the objective function $\mathcal{J}(t)$ in (8.4) and (8.5), which can be equivalently transformed into adjusting the weighting factors w_{ij}, α_i, and β_i to satisfy the following relationship:

$$\begin{aligned}&S_{i,\text{ref}}(t+\varsigma_{i,a}+\aleph_y)\\ &=P_{i,1}y_i(t-\varsigma_{i,s})+P_{i,3}\Delta\hat{V}_i(t+\varsigma_{i,a}|t-\varsigma_{i,s})\\ &\quad-\Xi_{i,d}R(t+\varsigma_{i,a}+\aleph_y)-\Theta_i(t+\varsigma_{i,a}+\aleph_y)\Xi_i e_i(0),\\ &=P_{j,1}y_j(t-\varsigma_{j,s})+P_{j,3}\Delta\hat{V}_j(t+\varsigma_{i,a}|t-\varsigma_{j,s})\\ &\quad-\Xi_{j,d}R(t+\varsigma_{i,a}+\aleph_y)-\Theta_j(t+\varsigma_{i,a}+\aleph_y)\Xi_j e_j(0).\end{aligned}\tag{8.16}$$

By taking (8.15) into (8.16), it is derived that

$$\begin{aligned}\hat{S}_i(t+\varsigma_{i,a}+\aleph_y|t-\varsigma_{i,s}) =& S_{i,\text{ref}}(t+\varsigma_{i,a}+\aleph_y)+P_{i,4}\Delta\phi_i(\cdot,t-\varsigma_{i,s}),\\ \hat{S}_j(t+\varsigma_{i,a}+\aleph_y|t-\varsigma_{j,s}) =& S_{i,\text{ref}}(t+\varsigma_{i,a}+\aleph_y)+P_{j,4}\Delta\phi_j(\cdot,t-\varsigma_{i,s}),\end{aligned}$$

which can be equivalent to

$$\begin{aligned}\hat{S}_i(t+\aleph_y|t-\varsigma_i) =& S_{i,\text{ref}}(t+\aleph_y)+P_{i,4}\Delta\phi_i(\cdot,t-\varsigma_i),\\ \hat{S}_j(t+\aleph_y|t-\varsigma_{ij}) =& S_{i,\text{ref}}(t+\aleph_y)+P_{j,4}\Delta\phi_i(\cdot,t-\varsigma_{ij}),\end{aligned}$$

where the last row is provided as

$$\begin{aligned}s_i(t+1) =& s_{i,\text{ref}}(t+1)+\mathcal{L}_{i,\varsigma_i+1}\Delta\phi_i(\cdot,t-\varsigma_i)\\ =& (1-\lambda_1 T)s_i(t)-\lambda_2 T\hbar_i(t)+\mathcal{L}_{i,\varsigma_i+1}\Delta\phi_i(\cdot,t-\varsigma_i),\\ s_j(t+1) =& s_{i,\text{ref}}(t+1)+\mathcal{L}_{j,\varsigma_{ij}+1}\Delta\phi_{ij}(\cdot,t-\varsigma_i)\\ =& (1-\lambda_1 T)s_i(t)-\lambda_2 T\hbar_i(t)+\mathcal{L}_{j,\varsigma_{ij}+1}\Delta\phi_{ij}(\cdot,t-\varsigma_{ij}).\end{aligned}\tag{8.17}$$

Then, Theorem 8.1 is presented here to analyze the asymptotic stability of sliding-mode variable $s(t)$ in (8.17).

Theorem 8.1 *System* (8.17) *can achieve the asymptotic stability if*

$$\Omega_{i,j,1} < 0, \quad \Omega_{i,j,3} - \Omega_{i,j,2}^{\mathrm{T}} \Omega_{i,j,1}^{-1} \Omega_{i,j,2} < 0, \tag{8.18}$$

where

$$\begin{aligned} \Omega_{i,j,1} &= 2(1-\lambda_1 T)^2 - 1, \\ \Omega_{i,j,2} &= \begin{bmatrix} -2(1-\lambda_1 T)\lambda_2 T & (1-\lambda_1 T)\mathcal{L}_{i,\varsigma_i+1} & (1-\lambda_1 T)\mathcal{L}_{j,\varsigma_{ij}+1} \end{bmatrix}, \\ \Omega_{i,j,3} &= \begin{bmatrix} 2\lambda_2^2 T^2 & -\lambda_2 T \mathcal{L}_{i,\varsigma_i+1} & -\lambda_2 T \mathcal{L}_{j,\varsigma_{ij}+1} \\ -\lambda_2 T \mathcal{L}_{i,\varsigma_i+1}^{\mathrm{T}} & \mathcal{L}_{i,\varsigma_i+1}^{\mathrm{T}} \mathcal{L}_{i,\varsigma_i+1} & 0 \\ -\lambda_2 T \mathcal{L}_{j,\varsigma_{ij}+1}^{\mathrm{T}} & 0 & \mathcal{L}_{j,\varsigma_{ij}+1}^{\mathrm{T}} \mathcal{L}_{j,\varsigma_{ij}+1} \end{bmatrix}. \end{aligned} \tag{8.19}$$

Proof By means of the Lyapunov stability theory, a definite Lyapunov function for system (8.17) is presented as

$$\mathscr{V}_{i,j}(t) = s_i^{\mathrm{T}}(t)s_i(t) + s_j^{\mathrm{T}}(t)s_j(t) \succ 0,$$

such that system (8.17) can achieve the asymptotic stability if $\Delta\mathscr{V}_{i,j}(t+1) < 0$, i.e.,

$$\begin{aligned} &\Delta\mathscr{V}_{i,j}(t+1) \\ &= \mathscr{V}_{i,j}(t+1) - \mathscr{V}_{i,j}(t) \\ &= 2(1-\lambda_1 T)^2 s_i^{\mathrm{T}}(t)s_i(t) - 2(1-\lambda_1 T)\lambda_2 T s_i^{\mathrm{T}}(t)\hbar_i(t) + 2\lambda_2^2 T^2 \hbar_i^{\mathrm{T}}(t)\hbar_i(t) \\ &- 2(1-\lambda_1 T)\lambda_2 T \hbar_i^{\mathrm{T}}(t)s_i(t) + (1-\lambda_1 T)s_i^{\mathrm{T}}(t)\mathcal{L}_{i,\varsigma_i+1}\Delta\phi_i(\cdot, t-\varsigma_i) \\ &- \lambda_2 T \hbar_i^{\mathrm{T}}(t)\mathcal{L}_{i,\varsigma_i+1}\Delta\phi_i(\cdot, t-\varsigma_i) + (1-\lambda_1 T)\Delta\phi_i^{\mathrm{T}}(\cdot, t-\varsigma_i)\mathcal{L}_{i,\varsigma_i+1}^{\mathrm{T}} s_i(t) \\ &- \lambda_2 T \Delta\phi_i^{\mathrm{T}}(\cdot, t-\varsigma_i)\mathcal{L}_{i,\varsigma_i+1}^{\mathrm{T}}\hbar_i(t) + \Delta\phi_i^{\mathrm{T}}(\cdot, t-\varsigma_i)\mathcal{L}_{i,\varsigma_i+1}^{\mathrm{T}}\mathcal{L}_{i,\varsigma_i+1}\Delta\phi_i(\cdot, t-\varsigma_i) \\ &- s_i^{\mathrm{T}}(t)s_i(t) + (1-\lambda_1 T)s_i^{\mathrm{T}}(t)\mathcal{L}_{j,\varsigma_{ij}+1}\Delta\phi_j(\cdot, t-\varsigma_{ij}) - \lambda_2 T \hbar_i^{\mathrm{T}}(t) \\ &\times \mathcal{L}_{j,\varsigma_{ij}+1}\Delta\phi_j(\cdot, t-\varsigma_{ij}) + (1-\lambda_1 T)\Delta\phi_j^{\mathrm{T}}(\cdot, t-\varsigma_{ij})\mathcal{L}_{j,\varsigma_{ij}+1}^{\mathrm{T}} s_i(t) \\ &- \lambda_2 T \Delta\phi_j^{\mathrm{T}}(\cdot, t-\varsigma_{ij})\mathcal{L}_{j,\varsigma_{ij}+1}^{\mathrm{T}}\hbar_i(t) + \Delta\phi_j^{\mathrm{T}}(\cdot, t-\varsigma_{ij})\mathcal{L}_{j,\varsigma_{ij}+1}^{\mathrm{T}} \\ &\times \mathcal{L}_{j,\varsigma_{ij}+1}\Delta\phi_j(\cdot, t-\varsigma_{ij}) - s_j^{\mathrm{T}}(t)s_j(t) \end{aligned}$$

$$
= \begin{bmatrix} s_i(t) \\ \hbar_i(t) \\ \Delta\phi_i(\cdot, t-\varsigma_i) \\ \Delta\phi_j(\cdot, t-\varsigma_{ij}) \\ s_j(t) \end{bmatrix}^{\mathrm{T}} \begin{bmatrix} \Omega_{i,j} & 0 \\ 0 & -1 \end{bmatrix} \begin{bmatrix} s_i(t) \\ \hbar_i(t) \\ \Delta\phi_i(\cdot, t-\varsigma_i) \\ \Delta\phi_j(\cdot, t-\varsigma_{ij}) \\ s_j(t) \end{bmatrix} < 0,
$$

with $\Omega_{i,j} = \begin{bmatrix} \Omega_{i,j,1} & \Omega_{i,j,2} \\ \Omega_{i,j,2}^{\mathrm{T}} & \Omega_{i,j,3} \end{bmatrix}$, where $\Omega_{i,j,1}$, $\Omega_{i,j,2}$, and $\Omega_{i,j,3}$ are provided in (8.19). On the basis of the Schur complement, $\begin{bmatrix} \Omega_{i,j} & 0 \\ 0 & -1 \end{bmatrix} < 0 \Longleftrightarrow \Omega_{i,j} = \begin{bmatrix} \Omega_{i,j,1} & \Omega_{i,j,2} \\ \Omega_{i,j,2}^{\mathrm{T}} & \Omega_{i,j,3} \end{bmatrix} < 0$, which can be further derived that

$$
\Omega_{i,j} < 0 \Longleftrightarrow \Omega_{i,j,1} < 0, \quad \Omega_{i,j,3} - \Omega_{i,j,2}^{\mathrm{T}} \Omega_{i,j,1}^{-1} \Omega_{i,j,2} < 0,
$$

such that the condition (8.18) is satisfied, which means that the system (8.17) can achieve the asymptotic stability.

This completes the proof. □

8.5 With Application to Flying-Around of Air-Bearing Spacecraft Simulators

There exist three ABSSs to take a flying-around experiment for illustrating the effectiveness and availability of the proposed TSM-HOFAS predictive control, where the dynamic models of three ABSSs are provided in (A.2) and the details of three ABSSs and its associated experimental platform are given in Appendix A.

Based on (8.2), a TSM-HOFAS predictive control for systems (A.2a) and (A.2b) is proposed as

$$
\begin{aligned}
F_{I,x_{i,\mathrm{ABSS}}}(t) &= -f_{i,x}(\cdot) + \Upsilon_i(A_{i,0\sim 1}, x_{i,\mathrm{ABSS}}(t)) + v_{i,x}(t), \\
F_{I,y_{i,\mathrm{ABSS}}}(t) &= -f_{i,y}(\cdot) + \Upsilon_i(A_{i,0\sim 1}, y_{i,\mathrm{ABSS}}(t)) + v_{i,y}(t),
\end{aligned} \tag{8.20}
$$

with

$$
\begin{aligned}
\Upsilon(A_{0\sim 1}, x_{1,\mathrm{ABSS}}(t)) &= 19.4x_{1,\mathrm{ABSS}}(t+1) - 0.3802x_{1,\mathrm{ABSS}}(t), \\
\Upsilon(A_{0\sim 1}, x_{2,\mathrm{ABSS}}(t)) &= 19.5x_{2,\mathrm{ABSS}}(t+1) - 0.3822x_{2,\mathrm{ABSS}}(t), \\
\Upsilon(A_{0\sim 1}, x_{3,\mathrm{ABSS}}(t)) &= 19.2x_{3,\mathrm{ABSS}}(t+1) - 0.3763x_{3,\mathrm{ABSS}}(t), \\
\Upsilon(A_{0\sim 1}, y_{1,\mathrm{ABSS}}(t)) &= 19.4y_{1,\mathrm{ABSS}}(t+1) - 0.3802y_{1,\mathrm{ABSS}}(t),
\end{aligned}
$$

$$\begin{aligned}\Upsilon(A_{0\sim 1}, y_{2,\mathrm{ABSS}}(t)) =& 19.5 y_{2,\mathrm{ABSS}}(t+1) - 0.3822 y_{2,\mathrm{ABSS}}(t),\\ \Upsilon(A_{0\sim 1}, y_{3,\mathrm{ABSS}}(t)) =& 19.2 y_{3,\mathrm{ABSS}}(t+1) - 0.3763 y_{3,\mathrm{ABSS}}(t).\end{aligned}$$

Based on (8.6), the terminal sliding-mode variable of systems (A.2a) and (A.2b) can be designed as $s_{i,x}(t) = \Xi_{i,x} e_{i,x}(t) - \vartheta_{i,x}\Xi_{i,x} e_{i,x}(0)$ and $s_{i,y}(t) = \Xi_{i,y} e_{i,y}(t) - \vartheta_{i,y}\Xi_{i,y} e_{i,y}(0)$ with $e_{i,x}(t) = x_{i,\mathrm{ABSS}}(t) - r_x(t)$ and $e_{i,y}(t) = y_{i,\mathrm{ABSS}}(t) - y_x(t)$, respectively, where $\Xi_{i,x}(q^{-1}) = \Xi_{i,y}(q^{-1}) = 0.05 - 0.03q^{-1} - 0.01q^{-2}$, $\vartheta_{i,x} = \vartheta_{i,y} = 0.9$, and $r_x(t)$ and $r_y(t)$ are the known desired reference signals. For the reference sliding-mode $s_{i,\mathrm{ref}}(t)$, the design parameters are provided as $\lambda_1 = 0.9$, $\lambda_2 = 0.01$, $\eth = 0.1$. For system (A.2c), only a stabilization control is needed to satisfy the requirement of $\psi_{i,\mathrm{ABSS}}(t)$ during the formation control. Hence, the cooperative control items are set as 0, and a stabilization control is designed in the form of (2.34), i.e.,

$$F_{I,T_{i,\mathrm{ABSS}}}(t) = -f_{i,T}(\cdot) + \Upsilon(A_{0\sim 1}, \psi_{i,\mathrm{ABSS}}(t)), \tag{8.21}$$

with

$$\begin{aligned}\Upsilon(A_{0\sim 1}, \psi_{1,\mathrm{ABSS}}(t)) =& 0.2629\psi_{1,\mathrm{ABSS}}(t+1) - 0.0717\psi_{1,\mathrm{ABSS}}(t),\\ \Upsilon(A_{0\sim 1}, \psi_{2,\mathrm{ABSS}}(t)) =& 0.2651\psi_{2,\mathrm{ABSS}}(t+1) - 0.0723\psi_{2,\mathrm{ABSS}}(t),\\ \Upsilon(A_{0\sim 1}, \psi_{3,\mathrm{ABSS}}(t)) =& 0.2596\psi_{1,\mathrm{ABSS}}(t+1) - 0.0708\psi_{1,\mathrm{ABSS}}(t).\end{aligned}$$

In this experiment, the related design parameters are provided as $T_s = 0.2$s, $w_{ii} = 0$, $w_{ij} = 1$, $\alpha_i = 1$, $\beta_i = 15$, $\Gamma_i = I$, $i, j = 1, 2, 3$, $\aleph_y = 5$, $\aleph_u = 3$. The communication constraints in the forward and feedback channels are given as $\varsigma_{1,a} = 8$, $\varsigma_{2,a} = 6$, $\varsigma_{3,a} = 5$, $\varsigma_{1,s} = 10$, $\varsigma_{2,s} = 5$, $\varsigma_{3,s} = 6$. Meanwhile, the desired circular orbit is shown in Fig. 8.2.

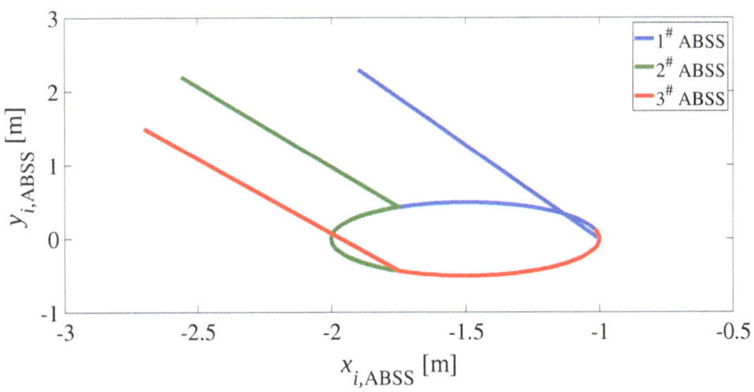

Fig. 8.2 The desired trajectory of three ABSSs

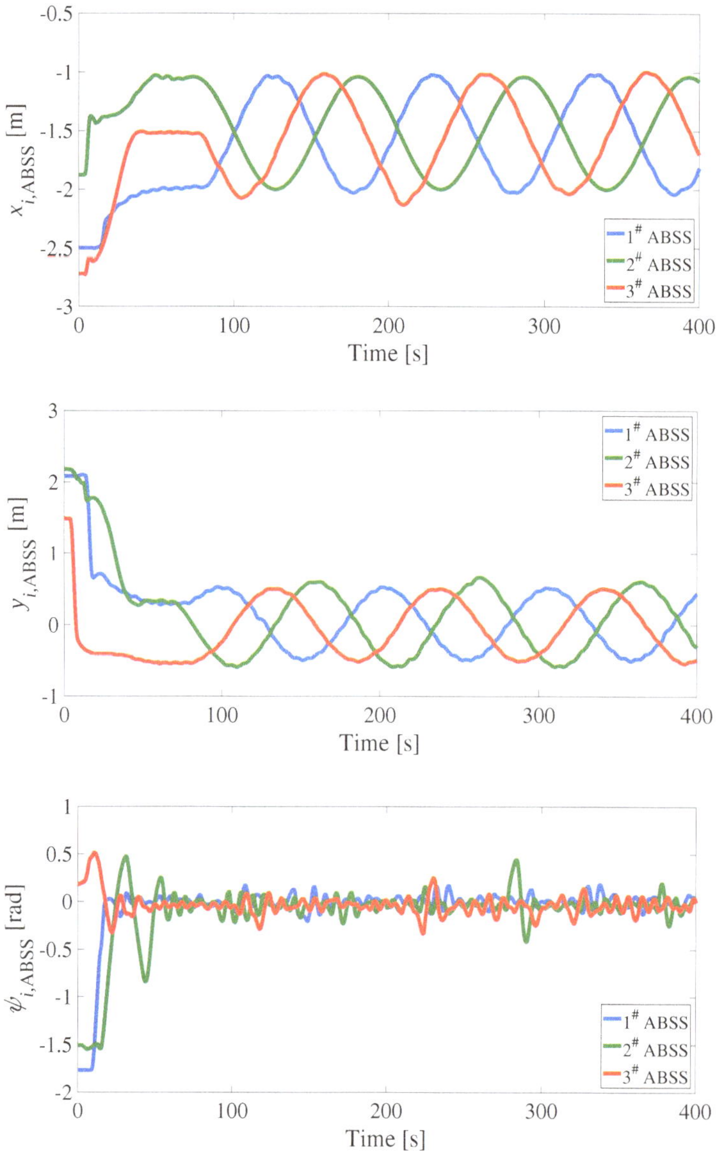

Fig. 8.3 The cooperative flying-around of three ABSSs by using the controls (8.20) and (8.21)

By using (8.20) and (8.21), the experimental results are provided in Figs. 8.3, 8.4, 8.5, 8.6.

Figure 8.3 shows the position and angle responses of cooperative flying-around of three ABSSs, which means that the position responses $x_{i,\text{ABSS}}(t)$ and $y_{i,\text{ABSS}}(t)$ can achieve the dynamical cooperative control under time-varying communication

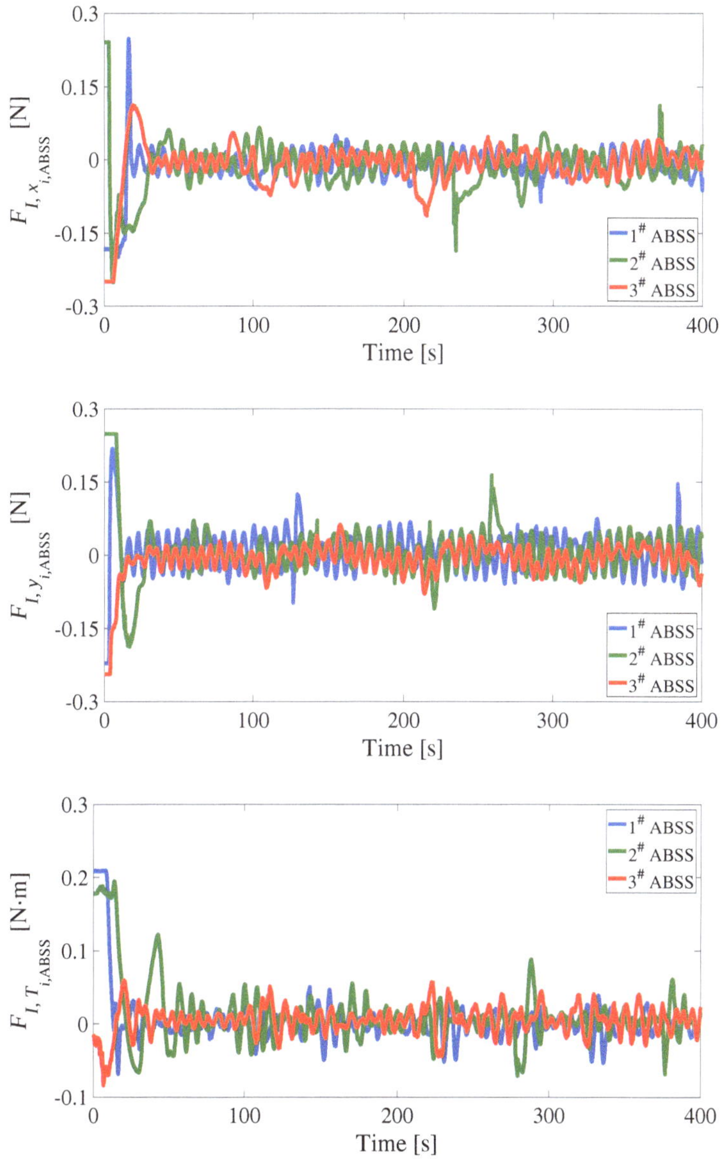

Fig. 8.4 The control inputs generated by the controls (8.20) and (8.21)

constraints and immeasurable states within the tolerant errors and their amplitudes and phases can be changed cooperatively. The angle responses $\psi_{i,\mathrm{ABSS}}(t)$ can realize the stabilization control with the allowable errors by adopting (8.21), but a shortcoming is that there exists the vibration during the steady process. The reason is that both the reaction forces of the thrusters and the airflow in the experimental

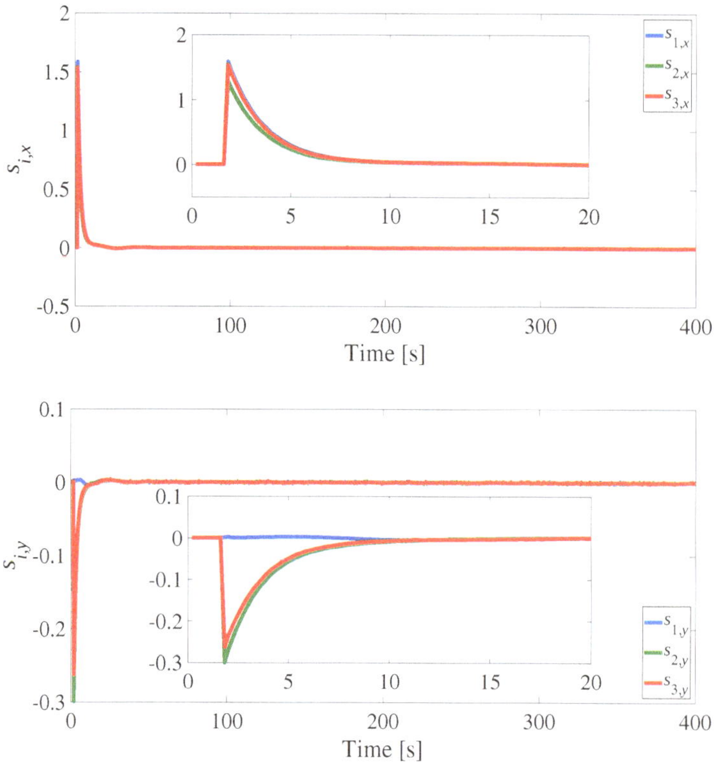

Fig. 8.5 The trends of terminal sliding-mode variables $s_{i,x}(t)$ and $s_{i,y}(t)$

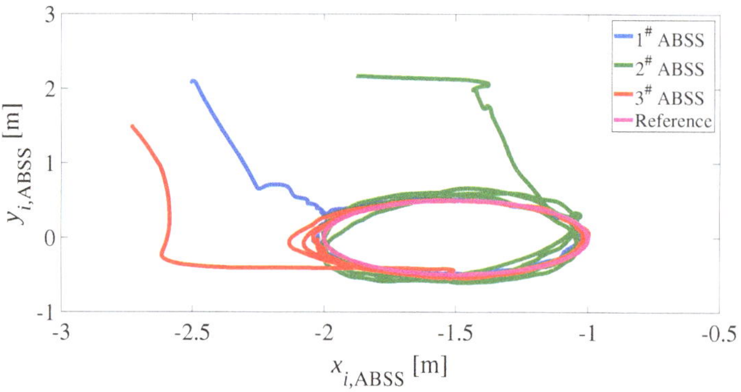

Fig. 8.6 The actual trajectory of three ABSSs

site affect the stabilization control performance of $\psi_{i,\mathrm{ABSS}}(t)$. The control inputs generated by (8.20) and (8.21) are shown in Fig. 8.4, where there are some vibrations because of the model uncertainties and external disturbances. Figure 8.6 provides the practical trajectory of cooperative flying-around of three ABSSs, which means that the proposed TSM-HOFAS predictive control (8.20) can achieve the desired flying-around mission and continue to carry out it by comparing with Fig. 8.2. Figure 8.5 provides the variation trends of $s_{i,x}(t)$ and $s_{i,y}(t)$, where $s_{i,x}(t)$ and $s_{i,y}(t)$ can converge to 0 and its convergence rate can be clearly improved comparing to Fig. 7.9.

According to the results in Figs. 8.3, 8.4, 8.5, 8.6, the effectiveness and availability of the proposed TSM-HOFAS predictive control can be fully verified, which provides a better foundation for the large-scale applications of practical spacecraft control.

8.6 Notes and References

This chapter has considered a robust cooperative control for the HUN-HOFAMASs. A TSM-HOFAS predictive control has been proposed to address this problem, so that the robust cooperative control performance can be optimized and the convergence rate can be accelerated. A sufficient condition has been constructed to discuss the simultaneous consensus and stability of the closed-loop HOFAMASs with the help of the Lyapunov stability theory and an LMI method. A highlight is that a terminal sliding-mode variable is adopted to further enhance the robustness and accelerate the convergence rate, and then an IHOFAS prediction model of terminal sliding-mode variable is developed via a type of Diophantine Equation, which enriches the HOFAS theory. The other is that a new idea is provided to develop the terminal sliding-mode control in the discrete-time domain by combining with the predictive control. Considering the better control performance, the proposed TSM-HOFAS predictive control will make the great contributions to practical applications of various fields.

Appendix A
Networked Control Experimental Platform for Multiple Spacecraft Systems

The air-bearing spacecraft simulator (ABSS) is a type of general simulation device of spacecraft at ground, which can be widely exploited to simulate the attitude joint orbit control and its relevant space tasks of spacecraft under the micro-gravity environment in space, such as rendezvous, capture, formation, detumbling, and flying-around, etc.. Because of its extensive use in the experimental verification of practical spacecraft control, a number of studies are devoted to the basic development of software and hardware for the ABSS (Santaguida and Zhu 2023; Wei et al. 2023; Huang et al. 2022; Papakonstantinou et al. 2022; Ousaloo et al. 2021). Meanwhile, there are also some literature that carry out the ABSS-based verification of spacecraft control. Concretely, Duan and Liu (2022), Cui and Duan (2024), Cui et al. (2024) developed an ABSS-based simulated device to verify the position and attitude control for a type of the combined spacecraft. Cao et al. (2023b,c), Chi et al. (2023) utilized three ABSSs to take an experiment of formation control for illustrating the practicability of the proposed control. Eun et al. (2021) adopted the ABSS to test the positive adaptive control approach for spacecraft proximity maneuvering. Wei et al. (2020) used two ABSSs to demonstrate the performance of collision avoidance resulted in by an analytical controller. Meanwhile, Ousaloo et al. (2016), Lyu et al. (2017), Huang et al. (2018) and the associated results also made contributions to basic development and experimental verification of the ABSS.

The hardware structure of the ABSS adopted in this book is shown in Fig. A.1, where the ABSS is placed on an ultra-flat granite monolith. The ABSS can be ensured to be under a micro-gravity environment and to carry out the frictionless motion because of a 2–3μm air-film between the ABSS and granite monolith when air flows from the bank to planar air bearings. The wireless actuator can receive and amplify the control signals from the networked controller to drive the solenoid valves, such that the corresponding thrusters can be driven. The optical markers are applied to the real-time positioning and tracking of the ABSS.

The relevant coordinated systems and the thrusters distribution of the ABSS are given in Fig. A.2, where $\mathcal{I}_I(O_I - I_x I_y)$ and $\mathcal{I}_B(O_B - B_x B_y)$ are the inertial and

D.-W. Zhang, G.-P. Liu, *Predictive Cooperative Control for High-Order Fully Actuated Multiagent Systems*, https://doi.org/10.1007/978-981-95-1695-7

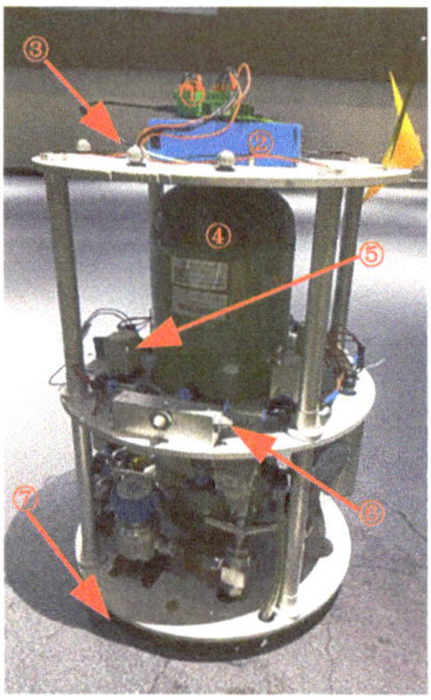

Fig. A.1 The hardware structure of the ABSS

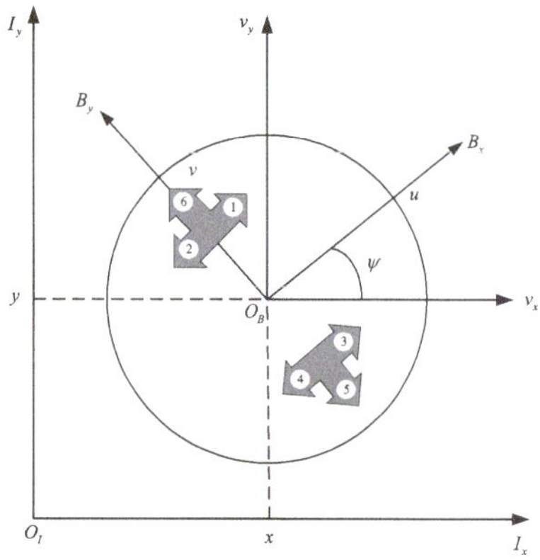

Fig. A.2 The related coordinate systems and the thrusters distribution of the ABSS

body coordinate systems, respectively, and the labels 1–6 represent the installation positions of 6 thrusters. In this experiment, the ABSS is with 3 degrees of freedom to be controlled, i.e., x, y (the position components of the xoy plane in the $\mathcal{I}_I$ coordinate system) and yaw angle ψ (rotating around the z axis). Meanwhile, ψ also establishes a relationship between $\mathcal{I}_I$ and $\mathcal{I}_B$ coordinated systems, i.e.,

$$\begin{bmatrix} F_{B,x} \\ F_{B,y} \\ F_{B,T} \end{bmatrix} = \mathcal{R}(\psi) \begin{bmatrix} F_{I,x} \\ F_{I,y} \\ F_{I,T} \end{bmatrix}, \quad \mathcal{R}(\psi) = \begin{bmatrix} \cos(\psi) & -\sin(\psi) & 0 \\ \sin(\psi) & \cos(\psi) & 0 \\ 0 & 0 & 1 \end{bmatrix},$$

where $F_{B,x}$, $F_{B,y}$, $F_{B,T}$ and $F_{I,x}$, $F_{I,y}$, $F_{I,T}$ denote the thrust and torque in the $\mathcal{I}_B$ and $\mathcal{I}_I$ coordinated systems, respectively. The PWM signal duty-cycle for 6 thrusters can be obtained by using the control allocation algorithm in Chen and Liu (2018) and the thrust and torque in the $\mathcal{I}_B$ coordinate system, i.e., $F_{B,x}$, $F_{B,y}$, $F_{B,T}$.

Based on the ABSS, a sketch of the networked control experimental platform of multiple spacecraft systems is provided in Fig. A.3, which is composed of VICON

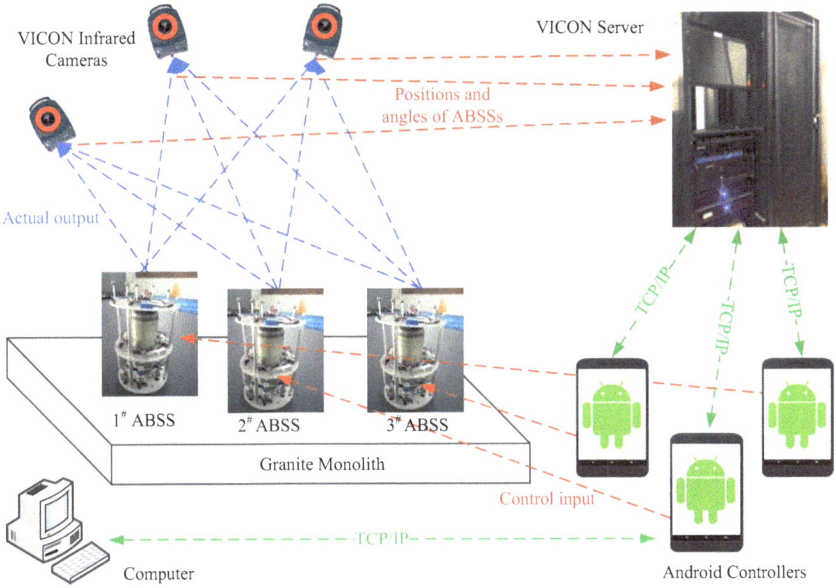

Fig. A.3 The networked control experimental platform of multiple spacecraft systems

Table A.1 The basic parameters of three ABSSs

Device	Mass ($m_{i,\mathrm{ABSS}}/\mathrm{kg}$)	Moment of Inertia ($J_{i,\mathrm{ABSS}}/\mathrm{kg}\cdot\mathrm{m}^2$)	Radius ($r_{i,\mathrm{ABSS}}/\mathrm{m}$)
1# ABSS	19.4 kg	0.239 kg · m^2	0.18 m
2# ABSS	19.5 kg	0.241 kg · m^2	0.18 m
3# ABSS	19.2 kg	0.236 kg · m^2	0.18 m

Infrared Cameras, VICON Server, three ABSSs, Android Controllers, Computer for Monitor. The working principle is summarized as follows. The VICON Infrared Cameras locate and collect the position and angle data (x, y and ψ) of the ABSS by applying the optical markers, and then transmit the position and angle data (x, y and ψ) to the VICON Server by using the local area network (LAN). The Android Controllers utilize the position and angle data (x, y and ψ) after resolving by the VICON Server to calculate the corresponding control input and also send the control input to the wireless actuator of the ABSS by adopting the LAN, so that three ABSSs can be driven. The basic parameters of three ABSSs are provided in Table A.1. The Computer is exploited to monitor, save and analyze the real-time data during the experiment. The experimental site is shown in Fig. A.4.

The proposed networked control experimental platform is a MATLAB/SIMULINK-based semi-physical simulation one. During the experiment, SIMULINK model can be transformed into the C program by utilizing the SIMULINK Coder, such that the C program can be directly complied, connected and run on the Android Controllers by adopting the NDK and other software.

Fig. A.4 The experimental site

Table A.2 The main parameters of Android controller

Controller Configuration	Controller Parameter
CPU Cores	4
CPU Frequency	1.4GHz
Operation System	Android OS v6.0
RAM	2 GB
ROM	16 GB
WLAN	WiFi 802.11 b/g/n, hotspot
Sensor	Gravity, light, distance
Display	5 inches
Home Screen Resolution	1280 × 720 pixels

Furthermore, the control program in the Android Controllers can be performed in the Linux kernel rather than Android virtual machine and can be coded in the C program instead of Java, which can ensure the real-time operation and communication between Android Controllers and wireless actuator via a TCP/IP protocol. The details have been reported in Chen and Liu (2020). The main parameters of Android Controller are shown in Table A.2 (Cao et al. 2020). For the Computer for Monitor, Netconview (Tan et al. 2018), a self-designed real-time monitoring software, is adopted in this proposed experimental platform to monitor, save and analyze the real-time data.

It is assumed that the origin of $\mathcal{I}_I$ coordinate system is located at the center of granite monolith. Based on Chen and Liu (2018), the motion equation of the i-th ABSS is established as

$$\begin{aligned} m_{i,\mathrm{ABSS}}\left(\ddot{x}_{i,\mathrm{ABSS}} - \dot{y}_{i,\mathrm{ABSS}}\dot{\psi}_{i,\mathrm{ABSS}}\right) &= F_{I,x_{i,\mathrm{ABSS}}}, \\ m_{i,\mathrm{ABSS}}\left(\ddot{y}_{i,\mathrm{ABSS}} - \dot{x}_{i,\mathrm{ABSS}}\dot{\psi}_{i,\mathrm{ABSS}}\right) &= F_{I,y_{i,\mathrm{ABSS}}}, \\ J_{i,\mathrm{ABSS}}\ddot{\psi}_{i,\mathrm{ABSS}} &= F_{I,T_{i,\mathrm{ABSS}}}, \end{aligned} \tag{A.1}$$

with $i = 1, 2, 3$. By using the forward difference operator $\ddot{x} = \frac{x(tT_s+2T_s)-2x(tT_s+T_s)+x(tT_s)}{T_s^2}$ and $\dot{x} = \frac{x(tT_s+T_s)-x(tT_s)}{T_s}$ to discretize the system (A.1), the dynamic model of the i-th ABSS in the discrete-time domain is provided as

$$m_{i,\text{ABSS}}x_{i,\text{ABSS}}(t+2) = f_{i,x}(\cdot) + F_{I,x_{i,\text{ABSS}}}(t), \tag{A.2a}$$

$$m_{i,\text{ABSS}}y_{i,\text{ABSS}}(t+2) = f_{i,y}(\cdot) + F_{I,y_{i,\text{ABSS}}}(t), \tag{A.2b}$$

$$J_{i,\text{ABSS}}\psi_{i,\text{ABSS}}(t+2) = f_{i,T}(\cdot) + F_{I,T_{i,\text{ABSS}}}(t), \tag{A.2c}$$

where T_s denotes the sampling period and is generally omitted in the corresponding representation, $i = 1, 2, 3$, and

$$\begin{aligned} f_{i,x}(\cdot) =& 2m_{i,\text{ABSS}}x_{i,\text{ABSS}}(t+1) - m_{i,\text{ABSS}}x_{i,\text{ABSS}}(t) \\ &+ m_{i,\text{ABSS}}(y_{i,\text{ABSS}}(t+1) - y_{i,\text{ABSS}}(t))(\psi_{i,\text{ABSS}}(t+1) - \psi_{i,\text{ABSS}}(t)), \\ f_{i,y}(\cdot) =& 2m_{i,\text{ABSS}}y_{i,\text{ABSS}}(t+1) - m_{i,\text{ABSS}}y_{i,\text{ABSS}}(t) \\ &+ m_{i,\text{ABSS}}(x_{i,\text{ABSS}}(t+1) - x_{i,\text{ABSS}}(t))(\psi_{i,\text{ABSS}}(t+1) - \psi_{i,\text{ABSS}}(t)), \\ f_{i,T}(\cdot) =& 2J_{i,\text{ABSS}}\psi_{i,\text{ABSS}}(t+1) - J_{i,\text{ABSS}}\psi_{i,\text{ABSS}}(t). \end{aligned}$$

Under the infinitesimal angular displacement motion, i.e., $\dot{\psi}_{i,\text{ABSS}} \approx 0$, system (A.1) can be simplified as a linear one, i.e.,

$$\begin{aligned} m_{i,\text{ABSS}}\ddot{x}_{i,\text{ABSS}} &= F_{I,x_{i,\text{ABSS}}}, \\ m_{i,\text{ABSS}}\ddot{y}_{i,\text{ABSS}} &= F_{I,y_{i,\text{ABSS}}}, \\ J_{i,\text{ABSS}}\ddot{\psi}_{i,\text{ABSS}} &= F_{I,T_{i,\text{ABSS}}}, \end{aligned} \tag{A.3}$$

by utilizing the forward difference operator again, the discrete-time model of system (A.3) is proposed as

$$m_{i,\text{ABSS}}x_{i,\text{ABSS}}(t+2) = L_{i,x}(\cdot) + F_{I,x_{i,\text{ABSS}}}(t), \tag{A.4a}$$

$$m_{i,\text{ABSS}}y_{i,\text{ABSS}}(t+2) = L_{i,y}(\cdot) + F_{I,y_{i,\text{ABSS}}}(t), \tag{A.4b}$$

$$J_{i,\text{ABSS}}\psi_{i,\text{ABSS}}(t+2) = L_{i,T}(\cdot) + F_{I,T_{i,\text{ABSS}}}(t), \tag{A.4c}$$

where $i = 1, 2, 3$, and $L_{i,x}(\cdot)$, $L_{i,y}(\cdot)$, $L_{i,T}(\cdot)$ are simplified as

$$\begin{aligned} L_{i,x}(\cdot) =& 2m_{i,\text{ABSS}}x_{i,\text{ABSS}}(t+1) - m_{i,\text{ABSS}}x_{i,\text{ABSS}}(t), \\ L_{i,y}(\cdot) =& 2m_{i,\text{ABSS}}y_{i,\text{ABSS}}(t+1) - m_{i,\text{ABSS}}y_{i,\text{ABSS}}(t), \\ L_{i,T}(\cdot) =& 2J_{i,\text{ABSS}}\psi_{i,\text{ABSS}}(t+1) - J_{i,\text{ABSS}}\psi_{i,\text{ABSS}}(t). \end{aligned}$$

Appendix B
Solution to Adjustment Parameters A_η in Remark 2.2

Based on the above studies, the adjustment parameters A_η, $\eta = 0, 1, \ldots, n-1$, play an important role in adjusting the control performances of the closed-loop system (2.3) by stabilizing the following system

$$y(t+n) = \Upsilon(A_{0\sim n-1}, y(t)) = \sum_{\eta=0}^{n-1} A_\eta y(t+\eta), \tag{B.1}$$

which is regarded as the nominal form of system (2.3), so that a better model foundation can be provided to construct a prediction model for improving the control performances of predictive control.

In fact, the stability of system (B.1) can be equivalent to that of the following system

$$\begin{bmatrix} y(t+1) \\ y(t+2) \\ \vdots \\ y(t+n) \end{bmatrix} = \Phi(A_{0\sim n-1}) \begin{bmatrix} y(t) \\ y(t+1) \\ \vdots \\ y(t+n-1) \end{bmatrix}, \tag{B.2}$$

where $\Phi(A_{0\sim n-1})$ is shown in (2.12), i.e.,

$$\Phi(A_{0\sim n-1}) = \begin{bmatrix} 0 & I & & \\ \vdots & & \ddots & \\ 0 & & & I \\ A_0 & A_1 & \cdots & A_{n-1} \end{bmatrix}.$$

D.-W. Zhang, G.-P. Liu, *Predictive Cooperative Control for High-Order Fully Actuated Multiagent Systems*, https://doi.org/10.1007/978-981-95-1695-7

System (B.2) can achieve the stability if and only if there exist a Schur matrix Λ and a nonsingular transformation matrix $\mathcal{V}_c = \begin{bmatrix} \mathcal{V}_0^{\mathrm{T}} \cdots \mathcal{V}_{n-1}^{\mathrm{T}} \end{bmatrix}^{\mathrm{T}}$ to guarantee that $\Phi(A_{0\sim n-1})\mathcal{V}_c = \mathcal{V}_c\Lambda$, which can be expressed as

$$\begin{aligned} \mathcal{V}_1 &= \mathcal{V}_0\Lambda, \\ &\vdots \\ \mathcal{V}_{n-1} &= \mathcal{V}_{n-2}\Lambda, \\ \sum_{i=0}^{n-1} A_i\mathcal{V}_i &= \mathcal{V}_{n-1}\Lambda. \end{aligned} \tag{B.3}$$

From (B.3), $\mathcal{V}_c$ can be rewritten as $\mathcal{V}_c = \begin{bmatrix} \mathcal{V}_0^{\mathrm{T}} \ (\mathcal{V}_0\Lambda)^{\mathrm{T}} \cdots \left(\mathcal{V}_0\Lambda^{n-1}\right)^{\mathrm{T}} \end{bmatrix}^{\mathrm{T}}$. Let $\mathcal{V} = \mathcal{V}_0$, $\tilde{A} = \begin{bmatrix} A_0 \ A_1 \cdots A_{n-1} \end{bmatrix}$ and $\mathcal{W}_c = \tilde{A}\mathcal{V}_c$, the last equation of (B.3) can be equivalently transformed into the following generalized high-order Sylvester Equation, i.e.,

$$\mathcal{V}\Lambda^n = \mathcal{W}_c.$$

By applying the solving method of the generalized high-order Sylvester Equation in Duan (2014), the solutions of $\mathcal{V}$ and $\mathcal{W}_c$ are provided as

$$\mathcal{V} = \mathcal{Z}, \ \ \mathcal{W}_c = \mathcal{Z}\Lambda^n,$$

where $\mathcal{Z} \in \mathbb{R}^{\tilde{n}\times\tilde{n}n}$ is an arbitrary parameter matrix and $\mathcal{V}_c$ can be further expressed as $\mathcal{V}_c = \begin{bmatrix} \mathcal{Z}^{\mathrm{T}} \ (\mathcal{Z}\Lambda)^{\mathrm{T}} \cdots \left(\mathcal{Z}\Lambda^{n-1}\right)^{\mathrm{T}} \end{bmatrix}^{\mathrm{T}}$. When $\det(\mathcal{V}_c) \neq 0$, i.e.,

$$\det\left(\begin{bmatrix} \mathcal{Z} \\ \mathcal{Z}\Lambda \\ \vdots \\ \mathcal{Z}\Lambda^{n-1} \end{bmatrix}\right) \neq 0,$$

$\tilde{A}$ can be solved as $\tilde{A} = \mathcal{W}_c\mathcal{V}_c^{-1}$, i.e.,

$$\begin{bmatrix} A_0 \ A_1 \cdots A_{n-1} \end{bmatrix} = \mathcal{Z}\Lambda^n \begin{bmatrix} \mathcal{Z} \\ \mathcal{Z}\Lambda \\ \vdots \\ \mathcal{Z}\Lambda^{n-1} \end{bmatrix}^{-1},$$

such that Eq. (2.13) is held.

Furthermore, in Remark 2.3, the considered system in the form of (B.1) is provided as

$$x(t+n) = \Upsilon(K_{0\sim n-1}, x(t)) = \sum_{\eta=0}^{n-1} K_\eta x(t+\eta),$$

its stability is also equivalent to that $\Phi(K_{0\sim n-1})\mathcal{V}_c = \mathcal{V}_c \Lambda$ with

$$\Phi(K_{0\sim n-1}) = \begin{bmatrix} 0 & I & & \\ \vdots & & \ddots & \\ 0 & & & I \\ K_0 & K_1 & \cdots & K_{n-1} \end{bmatrix},$$

where Λ is a Schur matrix and $\mathcal{Z}$ is an arbitrary parameter matrix. Following the above idea, it is also obtained that

$$\begin{bmatrix} K_0 \ K_1 \ \cdots \ K_{n-1} \end{bmatrix} = \mathcal{Z}\Lambda^n \begin{bmatrix} \mathcal{Z} \\ \mathcal{Z}\Lambda \\ \vdots \\ \mathcal{Z}\Lambda^{n-1} \end{bmatrix}^{-1}.$$

Appendix C
Recursive Solution of Diophantine Equation

The Diophantine Equation is a class of polynomial equations to commemorate the great Ancient Greek mathematician Diophantus, which is widely used in the polynomial equation method-based control design of discrete-time control systems, especially playing an important role in the predictive control design. In the Diophantine Equation (2.6), $\mathcal{E}_\eta\left(q^{-1}\right) = \sum_{\mu=0}^{\eta-1} e_{\eta,\mu} q^{-\mu}$ and $\mathcal{F}\left(q^{-1}\right) = \sum_{\mu=0}^{n} f_{\eta,\mu} q^{-\mu}$ are its solutions in the polynomial matrix form, which are generated by the prediction horizon η and the system polynomial matrix $\mathcal{A}\left(q^{-1}\right)$. Based on Clarke et al. (1987a,b), a recursive solving algorithm is provided here to calculate the $\mathcal{E}_\eta\left(q^{-1}\right)$ and $\mathcal{F}\left(q^{-1}\right)$.

By using (2.6), it is derived that

$$\mathcal{E}_\eta(q^{-1})\mathcal{A}(q^{-1})\Delta + q^{-\eta}\mathcal{F}_\eta(q^{-1}) = I, \tag{C.1a}$$

$$\mathcal{E}_{\eta+1}(q^{-1})\mathcal{A}(q^{-1})\Delta + q^{-(\eta+1)}\mathcal{F}_{\eta+1}(q^{-1}) = I. \tag{C.1b}$$

Subtracting (C.1a) from (C.1b) can be obtained that

$$\left(\tilde{\mathcal{E}}(q^{-1}) + \mathrm{e}_{\eta+1,\eta} q^{-\eta}\right)\tilde{\mathcal{A}}(q^{-1}) + q^{-\eta}\left(q^{-1}\mathcal{F}_{\eta+1}(q^{-1}) - \mathcal{F}_\eta(q^{-1})\right) = 0, \tag{C.2}$$

with

$$\begin{aligned}\tilde{\mathcal{A}}(q^{-1}) =& \mathcal{A}(q^{-1})\Delta \\ =& I + (A_{n-1} - I)q^{-1} + \cdots + (A_0 - A_1)q^{-n} - A_0 q^{-(n+1)} \\ =& I + \tilde{A}_1 q^{-1} + \cdots + \tilde{A}_n q^{-n} + \tilde{A}_{n+1} q^{-(n+1)}, \\ \tilde{\mathcal{E}}(q^{-1}) =& \left(\mathrm{e}_{\eta+1,0} - \mathrm{e}_{\eta,0}\right) + \left(\mathrm{e}_{\eta+1,1} - \mathrm{e}_{\eta,1}\right) q^{-1} \\ & + \cdots + \left(\mathrm{e}_{\eta+1,\eta-1} - \mathrm{e}_{\eta,\eta-1}\right) q^{-(\eta-1)},\end{aligned}$$

D.-W. Zhang, G.-P. Liu, *Predictive Cooperative Control for High-Order Fully Actuated Multiagent Systems*, https://doi.org/10.1007/978-981-95-1695-7

such that

$$\tilde{\mathcal{E}}(q^{-1}) + e_{\eta+1,\eta} q^{-\eta} = \mathcal{E}_{\eta+1}(q^{-1}) - \mathcal{E}_{\eta}(q^{-1}).$$

Hence, a further result from (C.2) is yielded that

$$\tilde{\mathcal{E}}(q^{-1})\tilde{\mathcal{A}}(q^{-1}) + q^{-\eta}\left(q^{-1}\mathcal{F}_{\eta+1}(q^{-1}) - \mathcal{F}_{\eta}(q^{-1}) + e_{\eta+1,\eta}\tilde{\mathcal{A}}(q^{-1})\right) = 0. \tag{C.3}$$

It is clearly that one of the necessary conditions to hold the (C.3) (Ding 2017) is that $\tilde{\mathcal{E}}(q^{-1}) = 0$ and

$$\mathcal{F}_{\eta+1}(q^{-1}) = q\left(\mathcal{F}_{\eta}(q^{-1}) - e_{\eta+1,\eta}\tilde{\mathcal{A}}(q^{-1})\right). \tag{C.4}$$

By comparing the coefficients of the same order terms on both sides of (C.4), it is obtained that

$$\begin{aligned} e_{\eta+1,\eta} =& f_{\eta,0}, \\ f_{\eta+1,k} =& f_{\eta,k+1} - e_{\eta+1,\eta}\tilde{A}_{k+1} = f_{\eta,k+1} - f_{\eta,0}\tilde{A}_{k+1}, \\ k =& 0, 1, \ldots, n-1, \\ f_{\eta+1,n} =& -e_{\eta+1,\eta}\tilde{A}_{n+1} = -f_{\eta,0}\tilde{A}_{n+1}, \end{aligned}$$

which can be further summarized as

$$\vec{f}_{\eta+1} = \vec{f}_{\eta}\bar{\mathcal{A}}, \tag{C.5}$$

with $\vec{f}_{\eta+1} = \left[\, f_{\eta+1,0} \cdots f_{\eta+1,n} \,\right]$, $\vec{f}_{\eta} = \left[\, f_{\eta,0} \cdots f_{\eta,n} \,\right]$, and

$$\begin{aligned} \bar{\mathcal{A}} =& \begin{bmatrix} -\tilde{A}_1 & -\tilde{A}_2 & \cdots & -\tilde{A}_n & -\tilde{A}_{n+1} \\ I & 0 & \cdots & 0 & 0 \\ 0 & I & \ddots & \vdots & \vdots \\ \vdots & \ddots & \ddots & 0 & 0 \\ 0 & \cdots & 0 & I & 0 \end{bmatrix} \\ =& \begin{bmatrix} I - A_{n-1} & A_{n-1} - A_{n-2} & \cdots & A_1 - A_0 & -A_0 \\ I & 0 & \cdots & 0 & 0 \\ 0 & I & \ddots & \vdots & \vdots \\ \vdots & \ddots & \ddots & 0 & 0 \\ 0 & \cdots & 0 & I & 0 \end{bmatrix}. \end{aligned}$$

Meanwhile, because of $\tilde{\mathcal{E}}(q^{-1}) = 0$, the recursive solution of $\mathcal{E}_\eta(q^{-1})$ can be represented as

$$\mathcal{E}_{\eta+1}(q^{-1}) = \mathcal{E}_\eta(q^{-1}) + \mathrm{e}_{\eta+1,\eta}q^{-\eta} = \mathcal{E}_\eta(q^{-1}) + \mathrm{f}_{\eta,0}q^{-\eta}. \tag{C.6}$$

By utilizing the (C.5) and (C.6), $\mathcal{E}_\eta\left(q^{-1}\right)$ and $\mathcal{F}\left(q^{-1}\right)$ in Diophantine Equation (2.6) can be obtained.

References

Abianeh AJ, Wan Y, Ferdowsi F, Mijatovic N, Dragičević T (2022) Vulnerability identification and remediation of FDI attacks in islanded DC microgrids using multiagent reinforcement learning. IEEE Transactions on Power Electronics 37(6):6359–6370

Ahmed Z, Ali N, Zhang W (2023) H_2 resilient consensus control of multiagent systems under deception attack. IEEE Transactions on Circuits and Systems II: Express Briefs 70(7):2530–2534

Amini A, Asif A, Mohammadi A (2021) RQ-CEASE: A resilient quantized collaborative event-triggered average-consensus sampled-data framework under denial of service attack. IEEE Transactions on Systems, Man, and Cybernetics: Systems 51(11):7027–7039

Amini A, Asif A, Mohammadi A (2022a) A unified optimization for resilient dynamic event-triggering consensus under denial of service. IEEE Transactions on Cybernetics 52(5):2872–2884

Amini A, Mohammadi A, Asif A, Hou M, Plataniotis KN (2022b) Fault-tolerant periodic event-triggered consensus under communication delay and multiple attacks. IEEE Systems Journal 16(4):6338–6349

An C, Su H, Chen S (2023) Leader-following exponential consensus for higher-order fractional-order MASs with mismatched disturbances and event-triggered input. IEEE Transactions on Systems, Man, and Cybernetics: Systems 53(10):6448–6459

Azarbahram A, Amini A (2022) Secure event-triggered tracking consensus under denial of service: A resilient periodically intermittent approach. IEEE Control Systems Letters 6:2786–2791

Belkacem K, Munawar K, Muhammad SS (2020) Distributed cooperative control of autonomous multi-agent UAV systems using smooth control. Journal of Systems Engineering and Electronics 31(6):1297–1307

Cai M, He X, Zhou D (2023a) An active fault tolerance framework for uncertain nonlinear high-order fully-actuated systems. Automatica 152:110,969

Cai M, He X, Zhou D (2023b) Fault-tolerant tracking control for nonlinear observer-extended high-order fully-actuated systems. Journal of the Franklin Institute 360(1):136–153

Cai M, He X, Zhou D (2023c) Low-power fault-tolerant control for nonideal high-order fully actuated systems. IEEE Transactions on Systems, Man, and Cybernetics: Systems 53(8):4875–4887

Cai M, He X, Zhou D (2024) Self-healing fault-tolerant control for high-order fully actuated systems against sensor faults: A redundancy framework. IEEE Transactions on Cybernetics 54(4):2628–2640

D.-W. Zhang, G.-P. Liu, *Predictive Cooperative Control for High-Order Fully Actuated Multiagent Systems*, https://doi.org/10.1007/978-981-95-1695-7

Cao L, Liu GP, Hu W, Bhatti JZ (2020) Design and implementation of an Android-based control laboratory. In: Proceedings of the 39th Chinese Control Conference, Shenyang, China, pp 4450–4455

Cao L, Pan Y, Liang H, Huang T (2023a) Observer-based dynamic event-triggered control for multiagent systems with time-varying delay. IEEE Transactions on Cybernetics 53(5):3376–3387

Cao L, Zhang DW, Ionescu CM, Liu GP (2023b) An output formation consensus control for leader–follower networked multi-agent systems under communication constraints and switching topologies. Asian Journal of Control 25(5):3978–3991

Cao L, Zhang DW, Liu GP (2023c) Cloud-based predictive formation control of networked multi-agent system and its application to air bearing spacecraft simulators. ISA Transactions 138:696–704

Cao Z, Wang Z, Niu Y, Song J, Liu H (2023d) Sliding mode control for sampled-data systems subject to deception attacks: Handling randomly perturbed sampling periods. IEEE Transactions on Cybernetics 53(11):7034–7047

Chai SC, Liu GP, Rees D, Xia Y (2008) Design and practical implementation of internet-based predictive control of a servo system. IEEE Transactions on Control Systems Technology 16(1):158–168

Chattopadhyay A, Mitra U (2020) Security against false data-injection attack in cyber-physical systems. IEEE Transactions on Control of Network Systems 7(2):1015–1027

Chen DL, Liu GP (2018) An adaptive control allocator for autonomous vehicles with parameter uncertainty. Proceedings of the Institution of Mechanical Engineers, Part I: Journal of Systems and Control Engineering 232(7):807–818

Chen DL, Liu GP (2020) A smartphone-based networked control platform: Design and implementation. In: Proceedings of the 39th Chinese Control Conference, Shenyang, China, pp 4437–4443

Chen J, Ling Q (2021) Bit-rate conditions for the consensus of quantized multiagent systems with network-induced delays based on event triggering. IEEE Transactions on Cybernetics 51(2):984–993

Chen WH, Yang J, Guo L, Li S (2016) Disturbance-observer-based control and related methods—an overview. IEEE Transactions on Industrial Electronics 63(2):1083–1095

Chen YJ, Li JN, Wu L (2023) Finite-horizon H_∞ output fault-tolerant consensus for multi-agent systems with switching topology and deception attacks. International Journal of Robust and Nonlinear Control 33(6):3589–3606

Cheng P, Ye S, Liu R, He S, Zhang W (2024) SMC-based bounded consensus tracking for multiagent systems under stochastic DoS attacks with applications to multiple DC motors. IEEE Transactions on Industrial Informatics 20(8):10,074–10,083

Cheng W, Jiang B, Zhang K, Ding SX (2021) Robust finite-time cooperative formation control of UGV-UAV with model uncertainties and actuator faults. Journal of the Franklin Institute 358(17):8811–8837

Chi C, Lin D, Ionescu CM, Liu GP (2023) Distributed sliding-mode cloud predictive formation control of networked multi-agent systems with application to air-bearing spacecraft simulators. Control Engineering Practice 137:105,580

Choi YH, Yoo SJ (2022) Distributed quantized feedback design strategy for adaptive consensus tracking of uncertain strict-feedback nonlinear multiagent systems with state quantizers. IEEE Transactions on Cybernetics 52(7):7069–7083

Clarke DW, Mohtadi C, Tuffs PS (1987a) Generalized predictive control—Part I The basic algorithm. Automatica 23(2):137–148

Clarke DW, Mohtadi C, Tuffs PS (1987b) Generalized predictive control—Part II Extensions and interpretations. Automatica 23(2):149–160

Cui KX, Duan DR (2024) High-order fully actuated anti-disturbance control for a type of combined spacecraft based in disturbance observer (in Chinese). Acta Aeronautica et Astronautica Sinica 45(1):628,892

Cui KX, Duan GR, Zhang DW, Gu DK (2024) Discrete-time high-order fully actuated adaptive stabilization control for a type of combined spacecraft with unknown parameters. IEEE Transactions on Aerospace and Electronic Systems 60(3):3379–3389

Cui Y, Liu Y, Zhang W, Alsaadi FE (2021) Sampled-based consensus for nonlinear multiagent systems with deception attacks: The decoupled method. IEEE Transactions on Systems, Man, and Cybernetics: Systems 51(1):561–573

Ding B, Pan Y, Lu Q (2023) Neural adaptive optimal control for nonlinear multiagent systems with full-state constraints and immeasurable states. Neurocomputing 544:126,259

Ding BC (2017) Theory and Method of Predictive Control (in Chinese). China Machine Press, Beijing, China

Dong S, Liu L, Feng G, Liu M, Wu ZG (2022) Quantized fuzzy cooperative output regulation for heterogeneous nonlinear multiagent systems with directed fixed/switching topologies. IEEE Transactions on Cybernetics 52(11):12,393–12,402

Dong Y, Xu S (2021) Cooperative output regulation problem of nonlinear multiagent systems with proximity graph via output feedback control. IEEE Transactions on Cybernetics 51(8):4201–4211

Du S, Xu W, Qiao J, Ho DWC (2023) Resilient output synchronization of heterogeneous multiagent systems with DoS attacks under distributed event-/self-triggered control. IEEE Transactions on Neural Networks and Learning Systems 34(3):1169–1178

Duan G, Liu GP (2022) Attitude and orbit optimal control of combined spacecraft via a fully-actuated system approach. Journal of Systems Science & Complexity 35(2):623–640

Duan GR (2014) Generalized Sylverter Equations—Unifined Parametric Solutions. CRC Press, Boca Raton, FL, USA

Duan GR (2021a) High-order fully actuated systems approaches: Part I. Models and basic procedure. International Journal of Systems Science 52(2):422–435

Duan GR (2021b) High-order fully actuated systems approaches: Part III. Robust control and high-order backstepping. International Journal of Systems Science 52(5):952–971

Duan GR (2021c) High-order fully actuated systems approaches: Part IV. Adaptive control and high-order backstepping. International Journal of Systems Science 52(5):972–989

Duan GR (2021d) High-order fully actuated systems approaches: Part V. Robust adaptive control. International Journal of Systems Science 52(10):2129–2143

Duan GR (2021e) High-order fully actuated systems approaches: Part VI. Disturbance attenuation and decoupling. International Journal of Systems Science 52(10):2161–2181

Duan GR (2022a) Discrete-time delay systems: Part 1. Global fully actuated case. Science China Information Sciences 65:182,201

Duan GR (2022b) Discrete-time delay systems: Part 2. Sub-fully actuated case. Science China Information Sciences 65:192,201

Duan GR (2022c) High-order fully actuated systems approaches: Part X. Basics of discrete-time systems. International Journal of Systems Science 53(4):810–832

Duan GR (2023a) Fully actuated system approaches for continuous-time delay systems: part 1. Systems with state delays only. Science China Information Sciences 66(1):112,201

Duan GR (2023b) Fully actuated system approaches for continuous-time delay systems: part 2. Systems with input delays. Science China Information Sciences 66(2):122,201

Duan GR (2023c) Robust stabilization of time-varying nonlinear systems with time-varying delays: A fully actuated system approach. IEEE Transactions on Cybernetics 53(12):7455–7468

Duan GR (2023d) Substability and substabilization: Control of subfully actuated systems. IEEE Transactions on Cybernetics 53(11):7309–7322

Duan GR (2024a) A FAS approach for stabilization of generalized chained forms: part 1. Discontinuous control laws. Science China Information Sciences 67(2):122,201

Duan GR (2024b) A FAS approach for stabilization of generalized chained forms: part 2. Continuous control laws. Science China Information Sciences 67(3):132,201

Duan GR (2024c) Fully actuated system approach for control: An overview. IEEE Transactions on Cybernetics 54(12):7285–7306

Duan GR (2024d) Fully actuated system approach for stabilization control of sub-strict feedback systems (in Chinese). Acta Aeronautica et Astronautica Sinica 45(1):629,552

Duan GR (2025a) Constrained unidirectionally connected FASs: Part I. Models. International Journal of Systems Science. https://doi.org/10.1080/00207721.2025.2466806

Duan GR (2025b) Constrained unidirectionally connected FASs: Part II. Sub-stabilization. International Journal of Systems Science. https://doi.org/10.1080/00207721.2025.2467223

Duan GR (2025c) Constrained unidirectionally connected FASs: Part III. Applications. International Journal of Systems Science. https://doi.org/10.1080/00207721.2025.2467221

Duan GR, Zhou B (2022) Fully actuated system approach for linear systems control: A frequency-domain approach. Journal of Systems Science & Complexity 35(6):2046–2061

Eun Y, Park SY, Lee T, Kim GN (2021) Experimental validation of positive adaptive-control approach for spacecraft proximity maneuvers. Journal of Aerospace Engineering 34(6):04021,096

Fan QY, Deng C, Ge X, Wang CC (2022) Distributed adaptive fault-tolerant control for heterogeneous multiagent systems with time-varying communication delays. IEEE Transactions on Systems, Man, and Cybernetics: Systems 52(7):4362–4372

Fang F, Li J, Liu Y, Park JH (2023) Resilient control for multiagent systems with a sampled-data model against DoS attacks. IEEE Transactions on Industrial Informatics 19(1):780–789

Fei J, Chen Y, Liu L, Fang Y (2022) Fuzzy multiple hidden layer recurrent neural control of nonlinear system using terminal sliding-mode controller. IEEE Transactions on Cybernetics 52(9):9519–9534

Feng S, Ishii H (2022) Dynamic quantized consensus of general linear multiagent systems under denial-of-service attacks. IEEE Transactions on Control of Network Systems 9(2):562–574

Franzè G, Tedesco F, Famularo D (2021) Resilience against replay attacks: A distributed model predictive control scheme for networked multi-agent systems. IEEE/CAA Journal of Automatica Sinica 8(3):628–640

Fu W, Qin J, Zheng WX, Chen Y, Kang Y (2021) Resilient cooperative source seeking of double-integrator multi-robot systems under deception attacks. IEEE Transactions on Industrial Electronics 68(5):4218–4227

Gong M, Zhou D, Sheng L, He X (2025) Multicontroller-based fault-tolerant control for uncertain high-order sub-fully actuated systems. IEEE Transactions on Cybernetics 55(7):3525–3536

Gong X, Li X (2024) Fault-tolerant practical prescribed-time formation-containment control of multi-agent systems on directed graphs. IEEE Transactions on Network Science and Engineering 11(1):352–365

Gu DK, Zhang DW (2020) A parametric method to design dynamic compensator for high-order quasi-linear systems. Nonlinear Dynamics 100(2):1379–1400

Gu DK, Zhang DW (2021) Parametric control to a type of quasi-linear high-order systems via output feedback. European Journal of Control 58:223–231

Gu DK, Zhang DW, Liu YD (2020) Parametric method to design dynamic compensator for descriptor high-order quasi-linear systems. IET Control Theory & Applications 14(19):3179–3192

Guo M, Xu D, Liu L (2022) Design of cooperative output regulators for heterogeneous uncertain nonlinear multiagent systems. IEEE Transactions on Cybernetics 52(6):5174–5183

Guo X, Zhang D, Wang J, Ahn CK (2021) Adaptive memory event-triggered observer-based control for nonlinear multi-agent systems under DoS attacks. IEEE/CAA Journal of Automatica Sinica 8(10):1644–1656

Han S, Zhu H, Zhong Q, Shi K, Kwon OM (2024) Secure sampled-data consensus of multi-agent systems under asynchronous deception attacks with application to unmanned surface vehicles. IEEE Transactions on Intelligent Transportation Systems 25(6):5462–5473

He W, Mo Z, Han QL, Qian F (2020) Secure impulsive synchronization in Lipschitz-type multi-agent systems subject to deception attacks. IEEE/CAA Journal of Automatica Sinica 7(5):1326–1334

Hong Y, Su Y, Cai H (2024) Internal model based cooperative robust resilient control under DoS attacks with application to vehicles formation. IEEE Transactions on Industrial Informatics 20(11):13,124–13,134

Hu L, Duan GR, Hou M (2023) Robust adaptive guaranteed cost tracking control for high-order nonlinear systems with uncertainties based on high-order fully actuated system approaches. International Journal of Robust and Nonlinear Control 33(13):7583–7605

Huang Q, Sun J (2023) Control of impulsive systems via high-order fully actuated system approach. Nonlinear Dynamics 111:17,961–17,971

Huang Z, Lu Y, Wen H, Jin D (2018) Ground-based experiment of capturing space debris based on artificial potential field. Acta Astronautica 152:235–241

Huang Z, Zhang W, Chen T, Wen H, Jin D (2022) Characterizing an air-bearing testbed for simulating spacecraft dynamics and control. Aerospace 9(5):246

Hwang CL, Abebe HB (2022) Generalized and heterogeneous nonlinear dynamic multiagent systems using online RNN-based finite-time formation tracking control and application to transportation systems. IEEE Transactions on Intelligent Transportation Systems 23(8):13,708–13,720

Jahangiri-Heidari M, Shahriari-Kahkeshi M, Shi P (2025) Resilient consensus of nonlinear multiagent systems under false data injection attack on communication channels: An attack detection and isolation-based approach. IEEE Internet of Things Journal 12(7):8219–8230

Jiang H, Duan GR, Hou M (2024a) Generalized proportional–integral extended state observer-based controller design for fully actuated systems. ISA Transactions 155:137–147

Jiang H, Duan GR, Hou M (2024b) State and disturbance observer-based controller design for fully actuated systems. IEEE Transactions on Circuits and Systems I: Regular Papers 71(11):5261–5270

Jiang H, Duan GR, Hou MZ (2025) Robust adaptive control based on reduced-order unknown input observer for fully actuated systems with uncertainties. IEEE Transactions on Circuits and Systems I: Regular Papers 72(9):4946–4956

Jiang W, Liu K, Charalambous T (2022) Multi-agent consensus with heterogeneous time-varying input and communication delays in digraphs. Automatica 135:109,950

Jiang Y, Liu Z, Chen Z (2023) Output synchronization of heterogeneous nonlinear multiagent systems with input quantization: A universal performance guaranteed control scheme. IEEE Transactions on Control of Network Systems 10(3):1590–1602

Jin XZ, Che WW, Wu ZG, Zhao Z (2022a) Adaptive consensus and circuital implementation of a class of faulty multiagent systems. IEEE Transactions on Systems, Man, and Cybernetics: Systems 52(1):226–237

Jin Z, Wang Z, Zhang X (2022b) Cooperative control problem of Takagi-Sugeno fuzzy multiagent systems via observer based distributed adaptive sliding mode control. Journal of the Franklin Institute 359(8):3405–3426

Kalman RE (1959) On the general theory of control systems. IRE Transactions on Automatic Control 4(3):110–110

Katsoukis I, Rovithakis GA (2022) A low complexity robust output synchronization protocol with prescribed performance for high-order heterogeneous uncertain MIMO nonlinear multiagent systems. IEEE Transactions on Automatic Control 67(6):3128–3133

Lederer A, Yang Z, Jiao J, Hirche S (2023) Cooperative control of uncertain multiagent systems via distributed Gaussian processes. IEEE Transactions on Automatic Control 68(5):3091–3098

Lei Z, Zhou H, Hu W, Liu GP, Guan S (2024) Web-based digital twin communication system of power systems for training and education. IEEE Transactions on Power Systems 39(2):3592–3602

Li D, Liu GP (2024) Coordinated predictive control of networked multiagent systems via distributed cloud computing with time-varying transmission delays. Systems & Control Letters 183:105,685

Li J, Wang L, Xu M, Fang Y (2023a) Adaptive event-triggered robust model predictive control for multiagent systems with time-varying delay under arbitrary network topology. IEEE Systems Journal 17(4):5381–5392

Li L, Shi P, Ahn CK, Kim YJ, Xing W (2023b) Tube-based model predictive full containment control for stochastic multiagent systems. IEEE Transactions on Automatic Control 68(7):4024–4037

Li M, Zhang K, Ma Y, Jiang B (2024a) Prescribed-time fault-tolerant control for the formation of quadrotors based on fully-actuated system approaches. International Journal of Systems Science 55(12):2541–2555

Li P, Duan GR (2024) High-order fully actuated control approach for servo systems based on dynamical compensator and extended state observer. IEEE/ASME Transactions on Mechatronics 29(5):3717–3726

Li S, Wang F, Er MJ, Yang Z (2022a) Approximate output regulation of discrete-time stochastic multiagent systems subject to heterogeneous and unknown dynamics. IEEE Transactions on Systems, Man, and Cybernetics: Systems 52(10):6373–6382

Li X, Tang Y, Zou Y, Li S, Zheng WX (2024b) Output-feedback multiagent consensus with intermittent communication on directed graphs. IEEE Transactions on Automatic Control 69(4):2537–2544

Li XM, Zhou Q, Li P, Li H, Lu R (2020) Event-triggered consensus control for multi-agent systems against false data-injection attacks. IEEE Transactions on Cybernetics 50(5):1856–1866

Li Y, Ding SX, Hua C, Chen J (2023c) Output-constrained consensus tracking for high-order nonlinear multiagent systems under switching networks. IEEE Transactions on Systems, Man, and Cybernetics: Systems 53(12):7608–7617

Li Y, Zhao Y, Liu W, Hu J (2023d) Adaptive fuzzy predefined-time control for third-order heterogeneous vehicular platoon systems with dead zone. IEEE Transactions on Industrial Informatics 19(9):9525–9534

Li Y, Ding SX, Liu G, Hua C (2024c) Sampled-data-based distributed output feedback leader–following consensus for time-delay multiagent systems. IEEE Transactions on Automatic Control 69(1):582–589

Li Y, Yu K, Lv M, Tong S (2025) Asynchronous coordination for output regulation in heterogeneous nonlinear MASs with jointly connected switching topologies. IEEE Transactions on Automatic Control 70(3):1859–1866

Li Z, Cao L, Pan Y, Zhang P (2022b) Adaptive resilient containment control for nonlower triangular multiagent systems with time-varying delay and sensor faults. Journal of the Franklin Institute 359(17):9759–9781

Li Z, Wang Y, Song Y, Ao W (2023e) Global consensus tracking control for high-order nonlinear multiagent systems with prescribed performance. IEEE Transactions on Cybernetics 53(10):6529–6537

Li Z, Wang X, Xi L, Li Y, Hua C (2024d) Event-triggered output-feedback control for high-order uncertain nonlinear multiagent systems subject to denial-of-service attacks. IEEE Internet of Things Journal 11(13):23,661–23,672

Liang H, Chang Z, Pan Y (2024) Dual-event-triggered intelligence security control for multiagent systems against DoS attacks with applications in mobile robot systems. IEEE Transactions on Artificial Intelligence 5(2):916–924

Liu C, Liu X, Wang H, Zhou Y, Gao C (2023a) Adaptive control for unknown HOFA nonlinear systems without overparametrization. International Journal of Robust and Nonlinear Control 33(6):3640–3660

Liu GP (2017a) Consensus and stability analysis of networked multiagent predictive control systems. IEEE Transactions on Cybernetics 47(4):1114–1119

Liu GP (2017b) Predictive control of networked multiagent systems via cloud computing. IEEE Transactions on Cybernetics 47(8):1852–1859

Liu GP (2020a) Coordinated control of networked multiagent systems with communication constraints using a proportional integral predictive control strategy. IEEE Transactions on Cybernetics 50(11):4735–4743

Liu GP (2020b) Predictive control of networked nonlinear multiagent systems with communication constraints. IEEE Transactions on Systems, Man, and Cybernetics: Systems 50(11):4447–4457

Liu GP (2022a) Coordinated control of networked multiagent systems via distributed cloud computing using multistep state predictors. IEEE Transactions on Cybernetics 52(2):810–820
Liu GP (2022b) Coordinated control of networked nonlinear multiagent systems using variable horizon learning predictors via cloud edge computing. IEEE Transactions on Control of Network Systems 9(4):1975–1986
Liu GP (2022c) Coordination of networked nonlinear multi-agents using a high-order fully actuated predictive control strategy. IEEE/CAA Journal of Automatica Sinica 9(4):615–623
Liu GP (2022d) Networked predictive control of nonlinear cyber physical sysems with time-varying communication constraints (in Chinese). Control Theory & Applications 39(1):145–153
Liu GP (2023) Tracking control of multi-agent systems using a networked predictive PID tracking scheme. IEEE/CAA Journal of Automatica Sinica 10(1):216–225
Liu GP (2024) Digital-twin predictive control of nonlinear systems with time delays, unknown dynamics, and communication delays. IEEE Transactions on Cybernetics 54(12):7198–7210
Liu GP, Mu JX, Rees D, Chai SC (2006) Design and stability analysis of networked control systems with random communication time delay using the modified MPC. International Journal of Control 79(4):287–296
Liu GP, Xia Y, Chen J, Rees D, Hu W (2007) Networked predictive control of systems with random network delays in both forward and feedback channels. IEEE Transactions on Industrial Electronics 54(3):1282–1297
Liu GQ, Zhang K, Li B (2022a) Fully-actuated system approach based optimal attitude tracking control of rigid spacecraft with actuator saturation. Journal of Systems Science & Complexity 35(2):688–702
Liu KZ, Teel AR, Sun XM (2024a) A stochastic hybrid framework for event-triggered nonlinear control systems with stochastic denial of service attacks. IEEE Transactions on Automatic Control 69(2):904–919
Liu L, Sun H, Ma L, Zhang J, Bo Y (2021) Quasi-consensus control for a class of time-varying stochastic nonlinear time-delay multiagent systems subject to deception attacks. IEEE Transactions on Systems, Man, and Cybernetics: Systems 51(11):6863–6873
Liu QZ, Zhang L, Sun B, Xiao Y, Fan GW (2024b) Fixed-time disturbance observer-based attitude prescribed performance predictive control for flexible spacecraft. IEEE Transactions on Aerospace and Electronic Systems 60(3):3209–3220
Liu QZ, Zhang L, Xiao Y, Zhang L, Fan GW (2025a) Predictive sliding mode control for flexible spacecraft attitude tracking with multiple disturbances. Control Engineering Practice 154:106,160
Liu W, Duan GR, Hou M (2022b) High-order robust command filtered backstepping design for strict-feedback systems: A high-order fully actuated system approach. International Journal of Robust and Nonlinear Control 32(18):10,251–10,270
Liu W, Duan G, Hou M (2023b) High-order command filtered adaptive backstepping control for second- and high-order fully actuated strict-feedback systems. Journal of the Franklin Institute 360(6):3989–4015
Liu W, Duan GR, Hou M (2023c) Concurrent learning adaptive command filtered backstepping control for high-order strict-feedback systems. IEEE Transactions on Circuits and Systems I: Regular Papers 70(4):1696–1709
Liu W, Duan GR, Hou M, Golestani M, Kong H (2024c) Control of uncertain high-order fully actuated strict-feedback systems: A backstepping approach with high-gain observer-based derivative approximation. IEEE Transactions on Cybernetics 54(12):7456–7468
Liu X, Chen M, Sheng L, Zhou D (2022c) Adaptive fault-tolerant control for nonlinear high-order fully-actuated systems. Neurocomputing 495:75–85
Liu X, Deng F, Wei W, Wan F (2022d) Formation tracking control of networked systems with time-varying delays and sampling under fixed and markovian switching topology. IEEE Transactions on Control of Network Systems 9(2):601–612

Liu X, Wang L, Cao J (2024d) Further results on fixed-time leader-following consensus of heterogeneous multiagent systems with external disturbances. IEEE Transactions on Systems, Man, and Cybernetics: Systems 54(1):416–425

Liu X, Chen M, Zhou D, Sheng L (2025b) Adaptive actuator fault-tolerant tracking control for stochastic high-order fully actuated systems. IEEE Transactions on Cybernetics 55(4):1848–1859

Liu Y, Zhang J, Jia Y (2024e) Adaptive containment control of heterogeneous high-order fully actuated multi-agent systems. International Journal of Robust and Nonlinear Control 34(7):4802–4819

Liu Y, Zhang J, Li M, Jia Y (2025c) Adaptive prescribed time containment control for fully actuated multiagent systems. IEEE Transactions on Aerospace and Electronic Systems 61(5):11,930–11,940

Liu Z, Li P (2025) Robust formation control of quadrotor uavs: A fully-actuated control approach. Unmanned Systems. https://doi.org/10.1142/S2301385025500918

Liu ZW, Shi YL, Yan H, Han BX, Guan ZH (2023d) Secure consensus of multiagent systems via impulsive control subject to deception attacks. IEEE Transactions on Circuits and Systems II: Express Briefs 70(1):166–170

Lu M, Liu L (2021) Consensus of heterogeneous second-order nonlinear uncertain multiagent systems under switching networks. IEEE Transactions on Automatic Control 66(7):3331–3338

Lu S, Tsakalis K, Chen Y (2023a) Development and application of a novel high-order fully actuated system approach—Part I: 3-DOF quadrotor control. IEEE Control Systems Letters 7:1177–1182

Lu X, Wang F, Liu Z, Chen C L Philip (2023b) Observer-based adaptive neural inverse optimal consensus control of nonlinear multiagent systems. Journal of the Franklin Institute 360(9):6296–6320

Lu Y, Zhang K, Jiang B (2024) Fully actuated system approach based prescribed-time fault-tolerant formation control for unmanned helicopters under fixed and switching topologies. IEEE Transactions on Circuits and Systems I: Regular Papers 71(11):5249–5260

Lui DG, Petrillo A, Santini S (2023) Bipartite tracking consensus for high-order heterogeneous uncertain nonlinear multi-agent systems with unknown leader dynamics via adaptive fully-distributed PID control. IEEE Transactions on Network Science and Engineering 10(2):1131–1142

Luo S, Xu X, Liu L, Feng G (2020) Output consensus of heterogeneous linear multi-agent systems with communication, input and output time-delays. Journal of the Franklin Institute 357(17):12,825–12,839

Lyu W, Dai S, Dong Y, Shen Y, Song X, Wang T (2017) Attitude motion compensation for imager on fengyun-4 geostationary meteorological satellite. Acta Astronautica 138:290–294

Ma Y, Zhang K, Jiang B (2023) Prescribed-time fault-tolerant control for fully actuated heterogeneous multiagent systems: A hierarchical design approach. IEEE Transactions on Aerospace and Electronic Systems 59(5):6624–6636

Ma Y, Zhang K, Jiang B (2024a) Neuroadaptive cooperative fault-tolerant control of heterogeneous multiagent systems based on fully actuated system approaches. IEEE Transactions on Cybernetics 54(8):4581–4592

Ma Y, Zhang K, Jiang B (2024b) Practical prescribed-time active fault-tolerant control for mixed-order heterogeneous multiagent systems: A fully actuated system approach. Automatica 166:111,721

Ma Y, Zhang K, Jiang B (2025) Prescribed-time fault-tolerant containment control of fully actuated heterogeneous multiagent systems without estimations of fault parameters. IEEE Transactions on Automation Science and Engineering 22:13,621–13,632

Mahdavi S, Panamtash H, Dimitrovski A, Zhou Q (2021) Predictive coordinated and cooperative voltage control for systems with high penetration of PV. IEEE Transactions on Industry Applications 57(3):2212–2222

Meng B, Shen L, Zhang K, Xia J (2025) Fully actuated system approach-based fault-tolerant formation reconstruction control and optimal task assignment for fixed-wing uavs. Nonlinear Dynamics 133:645–659

Miao Q, Zhang K, Jiang B (2024) Incremental fully actuated system approach-based prescribed-time fault-tolerant formation control of helicopters under multiple faults. Aerospace Science and Technology 151:109,334

Mu T, Pang ZH, Guo H, Liu GP, Han QL (2024) Output tracking predictive control of uncertain networked control systems. IEEE Transactions on Circuits and Systems II: Express Briefs 71(6):3141–3145

Ousaloo H, Nodeh M, Mehrabian R (2016) Verification of spin magnetic attitude control system using air-bearing-based attitude control simulator. Acta Astronautica 126:546–553

Ousaloo HS, Sharifi G, Akbarinia B (2021) Extended validation of a ground-based three-axis spacecraft simulator model. Proceedings of the Institution of Mechanical Engineers, Part G: Journal of Aerospace Engineering 235(2):151–170

Pang ZH, Bai CD, Liu GP, Han QL, Zhang XM (2021a) A novel networked predictive control method for systems with random communication constraints. Journal of Systems Science & Complexity 34(4):1364–1378

Pang ZH, Luo WC, Liu GP, Han QL (2021b) Observer-based incremental predictive control of networked multi-agent systems with random delays and packet dropouts. IEEE Transactions on Circuits and Systems II: Express Briefs 68(1):426–430

Pang ZH, Zhao XY, Sun J, Shi Y, Liu GP (2022a) Comparison of three data-driven networked predictive control methods for a class of nonlinear systems. IEEE/CAA Journal of Automatica Sinica 9(9):1714–1716

Pang ZH, Zheng CB, Li C, Liu GP, Han QL (2022b) Cloud-based time-varying formation predictive control of multi-agent systems with random communication constraints and quantized signals. IEEE Transactions on Circuits and Systems II: Express Briefs 69(3):1282–1286

Pang ZH, Xia CG, Zhang J, Han QL, Liu GP (2023) A prediction-based approach realizing finite-time convergence of networked control systems. IEEE Transactions on Circuits and Systems II: Express Briefs 70(7):2445–2449

Papakonstantinou C, Moraitis G, Lappas V, Kostopoulos V (2022) Design of a low-cost air bearing testbed for Nano CMG maneuvers. Aerospace 9(2):95

Parsa M, Danesh M (2021) Robust containment control of uncertain multi-agent systems with time-delay and heterogeneous Lipschitz nonlinearity. IEEE Transactions on Systems, Man, and Cybernetics: Systems 51(4):2312–2321

Qi T, Lu R, Chen J (2021) Consensus of continuous-time multiagent systems via delayed output feedback: Delay versus connectivity. IEEE Transactions on Automatic Control 66(3):1329–1336

Qi W, Lv C, Park JH, Zong G, Cheng J, Shi K (2022) SMC for semi-Markov jump cyber-physical systems subject to randomly occurring deception attacks. IEEE Transactions on Circuits and Systems II: Express Briefs 69(1):159–163

Qin D, Jin Z, Liu A, Zhang WA, Yu L (2024) Asynchronous event-triggered distributed predictive control for multiagent systems with parameterized synchronization constraints. IEEE Transactions on Automatic Control 69(1):403–409

Sakthivel N, Devi MM, Zhai G (2023) Non-fragile control for consensus of nonlinear multiagent systems under periodic denial of service attacks. Journal of the Franklin Institute 360(4):2702–2728

Santaguida L, Zhu ZH (2023) Development of air-bearing microgravity testbed for autonomous spacecraft rendezvous and robotic capture control of a free-floating target. Acta Astronautica 203:319–328

Shi X, Li Y, Du C, Shi Y, Yang C, Gui W (2025) Fully distributed event-triggered control of nonlinear multiagent systems under directed graphs: A model-free DRL approach. IEEE Transactions on Automatic Control 70(1):603–610

Su H, Chen J, Chen X, He H (2021a) Adaptive observer-based output regulation of multiagent systems with communication constraints. IEEE Transactions on Cybernetics 51(11):5259–5268

Su Y, Shi Y, Sun C (2021b) Distributed model predictive control for tracking consensus of linear multiagent systems with additive disturbances and time-varying communication delays. IEEE Transactions on Cybernetics 51(7):3813–3823

Sui S, Bai Z, Tong S, Chen C L Philip (2024) Finite-time adaptive fuzzy event-triggered consensus control for high-order MIMO nonlinear MASs. IEEE Transactions on Fuzzy Systems 32(2):671–682

Ta QM, Chea CC (2020) Multi-agent control for stochastic optical manipulation systems. IEEE/ASME Transactions on Mechatronics 25(4):1971–1979

Tan C, Zhang T, Li Y, Liu GP (2025) Time-varying group formation tracking control for uncertain nonlinear high-order fully actuated multiagent systems. Nonlinear Dynamics 133:2293–2314

Tan H, Huang Z, Wu M (2018) Development of a customizable real-time monitoring system for networked control systems. In: Proceedings of the 37th Chinese Control Conference, Wuhan, China, pp 6350–6355

Tan H, Wang Y, Wu M, Huang Z, Miao Z (2022) Distributed group coordination of multiagent systems in cloud computing systems using a model-free adaptive predictive control strategy. IEEE Transactions on Neural Networks and Learning Systems 33(8):3461–3473

Tang W, Wang X (2021) Optimal output consensus for nonlinear multiagent systems with both static and dynamic uncertainties. IEEE Transactions on Automatic Control 66(4):1733–1740

Thakoor O, Garg J, Nagi R (2020) Multiagent UAV routing: A game theory analysis with tight price of anarchy bounds. IEEE Transactions on Automation Science and Engineering 17(1):100–116

Thompson M, Dallas J, Goh JYM, Balachandran A (2024) Adaptive nonlinear model predictive control: Maximizing tire force and obstacle avoidance in autonomous vehicles. IEEE Transactions on Field Robotics 1:318–331

Tian G, Tan J, Li B, Duan GR (2024) Optimal fully actuated system approach-based trajectory tracking control for robot manipulators. IEEE Transactions on Cybernetics 54(12):7469–7478

Wang H, Zhang Q, Sun Z, Tang X, Chen IM (2022a) Continuous terminal sliding-mode control for FJR subject to matched/mismatched disturbances. IEEE Transactions on Cybernetics 52(10):10,479–10,489

Wang J, Sun J, Yang J, Li S (2024a) Periodic event-triggered model predictive control for networked nonlinear uncertain systems with disturbances. IEEE Transactions on Cybernetics 54(12):7501–7513

Wang M, Zhao C, Xia J, Sun J (2023a) Periodic event-triggered robust distributed model predictive control for multiagent systems with input and communication delays. IEEE Transactions on Industrial Informatics 19(11):11,216–11,228

Wang M, Lou X, Cui B, Suykens J (2025a) An attention-based approach for Koopman modeling and predictive control of nonlinear systems. ISA Transactions. https://doi.org/10.1016/j.isatra.2025.04.011

Wang P, Duan GR, Li P, Wang L (2025b) Adaptive formation control of nonlinear high-order fully actuated multiagent systems with full-state constraints and its application. IEEE Transactions on Cybernetics 55(10):5002–5013

Wang Q, Jin Y (2024) Fully actuated system approach for spacecraft rendezvous system with actuator saturation. International Journal of Systems Science 55(8):1709–1718

Wang Q, Hu J, Zhao Y, Ghosh BK (2020) Event-triggered consensus control of multi-agent systems with nonuniform communication delays via reduced-order observers. IFAC-PapersOnLine 53(2):3230–3235

Wang R, Li C, Li X, Deng R, Dong Z (2023b) GenAI4Sustainability: GPT and its potentials for achieving UN's sustainable development goals. IEEE/CAA Journal of Automatica Sinica 10(12):2179–2182

Wang S, Zhang H, Chen Z (2023c) Adaptive cooperative tracking and parameter estimation of an uncertain leader over general directed graphs. IEEE Transactions on Automatic Control 68(7):3888–3901

Wang W, Chen S, Shi Z, Wang Y (2024b) Neuroadaptive high-order fully-actuated system approach for roll autopilot with unknown uncertainties. Aerospace Science and Technology 155:109,567

Wang X, Duan GR (2023) High-order fully actuated system approaches: Model predictive control with applications to under-actuated systems. Journal of the Franklin Institute 360(10):6953–6975

Wang X, Duan GR (2024) Fully actuated system approaches: Predictive elimination control for discrete-time nonlinear time-varying systems with full state constraints and time-varying delays. IEEE Transactions on Circuits and Systems I: Regular Papers 71(1):383–396

Wang X, Wang H, Huang T, Kurths J (2023d) Neural-network-based adaptive tracking control for nonlinear multiagent systems: The observer case. IEEE Transactions on Cybernetics 53(1):138–150

Wang Y, Lu J, Liang J (2022b) Security control of multiagent systems under denial-of-service attacks. IEEE Transactions on Cybernetics 52(6):4323–4333

Wang Z (2022) Consensus of continuous-time agent dynamics with unknown input and communication delays. Applied Mathematics and Computation 412:126,563

Wei SY, Li YX, Ahn CK (2024) Prescribed finite-time output feedback consensus tracking for nonlinear multi-agent systems with time-varying delays. IEEE Transactions on Network Science and Engineering 11(1):1165–1175

Wei Y, Yang X, Xu Z, Bai X (2023) Novel ground microgravity experiment system for a spacecraft-manipulator system based on suspension and air-bearing. Aerospace Science and Technology 141:108,587

Wei Z, Wen H, Hu H, Jin D (2020) Ground experiment on rendezvous and docking with a spinning target using multistage control strategy. Aerospace Science and Technology 104:105,967

Wen G, Zhai X, Peng Z, Rahmani A (2020) Fault-tolerant secure consensus tracking of delayed nonlinear multi-agent systems with deception attacks and uncertain parameters via impulsive control. Communications in Nonlinear Science and Numerical Simulation 82:105,043

Wu HY, Liu Q, Park JH (2025) Observer-based secure consensus for multiagent systems under multimode DoS attacks with application to power system. IEEE Transactions on Cybernetics 55(3):1032–1044

Wu J, Peng C, Zhang J, Tian E (2024) A sampled-data-based secure control approach for networked control systems under random DoS attacks. IEEE Transactions on Cybernetics 54(8):4841–4851

Wu W, Tong S (2023) Collision-free adaptive fuzzy formation control for stochastic nonlinear multiagent systems. IEEE Transactions on Systems, Man, and Cybernetics: Systems 53(9):5454–5465

Wu Y, Wang Z, Zhang H, Huang C (2020) Output-based event-triggered consensus of general linear multi-agent systems with communication delay under directed graphs. Journal of the Franklin Institute 357(6):3702–3720

Wu Y, Liang H, Zhang Y, Ahn CK (2021) Cooperative adaptive dynamic surface control for a class of high-order stochastic nonlinear multiagent systems. IEEE Transactions on Cybernetics 51(11):5214–5224

Xi YG (2013) Predictive control (in Chinese), 2nd edn. National Defense Industry Press, Beijing, China

Xiao FZ, Chen LQ (2022) Attitude control of spherical liquid-filled spacecraft based on high-order fully actuated system approaches. Journal of Systems Science & Complexity 35(2):471–480

Xiao FZ, Chen LQ (2023) Fully actuated systems in terms of quaternions for spacecraft attitude control. Acta Astronautica 209:1–5

Xiao S, Dong J (2022) Distributed adaptive fuzzy fault-tolerant containment control for heterogeneous nonlinear multiagent systems. IEEE Transactions on Systems, Man, and Cybernetics: Systems 52(2):954–965

Xing M, Wu Y, Zhuang G, Wang Y (2023) Dynamic event-based sliding mode security control for singular semi-Markov jump LPV systems against deception attacks. ISA Transactions 133:116–133

Xing Y, Yin Z, Wei C (2024) Appointed-time safety-guaranteed control for spacecraft flying around non-cooperative target based on fully actuated system theory. International Journal of Systems Science 55(12):2570–2588

Xiong H, Chen G, Ren H, Li H (2025) Broad-learning-system-based model-free adaptive predictive control for nonlinear MASs under DoS attacks. IEEE/CAA Journal of Automatica Sinica 12(2):381–393

Yan B, Shi P, Lim CC (2022) Robust formation control for nonlinear heterogeneous multiagent systems based on adaptive event-triggered strategy. IEEE Transactions on Automation Science and Engineering 19(4):2788–2800

Yan Y, Zhang H, Sun J, Wang Y (2024) Sliding mode control based on reinforcement learning for T-S fuzzy fractional-order multiagent system with time-varying delays. IEEE Transactions on Neural Networks and Learning Systems 35(8):10,368–10,379

Yang H, Ye D (2022) Observer based fixed-time secure tracking consensus for networked high-order multiagent systems against DoS attacks. IEEE Transactions on Cybernetics 52(4):2018–2031

Yang H, Ju S, Xia Y, Zhang J (2021a) Predictive cloud control for networked multiagent systems with quantized signals under DoS attacks. IEEE Transactions on Systems, Man, and Cybernetics: Systems 51(2):1345–1353

Yang J, Yu X, Zhang L, Li S (2021b) A Lyapunov-based approach for recursive continuous higher order nonsingular terminal sliding-mode control. IEEE Transactions on Automatic Control 66(9):4424–4431

Yang J, Zhong Q, Wang Y, Shi K, Zhong S (2023) Nonfragile memory-based PD-like sampled-data consensus control for nonlinear multiagent systems with time-varying communication delays. IEEE Transactions on Systems, Man, and Cybernetics: Systems 53(7):4370–4380

Yang R, Zheng WX (2020) Output-based event-triggered predictive control for networked control systems. IEEE Transactions on Industrial Electronics 67(12):10,631–10,640

Yang Y, Li T, Yue D, Tian YC, Ding X (2021c) Distributed secure consensus control with event-triggering for multiagent systems under DoS attacks. IEEE Transactions on Cybernetics 51(6):2916–2928

Yang Y, Feng JE, Jia L (2024) Stabilisation of multi-agent systems over finite fields based on high-order fully actuated system approaches. International Journal of Systems Science 55(12):2478–2493

You X, Yan X, Liu J, Li S, Negenborn RR (2022) Adaptive neural sliding mode control for heterogeneous ship formation keeping considering uncertain dynamics and disturbances. Ocean Engineering 263:112,268

Yu Y, Liu GP, Huang Y, Chung CY, Li YZ (2024) A blockchain consensus mechanism for real-time regulation of renewable energy power systems. Nature Communications 15:10,620

Yuan L, Zhang K, B J (2024) Fully actuated system approach based prescribed-time fault-tolerant formation control for unmanned helicopters under fixed and switching topologies. IEEE Transactions on Circuits and Systems I: Regular Papers 71(11):5249–5260

Zhang D, Tang Y, Ding Z, Qian F (2021) Event-based resilient formation control of multiagent systems. IEEE Transactions on Cybernetics 51(5):2490–2503

Zhang DW, Liu GP (2022) Coordinated control of quasilinear multiagent systems via output feedback predictive control. ISA Transactions 128:58–70

Zhang DW, Liu GP (2023a) Predictive control for networked high-order fully actuated systems subject to communication delays and external disturbances. ISA Transactions 139:425–435

Zhang DW, Liu GP (2023b) Predictive sliding-mode control of networked high-order fully actuated systems under random deception attacks. Science China Information Sciences 66(9):190,204

Zhang DW, Liu GP (2024a) Disturbance observer-based predictive tracking control of uncertain HOFA cyber-physical systems. IEEE/CAA Journal of Automatica Sinica 11(7):1711–1713

Zhang DW, Liu GP (2024b) A high-order fully actuated predictive control approach of spacecraft flying-around under time-variant communication constraints (in Chinese). Acta Aeronautica et Astronautica Sinica 45(1):628,633

Zhang DW, Liu GP (2024c) Secure predictive control for networked high-order fully actuated systems under random DoS attacks. IEEE Transactions on Industrial Informatics 20:6935–6945

Zhang DW, Liu GP (2025) Secure tracking control of cyber-physical systems against hybrid attacks via FAS terminal sliding-mode predictive control. IEEE Transactions on Cybernetics. https://doi.org/10.1109/TCYB.2025.3569664

Zhang DW, Liu GP, Wang L (2025a) Anti-disturbance predictive tracking control for disturbed nonlinear fully actuated systems (in Chinese). Control Theory & Applications. https://doi.org/10.7641/CTA.2025.40437

Zhang F, Duan GR (2023) Coupled dynamics and integrated control for position and attitude motions of spacecraft: A survey. IEEE/CAA Journal of Automatica Sinica 10(12):2187–2208

Zhang H, Guo X, Sun J, Zhou Y (2023a) Event-triggered cooperative adaptive fuzzy control for stochastic nonlinear systems with measurement sensitivity and deception attacks. IEEE Transactions on Fuzzy Systems 31(3):774–785

Zhang J, Chai SC, Zhang BH, Liu GP (2022a) Distributed model-free sliding-mode predictive control of discrete-time second-order nonlinear multiagent systems with delays. IEEE Transactions on Cybernetics 52(11):12,403–12,413

Zhang JX, Yang GH (2022) Distributed fuzzy adaptive output-feedback control of unknown nonlinear multiagent systems in strict-feedback form. IEEE Transactions on Cybernetics 52(6):5607–5617

Zhang K, Miao Q, Jiang B (2025b) Learning-based fault-tolerant optimal formation control of helicopters: An incremental fully actuated system approach. IEEE Transactions on Cybernetics. https://doi.org/10.1109/TCYB.2025.3610020

Zhang L, Wang P, Hua C (2023b) Adaptive control of time-delay nonlinear HOFA systems with unmodeled dynamics and unknown dead-zone input. International Journal of Robust and Nonlinear Control 33(4):2615–2628

Zhang S, Jia R (2025) A self-healing predictive control method for discrete-time nonlinear systems. IEEE/CAA Journal of Automatica Sinica 12(4):668–682

Zhang S, Zhou X, Cai W, Qiu A, Zhang S (2025c) Predefined-time dynamic observer-based bipartite consensus sliding mode formation control of heterogeneous USVs-UAVs system. IEEE Transactions on Aerospace and Electronic Systems. https://doi.org/10.1109/TAES.2025.3613482

Zhang T, Liu T, Zhang E (2024) Adaptive optimal containment control for nonlinear multi-agent systems with time-varying output constraints (in Chinese). Control Theory & Applications 41(10):1899–1912

Zhang X, Liu J, Xu X, Yu S, Chen H (2022b) Robust learning-based predictive control for discrete-time nonlinear systems with unknown dynamics and state constraints. IEEE Transactions on Systems, Man, and Cybernetics: Systems 52(12):7314–7327

Zhang X, Pan W, Scattolini R, Yu S, Xu X (2022c) Robust tube-based model predictive control with Koopman operators. Automatica 137:110,114

Zhang Y, Wang G, Sun J, Li H, He W (2023c) Distributed observer-based adaptive fuzzy consensus of nonlinear multiagent systems under DoS attacks and output disturbance. IEEE Transactions on Cybernetics 53(3):1994–2004

Zhang ZC, Duan GR (2024) Stabilization controller of an extended chained nonholonomic system with disturbance: An FAS approach. IEEE/CAA Journal of Automatica Sinica 11(5):1262–1273

Zhao FJ, Gao YF, Wang XF, Gu HY, Sun XM (2025) Robust model predictive control for nonlinear systems with incremental control input constraints. IEEE Transactions on Automation Science and Engineering 22:9983–9993

Zhao G, Cui H, Hua C (2023a) Hybrid event-triggered bipartite consensus control of multiagent systems and application to satellite formation. IEEE Transactions on Automation Science and Engineering 20(3):1760–1771

Zhao H, Dai X, Zhou P, Yang T (2020) Distributed robust event-triggered control strategy for multiple high-speed trains with communication delays and input constraints. IEEE Transactions on Control of Network Systems 7(3):1453–1464

Zhao L, Yang GH (2020) Cooperative adaptive fault-tolerant control for multi-agent systems with deception attacks. Journal of the Franklin Institute 357(6):3419–3433

Zhao P, Dou C, Ma K, Zhang Z, Zhang B (2022) Distributed cooperative control based on multiagent system for islanded microgrids with switching topology and channel interruption. IEEE Systems Journal 16(1):362–373

Zhao Q, Duan GR (2022a) Fully actuated system approach for 6DOF spacecraft control based on extended state observer. Journal of Systems Science & Complexity 35(2):604–622

Zhao TY, Duan GR (2022b) Fully actuated system approach to attitude control of flexible spacecraft with nonlinear time-varying inertia. Science China Information Sciences 65:212,201

Zhao YZ, Ma D, Zhang YW (2023b) Adaptive asymptotic stabilization of uncertain nonstrict feedback nonlinear HOFA systems with time delays. Nonlinear Dynamics 111:14,139–14,153

Zheng CB, Pang ZH, Sun J, Liu GP, Han QL (2023) Time varying formation predictive control of second-order networked multi-agent systems with three-channel random communication constraints. IEEE Transactions on Circuits and Systems II: Express Briefs 70(9):3479–3483

Zheng S, Ahn CK, Jiang X, Yan H, Shi P (2025a) Nonlinear cooperative output regulation with input delay compensation. IEEE Transactions on Automatic Control 70(2):1336–1343

Zheng Y, Zhang Y, Li S, Luo M (2025b) Co-design of dynamic quantizer and small-gain-based distributed model predictive control of nonlinear continuous system. IEEE Transactions on Control of Network Systems. https://doi.org/10.1109/TCNS.2025.3526729

Zhong Q, Han S, Shi K, Cai X, Kwon OM, Zhong S (2022) Secure consensus switching control for multiagent system under abnormal deception attacks and its application to unmanned surface vehicle clusters. Expert Systems with Applications 205:117,702

Zhou B, Duan GR (2022) On the role of zeros in the pole assignment of scalar high-order fully actuated linear systems. Journal of Systems Science & Complexity 35(2):535–542

Zhou H, Tong S (2023) Adaptive neural network event-triggered output-feedback containment control for nonlinear MASs with input quantization. IEEE Transactions on Cybernetics 53(11):7406–7416